AUSTRALIA'S ANCIENT ABORIGINAL PAST

AUSTRALIA'S ANCIENT ABORIGINAL PAST
A Global Perspective

MURRAY JOHNSON

© 2020 Murray Johnson

Revised edition 2020

First published 2014 by
Australian Scholarly Publishing Pty Ltd
7 Lt Lothian St Nth, North Melbourne, Vic 3051

Tel: 03 9329 6963
enquiry@scholarly.info / www.scholarly.info

ISBN 978-1-925003-71-0

ALL RIGHTS RESERVED

Cover image: Tony Brown 'Mungo Sunset'

CONTENTS

Note to Second Edition	*vi*
Acknowledgements	*vii*
Abbreviations	*viii*
Introduction	*ix*
1. Archaeology and Archaeological Endeavour	1
2. Human Origins, Evolution and Global Dispersal	27
3. The Neanderthal Anomaly	55
4. The Hobbit Enigma	69
5. Colonisation of Sahul: The Archaeological and Skeletal Evidence	84
6. Demise of the Megafauna	109
7. Pleistocene Australia: Adaptation and Innovation	122
8. Holocene Australia and Regional Case Studies	146
9. Tasmania: An Isolated Trajectory	169
Bibliography	*191*
Notes	*218*
Index	*252*

NOTE TO SECOND EDITION

Unlike the evolution of *Homo sapiens* and our subsequent spread across the globe, science and technology have moved at a blistering pace within the last few years. Since this work first appeared in 2014 the hominid tree has become decidedly bushier, with a number of previously unknown species brought to light. Similarly, advances in genetics have provided new insights into our ancient past, and that includes our understanding of Aboriginal Australians. Research remains in a constant state of flux, so it become necessary at some point in time to call a temporary halt while we evaluate our current state of knowledge. I sincerely hope that readers of the first edition will appreciate this updated and revised work, which now bring us up to the present while reflecting back on what has gone before.

Dr Murray Johnson
Honorary Senior Research Fellow
School of Historical and Philosophical Inquiry
University of Queensland

ACKNOWLEDGMENTS

The purpose of this work was not only to write a general history of Aboriginal Australia prior to the permanent arrival of the British in 1788, but also to place it within the broader history of humanity. After all, the Aboriginal occupation of Australia or, more correctly, the ancient continent of Sahul, is merely one episode in an epic saga which has seen the human species penetrate to every corner of the world. Importantly, that expansion was also due in no small part to the role of our hominid ancestors. While there are numerous other works which focus on the Aboriginal presence in Australia, they all too often ignore that wider context. My intention was also to write a history that was intelligible to all interested readers, irrespective of their level of education. The late doyen of Australian archaeology, Professor John Mulvaney, had long held the view that too much emphasis on the science involved in understanding our ancient past tended to override the inherent social dimensions. Thousands upon thousands of generations have come and gone, but they were all *real* people living in a very *real* world. I thank Professor Mulvaney for the inspiration. So, too, must I thank the scholars with whom I have worked over the years at the University of Queensland, the Australian National University, and the University of Tasmania. The likes of Raymond Evans, W. Ross Johnston, Henry Reynolds and Mitchell Rolls immediately spring to mind. No less significant have been the many students who it has been my privilege to teach at the above institutions, a number of whom have made it even more worthwhile by going on to forge their own historical careers. Finally, a word must go to my wife Marianne, who has accompanied me on the rollercoaster ride of life longer than I care to remember. Her unflagging support has been appreciated more than mere words can express.

ABBREVIATIONS

BCE   Before the Common Era (formerly AD, *Anno Domini*)
BP   Before Present (technically before 1950)
CE   Common Era (formerly BC, Before Christ)
ENSO   El Nino Southern Oscillation system
ESR   Electron Spin Resonance
MYA   Million Years Ago
OSL   Optically Stimulated Luminescence

INTRODUCTION

Human beings have quite a number of unusual characteristics apart from their somewhat odd physical appearance which is something I wish to come back to later. For the moment, though, I would suggest that one of the most important things which separates us from all other members of the animal kingdom is our inquiring mind and our keen interest in trying to work out our relationship with the world around us. Many of us, and a great many at that, are almost obsessed with finding out where we have come from, which is amply demonstrated by the recent phenomenal growth of genealogical societies. One way or another most people at least want to learn something about their familial roots, but it also goes considerably further than that because to understand our relationship with the wider world we need to find out where we came from as a species. Throughout history, religions and mythologies have developed within virtually all human societies as a means of explaining those distant origins.[1]

In an important sense, the Dreaming Beings of Australian Aboriginal people are not necessarily all that different from the monotheism of Judaeo-Christian religion. We also need to bear in mind that the Western belief in a supreme creator was not seriously questioned until the mid-nineteenth century when Charles Darwin and Alfred Russel Wallace almost simultaneously formulated their theories of evolution.[2] Indeed, therein lies another similarity between the Western and Aboriginal belief systems. Although many northern Aboriginal groups readily acknowledge that their ancestors came to Australia from across the sea, numerous others, particularly in more southern parts of the continent, believe that they have always been here.[3] By this line of reckoning they were created by Dreaming Beings which arose from the ground or descended from the sky and embarked on their journeys across the landscape. The fact that those ancestral beings are often considered to have been anthropomorphic in itself suggests at least rudimentary evolutionary thought.[4]

As we are all members of a single species, *Homo sapiens sapiens*, it appears relatively easy to dismiss Aboriginal claims that they have always been present in Australia. After all, Australia is a continent of marsupials and monotremes, not placental mammals, and there is no evidence that primates ever existed on the southern land mass except, of course, for the mythical Yowie which appears in both Aboriginal and non-Aboriginal folk tales.[5] Yet there is at least one significant anomaly in all this. According to evolutionary theory hominoids (humans and primates) descended from a common ancestor which resembled the shrews found in many parts of the world today. They are small placental mammals, which once again appears to contradict the widespread Aboriginal belief that people have always lived in Australia. In the late 1990s, however, palaeontologists unearthed a fossil jaw south-east of Melbourne which has been dated to around 115 million years ago. The dentition indicates that it belonged to a small shrew-like placental mammal:[6] neither marsupial nor monotreme, it was an ancient inhabitant of the supercontinent of Gondwana before even those animals evolved. Even more extraordinary is the strong probability that elephants once roamed the ancient Australian landscape in significant numbers. Three pachyderm fossils have so far been discovered on opposite sides of the continent.[7]

Contrary to popular belief, humans did not evolve from primates, even though the nucleotide (DNA molecules) of both modern humans and chimpanzees differ by less than two per cent.[8] We are close, but not too close. The paths of hominids and primates probably separated around six or seven million years ago, with one line culminating in the great apes of today; the other passed through a range of human-like creatures until we reach the present time.[9] The current evidence suggests that *Homo sapiens sapiens* emerged as a distinct species less than 200,000 years ago,[10] and since then we have shared the planet with a number of other hominids, just two of which were the Neanderthals

Introduction

(*Homo neanderthalensis*) and the so-called 'Hobbit' (*Homo floresiensis*). Although the majority of palaeoanthropologists consider *Homo erectus* to be the immediate ancestor of modern humans,[11] it appears that this species co-existed with *Homo sapiens* until at least as recently as 50,000 years ago in South-East Asia.[12] And there are intriguing hints that it survived even later. Then there were the mysterious hominids known only as the Denisovans, a species related to, but genetically distinct from the Neanderthals. Named after the cave in southern Siberia where their physical remains were first unearthed, the Denisovans are now known to have inhabited many parts of Asia until at least 30,000 to 50,000 years ago. The presence of the Denisovans is still felt, as up to one-twentieth of their DNA is carried by a number of Melanesian groups from Papua New Guinea and the islands north-east of Australia, genetic evidence of an inter-relationship between two very different types of people.[13] It is also found in Australia's Aborigines, suggesting that this little-known hominid could have an important bearing on the original colonisation of the Australian continent.[14] As time goes on more and more hominid species are being brought to light, but we are extremely fortunate to have found what we already have because the chances of any hominid remains surviving from the distant past are extremely remote. Apart from the cranium and jawbone the remainder of the skeleton disappears relatively quickly, and conditions have to be just right for the long-term preservation of cranial or post-cranial remnants.[15]

Over the last two million years all hominids have shared a number of common characteristics. For one thing, they all walked upright on their hind legs which, as C. Owen Lovejoy rightly remarked, is a particularly 'unusual mode of mammalian locomotion'.[16] Monkeys, apes, and even bears can stand on their hind-legs – but humans do it all the time. Compared to body weight hominids have also been equipped with relatively large brains, the average in modern humans being in the order of 1,360 cubic centimetres, though they can range from 1,000 to 2,000 cubic centimetres without any loss of intelligence.[17] Even in the distant past a feature of hominids was their comparatively large brains in relation to body weight. Australopithecines, for example, were only the size of chimpanzees but their brains averaged around 480 cubic centimetres.[18] *Homo erectus*, which emerged some two million years ago, had an average cranial capacity of 1,100 cubic centimetres, and they were roughly the same physical size as modern humans.[19] Neanderthals, on the other hand, were slightly shorter than modern humans, but their brain was larger on average than our own. While that does not necessarily imply greater intelligence, we do know they were not the dim-witted creatures they were often portrayed during the late nineteenth and early twentieth centuries.[20]

Another feature which sets modern humans apart from most other animals is our curiously flattened face; even primates have faces which project forward. With the unique exception of the male Proboscis Monkey (*Nasalis larvatus*) of Borneo, where the elongated nose may be linked to sexual selection, the nostrils of primates are squat and forward-facing. Those of modern humans, on the other hand, turn downwards, which is not something that we often think about. It is just one of the many mysteries of evolution, because we still remain blissfully unaware of what advantage is gained. Modern humans are also remarkable for their apparent nakedness; although we are covered by hairs, they are so fine and short that to all intents and purposes we are naked. One would think that in cooler climates it would be advantageous to have a covering of hair, but the human species is very much the same right around the world. Lack of hair is almost certainly linked to the millions of microscopic sweat glands which carpet the body of modern humans, for our ability to sweat is an extraordinary evolutionary development.[21]

It is not just about our appearance, though, because human behaviour also clearly sets our species apart from all other animals. Bipedalism has allowed us to make free use of our forelimbs, and we have attained a remarkable degree of manipulative skill with our hands.[22] Our ability to make and do things is also dependent on the messages received from our brains via nerve fibres, but what really does set us apart is our ability to *choose* what we do. As Richard Leakey once perceptibly explained, while termites build intricate mounds which provide effective internal air-conditioning, they are locked in to building mounds only. Unlike modern humans they cannot choose to build an entirely different structure.[23]

Introduction

In a similar vein, humans are endowed with a sense of justice, of self-awareness and a sense of aesthetic pleasure. We have imagination, and on top of all this we largely communicate through spoken language which is characterised by a wide vocabulary and a complex grammatical structure. So in these ways modern humans are very different from all other members of the animal kingdom even though we share a common ancestor. Modern humans are also efficient predators, and unfortunately we are one of the few animals that kills for pleasure. Whether modern humans have evolved into nothing more than a 'killer ape' is a highly-contentious issue. Although many commentators agree that humans will ultimately save themselves, others are less optimistic and point out that we have already created sufficient technology to destroy our own species.[24]

Only time will tell what the outcome will be, and it is the concept of time that is central to this work. The emphasis here has been to take a broad approach to place the pre-European history of Australia within a global context. To that end the discussion will begin with the history of archaeology and developments in dating the remnants of the past. Although the collection of ancient artifacts has a very long lineage, the origins of archaeology lie in the eighteenth century and it was not until the later decades of the nineteenth century that it was established as a legitimate academic discipline. It was even more delayed in Australia, where the first major systematic excavation of an ancient Aboriginal site was not conducted until 1929,[25] and archaeology – along with serious studies of the ancient Aboriginal past – had to wait until the 1960s before they finally gained a firm footing.[26]

By taking a global perspective it will be necessary to investigate human evolution and hominid divergence. The majority of palaeoanthropologists contend that the origins of humanity lie in Africa, from which continent *Homo sapiens* spread throughout the world. Although the 'Out of Africa' theory still reigns supreme in Western intellectual thought, it has been increasingly challenged by multi-regionalists who counter that modern humans evolved long after their ancestral forebears had exited the African continent.[27] That said, it is in Africa where we gain our most useful understanding of hominid evolution. To maintain the broader

Australia's Ancient Aboriginal Past

view, consideration will also be given to the Neanderthals, a species or sub-species of hominid which apparently became extinct in the northern hemisphere while the Australian Aborigines were consolidating their occupation of an equally harsh environment in the southern. The focus will then be directed closer to Australia with the unusual hominid colloquially known as the 'Hobbit', or *Homo floresiensis*. This species existed on an Indonesian island until just prior to the Aboriginal people commencing their colonisation of the ancient super-continent of Sahul, a single land mass comprising today's Australia, Papua New Guinea and Tasmania. The discovery of this diminutive hominid owes much to Australian archaeologists, who were searching for traces of the Aborigines on the islands of the archipelago. The 'Hobbit' generated – and continues to generate – heated discussion about its rightful place in human evolution. Notwithstanding these debates, there can be no denying that it now plays an important role in Australia's ancient past.

This, of course, brings us directly to the human colonisation of Australia, or the ancient super-continent of Sahul, at least 50,000 years ago. Where the Australian Aborigines originally came from remains a mystery. Attempts to establish genetic links to Indigenous Asian people such as the Adivasis of the Andaman Islands in the Indian Ocean, the Vedda of Sri Lanka and the Ainu of Japan have so far proved fruitless.[28] Australian Aboriginal people possess blood groups A and O but very little B, and what there is appears to have entered the population in comparatively recent times. They share that characteristic with Native Americans, though even here they differ in a very significant way. Throughout the world the blood groups M and N, controlled by a single gene, are respectively around 55 and 45 parts out of 100. Native Americans are low in N and much higher in M, while the Australian Aborigines are the complete reverse, being low in M and high in N.[29] So who they are and where they originated remains elusive. Similarly, their initial entry point into ancient Sahul can only be conjectured.

Although present-day Papua New Guinea was the northernmost extremity of this huge landmass, a land-bridge extended almost to the island of Tanimbar in the east. The initial colonisers may have entered Sahul via these more northerly routes or through Timor directly into

Introduction

north-western Australia.[30] The latter would have involved a longer sea crossing, but the general consensus is that this was the most likely route taken, with the earliest archaeological sites now lying submerged under the Timor Sea. While a number of ancient coastal sites are also known from Papua New Guinea,[31] the earliest colonisers here were probably Melanesian rather than Aboriginal people.

Whether the founding population spread rapidly throughout the continent or initially settled the coastal regions before penetrating into the interior is another hotly-contested debate.[32] We do know that by 35,000 years ago the Aboriginal people had reached what is now south-western Tasmania, at that time making them the most southerly people in the world. The climate was even colder than today, with the first Tasmanians living and hunting in a sub-Antarctic environment.[33] Yet even though they were unquestionably modern humans, perceived morphological differences in archaic skeletal remains has led to suggestions that perhaps two very different groups of people initially inhabited the continental land mass. Others have argued that the physical disparity indicates successive migrations into Sahul, or that these supposed differences merely represent the extremes of modern humanity.[34]

Whoever they were and wherever they originated, the vanguard of Australian colonisers undoubtedly encountered a range of food sources with which they were already familiar. Maritime resources were one; plant foods were another, as many edible floral species are to be found on both sides of the Wallace Line, the transitional ecological zone which separates Asia and Australia.[35] Animals were a different matter again, for 50,000 years ago Australia was home to the megafauna. Giant mammals existed in many other parts of the world, but the Australian megafauna was unique. They were all marsupials, co-existing with strange reptilian and avian species, some of which were of gigantic proportions. A number of other animals, on the other hand, were only slightly larger than present forms or, in many instances, have survived unchanged to the present day. Emus, for example, were widespread throughout the continent, but they had a giant contemporary in *Genyornis newtoni*, a flightless bird which weighed up to 275 kilograms and resembled a giant goose. Among the mammals were the *Diprotodons*, two-tonne wombat-like creatures, kangaroos which stood almost three metres high, and the fearsome Marsupial Lion, the largest marsupial predator of all time. Reptiles were no less impressive, with the giant monitor lizard, *Megalania prisca*, possibly reaching more than five metres in length. A terrestrial crocodile, *Quinkana fortirostrum*, was also present, as was a five-metre python, *Wonambi naracoortensis*.[36]

Many of these animals had endured for hundreds of thousands of years, living through a series of Ice Ages and warmer interglacial periods. Then, apparently soon after the arrival of humans, at least three large reptiles, along with *Genyornis* and all marsupials exceeding 100 kilograms in weight, rapidly disappeared. Their extinction has been attributed to three possible causes: climate change, over-hunting by humans, or hunting combined with ecological alteration caused by anthropogenic fire regimes.[37] Similar scenarios were played out in North America and, to a lesser extent, Europe and Asia, but there can be no doubt that fire was a crucial tool of the Aboriginal colonisers of Sahul. While they may or may not have used fire indiscriminately at the outset, the Aboriginal people certainly refined its use over the following millennia. The development of effective fire regimes could also have been one of the reasons why Aboriginal people did not extend their horticultural practices into fully-fledged agriculture.

During the Pleistocene epoch the Aboriginal people certainly employed new technologies in their quest for sustenance. They also had sufficient leisure time to engage in intellectual pursuits, even though the evidence suggests they were far more mobile than their descendants in the succeeding Holocene epoch which commenced some 11,700 years ago. It was during the Holocene that Aboriginal people completed their conquest of the continent, settling permanently in the most arid areas of the interior, the coldest alpine regions, and colonising numerous offshore islands. There are indications that it was population growth in the mid-Holocene, coupled with environmental factors, which triggered a range of new strategies which included complex engineering projects.

The Holocene also witnessed considerable social change right across Australia, with people in distant regions interconnected through extensive trade networks. This was also the time that the islands of

Introduction

Torres Strait which lie between Cape York and Papua New Guinea were permanently settled by Melanesians who remain as Australia's second Indigenous people. While they maintained close contact with their Aboriginal neighbours and were brokers in a trade relationship which linked Australia with the wider world, the cultural development of the islanders played out along an entirely different path.[38]

At the opposite end of the continent, the Tasmanian Aborigines found themselves completely isolated around 10,000 years ago when warmer climatic conditions led to a shrinking of the polar ice caps and flooding of the Bassian Plain. Comprising nine separate socio-political groups,[39] isolation and environmental adaptation also projected the Tasmanians on a different trajectory from their mainland counterparts. Unlike the Aboriginal people in the cooler regions of the south-eastern Australian mainland, who wrapped themselves in warm possum-skin cloaks in winter, the Tasmanians wore nothing more than a wallaby or kangaroo skin cape draped over the shoulder.[40] They reduced the size of their toolkit to the basic essentials: they had no boomerangs, no spear-throwers and their stone tools became smaller. They abandoned the use of bone tools around 3,700 years ago for reasons that are still not understood. At that same time, however, the remains of fish disappeared from coastal middens suggesting a correlation between the two.[41] There is also a widespread belief that the Tasmanian Aborigines were incapable of making fire,[42] a myth which serves to show how our understanding of Australia's ancient Aboriginal past is often tainted by misconceptions and – at times – ignorance.

It is the purpose of this work to tease out many of the threads of that past and present them in a manner which is readily comprehensible to the general reader. Overall, we have come a long way from the time when Australia was seen as a non-event, a cultural backwater where the Aboriginal people were held to be frozen in the 'Stone Age'. We now know now that the situation was vastly different, with Aboriginal societies dynamic and in a constant state of flux, albeit, across immense spans of time. Archaeological work over the last fifty years has been instrumental in raising awareness of that rich past and its importance on the global stage. It is a story which resonates with meaning.

ARCHAEOLOGY AND ARCHAEOLOGICAL ENDEAVOUR

I

In any investigation of archaeology it is worth pointing out that humans are somewhat messy creatures. We tend to leave our rubbish lying around; we leave our marks on the landscape – or our carbon footprint in today's jargon. There seems to have nearly always been something left behind to say 'I was here'. One of the remarkable things about human history is that the accumulation of litter in one form or another has substantially increased over time. The more we delve back in to human history the less we find, but there is usually something even when we go back millions of years. At times it has been nothing more than our bones, but for all that it is fortunate we have this strange behaviour because it has allowed future generations to gain at least some knowledge of their forebears no matter how distant they might be. The picture, of course, can never be complete. The past is at best fragmentary, part of a massive jig-saw puzzle where most of the pieces are forever missing. Uncovering the few surviving pieces and attempting to make sense out of them is what archaeology is essentially all about.

While archaeology is painstaking work, its great attraction lies in the fact that it involves physical activity, often travel to exotic or at least little-known destinations, and it requires intellectual input in the study and/or laboratory. The blend of danger (which can be interpreted as some measure of hardship) and detective work has also made archaeology attractive to novelists and film-makers, perhaps best exemplified by the *Indiana Jones* films directed by Steven Spielberg. The only real element of truth in these representations is that archaeology is indeed a quest, often an exciting one, to gain knowledge of the distant past.[1]

Australia's Ancient Aboriginal Past

Archaeology is closely linked with anthropology, the study of living cultures, albeit, in the past tense. This further ensures that it is allied with history, except that the latter is useful for understanding just one per cent of the human past: the other ninety-nine per cent is almost totally dependent on archaeology. Written records first became available around 5,000 years BP and then only in western Asia. Archaeology provides meaning right back to the dawn of human history some 5 MYA. In Australia, apart from brief accounts by early mariners, written records have only been available since 1788.[2] So it is no surprise that archaeology has been crucial to our understanding of the ancient Aboriginal past. Archaeology and its allied disciplines have also reinforced Aboriginal oral histories, at least some of which may record events many thousands of years ago.[3]

Archaeology differs from conventional history in that its practitioners largely work with artifacts rather than documents which usually tell them nothing in themselves.[4] Although it is a truism that documents, whether ancient or modern, can be interpreted in numerous ways, the archaeologist is more like a scientist. They collect evidence or data, they conduct experiments, they formulate an hypothesis and test it, and they propose a paradigm which appears to offer the best explanation.[5] In short, they develop a plausible picture of the past, though there have been some notable exceptions to this general rule.

The Rosetta Stone, for example, was discovered by French soldiers in 1799 during Napoleon's campaign in Egypt. The Greek and Egyptian inscriptions later allowed Jean-Francois Champollion-le-Jeune to decipher hieroglyphics.[6] In a similar vein, the cuneiform script of ancient Mesopotamia was deciphered after Sir Henry Rawlinson spent the years 1835–1850 studying the tri-lingual Behistun inscription of Darius I on an almost inaccessible cliff face in Iran.[7] The point of all this is that archaeology combines the technical skill of the modern scientist with that of the historian. With the discipline's increasingly heavy dependence on the physical and biological sciences, however, the drift has been steadily away from the social sciences. Be that as it may, the origins of archaeology lie firmly in the social realm.

In the eighth century BCE the Greek 'farmer-poet', Hesiod, composed an epic verse known as *Works and Days* which structured the history of the world into five ages. At the beginning was the Age of Gold, literally a 'golden era' when everyone was content and had sufficient wealth to pursue leisurely activities. From that time on there was a gradual deterioration of living standards through the Age of Silver, Age of Bronze, Age of Epic Heroes and, finally, Hesiod's own era, the Age of Iron, when work and misery were constant companions. Although Hesiod's epic is open to multiple interpretations, at least one important strand harks back to the 'good old days', a recurring theme throughout human history.[8]

Even in ancient times there was a keen interest in the culture of past societies. Nabonidus, the last native-born king of Babylon, had a penchant for excavating and restoring temples from past eras during his reign from 556 to 539 BCE. Nabonidus has been described as one of the world's first archaeologists, and his interest in the past was inherited by a daughter, Bel-Shalti-Nannar. After being sent to the former Sumerian capital of Ur as High Priestess, Bel-Shalti-Nannar gathered together ancient artifacts and housed them in what may have been the world's first museum of antiquities.[9] These actions by father and daughter were nevertheless proto-archaeology, a detached interest in the past, and it was not until the Renaissance that developments began to take a far more serious turn.

At first it still followed closely in the footsteps of Nabonidus, with wealthy travellers or patrons employing collectors to fill their cabinets with an array of specimens. Ancient pots and other artifacts struggled for space alongside minerals, stuffed animals, shells and preserved plants, all of which fell under the general rubric of 'natural history'. Ancient sites in Greece and Italy were plundered of their treasures, while classical architecture was meticulously copied in northern European cities and on landed estates. At the same time, however, this interest in the distant past sparked an appreciation of ancient sites closer to home.[10] Megaliths at Carnac in France and Stonehenge in England were methodically surveyed and exploratory excavations conducted. William Stukeley's plans and illustrations of Stonehenge made between 1719 and 1724 were so accurate and detailed that they still remain useful today.[11]

Yet it was in North America rather than Europe that the first serious archaeological excavation was carried out in 1784 by Thomas Jefferson, later to become third President of the United States. In Jefferson's time there was considerable speculation over the hundreds of large burial mounds which dotted the landscape east of the Mississippi River. Many colonists refused to believe that Native Americans had been capable of such complex engineering feats, insisting they were the work of a mysterious vanished race of people who, for want of a better name, were simply dubbed the 'Mound Builders'.[12]

The wealthy Jefferson organised a team of workmen to dig a trench through one of the mounds on his property in Virginia. The excavation was meticulous enough to allow Jefferson to identify the different levels in the trench. The lower levels held human bones, and Jefferson hypothesised that the mound had been reused for burials over a very long period of time. He was convinced the mounds had been made by Native Americans and not a vanished race of people but, at the same time, Jefferson insisted that further research was necessary to confirm his findings.[13] Logical deduction based on careful excavation was well ahead of its time, and it was to be almost twenty years before his methodology was emulated.

In the first decade of the nineteenth century Sir Richard Colt Hoare excavated many of the ancient burial mounds scattered throughout Wiltshire in England and demonstrated they were the work of ancient Britons and not Romans as was generally believed.[14] The problem was that his work, like so many of his contemporaries, was severely constrained by a widespread acceptance of the Diluvian or Catastrophe Theory, which had been formulated to account for the presence of ancient fossils. All of them were held to have fallen victim to the Great Flood recorded in the Bible.[15]

In 1650 James Usher, then Bishop of Armagh in Ireland, had calculated the age of the Earth based on a close reading of the Old Testament. According to Usher and all other God-fearing people Creation had occurred on 23 October 4004 BCE, so all fossilised remains had to be subsequent to that date.[16] Short of committing heresy, Colt Hoare and other proto-archaeologists were forced to think within an extremely

Archaeology And Archaeological Endeavour

short chronology, but it was in the late eighteenth and early nineteenth centuries that a veritable flood of geological evidence began to wash away this powerful dogma. While geologists began to push back the age of the Earth it was a French naturalist with a particular penchant for palaeontology, Georges Cuvier, who paved the way.

In the first decade of the nineteenth century Cuvier carefully examined fossils in different geological strata and concluded there had to have been a whole series of violent upheavals, including devastating floods. Some localised events had annihilated all existing animals, with these regions later re-colonised by migrating forms. This accounted for the presence of woolly mammoths and rhinoceros in Europe. The great deluge of the Bible had merely been the last of these cataclysms, which meant that life on Earth had existed long before 4004 BCE.[17] Without seriously compromising the prevailing religious orthodoxy Cuvier adroitly demolished Usher's short chronology, though his own explanation for extinct life forms was soon to be discredited by the English geologist Charles Lyell, who refined the arguments of a Scottish predecessor named James Hutton.

As early as 1788 Hutton had published his *Theory of the Earth* based on a study of stratification, that is, the superimposed layers of rocks and sediments which became the basis of archaeological excavation already foreshadowed by Thomas Jefferson. It was Hutton who established the Principle of Uniformitarianism by showing that the stratification of sediments was an ongoing process in the ocean, rivers and lakes.[18] This was coupled with Steno's Law, whereby the layer above is younger than the one below. These ideas were developed further by Charles Lyell, who published the first of his three-volume *Principles of Geology* in 1830. Lyell reiterated Hutton's statement that the present is the key to the past: geological evidence could only be explained by reference to processes operating in the present day which were directly observable. His more sophisticated approach was so logical and so forceful that it became extremely influential,[19] and within a remarkably short span of time it was widely accepted that the Earth was not just many thousands of years old; it probably ran into the millions. Up to this point in time, however, little thought had been given to the possibility that the human species might itself be of great antiquity.

Although stone tools had been found among the bones of extinct animals from the early 1700s, it was assumed they were intrusive and could not have been contemporaneous. In 1858, however, William Pengelly, a schoolmaster and amateur geologist explored Brixham Cave near Torquay in England with Hugh Falconer, a professional palaeontologist. The pair again found stone artifacts among the bones of extinct animals, but in this instance they lay together under a thick layer of unbroken stalagmite. The discovery prompted British geologists to reassess the evidence of co-existence gathered in France by Jacques Boucher de Perthes. The French customs officer had published a paper on the subject in 1841 which had been dismissed out-of-hand or ignored because of his lack of scholarly credentials. That all changed in 1859 when two British geologists, Joseph Prestwich and John Evans, journeyed to France in the wake of the Brixham Cave discovery to see de Perthes evidence for themselves. They came away completely satisfied that de Perthes was correct, with both sites now confirming beyond any doubt that humans had more than just a history. They had, in fact, a *prehistory*, the first use of the word in a human context coming in 1865 when John Lubbock published *Prehistoric Times*, a book that quickly became a bestseller.[20]

By then another conceptual device essential for the discipline of archaeology had been formulated by the Danish scholar Christian Thomsen. In 1836 Thomsen published a guidebook to the collections held in the Museum of Northern Antiquities in Copenhagen (later the Danish National Museum). Faced with a bewildering array of ancient artifacts, Thomsen divided them into three chronological categories: the Stone Age, Bronze Age and Iron Age.[21] In many ways it was similar to Hesiod's 'ages' in *Works and Days*. This system of ordering whereby one group of artifacts is succeeded by another appears very basic, but it was extremely important. While Thomsen was not the originator of the idea he was the first to give it practical effect, and his system made it possible to say something about a specific period of the ancient past.[22] Thomsen's guidebook was later printed in English, and although there was resistance from German prehistorians who considered the origins of the Germanic peoples to have been quite different, his chronology was ultimately adopted throughout Europe.[23]

Archaeology And Archaeological Endeavour

By the mid-nineteenth century, then, the foundations of modern archaeology were beginning to fall into place. Careful excavation and recording was followed by knowledge of geological stratification and an acceptance that the world was perhaps millions of years old. It was known that humans had been contemporaneous with extinct animals and that they had a prehistory. It now required just one more intellectual thread to ensure that archaeology could truly become a discipline in its own right. That was the theory of evolution, which harmonised well with all preceding developments.

Charles Darwin was not the first to speculate about the processes of evolution, the origin and transmutation of species. Even his own grandfather, the physician Erasmus Darwin, had mused over the possibility that all living creatures shared a common ancestor. He had also thought deeply about how different species had diverged over time.[24] As early as 1809 the French naturalist, Jean-Baptiste de Lamarck, had published his own theory of evolution which briefly gained popular acceptance. Lamarck unfortunately based it entirely on the assumption that animals acquire characteristics during their lifetime which they pass on to their offspring. Giraffes, for instance, were held to have developed long necks because their forebears were continually reaching for higher branches. On the face of it there does not appear to be anything wrong with this idea, and even Charles Darwin later accepted that acquired characteristics could be inherited. Unlike Lamarck, though, Darwin did not base his own theory on the same line of reasoning. If we accept Lamarck's explanation it means that if a person had the misfortune to have one of their legs amputated it automatically followed that all the children they subsequently produced would be born with one leg. While obviously absurd, much of Lamarck's other theorising was quite sound,[25] but it was Darwin (and Alfred Russel Wallace) who developed the theory of evolution within a logical and plausible framework.

Darwin came from comfortable circumstances, the son of a country physician in Shropshire, England, who was related to the famous Wedgewood family. It was intended that Darwin would follow the family tradition and study medicine, but unable to tolerate the sight of blood he turned his attention to theology with the intention of entering the clergy. While studying at Cambridge University Darwin developed a passion for natural history, a pursuit that was encouraged by Professor John Henslow. The latter's recommendation helped Darwin secure a place as supernumerary on HMS *Beagle* which circumnavigated the world between 1831 and 1836. Contrary to popular accounts he was not the expedition's naturalist; that role was undertaken by the *Beagle*'s surgeon, Robert McCormack.[26] The main purpose of the voyage was to chart little-known waters for the Royal Navy, but it provided Darwin with the opportunity to amass a huge collection of natural history and geological specimens. After observing the minor differences between insular forms of finches and giant land tortoises on the Galapagos Islands off the coast of South America Darwin began to speculate about the transmutation of species.[27]

Darwin began formulating his theory of evolution on his return to England, but delayed publication for another twenty-two years. Although it has often been suggested that he feared a reaction from the religious establishment, it was criticism from the scientific fraternity that was of greater concern. Darwin was trying to make his name in the field of natural history and would have been well aware that his radical theory would rock the scientific community.[28] With nothing having been made public, Darwin was shocked to receive a letter from Alfred Russel Wallace in June 1858 which outlined the latter's own theory of evolution: it was virtually identical to his own. Knowing it was time to act and encouraged by his close confidants Charles Lyell and Joseph Hooker, a paper expounding the evolutionary theory of both Darwin and Wallace was read before the Linnean Society in London the following month.[29] A year later Darwin published the book for which he is most famous – *On the Origin of Species by Means of Natural Selection*. It was to have profound consequences.

In this work Darwin noted how the living world was in a constant state of flux, with new species emerging and others sliding into extinction. He argued that these changes were gradual and continuous rather than the result of sudden catastrophes. Darwin also put forward the idea of common descent: that all mammals shared a common ancestor, just as birds, reptiles and all other life-forms did. Building

Archaeology And Archaeological Endeavour

on that he questioned whether they might have all shared a common ancestor in the distant past. Finally, and of crucial significance, Darwin proposed that the mechanism for change was through natural selection, with individuals possessing advantageous characteristics passing them on to their offspring.[30]

This is where Darwin diverged from Lamarck, because natural selection – or 'survival of the fittest' in the words of the British social philosopher Herbert Spencer – can only operate when there is variation. In essence it meant that while all offspring will share many traits of their parents they are never completely identical, and occasionally – just occasionally – they are blessed with a physical characteristic that increases their chances of survival. Natural selection is not foolproof; offspring with enhanced characteristics can still fall victim to predators through simple misfortune. Overall, however, they tend to survive at a greater rate and leave more offspring of their own behind.[31]

Apart from the work of Lamarck, Hutton and Lyell, Darwin was also inspired by Thomas Malthus' 'principle of population', whereby population pressure results in increased competition. In Nature this equates to competition over available resources, with only the most successful variants surviving.[32] Darwin did not specifically mention humans until 1871, when he published *The Descent of Man*. Many others did, with evolutionary theory being applied to societies and cultures which, in turn, greatly influenced the leading archaeologists of the late nineteenth and twentieth centuries.[33]

In the 1860s, then, all the crucial elements of modern archaeology were firmly in place, forming a backdrop for the great discoveries of the ancient past, perhaps the best-known of which were Pompeii and Herculaneum. When Mount Vesuvius spectacularly erupted in CE 79 the city of Pompeii was buried under a thick carpet of volcanic ash. Residents who had failed to heed the earlier warning signs were asphyxiated by the heat of gases in a volcanic cloud which descended upon them, while their neighbours at Herculaneum boiled and drowned in hot volcanic mud.[34] Both settlements were buried and largely forgotten until 1710, when the Duc d'Elbeuf, an Austrian prince and military commander, heard rumours of worked marble being unearthed at what later turned out to be Herculaneum. He had workmen construct a labyrinth of shafts and tunnels which uncovered not just worked marble, but also statues and other works of art. Wholesale plundering – looting really – continued under the authority of King Charles III of Spain, particularly after Pompeii was discovered in 1748.[35] Nothing was documented until 1762, when the classicist, Johann Winckelmann, published a paper in which he excoriated the quality of the so-called 'excavations' at Herculaneum.[36]

Just two years earlier archaeological work at Pompeii and Herculaneum had finally commenced on an organised basis, and it was solely due to the efforts of Guiseppe Fiorelli. After being placed in charge of the excavations at Pompeii, Fiorelli strengthened and in some cases roofed over buildings to protect their interiors. Frescoes were left in situ where possible and everything was meticulously recorded to ensure its provenance. In 1864 Fiorelli devised a clever technique to fill cavities which had been left after human remains had decayed: with the hard volcanic ash serving as a mould, plaster of Paris was pumped in. The cast revealed the physical appearance and even details of the clothing worn by victims of the ancient disaster. This technique is still followed, albeit, with transparent fibreglass. Indeed, modern excavations at both Pompeii and Herculaneum roughly follow the pattern devised by Fiorelli, and despite the earlier plundering they stand together as the most complete archaeological excavation ever undertaken on an urban site anywhere in the world.[37]

Notwithstanding the many accounts which uncritically cite the example of Heinrich Schliemann and the discovery of the Homeric city of Troy in the early 1870s, documentary sources can also be important archaeological tools.[38] German-born Schliemann migrated to America in 1851 where he made a small fortune from banking during the California gold rush. He then speculated in real estate and invested in a range of mercantile enterprises with such success that he was able to retire at the age of just thirty-six.[39] Schliemann claimed that since childhood he had been infatuated with *The Iliad*, Homer's account of the Trojan War, and had long sought to fulfil his dream of locating the fabled city of Troy.[40] By his own account Schliemann had used the topographical details

Archaeology And Archaeological Endeavour

in *The Iliad* to determine that Hissarlick in western Turkey was the actual site of Troy, with subsequent excavations proving his assumption correct.[41] In fact, Schliemann's interest in the Homeric tale appears to have been sparked after his retirement from commerce and long after 1820 when Hissarlick had been identified as the likely site of Troy by the Scottish publisher and journalist Charles McLaren.[42]

In 1863 Frank Calvert purchased part of the site and began excavating. Lacking sufficient funds to embark on a full-scale project, Calvert approached the British Museum for assistance, but when his offer was rejected he was forced to continue on alone. He met Schliemann when the latter visited the region in 1868, convincing him to provide the financial backing. Schliemann willingly provided the funds and supervised much of the work himself, eventually confirming that Hissarlick was indeed the site of Troy – though not at the stratigraphical level he believed. Schliemann's wealth and skill as a self-publicist also relegated Calvert to the corridors of relative anonymity. While he has often been wrongly portrayed as the discoverer of Troy, Schliemann did establish the historicity of the Trojan War which itself had been dependent on Homer's text.[43] Having accumulated a hoard of treasure from the site, Schliemann next turned his attention to Greece where he discovered the lost Bronze Age Mycenaean civilisation.[44]

As in his dealings with Calvert, Schliemann's methods of excavation were just as unscrupulous, though few of his contemporaries were any better. Even Sir Arthur Evans, who became famous after excavating Knossos on Crete to reveal the Bronze Age Minoan civilisation in 1900, was guilty of compromising authenticity. Deciding to restore the city of Knossos to its former glory in 1905 Evans hired the Gillron's, a father and son team of artists, to assist in the reconstruction. Although he later claimed that recreations of the frescoes in the majestic Throne Room were based on archaeological evidence, they were in fact nothing more than the invention of his artists.[45]

Changes that were to raise the standards of modern archaeology were nevertheless already underway, particularly through the efforts of Augustus Pitt-Rivers and William Flinders Petrie. A retired Lieutenant-General of the British Army, Pitt-Rivers brought to the discipline military organisation and precision. In retirement he began excavating Saxon and Roman sites on the property he had inherited in Dorset, England, making concise plans and even models of the various features. Pitt-Rivers was meticulous in recording the position of every object uncovered by his workmen. He was not interested in treasure; the most mundane item was accurately plotted. Influenced by Darwin, he was one of the pioneers of typology, arranging similar artifacts together and tracing their evolution through time. In 1882 Pitt-Rivers was appointed Britain's first Inspector of Ancient Monuments, a position created by the parliamentarian and prehistorian John Lubbock, the connection between the two men cemented by Lubbock's marriage to one of the general's daughters. Pitt-Rivers worked on his estate for two decades before his death in 1900, the culmination of which was four large privately-printed volumes carefully documenting all the work that had been carried out. His collection of artifacts formed the basis of the Pitt-Rivers Museum, one of modern Oxford's leading attractions.[46]

William Flinders Petrie was similarly noted for his meticulous excavations and insistence that everything had to be collected, accurately plotted and described. With Flinders Petrie there is an Australian connection, somewhat tenuous though it may be. He was the maternal grandson of Matthew Flinders,[47] the first person to circumnavigate Australia and largely responsible for giving the continent its name. Flinders Petrie inherited his navigational skills from his own father, a civil engineer, who also trained him in the art of surveying. Working in Egypt, and later Palestine where he died in 1942, Flinders Petrie published full details of all his excavations and devised a system of sequential dating to provide a chronology. He achieved that by linking pottery styles to specific historical periods which could then be cross-checked from the written records.[48]

The reputation of Flinders Petrie has to some extent been overshadowed by one of his students, Howard Carter, who was equally meticulous with his record-keeping. In 1922 Carter discovered the tomb of Tutankhamen, one of the few treasure troves in Egypt which had experienced minimal losses from looters in antiquity.[49] Contrary to the legend, neither Carter, his financial backer, Lord Carnarvon, nor anyone

Archaeology And Archaeological Endeavour

else associated with the discovery fell victim to the 'Mummy's Curse';[50] Carter died in London from lymphoma – a rare type of cancer – in 1939 at the age of sixty-five.[51]

Another classical archaeologist who justly deserves mention was Robert Mortimer Wheeler, who raised the archaeological techniques of Pitt-Rivers from obscurity. Like his predecessor, Mortimer Wheeler applied military precision to his archaeological work on British hill forts during the 1920s and 1930s, as well as in India between 1944 and 1948. It was Mortimer Wheeler who invented the grid pattern for site excavation, one of the most basic practices in modern archaeology. He was also a great populariser of the discipline, bringing archaeology before enthusiastic mass audiences via books and the media, particularly television.[52]

These were just some of the great archaeologists – there were others – who took the discipline from amateurish beginnings to full maturity. They presided over the transition from an era of private funding and control by a single individual to one where excavations involved, and increasingly involve, teams of specialists from many fields. While all these developments were being played out on the global stage, however, few attempts were made to synthesise the growing body of information, particularly as it related to the earliest periods. One of the major exceptions was Vere Gordon Childe, an Australian archaeologist domiciled in Britain from the early 1920s to the mid-1950s, who examined the broad issues of change in the distant past and attempted to explain them. It was Childe who coined the terms 'Neolithic Revolution' and 'Urban Revolution' to describe the social and economic changes from hunting and gathering to agriculture, and from scattered agrarian settlements to urban centres. 'Revolution' in this context had nothing to do with Childe's well-known Marxist sympathies,[53] and although much of the theoretical edifice he built has since been torn down, his pioneering efforts provided a firm foundation for future investigations.[54]

When it comes to the very origins of humanity the name Leakey is perhaps unsurpassed. The patriarch of the family, Louis Leakey, was born in Kenya in 1903 and initially intended to follow in the footsteps of his missionary father. While studying at Cambridge University, however, Leakey became interested in fossils and joined a British Museum of Natural History palaeontological expedition to East Africa in 1924–1925.[55] With financial backing from Cambridge University Leakey began searching for hominid fossils in 1931, largely focusing on the promising site of Olduvai Gorge in Tanzania. He was joined there by British archaeologist Mary Nicol, who was to become his second wife in 1936.[56] The pair amassed a huge collection of stone artifacts, but the skeletal remains of their manufacturers eluded them until 1959. Thereafter they made a series of outstanding discoveries which included Australopithecines and early members of the genus *Homo*.[57] After the couple separated in the early 1960s Mary Leakey's reputation eclipsed even that of her formidable husband, who died in 1972. By the time of her own death in 1996 she had been credited with the discovery of fifteen new species of hominids, including an entirely new genus.[58] Their work was continued by son Richard, and through pushing back the known dates for the ancestors of modern humans by millions of years the Leakey family was instrumental in having Africa – rather than Asia – accepted as the most likely 'cradle' of humanity.[59]

During much of this time Australia was regarded as nothing more than an archaeological backwater, its Indigenous human inhabitants of interest only because they were held in many quarters to be living representatives of the Old Stone Age.[60] As such there could be no antiquity and no logical reason to carry out any excavations of Aboriginal sites. Given these widespread and erroneous beliefs it comes as some surprise to find that the first archaeological investigation in Australia dates to May 1788, just four months after the initial batch of European colonists were deposited on the shores of Sydney Harbour. Governor Arthur Phillip advised his superiors in London that he had opened an Aboriginal burial mound and from the appearance of ash he surmised they cremated their dead.[61] In accordance with official instructions Phillip and his officers were eager to understand the customs of the Indigenous people amongst whom they were thrown. They were also determined to establish cordial relations, a task which ultimately proved beyond their capabilities. Violence, disease and the rapid depletion of natural

Archaeology And Archaeological Endeavour

resources on which the Aboriginal people were dependent resulted in the survivors becoming fringe dwellers on the edge of an imposed society.[62] This was an unfortunate scenario that was to be played out right across the continent for the best part of 200 years.

Governor Phillip's innovative foray into archaeology was not repeated for more than a century. Apart from a few random excavations of no significance, the first solid archaeological evidence that Aboriginal people had occupied Australia for a considerable period of time emerged in 1896. This was due to the efforts of Robert Etheridge from the Australian Museum in Sydney, and the New South Wales government palaeontologist, J.W. Dun, who excavated a site at Shea's Creek near Botany Bay. Among other things they uncovered dugong bones bearing cut marks from stone tools.[63] Although this large marine mammal is normally found in northern Australian waters from Moreton Bay in the east to Shark Bay in Western Australia, they do occasionally wander as far south as Sydney.[64] Rather than dugongs, however, the real significance of this excavation was that Etheridge and Dun were able to demonstrate that Aboriginal people had lived in the area when the sea level was 1.5 metres lower than its modern level.[65] The following decade a collector of Aboriginal artifacts named Thomas Whitlegge noticed that backed blades he had gathered from coastal sandhills near Sydney were a different type from those known to have been made by local Aboriginal people during the colonial era.[66] So by the early 1900s it was finally beginning to dawn on the colonists that the Aborigines had lived in Australia for a very lengthy period of time.

The first person to deliberately probe into that antiquity was Norman Tindale, an ethnologist at the South Australian Museum, whose initial archaeological venture took place in 1922 when he excavated an Aboriginal shell midden on Groote Eylandt, off the Northern Territory coast. The dig itself yielded little, but it did provide Tindale with a grasp of stratigraphy which he directly applied to his seminal work at Tartanga and Devon Downs, on the lower Murray River just north of Mannum in South Australia, in 1929–1930. Along with Herbert Hale, the museum curator, Tindale was hoping to uncover fossilised human remains, and it proved to be a successful quest. The first excavation at Tartanga yielded a few stone artifacts as well as human skeletal material. Tindale compared the crania to the well-known Talgai Skull from Queensland which was rightly believed to be of considerable age. Having achieved his primary aim, Tindale followed up on H.L. Sheard's preliminary work in a rock shelter at nearby Devon Downs. In 1927 Sheard had dug a small test pit to expose charcoal and other evidence suggesting that it had been a well-used occupation site. With Hale mostly absent with his work at the museum, Tindale attempted to carry out a close examination of the various sediment levels. This was the importance of Devon Downs: it was the first rock shelter to be excavated in Australia and the first serious attempt to record the stratigraphy of an Aboriginal occupation site. Such was the state of archaeology in Australia at this time that Tindale's authority to dig was vested solely in a miner's right, and conditions for his twenty-five member team were extremely tough.[67]

The excavation against the wall of the shelter descended six metres, with all artifacts and organic matter meticulously recorded in relation to the level in which it was found. Petroglyphs exposed on the rock wall were treated in like manner, enabling Tindale to construct a reasonably detailed picture of technological change over time. Again, this was something which had never really been achieved in Australia before. According to Tindale, the excavation had uncovered four distinct 'cultural' sequences: Pre-Pirrian, Pirrian, Mudukian and Murundian. At the very least, it was a departure from previous practice, where the only distinction made was between the Old and New Stone Age. Tindale associated Pre-Pirrian 'culture' with bone tools and an absence of stone artifacts. Pirrian 'culture' retained bone tools but also included worked stone flakes. Mudukian was associated with backed blades, while Murundian 'culture' featured edge-ground axes.[68] The problem was that very few artifacts of any kind were unearthed at Tartanga and Devon Downs, so in effect Tindale extrapolated the supposed sequences from other locations in South Australia. Somewhat surprisingly he used metric measurements while the majority of other fieldworkers in Australia continued to use imperial measurements right up until the mid-1960s. Importantly, however, the excavations did reveal technological

Archaeology And Archaeological Endeavour

change over an extended period of time, notwithstanding that Tindale's 'cultures' were completely fallacious. Absolute dating methods were still decades away, and Tindale made no attempt to provide even an approximate date for the material he uncovered. With remarkable foresight he nevertheless retained samples of charcoal for the expected development of radiocarbon dating. This was also to be Tindale's last major archaeological work until 1961 when he was on the verge of retirement. Tindale undertook a minor salvage dig in 1936, but over the subsequent decades he was fully absorbed in his ethnographic work, particularly in central and northern Australia.[69]

A number of others continued what he had started. American anthropologist D.S. Davidson excavated two rock shelters in the Northern Territory in 1930; the following year the Australian Museum ethnologist W.W. Thorpe excavated Burrill Lake rock shelter in southern New South Wales. In 1934 E. Kennedy worked on another rock shelter at Pittwater, just north of Sydney. This brief flurry of activity was undertaken during the worst years of the Great Depression when little finance was available and a large sector of the population was struggling to survive. Clearly, archaeology was the preserve of the financially secure, and it was also partly inspired by events overseas. Carter's discovery of Tutankhamen's tomb in 1922 had caused a sensation, while from 1922 to 1934 Leonard Woolley's excavation of Ur in the Near East maintained the high level of interest. The romanticism attached to these archaeological wonders flowed into Australia.[70]

Frederick McCarthy's work in 1936 on a rock shelter at Lapstone Creek, in the lower Blue Mountains west of Sydney, was in many ways a pivotal point in the Australian archaeological saga. In the same vein McCarthy can rightly be regarded as the real 'father' of the discipline in the antipodes. As Curator of Anthropology at the Australian Museum in Sydney, he identified the problems preventing any major advance, and his first serious excavation at Lapstone Creek also resulted in a very different analysis from that of Tindale at Tartanga and Devon Downs. McCarthy avoided the trap of trying to associate 'cultures' with different stratigraphical levels, relying instead on what the artifacts themselves could tell him. He identified two specific types of stone tools

17

at the site, the earliest of which he named 'Bondaian industry' after the profuse number of Bondi points found in the lowest levels. Flakes, stone knives and edge-ground axes in the uppermost levels he referred to as 'Eloueran industry'. McCarthy rightly regarded them as evidence of technological change within a single culture.[71]

His work at the museum allowed McCarthy little time to conduct fieldwork, and that prompted him to reflect on the problems confronting archaeology in Australia. He noted that fieldwork was widely believed to be nothing more than a holiday in the bush, ensuring that research funding generally remained well out of reach. As McCarthy lamented, the discipline was not taught in Australian universities, there was no specialist archaeological journal to keep local researchers abreast of overseas developments, there was no legitimate archaeological association, no regular conferences and – importantly – few employment prospects.[72] Identifying the obstacles was one thing, but McCarthy played a crucial role in having them addressed.

When the Australian Institute of Aboriginal Studies was established in Canberra in 1964 McCarthy was invited to become the inaugural principal. The institute was granted government funding on an unprecedented scale, and although its task was to research all areas of Aboriginal studies, McCarthy made sure that archaeology was not ignored. Unable to personally authorise grants, he wrote to universities around the country, notifying them of grants available and encouraging them to apply for archaeological projects. By this means the institute supported archaeological fieldwork in places as far apart as Cape York in the north to Tasmania in the south; from Sydney in the east to Devil's Lair in the far south-west. Two particularly significant sites, Kow Swamp in northern Victoria and Lake Mungo in south-western New South Wales, were beneficiaries of the institute's funding. Under McCarthy's direction funds were also made available for the analysis and preservation of artifacts as well as the publication costs of reports. Of prime importance was the seed funding made available to the Australian National University for the establishment of Australia's first radiocarbon dating facility.[73]

The first archaeology department in an Australian university (and the only one until the 1960s) was established at the University of

Sydney in 1948, but the primary focus then, as of now, was southern Europe and the Near East. Trained at Cambridge University in England, Australian-born John Mulvaney was the first archaeologist appointed to an Australian university who was primarily interested in the ancient Aboriginal past. When he took up his posting at the University of Melbourne in 1953, however, it was as a member of the history department.[74] Mulvaney had gained valuable experience excavating sites in Britain before returning to Australia, where his first major dig was at Fromm's Landing in South Australia in 1956. This site was close to Devon Downs where Tindale had worked more than two decades before. While Edmund Gill had pioneered the use of radiocarbon dating in Australia the previous year, Mulvaney was the first to apply it to a stratified site. He distinguished two occupation periods, the oldest of which was between 4,850 and 3,240 years BP, convincingly showing the Aboriginal presence in Australia dated from at least as far back as the mid-Holocene.[75]

In 1960 Mulvaney turned his attention to Kenniff Cave in the interior of southern Queensland. The first radiocarbon dates of almost 9,000 years convinced him that occupation may have begun during the Pleistocene, and after digging through more than two metres of deposit the age was shown to be 16,130 years BP.[76] It is now known the Aborigines were present at Kenniff Cave 19,000 years BP.[77] This was a momentous time in Australian archaeology because it stimulated a number of other archaeological excavations across Australia. It also ushered in the era of 'cowboy archaeology', with fieldworkers venturing out to promising isolated regions hoping to record even earlier dates for the Aboriginal presence in Australia. Those results were certainly achieved. In 1968 four sites older than 20,000 years had been identified, and by the early 1970s two sites were confirmed to be older than 30,000 years.[78] Now it is in the order of 50,000, possibly 53,000 years,[79] and based on excavations at the Madjedbebe rock shelter in the Northern Territory, a number of researchers are convinced the Aborigines may have entered Australia up to 65,000 years ago.[80]

While Mulvaney's work at Kenniff Cave was unquestionably the catalyst which accelerated further archaeological research, it was built on the firm foundations laid by Frederick McCarthy. Between 1960 and 1964 a number of archaeologists were appointed to three Australian universities which, in turn, dramatically increased the number of graduate and postgraduate students. In 1965 J. Matthews of the Australian National University was awarded the first doctorate in archaeology from an Australian tertiary institution.[81]

Just as the discipline was expanding so, too, were the theoretical constructs of the ancient past. Like anyone else archaeologists are influenced to some degree by the social milieu in which they live, impacting upon their interpretations of past cultures and change. One of the most powerful theories of archaeology emerged at the very time the discipline was gaining maturity in the 1960s. That was Processual, or New Archaeology, the goal of which was to answer questions about the past in the same manner as anthropology. Practitioners went about this by speculating on cultural adaptation to environmental change.[82] In Tasmania, for instance, it was suggested that Aboriginal people dropped scale-fish from their diet around 3,700 years BP in response to cooler climatic conditions: henceforth they directed their attention to the capture of more energy-efficient foods such as seals. While this particular debate will be addressed more fully in a separate chapter on Tasmania, suffice to say now that this was just one of many issues raised by processual archaeologists. In the early 1980s, however, there was something of a revolution when younger archaeologists known as post-processualists began attacking the theoretical models of their predecessors. They insisted that previous constructs had been based on environmental determinism, with people merely passive agents in the process of change.[83] Processual archaeologists had portrayed past cultures as homeostatic, with no consideration given to factors such as gender, ethnicity or identity. Post-processual archaeology was a spin-off from post-modernism which adopted elements of neo-Marxism, feminism and a host of other 'isms' There is no single theory; rather, it was simply a critique of past practices.

In Australia the interpretations of Harry Lourandos allowed new insights into the ancient past, particularly in relation to Aboriginal eel fisheries in south-western Victoria. Lourandos argued that the complex

Archaeology And Archaeological Endeavour

canals and channels equipped with trapping devices were not constructed to maximise productivity, but to ensure a continual and reliable supply of food in order to satisfy social needs in an unpredictable environment.[84] In Lourandos' view local Aboriginal groups intentionally altered the landscape and were therefore active agents in the process of change. He successfully entwined ethnographic accounts from the colonial era with archaeological material to provide a more humanistic picture of the past,[85] as opposed to processual archaeology's emphasis on scientific methodology.

As the opponents of processual archaeology insist, there can be no accurate reconstruction of the past owing to the inherent bias of researchers. Seen in this light any interpretation of the past can only be as good as the next. While there is certainly sense in that argument, the main weakness of post-processual archaeology is its tendency to focus narrowly on isolated sites and the role of individuals. How an archaeologist – or anyone else for that matter – can tap in to the mind of an ancient individual is conveniently left unexplained.[86] Processual archaeology, on the other hand, generalises across a broader canvas in a bid to understand the picture as a whole. Put simply, there are positives and negatives in both approaches, a powerful reminder that reconstruction of the past is itself a continually evolving process.

A strange anomaly has been the growth of 'New Age' or alternative archaeology since the early 1970s, when Erich von Daniken published *Chariots of the Gods*. This was the first of twenty-six books which have sold many millions of copies world-wide. A television series followed, all of it based on von Daniken's assertion that many unusual relics of the ancient past are evidence of extra-terrestrial visitations. Aboriginal rock art figures from widely diverse regions of Australia were held by von Daniken to be actual representations of intergalactic travellers thousands of years ago.[87] We are not alone, and nor is von Daniken, for many other 'New Age archaeologists' insist that parts of Australia were once colonised by ancient Egyptians, 'evidence' of which can be found in 'hieroglyphic' inscriptions in the Hunter Valley of New South Wales and elsewhere. Another alternative view of the past has come from a return to Biblical Creationism and a short chronology for the existence

Australia's Ancient Aboriginal Past

of humanity.[88] Proponents of both 'New Age' archaeology and Biblical Creationism reach far larger audiences than conventional archaeologists and their influence continues to spread. Not surprisingly, they deny the accuracy of scientific dating methods which have been developed since the end of the Second World War.

It is all a question of time, and when it comes to dating the past there are two broad concepts. One is relative dating whereby an ancient object is held to be younger or older than another. Until the appearance of radiocarbon dating (C^{14}) the best that was available to archaeologists was fluorine dating. All soils contain fluorine which is gradually absorbed by bones, and where two pieces of bone were found in close association it was possible to determine which one was older – a relative date, the full extent of its usefulness.[89] Absolute or chronometric dating, on the other hand, can provide a reasonably accurate date for an ancient object. Crucial to its effective operation, however, was the necessity to determine a starting-point in time that was universally acceptable, no mean feat in itself. With Christian convention the broader sweeps of time are divided into two periods, previously BC (Before Christ) and AD (or *Anno Domini*, the Year of Our Lord). More recently, these have been expressed as BCE (Before the Common Era) and CE (Common Era),[90] the style adopted in this chapter. For followers of the Islamic faith, though, the starting-point in time is the Hegira, the prophet's departure from Mecca, which is reckoned in the Christian calendar as CE 622. The first Olympic Games in 776 BCE triggered the clock for the ancient Greeks while for the Maya of Meso-America (who devised the most accurate calendar of all) it was 3114 BCE in the Christian calendar.[91]

For counting backwards in archaeological terms the starting-point in time is BP (Before Present) which is 1950, not the actual present. It marks the first published radiocarbon dates by American chemist Willard Libby in 1949, for convenience rounded out to the following year.[92] The radiocarbon isotope was discovered in 1940, but it was Libby who recognised its potential for dating organic remains such as bone, shell, wood and even charcoal. Tiny amounts of C^{14} are constantly produced in the atmosphere by cosmic rays which bombard nitrogen and oxygen

Archaeology And Archaeological Endeavour

atoms. Without elaborating on the entire chemical process, suffice to say that when produced it bonds with oxygen to form carbon dioxide which filters down to be absorbed by plants through photosynthesis. In this way it enters the bottom of the food chain and consequently animals, so that C^{14} is present in all living tissue where it continually breaks down and is replenished. The process stops at death, and it takes 5,730 years for half the remaining radiocarbon atoms to disintegrate. By measuring the amount remaining in an organic sample it is then possible to work out roughly when it died.[93]

C^{14} is reasonably accurate up to 40,000 years, but there are a number of inherent problems. While it was initially believed that solar radiation has remained constant over time, this is now known not to have been the case. Largely due to periodic changes in the Earth's magnetic field it fluctuates considerably, and it has also been found that prior to 1,000 BCE all living matter was exposed to greater concentrations of C^{14} than is the case today.[94] Another problem is that C^{14} can be contaminated through younger atoms entering the sample in the field or even the laboratory. Contaminated samples can thus be thousands of years younger than their true age, though in recent decades scientists have developed complex cleaning techniques to remove most of the impurities.[95] Problems nevertheless continue, as radiocarbon can also have geographical limitations. For example, in early 2020 it was discovered that radiocarbon dates for the northern hemisphere do not hold true for the Mediterranean region. The offset means that our accepted dates for ancient Egyptian dynasties and the Minoan, Mycenaean and Greek civilisations are slightly later than the true figure.[96]

The accuracy of C^{14} up to around 40,000 years BP is particularly pertinent in Australia because the human presence falls just outside its limits. Moreover, at that extreme age the radiocarbon concentration in any given sample is reduced to approximately one part per thousand trillion, which is extremely difficult to date. From the mid-1970s the problem has been partly countered through accelerator mass spectrometry (AMS) which only requires a minute sample. Less than one milligram of material is sufficient, and AMS can date it with incredible speed. Keratin, a protein from a single human hair, can contain fifty million C^{14} atoms, and to provide a reasonably accurate date it requires 10,000 of them to be counted. Previously that took about a year to accomplish; it can be done with AMS in just one minute, and it has the added advantage of being able to process multiple samples at the same time.[97] Calibration of more recent C^{14} dates has also been possible through dendrochronology, the annual growth rings on trees, and this has the potential to be extended as far back as 17,000 years with long-lived species such as Celery-top, King Billy and Huon Pines from Tasmania.[98] Even with this there are inherent problems, for in some years there are no growth rings at all, while in other years two growth rings can appear.[99]

Another dating technique which has been widely used in Australia is thermoluminescence. All heated objects contain a certain amount of radioactive substances. As they break down the energy emitted is stored in the object, and when reheated that energy is released and can be accurately measured. Thermoluminescence has been extensively used overseas to date ceramics, and it has been applied in Australia to Aboriginal rock art. The main drawback is that the rate of change is influenced by temperature and the amount of moisture present in the soil, ensuring that results are difficult to interpret with a high degree of accuracy.[100] Both these factors also have a bearing on the accuracy of optically stimulated luminescene (OSL) which has been used to date stone tools manufactured from material such as quartz and feldspar. OSL measures the electrons trapped in the crystalline structure of minerals or, in some cases, a single grain of sand.[101]

When dealing with remains of the past that stretch into the millions of years potassium argon dating has been extremely useful. It has been widely utilised in Africa to date fossil remains and the stone tools of early hominids, but there has been less call on it in Australia because of its dependence on volcanic rocks. The latter contain a specific amount of radioactive potassium which breaks down into argon gas, and by measuring the amount of radioactive potassium remaining in a given sample, and the amount of argon gas trapped within, it is possible to determine its absolute age.[102] In Australia, electron spin resonance

Archaeology And Archaeological Endeavour

(ESR) has been increasingly used with success to date skeletal remains, particularly tooth enamel. ESR was developed as far back as 1967 and has been continually improved. At the present time it has a range of approximately two million years, but it is an extremely complicated process which lies in the realm of quantum physics and is understood by relatively few scientists.[103] These are just some of dating techniques currently available. There are many others – archaeomagnetism, racemisation, uranium series dating – the list goes on. Many more will undoubtedly appear in the future, and they are likely to exceed even ESR in complexity. For all that, we will gain even more valuable insights into the ancient human past, and to conclude this discussion it is worthwhile to demonstrate how the discipline of archaeology can impact upon daily life in the contemporary world.

In 1973 Dr William Rathje of the University of Arizona in the United States initiated the Tucson Garbage Project to determine patterns of urban consumption through a study of household refuse and to compare the results with answers from personal interviews. It was found that in the most socio-economically deprived suburbs of the city the standard of health care was far lower, and dietary habits substantially worse, than what the interviewees claimed. Right across the city those interviewed also stated they wasted little or no solid food: a study of their rubbish revealed that on average they wasted fifteen per cent. An interesting development occurred in 1987 when researchers noticed that people were purchasing less fresh red meat and discarding larger quantities of separable fat. This was in response to a report the previous year which warned that fat from red meat posed a possible cancer risk. The majority of people had turned to processed red meat in the form of hotdogs, sausages and salami – all of which contained large quantities of *hidden* fat. Finally, eighty-five per cent of interviewees claimed they did not drink beer, while the remaining fifteen per cent stated they consumed less than eight cans per week. In fact, only twenty-five per cent abstained from beer; twenty-one per cent drank no more than eight cans per week, while the remaining fifty-four per cent exceeded that amount.[104] Refuse archaeology, or 'garbology' as it is affectionately termed, has been adopted in Australia and a number of other countries to improve living standards. Much can be learned from a study of human refuse, regardless if it is from the modern era or the remote past. It is now time to follow the trail back to the very origins of humanity so many millions of years ago.

HUMAN ORIGINS, EVOLUTION AND GLOBAL DISPERSAL

II

This chapter explores the origin and evolution of the human species as well as the dispersal of *Homo sapiens sapiens* throughout the world. Australia features prominently in that diaspora, for it is here that we find some of the earliest indications of modern human behaviour outside Africa and the Near East. It is in Australia, or the ancient supercontinent of Sahul as it then was, that the first evidence of cremation appears. The earliest remains were also sprinkled with ochre, perhaps indicative of a belief in the afterlife. Ancient artworks testify to intellectualism and a sense of the aesthetic, and there is abundant evidence suggesting that Aboriginal people purposely altered the environment for their own advantage. These are all markers of modern human behaviour.

It is now known that when the Aboriginal people entered Sahul a number of other hominids still walked the planet. Rather than a family tree, human evolution was a thick bush from which all but one branch eventually withered and died. It was previously believed that modern humans had only reigned supreme in the last 15,000 years or so. New dating of the *Homo floresiensis* remains has suggested that we need to push this back a little (see Chapter 4), but we do know that our Neanderthal cousins (*Homo neanderthalensis*) held out on their rocky stronghold of Gibraltar until at least 29,000 years ago. Future discoveries may yet reduce the period of our presumed supremacy. And while all hominids and hominoids (primates) descended from a shrew-like ancestor in the depths of antiquity, their paths independently diverged from the common rootstock. The earliest-known primate is *Darwinius masillae*, affectionately known as 'Ida', a virtually intact 47 million-year-old specimen uncovered by a private collector from the shale beds of Germany's Messel Pit in 1982.[1] Until recently it was also thought that Old World monkeys split from the tree early in the Oligocene epoch some 38 MYA. The discovery of *Saadanius hijazensis* in western Saudi Arabia has now reduced the time of that divergence to somewhere between 28 and 24 MYA.[2] Apes were the next splinter group to follow just prior to the advent of the Miocene epoch. Fossil remains of *Proconsul*, a genus which bore a mixture of ape- and monkey-like features, first appeared around 23 MYA.[3] Finally, sometime between 14 and 7 MYA the evolutionary line which eventually led to modern humans also sheered off from the main stem. Despite the fragmentary evidence, much of it relying on chance events and even more fortunate finds, we know more about the hominid past than we do about the ancestral primates.

While both groups increased in size over time, the primates reached their physical peak in the Early to Middle Pleistocene (between two million and 300,000 years BP), with the emergence of *Gigantopithecus blacki* and *Gigantopithecus bilaspurensis*. The former is known from sixteen sites in China south of the Yangtze River, though its range possibly extended to Vietnam and northern Thailand. The distribution of the second species appears to have been restricted to modern Pakistan. Both are known only from their mandibles and dentition, enough to suggest that they were twice the size of modern gorillas, with an estimated body mass of between 200–300 kilograms.[4] Up to three metres in height, their massive bulk inhibited an upright stature,[5] and while they were truly formidable creatures, dental micro-wear has revealed that they were strictly herbivorous, feeding on a wide range of fruits, leaves, stems and possibly underground tubers in tropical and sub-tropical deciduous and evergreen forests.[6] It is also known that morphological changes in their dentition and the steadily increasing size of their teeth over time point to adaptive dietary behaviour, which could have been a response to ecological pressures, and possibly linked to their eventual disappearance. Alternatively, the demise of these terrestrial creatures roughly coincided with the arrival of *Homo erectus*, a hominid with both intelligence and appetite,[7] and while it may be pulling a rather long bow, it has been suggested that the frozen remains of *Gigantopithecus*

Human Origins, Evolution And Global Dispersal

could have inspired the legend of the Yeti in the Himalayas and adjacent regions.[8]

Apart from physical size, another characteristic shared by both hominids and the primates has been an increase in intelligence and complex social behaviour. The former has obviously been more pronounced in hominids than primates, but it did lead to opportunism in both groups. Baboons and chimpanzees, for example, exploit every available food source, and it may well have been an extension of this capability that allowed the first hominids, especially the line which ultimately led to modern humans, to thrive in an extremely competitive world.[9] One of the most successful of our distant ancestors were the Dryopithecines, ape-like creatures which evolved in Africa and flourished between 12 and 9 MYA. Their appearance coincided with a warmer climate, temperatures in more temperate regions averaging around 12° Celsius higher than today. It was even hotter in the tropics, and combined with high rainfall it ensured that lush forests covered much of Africa and Eurasia.[10] Those conditions allowed the Dryopithecines to spread rapidly from Africa into Europe, while a related genus, *Sivapithecus*, dominated Asia.[11] During the late Miocene epoch the world truly was a planet of the apes.

Successful though they undoubtedly were, Dryopithecines were relatively small creatures with an average body length of sixty centimetres and a weight of up to thirty-five kilograms. Most of their life was spent in trees where they consumed soft leaves and fruit. Unlike true apes, however, they did not walk on their knuckles: the structure of their limbs and wrist reveal that they walked on the flat of their hands.[12] But at the very height of their development climate change apparently spelt the beginning of the end for the Dryopithecines. Temperatures plummeted and the large tropical forests began contracting at a steadily increasing rate. Unable to adapt to their altered circumstances the Dryopithecines eventually disappeared,[13] but the recent discovery of one of their kind, *Danuvius guggenmosi*, which inhabited forests in Germany some 11.6 MYA, has provided new insights into erect postures and bipedalism. While *Danuvius* clearly had the ability to walk erect it was also equipped with long arms perfectly suited to hanging in trees. So whether this strange ape walked flat-footed along the ground or confined its upright locomotion to the tops of tree branches remains in some doubt. The issue is extremely clouded, as the patterns of movement and accompanying postures of Dryopithecines and many other ancestral apes lie beyond our comprehension. Evolutionary experimentation with locomotion literally moved in unimaginable ways,[14] and while climate change appears to have been responsible for the demise of the Dryopithecines, at least three new genera of ape-like creatures appeared in their wake.

One of them was *Ramapithecus*, the three known species of which inhabited dry forest environments of Africa, Europe and Asia. Studies of their dentition have shown that they ate tougher and far less nutritious foods than is usual for any of the primates, but just like their predecessors they were able to flourish. The fossil record documents their existence between 9 and 5 MYA, a remarkable success given that the Ramapithecines were even smaller than the Dryopithecines. Although weighing only around twenty kilograms, their skeletal features suggest they may have been far less arboreal than their predecessors.[15]

Unlike the Ramapithecines, the other two genera were much more restricted in their distribution. *Sahelanthropus tchadensis*, a single species, dates from around 7 MYA. This represents a critical point in human evolution, and it could be relevant that *Sahelanthropus* did not live in East Africa where the remains of virtually all of its predecessors – and successors – have been found. *Sahelanthropus* was discovered 2,400 kilometres to the west in sub-Saharan Chad. At that time the landscape was open woodland, and the skull of this species displays both ape- and human-like characteristics. It had a short face and a massive brow ridge, but the mouth and jaw did not protrude like other apes and it had relatively small canine teeth.[16] In other words, *Sahelanthropus* was physically advanced from all its known forebears, and while there has been considerable debate over its rightful position in the evolutionary bush, it is generally agreed that this creature was either a hominid or at the very least an extremely close ancestor.[17]

The third genus is similarly known from a single species, *Orrorin tugenensis*, dated to between 6.2 and 5.6 MYA. Skeletal remains of five individuals have been unearthed in Kenya, the first in the year 2000.

Human Origins, Evolution And Global Dispersal

From the molars and reduced canines it has been inferred that *Orrorin* lived principally on fruits and vegetables with an occasional meal of meat. Notwithstanding that all their fossil remains are extremely fragmented, and there is not even a partially complete skeleton, the general consensus is that this creature had the mechanical ability to walk upright. The conjecture is based on the shape of the femur, or upper thighbone, which was compared with 300 femurs from great apes, other extinct hominids and modern humans. Understandably, there are a few sceptics who insist that more skeletal evidence, particularly in the form of a pelvis, foot or spine is required before proof of bipedalism can be conclusively shown.[18] Despite the acrimony it could again be relevant that while *Orrorin* appears to have lived in a dense forest environment,[19] it was interspersed with more open areas.[20] There can be little question that such habitats had the effect of triggering further evolutionary change among the ancestral hominids.

This was clearly a major contributing factor between 5.8 and 5.5 MYA when yet another new genus of proto-hominids appears in the fossil record. There were at least two species of *Ardipithecus*, the more recent of which disappeared some 4.4 MYA, and they were clearly a major advance on what had come before. Skeletal fragments of *Ardipithecus ramidus*, the last known species, were first unearthed in Ethiopia in 1992, but since then further examples have been found elsewhere in eastern and northern Africa as far west as Chad. It was in Ethiopia, though, where a virtually complete skeleton of the species was discovered in January 1995.[21] This specimen, in particular, provided palaeoanthropologists with a much clearer understanding of their place in human evolution. *Ardipithecus* was not particularly intelligent, having a cranial capacity in the order of 300–350 cubic centimetres, roughly corresponding with that of a modern chimpanzee.[22] The dentition, on the other hand, was quite different. While they were certainly prominent, the upper canines were nowhere near as large nor as sharp as those of the chimpanzee. Furthermore, there was little appreciable difference in the size of the canines between the sexes. This has led to speculation that *Ardipithecus* may have been less aggressive and consequently more social than all previous proto-hominids. The general dentition also points to a less specialised diet. They were certainly omnivorous and perhaps opportunistic feeders which did not have the same reliance on fibrous plants, ripe fruit and hard abrasive food as primates.[23] It seems more likely they ate what they could easily obtain in the way of plants, insects and possibly meat.

The most distinctive physical feature of *Ardipithecus* is the base of its cranium, which shares a number of significant features with later members of the genus *Homo*. Rather than suggesting that *Ardipithecus* is an ancient ancestor of our own species, however, it is more likely that the characteristics of the cranial base are a form of parallel evolution among the apes following their split with the more direct ancestors of hominids.[24] Similar trends can be found in the feet and pelvis of *Ardipithecus*. Unlike the feet of chimpanzees which are specialised for grasping tree limbs, those of *Ardipithecus* were designed (at least to some extent) for walking upright. The shape of the pelvis serves to reinforce the capability of bipedalism, but it would be a mistake to claim that these proto-hominids spent a great deal of their time standing erect on two legs. They did not. The presence of a powerful grasping toe along with the structure of the hip and thigh leads to the conclusion that they probably used all four limbs when moving about in trees. On the ground their upright gait would have been awkward at best, and they would not have been capable of walking any great distance.[25] Running was entirely out of the question.

Importantly, though, it is with this genus that we see a marked divergence from the primates. Minor sexual dimorphism is a distinctively hominid trait, and their ability to walk upright in an open woodland habitat is of particular interest. Until the 1990s the leading theory was that climate change had dried out much of Africa where apes were dominant. Forests were replaced by dry savannah grasslands which (so the theory went), led directly to bipedalism. The ability to stand erect was held to give ape-like creatures a distinct advantage by allowing them to see over the grasslands to observe potential food sources as well as predators. At the same time, a vertical stance exposed less of the body to the harsh tropical sun. While all this made perfect sense, knowledge that a number of the more advanced proto-hominids, including *Ardipithecus*, inhabited open woodland and probably walked upright led to a major revision of the theory. It is now believed that climate change created a mosaic of open woodland and savannah grasslands. Such an environment allowed the primitive ancestors of modern humans to forage on grasslands and either advance or retreat to protective copses of trees. With their hands free they could carry items of food across open expanses. Literally taking this a step further, males with a superior walking ability might have carried food back to waiting females, thus enhancing their chances of winning a mate and passing on their genes through natural selection. The revised model has an element of plausibility without denying the likelihood that arboreal habits remained predominant.[26] At the very least these creatures climbed trees for safety, particularly when predators were in the vicinity. They may have also slept in trees when no other refuge was available, which is not dissimilar from the behaviour of many modern primates. Depending on the species and habitat, baboons find refuge at night on either rocky ledges or in trees.[27]

A major advance in human evolution came with the emergence of the Australopithecines around 4.4 MYA. There were a number of species belonging to two genera, the gracile *Australopithecus*, and the later more robust forms known as *Paranthropus*. The Australopithecines perhaps lasted until 1.5–2 MYA, indicative of their success as a whole.[28] What is important is that the majority of palaeoanthropologists agreed they were directly on the path which led to modern humans. The only question was whether the evolution of the robust forms was divergent or convergent – did *Paranthropus* evolve from the gracile Australopithecines, or were they an entirely separate evolutionary stream.

In 1924 skeletal remains of the first specimen, a juvenile *Australopithecus*, were discovered by a quarry worker at Taung in South Africa. They were studied by an Australian anatomist, Raymond Dart, who was based in Johannesburg: his report was published the following year. Dart recognised that a number of the skeletal features bore hominid characteristics, concluding that it represented an early human ancestor.[29] Dart's Australopithecine bore the specific name *africanus*, but his findings took many years to be accepted by the wider scientific community,[30] and that was largely due to the discovery of further Australopithecine fossils. They continue to come to light.[31] The most famous example, a gracile *Australopithecus afarensis* known as 'Lucy', was unearthed in 1974 in Ethiopia. Over a period of three weeks a joint American and French team managed to recover slightly less than forty per cent of the skeleton, a truly gruelling task.[32] Like all other Australopithecines 'Lucy' was a relatively small creature, standing just 1.1 metres tall. While 'Lucy' and her kin were roaming east Africa between four and 2.5 MYA, they had contemporaries in southern Africa, including *Australopithecus africanus* (3–2.5 MYA) and the earlier *Australopithecus prometheus* some 3.5 MYA.[33] On the basis of faunal correlation, U-Pb dating and palaeomagnetic data, yet another South African species, *Australopithecus sediba*, is understood to have been extant from around 1.78 to 1.95 MYA.[34] Although it cannot be demonstrated they were truly sympatric, *Paranthropus robustus* and a species of hominid with a cranial vault remarkably similar to that of *Homo erectus* were fellow travellers around this same period in time.[35] If the Australopithecines gave rise to the genus *Homo*, as is the current view, it does seem rather odd that both the gracile and robust forms should roughly co-exist with their intellectually superior successors, and that particularly applies to *Homo erectus*. What can be said for now, however, is that the robust members of the genus *Paranthropus* were slightly taller than the gracile Australopithecines, standing up to 1.4 metres in height,[36] with the cranial capacity of both genera ranging from around 400 to 530 cubic centimetres.

It is unanimously accepted that the Australopithecines walked upright, thus demolishing an old argument which held that large brains preceded bipedalism.[37] The latter clearly came first, and further evidence which strengthened the case of bipedalism in Australopithecines came through a chance discovery at Laetoli in Tanzania during 1974. A member of Mary Leakey's team searching for early hominid fossils noticed some unusual depressions on the surface of an ancient layer of volcanic ash. Careful excavation of the site revealed the tracks of long-extinct animals which had walked through the ash while it was still soft and damp, most likely after a light shower of rain.[38]

Human Origins, Evolution And Global Dispersal

This was an extremely fortuitous find. The ash was an unusual type known as carbonatite, and when it comes in contact with water – in this instance rain that was neither too heavy nor too light – it formed into a solution. When the water evaporated it left behind a mineral crystal called trona which hardened into concrete. The volcano then erupted again, laying down another protective layer over the top, with the entire process repeated. The fact that this had happened with animal tracks was rare enough, but as Leakey's team uncovered more of the layer they unexpectedly came upon a trail of human-like footprints extending for twenty-three metres. It was initially thought the tracks had been made by two individuals. Closer analysis, however, revealed that a third individual had purposely walked in the footsteps of one in front.[39] The indentations make it clear their heels were rounded, the arch was raised, the large big toe was aligned with the second toe, and that all toes gripped the ground in the same manner as modern humans.[40]

The Laetoli tracks have been dated to 3.5 MYA, and as bones and teeth belonging to *Australopithecus afarensis* have been found in the same general area and dated to approximately the same time, the footprints are assumed to be theirs – or at least made by members of the same species.[41] But this has been disputed on the basis of foot morphology as well as the fossilised remains of hominid feet.[42] Very little is known of the locomotor biomechanisms of early hominids. Modern humans clear the ground by tilting the pelvis, whereas the leg movement of Australopithecines appears to have been based around the hip joint which made their mode of locomotion more like a waddle.[43] More recent analysis of the Laetoli tracks suggest that the prints were made by hominids with a striding gait closely resembling that of modern humans. While the velocity was almost certainly slower,[44] it has nonetheless cast serious doubts on the widely-held belief that the tracks were made by Australopithecines.

Although the majority of gracile forms evolved first, the emergence of robust Australopithecines led to some overlap, with at least one species from each genera possibly contemporaneous throughout their entire co-existence. That in itself deserves some reflection because similar species living in a virtually identical manner cannot share the same environment without facing unacceptable competition from each other. It is simply not Nature's way, with one species invariably becoming extinct. Richard Leakey has argued that gracile Australopithecines were general foragers feeding on plants, insects, eggs, reptiles and possibly small mammals. *Paranthropus*, on the other hand, was more specialised, subsisting on plants and grubs, a restrictive diet which ultimately resulted in extinction through their inability to adapt. The dietary intake of both genera was confirmed through a close examination of their tooth enamel using an electron microscope, a procedure which reveals different types of scratch marks. Where both forms were contemporaneous they were ecologically separate. Robust Australopithecines appear to have primarily inhabited wooded areas while their gracile cousins foraged on the forest margins and the adjoining grasslands.[45] Australopithecines also fell prey to the large felines which co-existed with them. At one site in South Africa palaeoanthropologists discovered the remains of sixty *Paranthropus* individuals which had been devoured by leopards.[46] While this appears to confirm the woodland habitat of robust Australopithecines, further isotopic studies have shown that their diet was broad-based and included savannah grasses or at least animals which had consumed them. Rather than over-specialisation, other factors are therefore required to account for their eventual extinction.[47]

In 1964 Louis Leakey, Phillip Tobias and John Napier stumbled on something far more advanced than the Australopithecines at Olduvai Gorge in Tanzania. Based on very flimsy evidence, Leakey announced that the skeletal fragments belonged to an entirely new species of hominid which the trio named *Homo habilis*, or 'handy man'. It was so-named because the fragments were closely associated with a number of simple stone tools.[48] More skeletal remains have since been found to support the original classification, and the species is believed to have lived from around 2.3 to 1.4 MYA. That means it was contemporaneous with the later robust Australopithecines, though recent evidence suggests the gracile Australopithecines were actually the first hominids to manufacture stone tools.[49] Despite the inclusion of *habilis* in the same genus as modern humans, they stood only 1.5 metres high and weighed less than forty-five kilograms.[50] Early criticism of its placement within

Human Origins, Evolution And Global Dispersal

the genus *Homo* revolved around the relatively small brain capacity of 680 cubic centimetres – marginally below the accepted threshold of 700 cubic centimetres.[51] Leakey countered that the species displayed a number of morphological features that were distinctly human, and although his taxonomic classification has thus far stood the test of time it remains controversial.[52] There have also been attempts to classify specimens with slightly larger crania and dentition as a separate species, *Homo rudolfensis*.[53]

It is widely held that *Homo habilis* (aka *rudolfensis*), along with the Australopithecines, had some form of social organisation, and this is extremely important for a number of reasons. Until recently it was unanimously accepted that a later hominid, *Homo erectus*, was the first member of the genus to step foot outside the African continent. Modern humans, *Homo sapiens*, later followed in their footsteps to eventually spread across the globe – or so it was held. Research in South-East Asia is beginning to paint a slightly different picture. A careful examination of a dataset comprising crania, dentition and post-cranial remains from a variety of ancient hominids has suggested that the ancestor of the diminutive 'Hobbits' (*Homo floresiensis*) of Indonesia may not have been *Homo erectus* as most believed (and it needs to be noted that many still hold firm to that view). Rather than having been subjected to insular dwarfism over an extended period of time on their island home, it has been argued that the small stature of the species of just over a metre in height owed more to its only slightly larger ancestor, *Homo habilis*. The evidence seemingly points towards the 'Hobbits' having closer affinities with this species than any other member of the genus *Homo*,[54] and it may not have been unique, as another extinct diminutive hominid from the island of Luzon in the Philippines (discovered in 2007 but only confirmed as a separate species in 2019) has yet to undergo a similar comparative study.[55] While perhaps the majority of palaeoanthropologists still consider this implausible,[56] it is becoming increasingly apparent that *Homo habilis* or at least a derivative member of the clade could have actually been the first hominid to exit the African continent. This would not have been a conscious decision, but it did require exceptionally favourable environmental conditions, some form of cooperation amongst members of the species, and an advance in technology.

It is likely that *Homo habilis* either lived in small groups in a similar manner to primates, or more concentrated family units, with a radical divergence possibly stemming from the sharing of resources.[57] Primates very seldom share food with their own kind, chimpanzees being the major exception even though it is usually only given grudgingly. At some point in human evolution the hominids began to share their food resources, but whether this behaviour actually began with *Homo habilis*, the Australopithecines or even earlier cannot be known. All that can be surmised is that the success of the genus *Homo* was – and still is – at least partly due to a complex social organisation which included the sharing of resources. On the balance of probabilities *Homo habilis* appears to have been the first to develop that strategy, with food distribution having profound consequences for the future. But there are two differing lines of thought as to what triggered this alteration of lifestyle, with some researchers favouring the 'hunting hypothesis' while others place greater emphasis on food gathering.[58]

The 'hunting hypothesis' turns on the notion that early hominids advanced from scavenging to hunting larger game animals as their desire for meat increased. Meat is only a dietary supplement for primates, while for the majority of modern humans it is usually a significant component of the diet. The hypothesis appears to be strengthened if consideration is given to the hunting activities of certain non-human carnivores such as wolves, lions or even dingoes, which work together and share the spoils. Conversely, other non-human predators – bears and leopards are useful examples – generally do not. The 'hunting hypothesis' also tends to place too much emphasis on male aggression. By following this theory through it can be argued that hunting large game animals stemmed from a desire to kill, or a culture of killing. Yet for the majority of extant hunter-gathering societies it is women who play a pivotal role in the survival of the group as a whole. Plants constitute the bulk of the diet, with game meat often an irregular addition.[59]

So it could just as easily be asked whether food sharing among early hominids arose from an ever-increasing period of child dependency. In

Human Origins, Evolution And Global Dispersal

other words, mothers would have been forced to increase the scope of their gathering activities to provide food for dependent offspring. There is also another way of considering this issue. While human brains average only two per cent of total body weight they consume approximately twenty per cent of all the energy produced. The ratio is even greater with children, foetal brains consuming up to seventy per cent of all energy coming from the mother. Nor does it stop there: during the first year of infancy the brain still consumes sixty per cent of a child's total energy. As the brains of hominids increased in size around 500,000 years BP it was females who paid the highest price. Having infants, particularly after they began maturing later, meant that mothers had to rely more heavily on others – and they required higher quality foods such as game that was rich in protein. This bequeathed two possibilities: increased meat consumption and a greater dependency on males.[60]

The problem here is that the first tools, whether manufactured from stone, bone or wood, were not used for hunting large game animals. On the contrary, they were employed to gather plants and small prey as well as dismembering carcasses. Hands and tools merely replaced some of the functions of teeth, but if the 'gathering hypothesis' is accepted there is once again an over-emphasis on one aspect of survival at the expense of the other. Perhaps it involved both, because evolutionary success results from maintaining and/or improving access to food. Early hominids certainly expanded their range of foodstuffs,[61] and that gave them a distinct advantage over the primates which were evolving alongside them. It is therefore likely that the early hominids were principally scavengers, eating meat killed by other carnivores which had already eaten their fill or been driven off through co-operative aggression. Even though *Homo habilis* apparently developed a co-operative social organisation, their ability to obtain concentrated protein and fat could well have relied heavily on scavenging.[62]

The genus *Homo* has traditionally been associated with the acquisition of culture, reduced mastication, bipedalism and,[63] of course, a cranial capacity above 700 cubic centimetres. *Homo habilis* could have been endowed with most of these attributes. Compared with modern humans the species had disproportionately longer arms, much like the gracile Australopithecines from which they probably evolved. The face, however, did not protrude anywhere near the extent of its predecessor and was far more akin to modern humans. So, too, was the dentition.[64] The main difficulty remains with its relatively small cranial capacity which fell into the maximum reached by the Australopithecines. Not that this necessarily reflected their level of intelligence.[65]

One of the ways to estimate cranial capacity is by filling the cast of a braincase with millet seed and measuring it. This system is obviously not foolproof and estimates can vary widely. On the other hand, over the last few decades there has been a greater understanding of early hominid brains. While the brain itself does not survive in the archaeological record, it does leave distinctive impressions on the inside of the braincase. Both halves of all hominoid brains are divided into four lobes and a few general statements can be made about the function of each. The frontal lobe controls movement and to some extent the emotions, while the occipital lobe at the back of the brain is responsible for vision. The temporal lobe is crucial for memory, and the parietal lobe collates, compares and integrates all information flowing into the brain via the sensory channels – sight, hearing and touch. The parietal and temporal lobes predominate in hominids whereas in primates they are smaller and of less importance.[66]

Keeping these guidelines in mind, Ralph Holloway of Columbia University in New York examined the braincases of Australopithecines and a number of other early hominids, including *Homo habilis*. He found that while they were certainly smaller their architecture was remarkably similar to modern humans. This also had important implications for their ability to speak. In modern human brains there is a section located near the front of the left hemisphere known as Broca's area which controls the muscles of the mouth, tongue and throat during speech. Another section at the side of the left hemisphere known as Wernicke's area collates information from the eyes and ears to structure and make sense of language. Both these anatomical features are well developed in modern humans, but Holloway was surprised to find the unmistakable impression of Broca's area on a cranium of *Homo habilis* known as

Human Origins, Evolution And Global Dispersal

skull 1470. Although there was no impression of Wernicke's area, its absence could have been due to the antiquity and poor condition of the braincase. This suggests that *Homo habilis* may have had some form of rudimentary speech, and even more surprising was the distinct impression of an enlarged corresponding feature on Australopithecine crania.[67]

It does need to be noted, however, that there is a swelling in the brain of modern apes which roughly corresponds to the position of Broca's area in hominids. The brains of modern apes also differ by having one hemisphere – usually the right – larger than the other, but what purpose is served by the swelling in the brain remains a mystery.[68] So whether the Australopithecines and *Homo habilis* did have the ability to speak must remain in doubt. All that can be said is that both Broca's area and Wernicke's area have developed steadily up to the present time. Unlike all other animals it is speech which has become the main channel for the flow of information among modern humans, and this has been further enhanced by the position of the larynx, which is ideally located to act as a sound source. Such an evolutionary refinement has nonetheless come at a high price. The position of the larynx means that it can, and often does, interfere with chewing and eating. When food falls into the windpipe it causes choking, occasionally with fatal consequences.[69]

It is more likely that the Australopithecines and *Homo habilis* had the ability to make sounds even if it was not actual speech. Viewed in this light it can also be said that as speech became increasingly important as a means of communication, the biological mechanisms were even further refined in the immediate ancestors of modern humans. This begs the question at to why speech developed in the first place. Apes do not require speech for communication, and yet modern humans clearly do, which suggests that it could be linked to a higher degree of socialisation.

It was once believed that language evolved through co-operative activities, particularly hunting, which required an efficient means of communication between the participants. Yet carnivorous animals which hunt in packs, and the Australian wild dog or dingo (*Canis familiaris dingo*) is a good example, do not necessarily communicate vocally. Dingoes manipulate their group size and alter their hunting strategies to maximise success without the benefit of any obvious vocal communication.[70] Moreover, the majority of human hunters rarely communicate by speech during an organised hunt, usually relying on hand signals. Speech, then, could have had its genesis in food-sharing. If it is accepted that social organisation led to a hunter-gathering society with a gendered division of labour – and that it resulted in temporary home bases and leisure activities – language would have proved extremely beneficial.[71] Knowledge is more easily transmitted through vocal communication, and that applies equally to other highly-social animals including bees, which have developed a sophisticated system for the exchange of information through sound waves.[72] Higher intelligence has merely taken it to another level in modern humans, and although the vocabulary of early hominids may have been rudimentary at best it was without doubt a major evolutionary – not to say revolutionary – step.

And it was reinforced by the use of stone tools. While the Australopithecines may have used only naturally flaked stone for cutting,[73] *Homo habilis* invented Oldowan technology by striking quartz, quartzite and volcanic stone cores to produce sharp flakes. Some were only two or three centimetres in length, but they were sufficient to butcher a carcass the size of a cow. Named after Olduvai Gorge in Tanzania where tools of this type were first discovered, Oldowan technology seems to have signalled the beginning of a totally new economic order and perhaps provided *Homo habilis* with the means to expand beyond the African continent. Their technology was not to be superseded until around 1.6 MYA when Acheulean tools first appear in the archaeological record.[74] Oldowan technology distanced hominids even further from the primates, but it did not guarantee protection from other predators. There is evidence suggesting that *Homo habilis* regularly fell prey to leopards, the sabre-toothed *Megantereon*, and hyenas.[75]

Life was deadly in Africa, and then just prior to 2 MYA a splinter group of *Homo habilis* within the continent evolved into an entirely new species which is generally recognised as the first globe-trotter, eventually finding their way as far east as China and as far north as Germany.[76] The newcomer was *Homo erectus*, the earliest forms of which are also known as *Homo ergaster*.[77] Later types are currently understood to be the immediate ancestor of *Homo sapiens sapiens*, and given the enormous span of time *Homo erectus* walked the earth – from 2 MYA to perhaps as recently as 27,000–53,000 years BP – it was the most successful member of the genus *Homo*.[78] The latter figures nevertheless need to be qualified, as the most recent evidence of the species in Africa is around 1 MYA, while in mainland Asia it was accepted that *Homo erectus* became extinct some time before 500,000 years BP. In December 1996, however, C.C. Swisher III and associates announced that electron spin resonance and mass spectrometric dating of fossil bovid teeth from hominid-bearing levels at two sites in central Java were evidence that *Homo erectus* had long outlived its mainland relations.[79] These dating techniques do have their problems, and a later revised estimate suggested the true figure is closer to 110,000 years BP,[80] which is still fairly recent and long after the disappearance of the species on the Asian mainland.

Nor is it surprising that there was substantial biological variation between the earliest and later members of this species. The archaic type, *Homo ergaster*, had a slightly more protrusive face, thinner bones and a smaller brain capacity of somewhere between 800 and 900 cubic centimetres. From the neck down the classic form of *Homo erectus* was not all that different from modern humans. They stood around 1.8 metres tall and were slightly more robust than their modern descendants. When the later type emerged the brain capacity had expanded to an average 1,100 cubic centimetres. Above the neck they differed from modern humans by having a low sloping forehead, heavy brow ridges and an extremely weak chin.[81]

It has been argued that *Homo erectus* lacked any obvious covering of body hair, and if that was the case they probably had dark skin. The species arose in a tropical environment where darker pigmentation is essential protection against the harmful effects of ultraviolet rays. At the same time, though, all hominids require at least some measure of vitamin D, so it is reasonable to assume that as *Homo erectus* spread into more temperate regions their pigmentation became lighter in response to weaker sunlight.[82] Of course, it is not known with any certainty that this species lacked a protective covering of thick hair, but as one of the most immediate ancestors of modern humans such an assumption is not entirely unreasonable.

Probably originating in east Africa (despite the earliest remains recently uncovered in the Drimolen Main Quarry in north-eastern South Africa),[83] *Homo erectus* first came to light in Asia and owe their discovery to the remarkable determination of Dutch anatomist Eugene Dubois. A lecturer at the University of Amsterdam, Dubois was consumed by an interest in the ancestors of modern humans, and his choice of Asia as the possible cradle of humanity was heavily influenced by the writings of Alfred Russel Wallace, Darwin's co-proponent of evolutionary theory. The presence in Asia of Orangutans – or 'men of the forest' as they were termed in Malay – convinced Wallace that ancestral humans were likely to have inhabited South-East Asia.[84]

Unable to gain sponsorship for a private survey, Dubois enlisted in the Dutch East India Army as a physician in 1887 and was first posted to Sumatra. With ample leisure time he excavated many remote caves on the island and accumulated a huge collection of fossils from long-extinct fauna.[85] Human remains were a very different matter, and it was not until Dubois was transferred to Java that he finally found what he was searching for in 1891. Digging into the bank of the Solo River at Trinil, his workmen uncovered an archaic hominid braincase and a legbone which Dubois subsequently named *Pithecanthropus erectus*, or 'ape-man who walks erect'.[86] Java was to yield many more examples of this hominid, but it was not until 1960 that they were finally classified as members of the genus *Homo*.[87]

In the late 1920s the distribution of what was to become known as *Homo erectus* was extended to China after Davidson Black, a Canadian anatomist, conducted his own quest for early hominid remains. In 1927 Black examined a lower molar hominid tooth found by Dr Birger Bohlin at Zhoukoudian and boldly announced the discovery of an entirely new species which he named *Sinanthropus pekinensis*, or 'Peking Man'. Fortunately for Black's reputation, the first of a number of crania was uncovered the following year, confirming that it was indeed a hominid,[88] but what is surprising is that Black adhered to the new generic name even though it was obvious from the outset that the fossils differed little

Human Origins, Evolution And Global Dispersal

from Dubois' *Pithecanthropus*.[89] Since then many more specimens of *Homo erectus* have been found throughout Asia,[90] with phylogenetic studies suggesting that the Asian branch eventually became extinct while the African population evolved into archaic *Homo sapiens*.[91] Once again, however, there is no certainty in any of this.

And just like *Homo habilis* (or members of its clade) it is not known what factors triggered the exodus of *Homo erectus* from Africa. It was once suspected that increased intelligence had resulted in new technological advances, evidenced by the appearance of Acheulean tools around 1.6 MYA. The most obvious examples were hand axes which had been worked symmetrically on both sides and were useful for a variety of purposes.[92] These tools have been found in association with *Homo erectus* in many areas of Africa, Europe, the Near East and on the Indian sub-continent. They take their name from St Acheul, a suburb of Amiens in northern France, where this stone technology was first identified.[93] The theory was that with these more sophisticated tools *Homo erectus* could exploit a wider range of food sources and was their ticket of Africa. The problem is that Acheulean tools have not been found at all *Homo erectus* sites, and nor are they known from South-East Asia.[94]

The late Australian palaeoanthropologist, Alan Thorne, suggested that Acheulean technology may have been superseded by tools made from less durable materials such as bamboo before the species reached South-East Asia. In some instances such tools are superior to stone technology and they are definitely far more versatile.[95] Yet if it was advanced stone technology which possibly allowed *Homo habilis*, and more definitely *Homo erectus*, to exit Africa it is rather odd that the latter's tools should disappear altogether. This leaves open the possibility that it was climate change rather than technology which contributed to the expansion and success of *Homo erectus*. There is evidence of faunal dispersals through corridors which periodically opened between East Africa and Asia Minor, and it is quite possible – if not highly-likely – that *Homo erectus* followed prey species through these temporary passages.[96] This argument is linked to an increasingly carnivorous diet, because carnivores require larger home ranges,[97] a consequence of which is territorial expansion.

On a geological timescale it would not have taken *Homo erectus* (or its predecessor) all that long to reach Asia. An advance of just ten kilometres every generation would have been sufficient to accomplish the journey in 25,000 years.[98] Expansion was probably a lot quicker than that, with each generation simply moving further afield to stake out its own territory, whether it was to the north or the east. All this has given rise to a debate whether *Homo sapiens* evolved only in Africa – or whether there were multiple evolutions. Proponents of the 'Multiregional' thesis argue that if modern humans descended from *Homo erectus* it could just as easily have happened in Asia as Africa, and probably around the same time in both regions. Although these populations were widely separated they believe there was sufficient contact for interbreeding and flow of genetic material. 'Out of Africa' theorists, on the other hand, maintain there were two (now possibly three) hominid migrations from Africa, with *Homo sapiens* the most recent. There is no denying the fact that 'Out of Africa' is the strongest theory, because if modern humans evolved in both Africa and Asia there is virtually no possibility of these widely-separated populations being identical.[99] The existence of the Neanderthals in Europe nevertheless remains a problem, as do the mysterious Denisovans of Asia as well as *Homo floresiensis* in Indonesia, where stone tools remarkably similar to Acheulean technology have also been found.[100]

While members of either *Homo erectus* (or the *Homo habilis* clade) appear to have survived until at least 50,000 years ago on the islands of Flores and Luzon in South-East Asia, there is no clear reason why *Homo erectus* became extinct. The key to the success of the species lay with its superior intellect and co-operative social organisation, both of which are abundantly clear in the archaeological record. We can also be sure that meat became an important part of the diet due to their ability to butcher large animals with superior stone tool technology.[101] Nor is there any doubt that *Homo erectus* exploited a wider range of resources than any of its predecessors. Examination of their dentition under an electron microscope has shown that their diet also included roots, tubers and bulbs, underground food sources which required a considerable degree of ethnobotanical knowledge and the use of wooden implements.

Human Origins, Evolution And Global Dispersal

Interestingly, those plant foods occur as far north as 50° latitude, perhaps not coincidentally the northernmost limit of *Homo erectus* remains.[102] Rather than relying on scavenging this hominid actively hunted its food, though an increasing meat intake initially led to some mistakes. One of the most complete skeletons of *Homo erectus* was excavated in Kenya and dates from approximately 1.5 MYA. The leg bones show that this particular individual was afflicted by disease, with new bone having grown over the old. The condition has been identified as a toxic overdose of vitamin A, and although rare it still occasionally occurs in modern humans. One of the most common ways of contracting the disease is through the consumption of large quantities of raw liver, an organ particularly rich in vitamin A. Given the age of the specimen from Kenya, and that the disease has not been detected in younger examples, it can be surmised that this was a dietary error eventually avoided through experience.[103] And even though *Homo erectus* had nowhere near the vocal range of modern humans, it was knowledge that could have been passed on through verbal communication.

Archaeology has also disclosed three examples of co-operative and specialised hunting by *Homo erectus*. Two sites are in Spain, where the butchered remains of horses, oxen, deer, rhinoceros and elephants have been found. Tell-tale cut marks on the bones indicate ancient feasts dating back to 300,000 years BP. Both sites are located in valleys which once contained large swamps, and it appears the animals were chased into the water where they were immobilised in the mud before being killed.[104] The third site, Olorgesailie in Kenya, is quite different, for here the remains of ninety extinct giant baboons have been found among thousands of Acheulean hand axes manufactured by *Homo erectus*. The remains date from between 400,000 and 700,000 years BP and suggest a series of hunts which took place over a lengthy period of time. Why the giant baboons were targeted remains a mystery, as they were formidable creatures roughly the size of a female gorilla and equipped with large canine teeth. Modern baboons are aggressive animals which live in troops, so it can be assumed that their giant ancestors exhibited similar behaviour. Yet despite the presence of cut marks on the bones these animals may not have been hunted for food.

The butchering was carried out in a very inefficient manner, and it could be that these were specialised hunts – possibly conducted at night – for a purpose unknown.[105] As one could only expect, this scenario also has its detractors.[106]

In China, when climatic conditions differed only marginally from the present time with hot summers and frigid winters, groups of *Homo erectus* used a large cavern at Zhoukoudian as a winter refuge. Evidence of occupation extends from 500,000 down to 200,000 years BP, with the cavern providing comfortable living quarters for as many as twenty individuals at any one time. They cooked their food on what are unmistakably stone hearths,[107] a similar activity played out at Terra Amata in what is now the French Riviera. Located just outside the city of Nice, Terra Amata offers a commanding view of the Mediterranean, though when it was occupied by *Homo erectus* some 400,000 years BP the shoreline was approximately twenty-five metres higher than it is today. The climate was also considerably colder. Archaeological excavations have revealed traces of eleven carefully constructed dwellings grouped around a freshwater spring. The huts were oval in shape, roughly twelve metres long by six metres wide. The walls were made from intertwined branches and the structures supported in the centre by a row of solid posts. Although the interpretation is entirely conjectural, it is believed that large rocks at the site were placed around the perimeter of the huts for additional support. The inhabitants may have used animal skins for extra warmth, and traces of ochre suggest they decorated their bodies.[108]

The residents at Terra Amata certainly ate well. The bones of elephant, rhinoceros, red deer, mountain goats and wild boar, mostly from young animals, litter the site along with Acheulean tools. They also feasted on oysters, mussels and limpets gathered on the rocky shore. The fossilised faeces of the inhabitants contain pollen from broom, a shrub which only flowers in spring. Terra Amata was apparently only occupied at this time, just one more seasonal campsite for a band of *Homo erectus* following a well-established hunter-gatherer lifestyle.[109] Along with their superior intellect and co-operative organisation, the success of this species also depended on an extensive knowledge of the environment.

Human Origins, Evolution And Global Dispersal

While it can be accepted that populations of *Homo erectus* appear to have evolved into archaic *Homo sapiens*, it has yet to be adequately explained why this had to happen. It also leaves us with the where and when, with Asia unable to be discounted from the final equation. After all, *Homo erectus* colonised wide areas of Eurasia and successfully adapted to diverse climatic conditions.

Indeed, it is likely that a number of species split from the *Homo erectus* rootstock. *Homo antecessor*, a tall hominid weighing up to ninety kilograms, first appears in the fossil record between 1.1 and 1.2 MYA and continued in existence until 800,000 years BP. The species is known only from Spain and its cranial capacity was equivalent to the maximum reached by *Homo erectus*.[110] *Homo antecessor* may have evolved into *Homo heidelbergensis*, whose range extended into northern Europe.[111] They, too, were tall – up to 1.8 metres in height – and far more muscular than modern humans, whose cranial capacity they matched. *Homo heidelbergensis* roamed Europe between 600,000 and 400,000 years BP, and are probably the direct ancestor of the Neanderthals, *Homo neanderthalensis*.[112] Around 300,000 years BP yet another hominid, *Homo rhodesiensis*, emerged in Africa and was successful enough to colonise wide areas of the continent before disappearing from the fossil record. One argument is that *Homo rhodesiensis* was the immediate ancestor of *Homo sapiens*,[113] which only emerged as a distinct species between 150,000 and 200,000 years BP.[114]

The survival of modern humans to the present day could also have been due to a mere stroke of luck or their ability to adapt more readily to climate change. The earliest evidence of their existence comes from the vicinity of Mossel Bay in South Africa, a site securely dated to 164,000 years BP. It is currently believed that this population of archaic *Homo sapiens* was forced to the coast by cooler drier conditions which began around 200,000 years BP, and severely impacted on the African continent. The effect was so widespread and devastating that hominid populations survived only in small enclaves, one of which was Mossel Bay. It was here the ancestors of modern humans radically altered their lifestyle, relying heavily on molluscs and other marine resources until the climatic pattern finally reversed to allow re-colonisation of the interior. Their lengthy sojourn on the coast marked a crucial point in time when *Homo sapiens* came close to extinction,[115] while other hominid species either vanished completely or had their numbers so reduced that extinction was inevitable.

What tends to reinforce this doomsday portrayal is that the gene pool of modern humans, particularly mitochondrial DNA, can be traced back to a very small population in southern Africa.[116] Mitochondrial DNA is inherited through the maternal line, with mutations occurring both randomly and irregularly through time. The largest number of mutations is in Africa, which is yet another reason why that continent is favoured as the cradle of humanity. It was also why geneticists began analysing sequences of mitochondrial DNA during the 1980s in an attempt to trace the human lineage back to a mitochondrial 'Eve' – not the actual mother of humanity – but rather the original molecule. It was a path fraught with immense difficulties. Apart from significant moral and ethical issues, DNA sequences are often scrambled and although samples were extracted from different populations right around the world they were not representative of the whole.[117] The project failed to achieve its objective as the original molecule was found to extend far beyond the existence of *Homo sapiens* as a distinct species.[118]

The dispersal of *Homo sapiens* from the African continent presented its own set of problems, as there have been very few occasions during the entire history of the species when an exit was possible. Routes to the south, east and west have been (and still are) blocked by the sea, while waterless stretches of desert usually barred a path through the north. Around 115,000 years BP, however, moister and cooler conditions opened a corridor between East Africa and the Levant, and it is perhaps not surprising to find that the oldest remains of *Homo sapiens* outside Africa, dating to between 90,000 and 100,000 years BP, have been found in Israel. This pioneering population may have been trapped in the Levant when conditions again became extremely dry; completely isolated from others of their kind they eventually died out.[119]

Another opportunity to move out of Africa did not present itself until 70,000 years BP, and this time there were two possible routes that could have been taken. One was again through Egypt into the Levant,

Human Origins, Evolution And Global Dispersal

the other was across the Red Sea, where a narrow gap then existed between Africa and the Arabian Peninsula. While there is evidence that at least one group of *Homo sapiens* undertook the short sea crossing and moved east along the fertile southern tip of the Arabian Peninsula,[120] it is almost certain that others used the corridor to the Levant. The eastern dispersal certainly occurred at a relatively rapid rate: Australia was seemingly reached prior to 50,000 years BP, and Japan was colonised approximately 10,000 years later,[121] when *Homo sapiens* is also known to have spread throughout Asia to northern China. The Tibetan Plateau, with an average elevation of 4,000 metres above sea level, average annual temperatures close to freezing and a rarified atmosphere, offered a particularly formidable obstacle. It had been accepted that *Homo sapiens* was unable to permanently settle this region until as recently as 12,000–15,000 years BP, and was only possible following the domestication of barley and the yak. Recent genetic studies, however, paint a very different picture. It has been argued that archaic humans were living at these extremely high altitudes as early as 30,000–40,000 years BP, a feat only made possible through interbreeding with the Denisovan cousins of Neanderthals, who had long been adapted to extremely frigid conditions.[122] The jury remains out, but a parallel scenario may have taken place in Europe 40,000 years BP when pioneering populations of archaic *Homo sapiens* first encountered the Neanderthals, who were similarly adapted to living in the prevailing bitterly cold conditions.[123]

The American continent offered its own unique barriers to human colonisation. The general consensus has been that *Homo sapiens* was unable to reach the Americas until as recently as 12,000–15,000 years BP, when warmer weather at the end of the Last Glacial Maximum permitted ingress across the Beringia land-bridge and expansion south along an ice-free coastal corridor.[124] A more recent (and debatable) line of thought is that the Americas were reached by watercraft, an hypothesis based on the discovery of stone tools and animal remains at Cooper's Ferry in western Idaho which are reputed to be up to 16,650 years old.[125] But an even more contentious claim for the early arrival of *Homo sapiens* in the Americas comes from Pedra Furada in Brazil, where it is held in some quarters that evidence of human occupation dates back to 50,000 years BP. Thus far no skeletal remains have been uncovered and the alleged quartz and quartzite tools are difficult to distinguish from naturally fractured specimens. If further research does confirm the antiquity of the site, however, our current theories of human dispersal will require a major overhaul. That will be even more imperative if the several hundred cave paintings at Pedra Furada are found to date from this same early period.[126] While the ability to produce art was once believed to be a distinctly human trait, it is now known that the Neanderthals were producing recognisable artworks in three Spanish caves at least 20,000 years before the arrival of archaic humans.[127] Moreover, while the earliest traces of paintings by *Homo sapiens* extend as far back as 100,000 years BP, it is only within the last 30,000 years that it emerged as a common feature of modern human behaviour. It was art and particularly its derivative – writing – which allowed humans to store and analyse information outside the brain.[128] Above all else, it is comprehensible written words that make us so unique.

The search for the origins of humanity is a fascinating quest even though the full details may never be known. The human story has also been further confused by a few deliberate frauds, the most notable of which was the infamous 'Piltdown Man' hoax of 1912. In that year an amateur archaeologist named Charles Dawson announced the discovery of an archaic human skull in a gravel pit at Piltdown in Sussex, England. The site also yielded the bones of long-extinct animals thought to have been contemporaneous. The skull was reconstructed by two leading anatomists, one of whom was Sir Arthur Keith, the other an Australian, Grafton Elliot Smith, at that time Professor of Anatomy at the University of Manchester. They agreed that while the cranium appeared to be modern the jaw was ape-like, the chin undeveloped, and the molars projected forward. A canine tooth was later found separately by Father Pierre Teilhard de Chardin, a Jesuit priest.[129] In the opinion of Keith and Elliot Smith there could be no doubt that this was a primitive hominid which had roamed the British countryside long before the arrival of *Homo sapiens*. Importantly, the discovery endowed the British scientific establishment with considerable prestige,

Human Origins, Evolution And Global Dispersal

the 'Piltdown Man' widely proclaimed as the 'missing link' on the evolutionary ladder.[130] Continental Europeans had their Neanderthals, but Britain had something of even greater significance.

As early as 1915 an American mammalogist named Gerrit Miller had cast doubt on the veracity of the claim, insisting that the cranium was that of a modern human, and the mandible belonged to a chimpanzee.[131] His objections (and a number of others) were dismissed by the British scientific establishment, and it was not until 1953 that three British physical anthropologists unaffected by national prestige conducted a detailed examination of the 'Piltdown Man'. Miller had been very close to the mark: the skull was indeed from a modern human, but rather than a chimpanzee the mandible was that of an orangutan. The molars had been carefully filed down and the bones stained to give the impression of great antiquity. Genuine fossilised animal bones had been planted in the gravel bed to complete the illusion of a primordial environment. The identity of the actual perpetrator (or perpetrators) remains unknown: Dawson, de Chardin, Keith, Grafton Smith, and even Sir Arthur Conan Doyle of *Sherlock Holmes* fame, who lived close by, have all been named as prime suspects.[132] Phillip Tobias, argued that the hoax was concocted between Dawson and Sir Arthur Keith after the latter's applications for a fellowship of the prestigious Royal Society of Great Britain had been rejected in 1911 and again in 1912. Prompted by revenge Keith sought to fool the British scientific establishment, the fake skull so well crafted that it took an unexpected forty years to expose the fraud.[133] More recently, however, an exhaustive examination of all the available evidence by John Walsh has concluded that Charles Dawson was the sole perpetrator.[134]

These days, of course, new finds are publicly declared and other palaeoanthropologists are invited to access the site. Casts are usually made of the skeletal material and distributed for further comment, and although it does not prevent disagreement it generally results in a reasoned assessment being made. In the case of one genuine archaic hominid from Europe that took more than a century to be achieved. Almost since their discovery the Neanderthals have suffered an identity crisis, invariably portrayed as lumbering dim-witted brutes who were little more than an evolutionary dead-end. More recent research suggests something very different, but their disappearance following the arrival of *Homo sapiens* could also have important implications for Australia's ancient past. It is to the Neanderthals, then, that we next need to turn.

THE NEANDERTHAL ANOMALY

III

Neanderthals are perhaps the best-known of all the extinct hominids, and notwithstanding their close relationship with modern humans, their evolutionary path probably diverged at least 500,000 years BP. By 400,000 years BP the distinctive morphological features of the Neanderthals began to appear in the fossil record, and around 130,000 years BP the classic form of this species reigned supreme in Europe, the Near East and western Asia.[1] They maintained their dominance until archaic *Homo sapiens* began venturing into these regions between 50,000 and 40,000 years BP, and by 29,000 years BP the Neanderthals appear to have become extinct.[2] Their reasonably abrupt disappearance has sparked claims that this remarkable hominid was either exterminated or assimilated by archaic humans.[3] Many researchers have tended to favour the 'blitzkrieg theory' and a violent end, but there is increasing evidence that Neanderthal genes have been inherited by their usurpers, thus pointing to a more benign exit from the global stage.

From the time their existence first became known in the mid-nineteenth century, and continuing right up until the 1950s and beyond, Neanderthals were invariably portrayed as brutish dim-witted creatures. Even today, to be called a Neanderthal is often considered an insult of the highest order.[4] They were the simple cave people of cartoons, popular articles and stories, but as we now know they were much more complex. Neanderthals were like us, but so very different from us. On average they were slightly shorter than modern humans, males reaching a maximum height of 169 centimetres, females 160 centimetres, though there was a degree of regional variation in stature. What all of them shared, however, was a powerful physique and prodigious strength.[5]

In October 2007 researchers at Leipzig University in Germany announced they had isolated a pigmentation gene from the DNA of two Neanderthals, one from Spain, the other from Italy. This particular gene, known as MCIR, indicated that at least some Neanderthals had red hair, fair skin and possibly freckles. Yet MCIR was totally different from the gene found primarily in red-haired European people today, and probably evolved quite independently as a means of increasing vitamin D intake in the colder regions which Neanderthals called home.[6]

As well as their remarkable physique, Neanderthals were endowed with a prominent nose and massive jaws, while their teeth projected further forward than they do in modern humans. The cheekbones also sloped backward rather than being angled as in the 'high cheekbones' of northern European people today. Instead of rising abruptly, the foreheads of the Neanderthals similarly sloped back and were marked with heavy brow ridges.[7] At the back of the skull was a pronounced bulge known as the occipital bun, which is usually associated with delayed posterior brain growth.[8] On the other hand, it could be linked to the accommodation of their large braincase, as Neanderthal brains averaged around 1,400 cubic centimetres, marginally above that of modern humans.[9] The brain architecture on Neanderthal crania also shows little difference from that of their successors, so they could have been equally intelligent. It is possible, however, that the Neanderthals required more brain cells to coordinate their larger body mass.[10]

While that remains in the realm of speculation, a number of their morphological features were clearly biological adaptations to cold climatic conditions. The large nose of the Neanderthals contained three unusual bones structures in the nasal passage which are not found in modern humans. Along with their large sinuses, these bones are believed to have assisted in warming inhaled air,[11] because cold dry air heats up and moistens as it passes over warm tissue; the larger the area the more beneficial it becomes. By this means the sensitive tissue of the throat and lungs were protected.[12] Barrel-shaped chests and wide ribcages were yet another adaptation to living in cold regions, and their large lungs were necessary to sustain an exceptionally high level of physical activity. Compared to modern humans, Neanderthal limbs were comparatively

The Neanderthal Anomaly

short in relation to body size, but that reduced the overall surface area and helped to maintain body heat. More generally, their bone structure was extremely sturdy and it was held together with substantial muscle.[13]

Could the Neanderthals talk? Although it has been argued they might not have the full vocal repertoire of modern humans, Neanderthals arguably had some form of verbal communication even if they were unable to pronounce the vowel sounds *a*, *i* and *u*. Nor would their more elevated larynx have impacted on the ability to speak.[14] Unfortunately, voice boxes and vocal tracts do not survive in the fossil record, but a small bony structure at the back of the tongue occasionally does. The voice box hangs off the hyoid bone, which is approximately thirty-five millimetres in length and resembles a wishbone. In 1983 an intact hyoid bone was found among the skeletal remains of a 60,000-year-old Neanderthal in Israel: it was virtually identical to the hyoid bone found in modern humans.[15] More recently a gene known as FOXP2 has been recovered from Neanderthal DNA. That, too, is similar to a gene found in modern humans which acts in the brain and on the nerves which control facial muscles to assist with speech. Although the available evidence is limited, it could have served the same function in Neanderthals.[16] The problem for many Neanderthals was finding someone to talk to, as demographic estimates suggest there may have been as few as 15,000 individuals at their peak. Moreover, Neanderthals were scattered from Britain in the west to central Asia in the east, and south as far as Israel,[17] the latter location reoccupied between 70,000 and 50,000 years BP.[18]

Skeletal remains of what might have been Neanderthals began turning up in Europe from at least the early 1700s. In 1829 definite remains were uncovered in Belgium, and in 1848 on the north face of Gibraltar. Both finds languished in virtual obscurity, and it was not until 1857 that Neanderthals first began to become widely known.[19] The previous year quarry workers mining limestone in Germany's Neander Valley near Dusseldorf came across what was possibly an almost complete Neanderthal skeleton. Unfortunately, their interest was in the task at hand and only the skullcap, ribs, part of the pelvis, and a few limb bones were saved from destruction by Wilhelm Beckershoff, co-owner of the quarry. They were passed on to a local schoolteacher named Johann Fuhlrott, who realised they were from an archaic human.[20] Aware that his lack of academic credentials would weaken the credibility of any such claim, Fuhlrott contacted Hermann Schaaffhausen, Professor of Anatomy at Bonn University, who agreed they were indeed from an archaic form of humanity.[21] The discovery was jointly announced by Schaaffhausen and Fuhlrott in 1857.[22]

This was two years before Darwin published his theory of evolution, and both Schaaffhausen and Fuhlrott were among the majority who firmly believed in a comparatively recent biblical creation. Schaaffhausen nevertheless published an important paper on the skeletal remains and exhibited them before a number of learned scientific societies, thus generating considerable interest. Despite his efforts, few were convinced the bones belonged to an ancient hominid which predated modern humans. Perhaps not surprisingly, a number of sceptics disputed the antiquity of the bones, claiming they belonged to a modern human who had been deformed by some strange disease. In 1864 German anatomist August Mayer pulled the longest bow of all when he claimed the remains were those of a man who had been afflicted with rickets, whose bowed legs were clear evidence of a lifetime spent on horseback. Taking it further, Mayer speculated whether the deceased had been a Mongolian Cossack from the Russian cavalry who had pursued Napoleon's forces back across the Rhine in 1814, before deserting and making his way to the Neander Valley. Prior to death he had also broken an elbow, with the pain becoming so intense he had knotted his brow which had subsequently ossified.[23] In this way, Mayer adroitly explained the presence of heavy brow ridges. Nobody could accuse the anatomist of lacking imagination.

Only one expert suspected otherwise. Dr William King, Professor of Anatomy at King's College in Ireland, initially agreed the bones belonged to an extinct hominid which he named *Homo neanderthalensis* after the discovery site. Unfortunately, King retracted his opinion after reading the report of world-renowned German anatomist, Rudolf Virchow.[24] According to Virchow the bones were comparatively recent and belonged to a man who had suffered from rickets in childhood and arthritis in old age. On top of that he had received a number of heavy blows to the head during his lifetime. Virchow's reputation was so formidable that his conclusions stifled any further speculation until 1886, when two more Neanderthal skeletons were discovered in a Belgian cave. Virchow dismissed the find as simply diseased modern humans, but by this time other researchers were beginning to have doubts. It appeared too much of a coincidence that these unusual and widely-separated skeletal remains could be from diseased humans, particularly when all of them were associated with ancient stone tools and the bones of extinct animals.[25]

Then, around 1900, skeletal remains of up to eighty Neanderthals were discovered in a Croatian cave.[26] From 1908 large numbers also began turning up in the Dordogne region of southern France. Now armed with a wealth of new material French researchers believed that a full reconstruction was finally possible. Although an almost complete Neanderthal skeleton from La Chapelle-aux-Saints was selected, it was unfortunate they belonged to an elderly individual and that the task of re-articulation was given to the respected anatomist and palaeontologist, Marcellin Boule. Despite his unquestionable expertise, Boule was completely carried away by his own preconceptions. He concluded the Neanderthal had prehensile feet and was unable to fully extend its legs. Boule's drawings portrayed the Neanderthal with a stooped posture, the head bent so far forward it would have fractured its neck looking at the sky. The facial features also had simian qualities, distancing the Neanderthals even further from modern humans.[27]

It was an image that was to influence all other depictions of Neanderthals until 1957 when two anatomists, William Straus and A.J.E. Cave, re-examined Boule's original specimen. They quickly realised the Frenchman had seriously erred by failing to recognise that it was only severe arthritis which prevented this particular individual from standing fully erect. The facial features were not ape-like, and nor was it endowed with prehensile feet. They believed that if the Neanderthal was living, cleaned, and dressed in modern clothes it would have drawn no more attention in a New York subway than other city commuter.[28] Whether or not this was an indictment of the 'Big Apple' is unclear, but there was a subsequent trend to increasingly humanise the Neanderthals and perhaps taking things too far the other way. They were not modern humans, and Neanderthals were further distinguished by their unique culture and general lifestyle which contributed to a phenomenally high incidence of traumatic injury.

They certainly appear to have eaten reasonably well. Studies of the dental calculus (i.e. hardened plaque) of fossilised Neanderthal teeth from sites as far apart as Belgium and Iraq have revealed that grain, roots and tubers were a regular part of the dietary intake. Many of the particles had also undergone physical change which matched experimentally cooked starch grains. While the full range of their plant foods may never be known, and although there is no evidence that the Neanderthals practised agriculture (or even horticulture) they definitely harvested and cooked vegetables and grain. A number of stone artifacts also suggest they were used for crushing and grinding plant foods as part of the preparatory process.[29] With one notable exception, however, there is no denying that meat formed the major component of the Neanderthal diet.

The coastal site of Figueira Brava, 30 kilometres south of Lisbon in Portugal, contradicts this pattern. Between 86,000 and 106,000 years BP Neanderthals visited this location to exploit marine resources, albeit, while still hunting large terrestrial game further inland. In March 2020 archaeologists reported that the Neanderthal diet here included molluscs (both gastropods and bivalves), Brown Crabs (*Cancer Pagurus*), Spider Crabs (*Maja Squinada*), a variety of fish, birds (both waterfowl and marine) as well as the occasional seal and dolphin, the latter possibly scavenged. Importantly, seafoods are rich in omega 3 fatty acids which promote the development of brain tissue and cognitive behaviour. Inland they targeted land tortoises, deer, ibex, horses and auroch, while the Neanderthal hearths also contain the remains of olive trees, vines, figs and the cones of Stone Pine (*Pinus pinea*). The cones are of particular interest, for had they been used as fuel they would have been totally consumed by fire. Instead, the bracts have frequently preserved their anatomical shape, which implies roasting rather than burning. As mature cones can only be obtained in the canopy, it also suggests that the Neanderthal inhabitants climbed the trees in autumn and winter to harvest this plant resource. Until further Neanderthal coastal sites are discovered and fully analysed it cannot be known with certainty whether this behavior was restricted to the Iberian Peninsula or was perhaps more widespread. All that can be said at present is that Neanderthals do not appear to have relied on marine resources anywhere near to the same extent as their *Homo sapiens* successors.[30]

Meat, on the other hand, was the general rule. Apart from the Figueira Brava site, and until the very twilight of their existence, the Neanderthals largely ignored small game such as hares, birds and even fish. Theirs was a specialised food regime in which the focus fell on medium to large mammals which flourished in the often tundra-like conditions of Europe and western Asia. During periods of intense cold, woolly mammoths and woolly rhinoceros were targets for Neanderthal spears. In warmer interglacial interludes they hunted hippopotamus and elephants which roamed as far north as Britain. Allowing for regional specialisation, their most common prey species included horses (which were slightly smaller than modern varieties), bison, reindeer, wild boars and the giant Irish elk, mature stags standing two metres at the shoulder with antlers spanning up to 3.5 metres. In mountainous regions they occasionally targeted chamois, while Ibex was sometimes hunted in rocky areas. The most favoured prey of all, however, may have been the auroch, the extinct ancestor of modern cattle.[31] Importantly, there was a good reason why they targeted these large, gregarious and migratory animals. A typical Neanderthal male required up to 5,000 calories per day to support his body mass in a generally frigid environment. To put it another way, the average Neanderthal male burnt up almost as much energy per day as a cyclist does in the Tour de France.[32]

Many of the animals they hunted were extremely dangerous, and even when juveniles were the selected prey the Neanderthal hunters still had to contend with enraged mothers. The auroch was not only dangerous, it was extremely aggressive and inclined to charge anything on sight. Adults stood around two metres at the shoulder, weighed in at 1,000-kilograms, and were equipped with two large forward-facing horns. The habits of the auroch have been well documented because they survived until the early seventeenth century: the last one, a female, died in Poland in 1627.[33] Hunting such formidable beasts required co-operative tactics which may have involved women and children as there appears to have been no strict gendered division of labour in Neanderthal society. Tellingly, evidence of traumatic injury is found across all age groups and among both sexes.[34] As they lived in small bands the assistance of women and children to drive herd animals, particularly horses, to their doom would have been crucial for survival. Where possible, the Neanderthals probably utilised natural features such as swamps and high banks to immobilise and trap their prey.[35]

From a chance discovery in a German peat bog it is known the Neanderthals used heavy spears up to 2.5 metres in length. They were thrusting, rather than throwing spears,[36] a preferred strategy also found among a number of modern human groups, including the Maori of New Zealand.[37] This meant the Neanderthals had to close with their prey to inflict a fatal wound, thereby placing themselves at considerable risk. While surrounding and confusing prey is a classic tactic used by animal predators,[38] it is extremely rare among hominids. Although the Neanderthals possessed great strength and endurance, the majority of their skeletal remains reveal an exceptionally high incidence of traumatic injury – particularly to the head and upper body. Thomas Berger and Erik Trinkaus analysed the bones from seventeen Neanderthals who between them had sustained twenty-seven serious injuries. Comparing the results with modern humans who had experienced similar traumatic events they were surprised to discover an almost perfect match: rodeo riders.[39] Some of the injuries were quite extensive. The bones of one elderly Neanderthal (who had to be tough to survive into his forties) were covered with serious lesions. The bone around his left eye and cheek had been crushed and healed over, suggesting either blindness in the eye or permanent double vision. His right arm was withered from the shoulder down as a result of having been broken in two places above the elbow, the fractures failing to heal. He also had severe arthritis in his right ankle and big toe, and there was a healed fracture on the outside of the foot. Having occurred years before death, this particular individual would have limped painfully through the remainder of his

The Neanderthal Anomaly

life.⁴⁰ At least some assistance would have been required for him to keep up with the group, which illustrates another dimension to Neanderthal society. These hominids clearly cared for one another, and that level of care extended beyond mortal life.

It is with the Neanderthals that we have the first evidence of ritual burials. Many of the remains indicate the dead were laid to rest in a deliberate and possibly reverential manner. At Le Moustier in France a teenager was lowered into a pit and placed on his right side, the head resting on his arm as if he had quietly gone to sleep. A pile of flint tools served as a pillow and the auroch bones scattered around his body may have held meat to sustain him in the afterlife. At Teshik Tash in Uzbekistan a young child was laid among ibex bones, with six pairs of horns forming a ring around his head. Red ochre, which is present at other burial sites, possibly decorated the bodies of the deceased,⁴¹ and one of the most interesting Neanderthal burials of all took place at Shanidar Cave in modern Iraq.

Pollen samples have revealed that the body of a Neanderthal male had been carefully laid to rest on a bed of wildflowers comprising yarrow, cornflower, St Barnard's thistle, ragwort, grape hyacinth and hollyhock. Together these species would have effected a delicate blend of white, yellow and blue against a backdrop of green from woody horsetail, the pollen of which was also present. On the other hand, it may not have been solely about aestheticism, because the majority of these plants also have important medicinal properties which are still utilised by people living in the region today.⁴² That, however, is one side of Neanderthal society. Two sites in Croatia and one in France suggest a much darker side to the Neanderthal world.

A cave at Moula-Guercy overlooking the Rhone River in France contains the remains of six Neanderthals who died there approximately 100,000 years ago. What is particularly significant about this site is that the expert butchery skills of these hominids were applied to their own kind. Cutmarks show that the chewing muscles from the heads of two young individuals had been filleted, and the tongue from at least one of them had been sliced out. The leg and arm bones of the four adults had been smashed open on a stone anvil to extract marrow, while the braincases of all six individuals had been broken open to extract the brains.⁴³ The two sites in Croatia contain similar evidence of systematic cannibalism, and at all three locations the flesh had either been consumed raw or cooked after separation from the bone. That in itself is unusual, as Neanderthals are known to have made good use of fire to cook their meat. The full meaning behind these anthropophagic feasts remains obscure, and as Fred Smith from Northern Illinois University has aptly pointed out, it is unfortunate that only actions are preserved in the archaeological record – not the intentions.⁴⁴

Whether these Neanderthals had been slain or succumbed to natural causes prior to butchering also remains unclear. One explanation is that the deaths occurred at the end of winter, when the surviving members of their bands were desperate for dietary fat and protein to sustain them until the onset of warmer weather. Both brains and marrow are extremely rich sources of fat and protein.⁴⁵ It is possible, however, that they were deliberate victims, perhaps members of a hostile group. Yet, as they appear to have been isolated events, cannibalism appears to have been anything but the norm in Neanderthal society. It also needs to be borne in mind that anthropophagy has been practised by many modern human societies right around the world for a wide variety of reasons.⁴⁶

The cutting tools employed for butchering were part of an elaborate stone toolkit comprising sixty-three types of implements unique to the Neanderthals.⁴⁷ Known as the Mousterian tradition after the site in France where they were first found, some of the tools are quite exquisite, while those made from flint were superior to all previous stone technologies. Flint posed a number of problems. Good supplies were relatively scarce, so scarce in fact, that Neanderthal hunters often carried their smaller prey to the quarries before butchering. Flint is also a difficult material to work with precision because it fractures different ways depending on conditions. The ability to strike suitable flakes from a core often requires years of practice.⁴⁸

Neanderthals are also known to have worked extensively with wood, though apart from spears, few of their artifacts have survived.⁴⁹ Bone tools have also been found at a number of later Neanderthal

The Neanderthal Anomaly

sites, and although it was long suspected that their presence either reflected cultural transfer from archaic humans or were actually made by the latter, a number of researchers are no longer quite so sure. Four fragments of bone from south-western France dating between 42,000 and 51,000 years ago are said to be *lissoirs* (smoothers) manufactured by Neanderthals for making animal hides tougher and more water-resistant – similar to modern leatherworking tools.[50] Another useful tool was their strong forward-projecting teeth, all of which exhibit a considerable degree of wear. They functioned almost as a third hand, or vice, allowing the Neanderthals to hold objects being worked with stone tools.[51]

It was long-believed that the Neanderthals lacked the artistic expression which is held to be a hallmark of modern humanity. That is no longer the case. As noted in the previous chapter, paintings attributed to the Neanderthals in three Spanish caves date from more than 64,000 years ago – at least 20,000 years before the arrival of *Homo sapiens* on the Iberian Peninsula. The outline of a hand and an array of lines might not be considered high art, but they nevertheless represent symbolic expression. A fourth Spanish cave has also yielded pierced shells stained with pigment which, it has been argued, could have been used for body ornamentation. They are even older than the paintings,[52] but regardless of their actual use it can be said that taken together these caves provide evidence of a level of cognition which is far removed from the dim-witted brutes the Neanderthals have often been portrayed.

While the vast majority of known Neanderthal campsites are located in caves and rocky overhangs, most of their activities were almost certainly conducted in more open areas. They were nomadic people who pursued herds of large animals across the landscape well away from rocky shelters, with exposed sites rarely preserving any indication of their transient occupation.[53] They are more frequent in France, Germany, the Czech Republic and the Ukraine, but either rare or entirely absent elsewhere.[54] It has been surmised that the Neanderthals constructed shelters from wood or perhaps mammoth bones, the shape of which resembled the tepee of Native American. A posthole in southern France provides a unique glimpse of Neanderthal housing in more expansive areas.⁵⁵ At this location and others ancient cooking hearths have also been identified, sophisticated enough to efficiently draw air and thus promote combustion.⁵⁶ Fire was essential for survival, and some of the caves used by Neanderthals contain compressed layers of ash more than a metre thick. Crushed animal bones provided fuel when wood was in short supply.⁵⁷

Overall the Neanderthals were extremely well-adapted, reinforced by their dominance of the European and western Asian landscapes for the greater part of 100,000 years. Around 50,000 years BP modern humans began advancing into western Asia, where the Neanderthals rapidly disappeared. A similar scenario was played out 10,000 years later when the first anatomically modern humans, known as Cro-Magnons, ventured into Europe and displaced the Neanderthals by 29,000 years BP.⁵⁸ What happened during that 11,000-odd years of coexistence in Europe continues to puzzle researchers. There can be little doubt that when the first modern humans entered the domain of the Neanderthals both species sought to exclude the other from the landscape.⁵⁹ Early Cro-Magnons were substantially taller than Neanderthals and more robust than modern humans. Importantly, however, they had superior technology and, perhaps the most crucial factor of all, greater numbers.⁶⁰

On the other hand, there are two lines of reasoning which can account for the disappearance of the Neanderthals without violence. Svante Paabo, Director of Genetics at the world-renowned Max Planck Institute for Evolutionary Anthropology at Leipzig in Germany, is among a number of researchers who lean towards assimilation. Neanderthal genes are slightly different from modern humans, and it was once assumed that the productivity of any union between the two species would be highly unlikely. One argument was that any offspring would assuredly be infertile, and claims that a number of early human remains bore Neanderthal features were generally dismissed on the basis that all of them fell within the broad range of either Neanderthal or *Homo sapiens* morphology. Given the length of time that has elapsed since the Neanderthals disappeared from the European landscape it was also thought that any trace of their DNA in modern humans would have become so diluted it would be virtually impossible to detect.⁶¹

The Neanderthal Anomaly

That can no longer be upheld. Technological advances, including the application of high-throughput sequencers, reduced costs and new methods of dealing with old and degraded DNA has enabled geneticists to sequence the entire Neanderthal nuclear genome. And the results have been totally unexpected. Genes did indeed flow from Neanderthals to humans. And they have left a legacy, with Neanderthal genes comprising between one and four percent of the DNA of modern humans living outside the African continent.[62] This means that interbreeding occurred after the human exodus from Africa and that modern humans without African ancestry are two percent Neanderthal. There is also evidence that certain genes inherited from Neanderthals have provided their successors with some measure of protection against illnesses such as high cholesterol, autism and depression. It is also possible that while people with genetic variants have gained immunity to some medical conditions they can also be susceptible to a number of allergies. Bearing in mind that the Neanderthal populations were small and widely dispersed, it can reasonably be argued that interbreeding with humans led to the disappearance of the Neanderthals as their DNA became steadily diluted.[63] But in some ways they are still with us.

We also know that the last physical bastion of the Neanderthals was in the caves of Gibraltar, where they underwent a radical transition in their lifestyle before disappearing around 29,000 years ago. No longer able to pursue large animals as their forebears had done, they became almost totally dependent on small game such as rabbits and land tortoises. At Gorham's Cave mussel shells litter the floor, along with dolphin bones and skeletal fragments of a seal which had been dismembered with Mousterian tools.[64] Vanguard Cave also contains large numbers of mussel shells, but here there are also limpets, cockles and a small number of barnacles. Some of the shells are either burnt or show clear indications of having been heated.[65] More recent excavations at Gorham's Cave have shown that the Neanderthals hunted and ate rock doves, the ancestors of today's feral pigeons, with dating of the remains indicating that they exploited these birds over a period of almost 40,000 years.[66] It also made sense, as rock doves, just like their modern descendants, rapidly reproduce and live in high population densities which made them a highly-sustainable resource.

On the other side of the world the Aborigines had colonised virtually every part of the ancient continent of Sahul long before the last bastion of the Neanderthals fell. The Aborigines had also adapted to bitterly cold glacial conditions in the far south which would have favoured the Neanderthals. The former not only survived, they prospered. On their journey to the continent they were soon to call home, the Aboriginal people came into contact with a close relative of the Neanderthals, a mysterious hominid known as the Denisovans. They may also have chanced upon yet another species of the genus *Homo* which differed markedly from both themselves and their Eurasian contemporaries. The so-called 'Hobbits' of Flores, an island in the Indonesian archipelago, were diminutive creatures quite the physical opposite of the Neanderthals in the Northern Hemisphere. Importantly, their own forebears had passed through this island chain heading east long before the arrival of the Aborigines. Flores, then, is the final stepping-stone on the journey to the Australian continent and its ancient past.

THE HOBBIT ENIGMA

IV

In 1995 Mike Morwood, an archaeologist at the University of New England in Armidale, New South Wales, gazed across the waters of the Timor Sea from his camp on Anja Peninsula in the Kimberley region of north-western Australia, and contemplated searching for evidence of the Australian Aborigines in distant Indonesia. While it was (and is) generally accepted that the Indonesian islands were stepping-stones to the ancient southern continent of Sahul, Morwood put his thoughts into action in 2003 when he began excavations at a number of sites on the island of Flores.[1] A relatively large volcanic island, 360 kilometres in length and up to seventy kilometres wide, Flores has an area of approximately 14,000 square kilometres.[2] Morwood and his team failed to find any evidence of the Australian Aborigines: instead, they found an entirely new species of humanity. Initial dating suggested that they had survived on their island home until as recently as 12,000 years ago.[3] Later dating of sediments containing stone artifacts, however, pushed their final presence back to around 50,000 years,[4] a date roughly corresponding with the currently accepted arrival in Australia of the first wave of Aboriginal colonisers.

The hominids of Flores were like no other. While they possessed a number of morphological features which appeared to place them within the genus *Homo*, they also had close affinities with the Australopithecines.[5] They were tiny creatures standing just over a metre in height, which is why they were quickly dubbed the 'Hobbits', after J.R.R. Tolkien's fictional creations.[6] After a careful examination of the skeletal remains Peter Brown (also from the University of New England), was convinced that they still fell within the parameters of the genus *Homo* despite their relatively small brain and accordingly provided the specific name *floresiensis* after their island home.⁷ The broader scientific community nevertheless remains divided over their precise place within the evolutionary framework, and it was only in 2017 that some measure of clarity on this issue finally began to emerge.

If the island of Flores was directly on the route taken by the Aborigines as they made their way east to the supercontinent of Sahul it could also have important implications for the human colonisation of Australia. There are three likely entry points into northern Australia, one of which included the island of Timor where the earliest human occupation sites have been dated to around 42,000 years BP.⁸ At present there is no evidence of a modern human presence on Flores prior to 11,000 years BP,⁹ but the existence of *Homo floresiensis* could mean that Australia might have been initially colonised by their forebears rather than modern humans,¹⁰ or possibly by *Homo erectus* or the mysterious Denisovans whose DNA is present in both the Australian Aborigines and Papua New Guineans. In fact, it was the search for *Homo erectus* on Flores which provided the groundwork for the eventual discovery of the diminutive Hobbits.

The story began with Father Theodor Verhoeven, a Dutch priest trained in classical archaeology who entered the Catholic seminary on Flores in 1950. Shortly after his arrival on the island Verhoeven was shown a number of stone artifacts by local villagers, and knowing that *Homo erectus* had inhabited Java he identified them as examples of Oldowan technology. To confirm his assumption Verhoeven commenced a series of excavations which continued until his return to Holland in 1967. In 1959 the Catholic priest investigated an open site known as Mata Menge in central Flores, where he uncovered Oldowan stone tools in association with the skeletal remains of pygmy stegodon, an extinct form of elephant. Both the tools and bones lay in a sandstone deposit sandwiched between layers of volcanic ash.¹¹ As stegodons and *Homo erectus* were known to have co-existed on Java 750,000 years BP, Verhoeven concluded that a similar situation existed on Flores around the same time. Along with a detailed account of the excavations, Verhoeven published his deductions in *Anthropos*, a leading scholarly journal, only to find his claims either dismissed or

The Hobbit Enigma

ignored. Despite training in archaeology Verhoeven was regarded as an amateur and serious doubts were cast on his identification of the stone tools as products of Oldowan technology, as well as their association with stegodon bones.[12]

At that time it was not known when stegodons had become extinct on Flores, and while it was accepted that *Homo erectus* had inhabited Java, it was widely agreed that migration further eastwards had been blocked by insurmountable water barriers. At no time in the past has Flores ever been connected to the ancient continent of Sunda, and at the very least nine kilometres of treacherous waters had separated it from the nearest island of Sumbawa.[13] A capacity for language and intelligent organisation were necessary prerequisites for *Homo erectus* to accomplish such a journey, and to endow this species with both traits would have required a complete rewrite of human evolution. No one was prepared to go that far. Moreover, after seventeen years of excavations Verhoeven had been unable to locate the skeletal remains of the Flores toolmakers, a discovery that would have considerably strengthened his thesis.[14]

In 1994 a Dutch team began investigating the ancient fauna of Flores, and they found that the pygmy stegodon (*Stegodon sondaari*) and a giant land tortoise (*Geochelone sp.*) had flourished on the island until 900,000 years BP, when both animals suddenly slid into extinction. Their demise coincided with the appearance of stone tools, but this is not to suggest that human predation was necessarily a factor in their disappearance.[15] The pygmy stegodon, an animal roughly the size of a cow, was succeeded by a larger form standing three metres high at the shoulder (*Stegodon florensis*), and it is the remains of these animals which are directly associated with the stone technology.[16] Stegodons existed throughout Asia from 11.6 MYA until as recently as 11,000 years BP. The majority were larger than modern elephants, averaging eight metres in length and standing around four metres high at the shoulder. Their tusks were up to three metres long, and like modern elephants the stegodons were powerful swimmers, capable of crossing formidable sea barriers to colonise islands. As the oceanic currents in the Indonesian archipelago flow from north to south, it is surmised that the successors of the pygmy form recolonised Flores from Sulawesi.[17]

More recently, it has been argued that *Homo erectus* did in fact have the intellectual capacity to accomplish sea crossings in pursuit of stegodons, one of their favourite prey species.[18] This posed two important questions. The first is whether the expansion of *Homo erectus* continued eastward, the second is whether a population remained behind on Flores and steadily diminished in size like the pygmy stegodons. It all comes down to a concept known as the 'island rule', whereby large species – notably mammals – tend to become smaller on islands owing to limited or restricted resources. It is driven by natural selection, a means of reducing calorie intake and energy requirements.[19] Geologically speaking, insular dwarfism can be relatively rapid. On the Mediterranean islands of Crete, Sicily and Malta four-metre-high elephants dwarfed to just one metre in 5,000 years. At the same time small species often head towards gigantism, particularly where predators are either non-existent or few in number.[20] Examples of gigantism also occurred on Flores, where there were once four species of giant rats, only one of which has survived to the present day. The Flores Giant Rat (*Papagomys armandvillei*) is twice the size of the Common Brown Rat (*Rattus norvegicus*), with a body length of forty-five centimetres. With its seventy centimetre tail, this species is slightly over one metre long.[21]

What is unusual about Flores is that there were – and still are – highly-efficient predators. The Komodo dragon (*Varanus komodoensis*) is a monitor lizard that reaches three metres in length, and is known to have existed on Flores since at least 900,000 years BP. A small population still lives on the island, albeit, largely confined to the north and west coasts.[22] There was also a slightly smaller species of monitor lizard (*Varanus hooijeri*) which is now extinct, a fate which also befell the Giant Marabou Stork (*Leptoptilis robustus*), a flightless bird which stood 1.8 metres high and is known to have been carnivorous.[23] This avian predator, which probably relied more on carrion than live prey, disappeared around 18,000 years BP.

For the 'island rule' to function, members of a species have to be totally isolated from others of their kind. In the case of *Homo floresiensis*, this meant the island had to be remote enough to avoid any influx of newcomers who would have broadened the gene pool.[24]

The Hobbit Enigma

There is of course the possibility that rather than island-hopping, the founding hominid population was washed ashore on Flores by a tsunami following a volcanic eruption. This was highlighted in December 2004 when a tsunami struck Banda Aceh on the northern tip of Sumatra and a number of people were washed hundreds of kilometres out to sea. They survived for lengthy periods by clinging to tree trunks and other flotsam.[25] The main problem with this scenario is that primates are even more likely to survive a similar natural catastrophe, and there is no endemic species of primate on Flores. The macaque monkeys which flourish on the island today were introduced comparatively recently by modern humans.[26]

It is possible that the diminutive 'Hobbits' occasionally fell victim to the endemic predators, notably the Komodo dragons which are stealthy and formidable hunters. These giant lizards often ambush their victims along game trails or at waterholes. Although equipped with razor-sharp teeth, the Komodo dragons seldom kill their prey outright. Bacterium in the saliva infects the wounds made by the initial bite and death occurs from septicaemia – usually days later. Despite that, Komodo dragons are adept at locating the corpse, and it is not unusual for a number of these reptiles to converge on the body where they feast together. While fully-grown Komodo dragons are quite capable of bringing down adult male buffaloes, deer and goats, they prefer to target pregnant females at the point of giving birth before they attack.[27]

While there can be little doubt that Komodo dragons also fed on the extinct stegodons, they may have experienced some difficulty in hunting down the 'Hobbits'. These hominids were armed, and even today tourist guides on the islands of Komodo and Rinca easily keep these lizards at bay with long forked sticks. Conversely, *Homo floresiensis* may have had little trouble despatching Komodo dragons. In the warmer hours of the day the reptiles are forced to remain inactive to avoid overheating, while at night they are equally vulnerable when their bodies have cooled. At present the relationship between the 'Hobbits' and the Giant Marabou Stork remains unclear, but what we do know from microscopic residue on their stone tools is that *Homo floresiensis* utilised a wide variety of plant foods. As yet there is no evidence of these hominids having exploited coastal resources or even the land and freshwater molluscs which feature regularly in the diet of the island's modern human inhabitants,[28] emphasising that much of their culture and lifestyle remains shrouded in mystery. More to the point, their very discovery generated a host of controversies, many of which remain unresolved today. They are certainly enigmatic creatures.

Just a year after Mike Morwood looked out across the Timor Sea from his camp in the Kimberleys he had joined with Indonesian archaeologists to redate hominid artifacts and extinct animal bones at sites first investigated by Verhoeven in the central districts of the island. Two years later he received a grant from the Australian Research Council to undertake a thorough geological survey of the Soa Basin, where it was ascertained that layers containing both artifacts and fossil bones disappeared around 680,000 years BP. All subsequent deposits are much more recent, so to unravel what had happened in the intervening period Morwood and his Indonesian co-workers turned their attention to other areas, including sites first recorded by Verhoeven.[29]

One of them was a large spectacular limestone cavern located thirty kilometres from the west coast called Liang Bua, which translates as the Cool Cave. It is so roomy and comfortable that it was used as an elementary school for local children until the late 1950s. After the school closed down Verhoeven excavated the floor to a depth of two metres and found bronze artifacts and grave goods left by modern humans. Between 1978 and 1987 Indonesian archaeologists also worked the site, penetrating no deeper than 3.5 metres. Morwood was convinced they had not dug deep enough, and that a more extensive excavation could possibly locate ancient skeletal remains.[30] As luck would have it his supposition proved correct, with the Indonesian members of Morwood's team uncovering the bones of *Homo floresiensis*.

It was not until 2003, however, and only after Morwood's team had reached the six metre level, that they first came to light. Owing to their great antiquity and the damp environment the bones had the consistency of blotting paper. They had to be exposed in situ for three days before even hardener could be applied,[31] and it was almost immediately apparent that these were no ordinary bones. They belonged

The Hobbit Enigma

to an individual of exceptionally small stature who possessed a range of primitive physical features, including the absence of a chin. Standing just over a metre high, in life it probably weighed less than twenty-five kilograms. Judged by the facial features and dentition it seemed to fit within the genus *Homo*, and was widely touted as a dwarfed form of *Homo erectus*: some authorities still hold that view.[32]

Known as LB1 (Liang Bua One) the dentition also suggested the individual was around thirty years of age when it died, and the pelvic structure revealed that 'it' was a female. Initial estimates of the cranial capacity were as low as 380 cubic centimetres – roughly equivalent to a modern chimpanzee.[33] Although this was well below the 700 cubic centimetre threshold for inclusion in the genus *Homo*, the archaeological record had shown that these creatures were not only capable of manufacturing stone tools, they had also mastered the use of fire. Sediments in Liang Bua Cave which contain stone tools have been dated to between 50,000 and 190,000 years ago, and evidence of their cooking hearths exists at all levels. A number of the stegodon bones bear cut marks where they were de-fleshed with stone tools, though it is possible, if not probable, that the 'Hobbits' also used wood or bamboo implements which have long since rotted away.[34] Importantly, the stone tools at Liang Bua Cave are quite sophisticated. They include elongated flakes made by rotating core stones and striking downwards, as well as pointed tools with retouched edges. The technology is virtually identical to the stone toolkit unearthed at Mata Menge in central Flores,[35] where 'Hobbit'-like remains dating back to 700,000 years ago were discovered in 2014.[36] Based solely on some teeth and a partial jaw (always a risky business) the discoverers maintained that these earlier hominids had closer affinities to *Homo erectus* than *Homo habilis*, but until sufficient postcranial remains are unearthed any inference must necessarily be treated with due caution.[37]

That said, however, the majority of the stegodon bones at Liang Bua, along with those of Komodo dragons belong to juvenile animals, evidence that *Homo floresiensis* was a highly-selective hunter who usually avoided tackling adult animals. Hunting was clearly a well-organised activity,[38] which at times might have involved highly-sophisticated techniques, especially for the giant rats whose bones have been found in every sediment level at Liang Bua. While excavations were underway a curious local villager arrived at the site with a Giant Flores Rat dangling from an ingenious trap that used tightly-stretched wire to snap shut a pair of jaws on the unsuspecting rodent. Morwood was so intrigued that he followed the rat-catcher back to his village and watched as the animal was split open and barbecued. Nothing was wasted; even the smaller bones were gathered up and boiled into a soup.[39] Whether the 'Hobbits' used similar traps to ensnare their prey is open to speculation, but they certainly did not lack the wherewithal to do so.

The remains of up to six more 'Hobbits' have been unearthed at Liang Bua since the discovery of LB1, and the cubic capacity of the braincase has been revised to a maximum of 420 cubic centimetres – still very tiny in comparison with other members of the genus *Homo*.[40] That does not necessarily mean they lacked intelligence. Impressions of the highly-convoluted frontal lobes, the section of the brain associated with self-awareness and a good indicator of intelligence, are almost equal in size to those of modern humans.[41] Taken together, it appeared the joint Indonesian-Australian team had made the archaeological find of the century with their discovery of *Homo floresiensis*, a short-statured hominid that had survived almost to the very time that the vanguard of modern humanity had passed by to reach the ancient southern continent of Sahul. (At that time, of course, dating suggested that it had survived on the island until as recently as 12,000 years ago). The find made headlines around the world, but almost before the ink had dried critics began launching a series of attacks aimed at discrediting the sensational announcement.

Under an agreement between the University of New England and Indonesia's National Centre for Archaeology in Jakarta, the type specimen was to be held in the latter institution. Yet even before Morwood's team had completed their initial research, pieces of LB1 were whisked off to the Gadja Madu University at Yogyakarta in central Java after pressure was placed on the National Centre for Archaeology by Indonesia's so-called 'king of palaeoanthropology', Professor Teuku

The Hobbit Enigma

Jacob. Up to this time Jacob had not been associated in any way with the project on Flores,[42] and the following year he confidently announced that the bones were not those of an ancient hominid. On the contrary, said Jacob, they were from a modern human who had suffered from a serious genetic brain disorder known as microcephaly,[43] an abnormal growth on the brain which is sometimes triggered by maternal alcoholism, diabetes, chickenpox, rubella or radiation poisoning while the foetus is being carried in the womb. It can also arise from abnormalities in the chromosomes, but whatever the cause it results in the head failing to achieve its full growth.[44] The cubic capacity of the brain does not exceed 700 cubic centimetres, and those who suffer from microcephaly are usually intellectually-impaired and short in stature; most die young.[45]

While Jacob had the remains in his possession he invited two Australian scientists to examine them. Both had been critical of Morwood and Brown's findings. One was Alan Thorne from the Australian National University in Canberra, while the other was Maciej Henneberg, Adelaide University's Professor of Biological Anthropology and Comparative Anatomy. After concurring with Jacob's assessment, Thorne made a public statement on Channel Nine's *Sixty Minutes* television program that he was soon to regret. According to Thorne, Morwood's team had not been able to recognise 'a village idiot when they saw one'. The timing was unfortunate, because shortly afterwards the project team on Flores began unearthing the skeletal remains of more specimens, all of which bore the same physical characteristics as LB1. Rather than the type specimen being a village idiot, it seemed that Liang Bua contained an entire village of idiots.[46] Jacob responded by returning to the National Centre of Anthropology to remove the remaining fragments of LB1. Thorne and Henneberg jointly published an article in an online journal which agreed with Jacob that the 'Hobbit' was nothing more than a microcephalic, comparing the skull of LB1 with one belonging to an ancient Minoan from Crete.[47]

Brown and Morwood defended their findings in the same journal,[48] but they also received considerable support from Dean Falk and her colleagues at Florida State University. Falk is a leading authority on brain evolution. Using CT scans and endocasts of the 'Hobbit's' cranium, Falk's co-workers (who included Brown and Morwood) also made their own comparisons with modern humans (including a microcephalic and a pygmy), as well as hominids such as *Homo erectus* and the Australopithecines. According to these findings the closest match was *Homo erectus*; the most distant the microcephalic. The results were published in the highly-respected journal *Science*, though Falk and her colleagues emphasised that the 'Hobbit's' brain was not simply a miniature replica of *Homo erectus*. It possessed a number of very different and rather unusual features.[49]

When Jacob, Thorne and Henneberg returned to the fray in 2006 they repeated their arguments regarding microcephaly, but now LB1 was considered to be a descendant of a population of modern pygmies which had once inhabited the island of Flores.[50] The anatomist, Gary Richards, also entered the debate by suggesting the Hobbit might have been a victim of Laron syndrome, a condition which also results in dwarfism.[51] His argument received formidable support from three other researchers, one of whom was no less than Zvi Laron, the Israeli endocrinologist who had first described the syndrome.[52] The only way of proving this hypothesis, however, was to test the 'Hobbit's' DNA for defective genes; unfortunately all DNA extracted from these diminutive creatures thus far has been contaminated by modern human DNA.[53]

By the time Richards had raised the possibility of Laron's syndrome, Jacob had returned the remains of LB1 to the National Centre for Archaeology. They did not return intact, as moulds taken in his laboratory had seriously damaged the skeletal fragments. A jawbone, for instance, had been broken in half and wrongly glued back together. Not only was it misaligned; some of the pieces had disappeared altogether. Two leg bones were also missing, while the left side of the pelvis had also been smashed, destroying crucial evidence of body shape and locomotion. Jacob denied any wrongdoing, insisting the damage had been done while the remains were in transit and not in his laboratory.[54] Few were convinced, and the outrage grew so intense that the Australian scientists were banned from working in Indonesia until tensions eased. It was not until Jacob died in early 2007 that work finally resumed at Liang Bua.[55]

The Hobbit Enigma

While all these scientific arguments were raging, Australian wildlife artist Peter Schouten published an illustration of a male *Homo floresiensis* with a giant rat slung over its shoulder, an image that was flashed around the world. It, too, proved controversial. Schouten had based his depiction on LB1, the type specimen, which of course was a female. Feminists were among those who were outraged at Schouten's male bias, and there were even suggestions that the creature should be colloquially renamed 'Flo' after its island home.[56] Unfortunately for the proponents, it did not have quite the same appeal as 'Hobbit', and the appropriation from Tolkien remained intact.

The inaccurate drawing was soon forgotten when those critical of the discovery began advancing new arguments in their bid to further undermine the unique status of these creatures. In 2008 Henneberg struck back with the extraordinary claim that one of the 'Hobbit's' teeth – the first lower left molar – bore evidence of dental work carried out in the 1930s. Although he had previously examined the Hobbit's teeth in Jacob's laboratory after the specimen had been hijacked in 2005, Henneberg waited three years before making this astounding revelation to the media.[57] He insisted that a filling in the tooth had been made with dental cement rather than metal amalgam, which is dark in colour and thus stands out clearly. The only support came from his close associates, including Thorne, who were collectively known as the Pathology Group.[58] Henneberg's claim was dismissed by specialists who had closely studied the dentition of *Homo floresiensis*. If dental work had been conducted in the 1930s it was nothing short of incredible that the skull fragments would have been buried under six metres of sediment among the fossilised bones of extinct animals and ancient stone tools.[59]

There the matter might have rested, except that Henneberg and John Schofield published a book called *The Hobbit Trap*, a work which says more about Henneberg than the archaic little hominid. He condemned the scientific establishment generally and the funding received by Morwood and his team in particular. As a number of reputable journals had refused to publish Henneberg's articles on the 'Hobbits', he interpreted this as part of a wider conspiracy to destroy the credibility of the Pathology Group. Having been closely associated with Jacob's appropriation of LB1, Henneberg also failed to understand why he was not 'welcomed back with open arms' to examine the more recent skeletal material from Liang Bua.[60] Moreover, Henneberg has continued to dispute the authenticity of *Homo floresiensis*. In 2014, for instance, Henneberg and a number of associates moved away from microcephaly to pronounce LB1 to be nothing more outstanding than an early human with the developmental disorder known as Down syndrome.[61] Again, though, it appears that Liang Bua must have contained an entire community of similarly afflicted individuals, and in this instance Mike Morwood could no longer respond to the critics. He had lost his battle with cancer in July 2013.[62]

A far more legitimate argument was that the 'Hobbits' suffered from endemic cretinism, an iodine deficiency which destroys the thyroid gland in infancy and seriously retards bone growth and brain size. That conclusion was reached by a number of researchers who had not examined the skeletal evidence first-hand, relying instead on data which had been published for very different reasons. For all that, this line of reasoning has still not been dispelled.[63] Around the same time it was discovered that the carpel bones in the wrists of the 'Hobbits', the bones which allow the wrist to move and rotate vertically, were remarkably similar to those of the Australopithecines.[64] The limb bones of the 'Hobbits' also lack a number of features which are found in all other archaic hominids that have roamed the planet within the last 800,000 years. Their feet are unusually flat and very lengthy in proportion to the body. In modern humans, for example, the foot is approximately fifty-five per cent of the length of the short femur bone in the leg; in the Hobbits it is seventy per cent. As these creatures could not bend their knees as far back as modern humans it has been conjectured that their steps were high – a little like walking with a pair of over-sized shoes – which meant that running would have been difficult and, one would assume, very tiresome. The toes of the 'Hobbits' are also oddly-shaped, while the big toe is exceptionally short.[65]

This raised questions as to whether the 'Hobbits' were dwarf *Homo erectus*, a form of Australopithecine, or perhaps a unique branch of the human bush whose ancestors still await discovery. Before his death, Mike Morwood and his co-worker Peter Brown had shifted to the latter line of reasoning, both suggesting that the ancestors of the 'Hobbits' may have left Africa and spread to Asia before the genus *Homo* even evolved.[66] To confuse the issue even further, in 2008 a team led by Lee Berger of Witwatersrand University in South Africa claimed to have uncovered 'Hobbit'-sized remains in burial caves on the Palauan Archipelago in Micronesia. Although they possessed a number of morphological features similar to the 'Hobbits' of Flores, Berger maintained they were modern humans of remarkably short stature.[67] He was correct on all counts but the last: they proved to be nowhere near as small as the 'Hobbits'.[68]

However, the previous year a 67,000-year-old third metatarsal (a foot bone) belonging to another unknown member of the genus *Homo* had been discovered in Callao Cave on the island of Luzon in the Philippines. Like Flores, entry to Luzon at any time during the past required a passage over water,[69] but it was not until 2019 that the full significance of this find became apparent. It was only then that enough skeletal material had been uncovered to classify it as a distinct species – *Homo luzonensis*. More to the point, the available evidence suggests that it is also of diminutive proportions and has skeletal anatomical traits either rare or absent in all other members of the genus except for the 'Hobbits' of Flores. As with the 'Hobbit' it shares some affinities with the Australopithecines, and just like *Homo floresiensis* this species survived on its island home until around 50,000 years ago.[70] What caused their extinctions still remains unexplained, though some measure of clarity was seemingly thrown on the origins of *Homo floresiensis* in 2017.

As mentioned in Chapter 2, Debbie Argue and Colin Groves of the Australian National University (along with Michael Lee and William Jungers) closely analysed the phylogenetic characteristics of a host of archaic hominids and rejected the possibility of any relationship between the 'Hobbits' and *Homo erectus*. On the contrary, they found remarkable similarities between *Homo floresiensis* and *Homo habilis*, which also has a number of Australopithecine traits. Although clearly separate species they were still close,[71] which provided support for the argument that *Homo habilis* exited the African continent long before its successors.[72] Many others, however, consider this earlier migration to be implausible, so confirmation still awaits further discoveries.[73]

And there still remains the question as to whether these small-statured insular hominids survived beyond the 50,000-year mark. Although modern humans did not colonise the Indonesian island of Flores 11,000 years ago, a folk tale relating to the presence of small hairy people known as the *ebu gogo*, who lived in caves, has persisted to the present day. According to the oral tradition both groups lived in relative harmony until the *ebu gogo* began systematically raiding the crops of the villagers and abducting some of their children. Enraged by their actions the villagers trapped their small hairy adversaries in a cave, lighting fires at the entrance which suffocated them. So the story ends. It has been estimated that this sequence of events took place sometime between CE 1750 and 1820, and while it may be no more than a fanciful tale it could contain an element of truth. It needs to be remembered that this story and others concerning the *ebu gogo* were circulating long before the discovery of *Homo floresiensis* in September 2003.[74]

A similar oral tradition about little people standing just over a metre high is found on Sumatra, where they were known as the *orang pendek*.[75] The discovery of *Homo luzonensis* reinforces the possibility that other diminutive forms of humanity may have lived on similarly remote islands of South-East Asia and perhaps on those even further to the east and south. This leaves open the possibility – not to say probability – that the parent species continued its own migration eastwards and was followed by others long before the evolution of *Homo sapiens*.

Lengthy sea crossings were clearly not insurmountable, and the Aboriginal people right across northern Australia, from Broome in the west to Cairns in the east, have very similar tales to the modern inhabitants of Flores and Sumatra concerning the presence of 'Little People' who spoke strange languages. Despite the geographical enormity of northern Australia, the Aboriginal oral histories have a remarkable consistency. In some instances, just as on the Indonesian island of Flores, the 'Little People' were destroyed by the Aborigines when tensions between the two groups reached breaking-point. Conversely, other Aboriginal groups insist that the 'Little People' still exist in the remote fastness of their territories.[76] In the Aboriginal Dreaming, ancient times can be conflated with the present (and projected into the future),[77] and could simply mean that the oral histories are but distant memories of encounters during the Aboriginal migration to Australia. But the possibility of diminutive forms of humanity on the Australian continent – at least in antiquity – is intriguing. It is also interesting that both *Homo floresiensis* and *Homo luzonensis* appear to have disappeared on their island homes when the Aboriginal people were embarking on their colonisation of an entire continent to the south. How they accomplished that extraordinary feat is the next step on the journey into Australia's ancient Aboriginal past.

COLONISATION OF SAHUL: THE ARCHAEOLOGICAL AND SKELETAL EVIDENCE

V

Our knowledge of the colonisation of the supercontinent of Sahul is entirely dependent on archaeological sites and skeletal evidence, and given our limited understanding of this crucial episode the possibility that modern humans were not the first people to step foot on the antipodean shores should not be lightly dismissed. Speculation as to whether *Homo erectus* or archaic *Homo sapiens* preceded the Aborigines was often discussed in the past but is seldom heard today. Many Aborigines, of course, insist they have always lived in Australia, so to suggest there may have been an earlier hominid on the continent is to open a veritable Pandora's Box. Yet to raise this issue does nothing to detract from the extraordinary antiquity of the Aboriginal presence in Australia, nor of their magnificent achievements. It is simply a subject that is relative to human evolution more broadly and to Australia's ancient human past more specifically. As such it deserves scholarly attention, particularly in view of our more recent knowledge of the existence of the Denisovans.

The 'Hobbits' of Flores and *Homo luzonensis* have clearly demonstrated that at least one early form of hominid was capable of making lengthy and dangerous journeys across sea barriers. *Homo erectus* was present in Java at least 1.7 million years BP and the island of Flores had been reached by either a clade of *Homo habilis* or *Homo erectus* some 840,000 years BP. The ancestor of *Homo luzonensis* had also reached that isolated island in the Philippines at roughly the same time. In both instances dwarf stegodons, giant tortoises (and on Luzon also a unique pig with four tusks) disappeared shortly after the arrival of hominids.[1] Whether these pioneering members of the genus *Homo*

Colonisation Of Sahul: The Archaeological And Skeletal Evidence

continued further in pursuit of stegodons, population pressure or even sheer curiosity is more problematic. At this point in time we simply do not know, and if an early species of hominid did in fact reach the shores of Sahul its ultimate fate remains just as uncertain as that of the Neanderthals of Europe. That is why the Neanderthals were deliberately included in this work: it is not beyond the realm of possibility that a similar scenario was played out on ancient continental Australia.

What we can say is that whoever the original colonisers were they definitely entered Sahul from the adjacent supercontinent of Sunda, the residue of which is present-day South-East Asia. In the face of uncertainty, however, it is only possible to focus on modern humans, and although the more recent origins of the Australian Aborigines are unknown, DNA studies have conclusively shown that they fall within the mitochondrial founder branches M and N. Their Y chromosomal founders C and F also directly link these people to the exodus of modern humans from Africa around 70,000 years BP. This applies equally to modern Papua New Guineans, which means that both groups are descended from the same founding population. Moreover, the mitochondrial founding branch M has a variant nucleotide known simply as 13500 which is found only among the Australian Aborigines, Papua New Guineans and other neighbouring Melanesians. It occurs nowhere else in the world, so while they appear to be physically distinct there is a very close genetic link between the Australian Aborigines and their Melanesian neighbours to the north.[2] And just as the DNA of northern Europeans is around three per cent Neanderthal, that of the Australian Aborigines, Papuan New Guineans and other closely related Melanesian groups is between three and four per cent of the Neanderthal's close cousin, the Denisovans.[3]

Regardless of whom the first colonisers were, the occupation of Sahul occurred during the Pleistocene epoch which began some 2 MYA and drew to a close around 11,700 years BP, when an entirely new phase of the Quarternary period commenced. Known as the Holocene, it is the epoch we live in today. The Pleistocene was marked by nineteen climatic cycles – frigid Ice Ages interspersed by warmer interglacial interludes, with sea levels around the world rising and falling by as much as 100 metres. Between 18,000 and 120,000 years BP the seas were on average sixty-five metres lower than at present, and if the Australian Aborigines entered Sahul between 50,000 and 60,000 years BP the seas were at that time between sixty and eighty-five metres lower than today.[4] The Aborigines had certainly occupied the continent long before the Last Glacial Maximum which began sometime between 25,000 and 30,000 years BP and finally drew to a close between 12,000 and 15,000 years BP. Subsequent global warming resulted in the seas rising to their present levels around 6,000 years BP.[5]

At no time during the Pleistocene were the two supercontinents of Sahul and Sunda connected. They came reasonably close on a number of occasions, but there was always a marine barrier separating them known as the Wallace Line. Although its boundaries are far from rigid, the indigenous mammalian fauna on both sides are distinct. Placental mammals dominated Sunda; marsupials and monotremes reigned supreme on Sahul. Despite their swimming prowess stegodons never reached Sahul. The only placental mammals to do so prior to human colonisation were rodents and bats, the former almost certainly drifting across on flotsam.[6]

During the interglacial phases of the Pleistocene the north-west monsoons were significantly stronger than today, a factor that would have greatly assisted watercraft voyaging from Sunda to Sahul.[7] It certainly helped the transmigration of rodents and bats, and was therefore no less relevant to the human story. There is a caveat in all this, however, as while it is often assumed that any migration to Sahul probably depended on low sea levels the very opposite may have actually been the case.[8] Rising seas could just as easily have triggered an exodus from islands lying between the supercontinents by submerging large tracts of land and coastal resources, concomitantly restricting available living space. Whatever the precise reasons there would have been an awareness of land over the horizon. Ocean currents, flotsam, bird migrations and even natural bushfires were all important indicators.[9] While the islands of Flores and Luzon could have been colonised by an early hominid following a volcanic eruption and accompanying tsunami, the settlement of Sahul was unlikely to have been a matter of chance. The distance was too great and scattered individuals would have had little hope of forming a viable population.

Colonisation Of Sahul: The Archaeological And Skeletal Evidence

It can be inferred from all this, then, that the colonisation of Sahul was a deliberate and organised accomplishment involving watercraft more sophisticated than mere logs. Rafts may have been used, but the material used in their construction can only be conjectured. Palm trunks and bamboo would have been ideal owing to their buoyancy, but the natural distribution of bamboo, in particular, may not have extended beyond Java during the Pleistocene epoch.[10] Not all the voyagers are likely to have survived the journey: lengthy sea crossings by raft or other similar watercraft run considerable risks, not the least of which are adverse weather conditions. It needs to be added, though, that in more recent times Aboriginal people along the north coast of Australia regularly made off-shore voyages of up to thirty kilometres on log rafts and flimsy sewn bark canoes.[11] These trips were admittedly conducted in relatively shallow coastal waters as opposed to deep ocean troughs, but given the assistance of strong north-west monsoons and favourable currents longer voyages would not have been extraordinarily difficult.

While it is almost certain there was more than one wave of migrants, studies of Polynesian colonisation in the Pacific have shown that where the rule of monogamy had been removed a primary group consisting of just one man and two women at the beginning of their reproductive lives had a three-in-four-chance of surviving lengthy sea voyages and populating large islands.[12] It does not take that many more to populate an entire continent if time is not a factor. That leads to the three, possibly four, routes which could have been taken to colonise the ancient supercontinent of Sahul as first proposed by Joseph Birdsell.[13] The northern routes from Sulawesi to what is now Papua New Guinea were the shortest and probably safest, but most researchers favour one of the two more southerly alternatives. Both followed the Indonesian archipelago to Timor, where one route continued directly east through another chain of islands to Tanimbar, followed by a voyage of forty kilometres to a landfall now submerged beneath the waters of the Arafura Sea. The second route would have involved a direct eighty-kilometre voyage from Timor to the north-west tip of Sahul.[14] The latter has received the greatest attention even though a crossing via the Tanimbar Islands appears to make more sense.

From raised coral terraces along the Huon Peninsula it is known that modern humans inhabited coastal Papua New Guinea (then the northern section of Sahul) at least 40,000 and possibly 50,000 years BP, and by 25,000 years BP there are hints of rudimentary horticultural activities being practised in the Papua New Guinean highlands.[15] This development did not filter south despite the absence of a sea barrier because much of present-day Australia was either completely arid or consisted of dry grass and shrublands until 18,000 years BP. Prior to that time the Papua New Guinea highlands were probably the most fertile region of Sahul, consisting of rainforest and more open country suitable for horticultural and, later, agricultural production.[16] It is worth noting, however, that even today agriculture in Papua New Guinea is frequently subsidised by hunting and gathering activities.[17]

Timor, the point of divergence for both southern routes into Sahul, was certainly an attractive stepping-stone if not a permanent place of residence. Pleistocene fauna included the stegodons which were the favourite prey species of Asian *Homo erectus*, giant land tortoises and rodents – including giant rats.[18] As previously stated, the modern human presence on Timor dates back to at least 42,000 years BP, but it may be relevant that stone tools have been found on the island which reputedly differ from the stone technology of *Homo sapiens*. They have yet to be accurately dated, but from the published descriptions they bear a remarkable similarity to Oldowan stone tools, and all of them have been recovered from the same gravel beds as the bones of extinct stegodons.[19]

There were a number of additional factors which made Timor a favourable springboard to Sahul. The deep Timor Trough which separates the island from modern Australia was far less turbulent before 12,000 years BP as there was no through current from the Pacific. Torres Strait and the Arafura Sea were both part of the Sahul land mass, so in many ways the Timor Trough was little more than a huge estuary despite its considerable depth.[20] Coupled with the stronger north-west monsoons and a prevailing southerly current the crossing to Sahul would not have been anywhere near as formidable as it is today. A case in point is offered by the island of Buka on the opposite side of the great southern continent. Buka is one of the northern Solomon Islands,

Colonisation Of Sahul: The Archaeological And Skeletal Evidence

which throughout the Pleistocene was separated from the nearest land to the west – New Ireland – by 180 kilometres of ocean. Yet it is known that modern humans reached Buka from New Ireland at least 28,000 years BP.[21]

The earliest evidence of people of one form or another on Sahul now lies beneath the sea. Moreover, if the founding population had been small, as seems likely, there would be so little evidence of their presence that they will remain archaeologically invisible.[22] An exception is Boodie Cave on Barrow Island, off the north-west coast of Australia. Optically stimulated luminescence dating of sediments in 2015 provided an occupation date of approximately 53,000 years BP – and this was said to have been a conservative figure. Importantly, the sediments are strewn with thousands of tiny artifacts, and according to lead archaeologist Peter Veth, there is no longer any question that the Aboriginal people arrived in Australia before 50,000 years ago.[23] On the mainland itself, the oldest archaeological site which has been securely dated lies near the shore of Lake Gregory on the edge of the Great Sandy Desert in north-western Australia. Artifacts uncovered there have been conservatively dated to between 45,000 and 50,000 years BP.[24] A number of other early sites are also known from north-western Australia, supporting the notion that it was this region which experienced the first influx of colonisers. One of them is Minjiwarra, a large sedimentary outcrop rising six metres on the lower catchment of the Drysdale River in the north-eastern Kimberley region. Evidence of Aboriginal occupation extends from approximately 7,700 years BP to around 50,000 years BP, and importantly, the researchers (again led by Peter Veth) applied a number of dating techniques to reach their conclusion regarding the great antiquity of the site.[25] Sediments with artifacts dated to around 40,000 years BP have also been found at Carpenter's Gap rock shelter in the Napier Ranges,[26] and a similar age has been obtained from charcoal in stone hearths at Mimi Caves, just to the south-west of Fitzroy Crossing.[27] Despite this concentration in the north-west, it does need to be added that even earlier dates have been obtained at Devil's Lair in the Leeuwin-Naturaliste Ranges, 260 kilometres south of Perth.[28]

For all that, there can be little doubt that the initial entry point was somewhere in the north where the pioneering population encountered a climate similar to the one they had left behind. They also brought with them knowledge of making fire, language and stone tool technology. A number of edible plants would probably have been familiar, though the same cannot be said for the terrestrial fauna.[29] Sahul was home to the unique megamarsupials, some of which reached truly gigantic proportions. Yet, apart from a few fearsome predators, most were relatively harmless and many could be hunted for food. Their disappearance within a relatively short span of time will be explored in the following chapter.

A number of theories have been put forward to explain how the settlement of Sahul was achieved. In 1977 Sandra Bowdler proposed her 'coastal colonisation' model, in which she argued that as the pioneers were seafarers they sensibly followed the coast to exploit marine resources. Only later did they begin venturing inland along the river systems and settling the interior. To support her hypothesis Bowdler drew on one of Australia's best-known and most important archaeological sites at Willandra Lakes in south-western New South Wales. Here the ancient inhabitants relied heavily on aquatic resources provided by the river and lakes,[30] only utilising the back country on a sporadic basis. Terrestrial animals, Bowdler insisted, were of secondary importance, but this theory tends to underrate the intelligence of the founding population, which would have quickly recognised and begun to exploit land-based resources which yielded a high return for the energy expended.[31] That included the smaller marsupials, and especially the giant herbivorous megafauna.

An alternative model is the 'fast tracker hypothesis', whereby vast areas of the continent were rapidly explored and settled.[32] From the more recent dates obtained at Devil's Lair in south-western Australia it is now known that the region was inhabited 47,000 or 48,000 years BP,[33] and by 35,000 years BP the Aborigines had reached their southernmost limit in south-western Tasmania.[34] In both instances their economies were firmly terrestrially-based. The available evidence suggests that virtually all the physical and environmental barriers could have been overcome

Colonisation Of Sahul: The Archaeological And Skeletal Evidence

within a relatively short period of time,[35] with perhaps the only limiting factor the rate of reproduction. It is interesting, too, that around 1914 three unusual rock engravings were recorded at two sites east of Port Augusta in South Australia. One features a saltwater crocodile, the second a sea turtle, while the third has been identified as a marine fish. At the time it appeared to offer proof that the Aborigines had been present in Australia when those animals had existed in these southern climes.[36] The problem is that when they did swim in such southerly latitudes modern humans had not even evolved. It is far more likely that their images were etched in stone by people who had travelled from the north coast, which again suggests fairly rapid movement directly through the interior.

In many ways it was similar to the human colonisation of the Americas, where almost the entire landmass was settled within a remarkably short span of time. To achieve that the colonisers had to adapt to a whole range of different environments ranging from freezing sub-Arctic tundra in the north, through temperate forests, deserts, tropical jungles, high altitudes, and finally a return to frigid conditions in the sub-Antarctic south.[37] One way of explaining the rapid settlement of the Americas has been through the 'big game tracker' hypothesis, which proposes that the first Americans pursued localised populations of giant megafauna to extinction before moving on to new areas and repeating the process.[38] Unlike Sahul, the American megafauna consisted of placental mammals – mammoths, mastodons, camels, bison and ground sloths – just to name a few. This theory still fails to explain how those pioneering human groups managed to adapt so quickly to such a diverse range of environments. On the other hand, more than fifty per cent of the American megafaunal species did become extinct shortly after the appearance of modern humans,[39] a repetition of what had already played out on the opposite side of the Pacific.

Since the 1970s it has almost become a fad amongst archaeologists to claim the discovery of the earliest evidence of the human presence in Australia, often making a premature announcement in the popular media. In many cases new claims have been made and just as quickly dismissed by other archaeologists applying a different – and sometimes a more reliable – dating technique to the same material. The current procedure is to publish the results of any new find in a peer-reviewed journal, allowing discussion and balanced checks to take place before the information enters the public domain. Any claim also has to meet two important criteria. One is that any assumed artifact actually is an artifact shaped by human hands. The second is that if those artifacts cannot be dated they must be clearly shown to be the roughly same age as their associated surroundings.[40] This may sound simple, but at times it causes enormous headaches. In northern Australia, for example, tunnels made by termites often collapse, a process known as bioturbation which results in artifacts filtering downwards to much earlier levels. Worms and other burrowing animals can have the same effect right across Australia.[41]

To take the first point, it can be said that the majority of stone artifacts can readily be distinguished from naturally-broken stone. Flakes struck from a core have a distinctive conchoidal, or shell-like form or markings. Some of the material which was used to make stone tools can itself be distinctive. Flint and chert, for instance, are both isotropic, with their mechanical properties the same in any direction. That is exactly why they were often chosen by the original makers, because flakes could be struck from the core regardless of which way it was struck. That type of flaking is extremely rare under natural conditions, and it never creates the distinguishable pattern of flakes seen in Aboriginal stone quarries. The earliest stone tools were frequently made from quartz, which readily fragments when struck and can also fracture naturally. Even then, however, it seldom leaves the distinctive conchoidal marking.[42]

In 1960 the earliest known evidence of the Aboriginal presence dated to 8,700 years BP at Cape Martin in South Australia.[43] While a number of other sites were suspected of being much older they could not be accurately dated, the unique Kartan culture of Kangaroo Island and the South Australian mainland being just one example. The Pleistocene barrier was finally broken by John Mulvaney in 1962, when radiocarbon was used to date material from Kenniff Cave in southern Queensland. At first it was 10,000 years BP, but two years later occupation of the site was pushed back to 16,000 years BP and then to 19,000 years BP.[44]

Colonisation Of Sahul: The Archaeological And Skeletal Evidence

If the Barrow Island dates are correct the initial colonisation of Sahul by Aboriginal people can now be extended just beyond 50,000 years BP, though a number of researchers still favour a date in the order of 60,000 years BP.[45]

If modern humans first exited the African continent around 70,000 years BP, however, the settlement of Sahul probably occurred between 50,000 and 55,000 years BP. It would of course be a very different matter if the continent was first colonised by a pre-human hominid such as *Homo erectus*. While there is currently no direct evidence of that having happened, it does need to be added that no evidence is merely the weakest evidence of all.[46] The lowest sea level between the ancient supercontinents of Sunda and Sahul was reached around 160,000 years BP, which is far too early for modern humans.[47] It could have proved beneficial for other hominids, and there are tantalising hints of their presence in skeletal remains which will shortly be considered. For the moment, though, it can be said that while archaeological sites offer no such clues, the significant Australian Pleistocene locations have still managed to generate their own controversies.

There can be no question that one of the most important sites is Lake Mungo, one of thirteen interconnected former lakes in south-western New South Wales. Evidence of ancient occupation was first noticed in 1968 by Jim Bowler, a geomorphologist studying the sediments of the Willandra Lakes complex to determine climate change over the last 100,000 years. The lakes were once filled by overflow from the Lachlan River, but they have been dry for the last 15,000 years and today the entire region is extremely arid.[48] Bowler stumbled on a few bones which had been exposed by wind erosion which he reported to archaeologists at the Australian National University in Canberra. He suspected they were kangaroo bones remaining from an ancient Aboriginal meal, so his information initially aroused little interest. The following year John Mulvaney, Rhys Jones and Alan Thorne decided to make the long drive from Canberra to investigate the find, quickly identifying the bones as human.[49] Stone tools were also located close by. The trio was so ill-equipped with what was soon to become a major archaeological discovery that the delicate bones had to be transported back to the

Australian National University in Mulvaney's suitcase. Indeed, Lake Mungo is now regarded as so significant that the suitcase is lodged in the National Museum of Australia.[50]

Early radiocarbon dates of the skeletal material indicated the individual – a female – died around 26,000 years BP. Another virtually complete skeleton, this time a male, was discovered in 1974 and dated between 28,000 and 32,000 years BP.[51] New techniques have since shown that the original dates were far too conservative. In 1999 a team led by Alan Thorne published a sensational report that Mungo 3, the male, had died approximately 62,000 years BP. As can only be expected in the volatile world of archaeology the claim was quickly dismissed by a second team which included Jim Bowler, whose findings indicated death at 42,300 years BP, plus or minus 4,400 years.[52] This was still a lot further back in time than the original radiocarbon dates had suggested. Further studies at Lake Mungo and elsewhere in the Willandra Lakes have also allowed archaeologists to construct one of the most comprehensive pictures of life in Pleistocene Australia. Importantly, Lake Mungo provided unequivocal evidence that the Aborigines were firmly established in the inland regions by at least 40,000 years BP. Sandra Bowdler drew on this site to support her 'coastal colonisation' model for the settlement of ancient Sahul, and if one accepts her conclusions it means that the first inhabitants of this area had made an arduous journey from the southern coast of Australia, as the Lachlan River is on the western watershed of the Great Dividing Range.

Despite Devil's Lair in the far south-west of the continent being located relatively close to the sea there is little evidence of a maritime economy. The site takes its name from the large quantities of Tasmanian devil bones in the upper levels of the deposits,[53] a reminder that both the devil and thylacine were once distributed right across Sahul from present-day Papua New Guinea to Tasmania. These animals became extinct on the Australian mainland and in Papua New Guinea following the respective arrival of the dingo and the New Guinea singing dog around 4,000 years BP. They survived into historical times only on the island of Tasmania.[54] Excavations at Devil's Lair, a large limestone cavern, have been continuing since 1973. Now situated just five kilometres from the

Colonisation Of Sahul: The Archaeological And Skeletal Evidence

Indian Ocean, at the height of the Last Glacial Maximum the sea was at least twenty-five kilometres distant. The sediments are littered with ancient animal remains, at least some of which were consumed by the Aboriginal inhabitants. Although limited quantities of shellfish were carried back to the site, the economy was overwhelmingly terrestrially-based right throughout its 47,000–48,000 year human history.[55]

The economy of the Aboriginal people living in the south-west of Tasmania from 35,000 years BP was similarly focused on land-based resources. In this instance the major prey species was the red-necked pademelon, a food source supplemented with wombat and many smaller animals. The inhabitants were at that time further south than anyone else in the world, with the environment primarily consisting of alpine heath.[56] At the height of the Last Glacial Maximum glaciers slowly carved their way through the landscape, and the ability to live in this hostile region was a truly remarkable human achievement. Apart from the most inhospitable regions further north it also essentially completed the colonisation of ancient Sahul by the Aboriginal people. This leads us back to the beginning of that process, owing to claims that the arrival of the Aborigines occurred much earlier than the majority of archaeologists are willing to accept. Some have been easily dismissed; others hint at very different possibilities.

In 1972 Rhys Jones conducted a brief archaeological survey of a sandstone shelter known as Nauwalabila, which now lies within the boundaries of Kakadu National Park in the Northern Territory. A thorough investigation was delayed until 1981 when a team led by Jones excavated the floor of the shelter to a depth of three metres, uncovering artifacts at all levels. Charcoal disappeared halfway through the deposits while artifacts continued to appear, so the age of the lower levels could not be determined. Jones was convinced they could be as old as 30,000 years BP, but lacking proof he decided to excavate another rockshelter eighty kilometres away then known as Malakunanja II (now Madjedbebe) in the hope of locating charcoal lower down. Although this proved unsuccessful, his team did unearth pieces of haematite, or iron ore, which is still used by Aboriginal people as a source of red ochre for painting and body decoration. Jones reasoned that it probably served the same purposes 30,000 years BP, which would have clearly placed the Aborigines in the vanguard of artists on the global stage.[57]

By then he was convinced the Aboriginal presence at both sites extended even further back in time, an assumption which appeared to be confirmed when thermoluminescence dating of the material provided dates of 55,000 to 60,000 years BP. As thermoluminescence is difficult to interpret with precision, Jones also employed optically stimulated luminescence (OSL), at that time a new and revolutionary technique which measures radioactive energy trapped in grains of sand. OSL gave dates of between 53,000 and 60,000 years BP, which would have made Nauwalabila and Malakunanja II the oldest known archaeological sites in Australia. Yet even Jones, who was known as the 'cowboy' of Australian prehistory, insisted that these results had to be treated with caution.[58] He was right. Using a different dating technique, evidence of the Aboriginal people at Nauwalabila did not extend beyond 40,000 years, and 45,000 years at Madjedbebe.[59] These were still very respectable figures, but then another team of researchers went back to Madjedbebe and, sticking with OSL, confidently announced in 2017 that the Aboriginal occupation of Australia had commenced prior to 65,000 years BP.[60] No real surprise there: a similar date from the same dating technique, which had been found to be in error thirty-six years before.

But in 1996 there was an even more extraordinary claim. In that year yet another team of archaeologists excavated Jinmium rockshelter just inside the Northern Territory-Western Australian border. Thermoluminescence was used to date the material, and on this occasion all caution was thrown to the winds, with the preliminary dates of 116,000–117,000 years BP leaked to the press.[61] The *Sydney Morning Herald* newspaper boldly declared the discovery of an 'Australian Stonehenge', an inference that Aboriginal cultural achievements require measurement against a European reference point when in fact they have significant value in their own right.[62] Predictably, critics did not take long to strike back. Both radiocarbon and OSL was applied to the material, and although radiocarbon is only accurate to 40,000 years BP it did not need to reach anywhere near its maximum limits. Both techniques

Colonisation Of Sahul: The Archaeological And Skeletal Evidence

convincingly revealed that the Aboriginal presence at Jinmium did not extend beyond 10,000 years BP.[63]

Although this site no longer has any relevance to the antiquity of Aboriginal colonisation, there is a remarkable similarity between the original dates and the findings of palynologists in eastern Australia. Palynology is the study of pollen, an organic substance which is not only virtually indestructible but very distinguishable between different floral species. Pollen accumulates as sediment, allowing specialists to identify plant communities across vast spans of time.[64] Sediment cores collected at Lake George in southern New South Wales during 1981–1982 showed the environmental patterns over the last 730,000 years, with an abrupt change occurring at 130,000 years BP. Charcoal fragments dramatically increased, with fire-sensitive trees such as southern beech replaced by fire-resistant species such as eucalypts. This vegetative transition did not correspond with any known climatic change, and it was suggested that it could indicate human agency.[65] Others have questioned the accuracy of Singh and Geissler's study, with Richard Wright contending that the change is likely to have been more in the order of 60,000 years BP.[66] If it was a non-natural event it still occurred prior to the arrival of the Aborigines, which leaves open the possibility that another hominid with fire-making skills could have been present on Sahul. To further pursue that line of inquiry it is necessary to consider the available skeletal evidence.

Among other things, Charles Darwin's theory of evolution brought in its train growing speculation about the origins of the Australian Aborigines. It was readily apparent to the European colonists that numerous physical differences existed throughout the continent, and to account for the obvious heterogeneity the idea of successive waves of immigrants in the distant past was slowly formulated. One of the most original thinkers on this subject was John Mathew, a Presbyterian minister and ethnographer, who published a small book on the origins of the Australian Aborigines in 1899. In *Eaglehawk and Crow* Mathew argued there had been three separate migrations of pre-European people into the continent, the first of which consisted of Papuan stock. These people had penetrated to the southernmost regions of Australia, with a remnant surviving in Tasmania. Although it was not known at the time, Mathew correctly surmised that a land bridge had once connected Tasmania with the Australian mainland.[67]

His second wave of immigrants consisted of Dravidians from the Indian sub-continent, an early group of people whose own origins remain obscure. Speakers of Dravidian languages are today found throughout southern and eastern India as well as Sri Lanka, Bangladesh, Pakistan, Afghanistan and Iran. According to Mathew these migrants were considerably taller than the Papuans, with straight hair and slightly fairer complexions. They were also more aggressive, partly eliminating and partly assimilating the first wave of colonisers. Prior to their arrival, however, Tasmania had been separated from the Australian mainland, effectively blocking the Dravidians from completing their conquest of the entire continent.[68]

Mathew's third and final wave of pre-European immigrants were of Malay stock, whose influence was far less dramatic and largely confined to the most northerly regions of Australia. Mathew drew on a close study of Aboriginal cultural and social characteristics, including language, to formulate his tri-hybrid theory. What particularly distinguished this explanation of Aboriginal diversity was his emphasis on myths and legends as valid forms of oral evidence. Mathew found that right across south-eastern Australia there was an Aboriginal tale of a conflict between an aggressive and lighter-coloured eaglehawk and a weaker, darker crow – hence the title of his work. For Mathew this tale represented a distant memory of a Dravidian migration to Australia and their dominance over the original Papuan colonisers.[69]

It is now known that the bulk of Mathew's theory has little basis in fact even though there are a few minor valid elements. On the other hand, his attempt to critically analyse Aboriginal Dreaming stories in a bid to gain some understanding of their external origins was a genuinely novel approach. From 1906 this path was pursued by J.W. Gregory, Professor of Geology and Mineralogy at the University of Melbourne. Unfortunately, Gregory's methodology was constrained by his firm conviction that the Aborigines were comparatively recent arrivals from India or Egypt and his work in this direction ultimately led nowhere.[70]

Colonisation Of Sahul: The Archaeological And Skeletal Evidence

The same can be said for the tri-hybrid theory even though it underwent a major resurgence in the twentieth century, particularly in the hands of the American anthropologist and population geneticist Joseph Birdsell.

Birdsell commenced his studies of the Australian Aborigines in 1938 and produced his final report in 1993. During those fifty-five years Birdsell's research ranged from craniometric measurements to studies of blood groups and, finally, modern genetics.[71] The latter has provided particularly strong evidence for the arrival of immigrant people in the mid-Holocene, probably in the last 4,000–5,000 years, but not in the Pleistocene as Birdsell contended. There are also a number of significant problems relating to Birdsell's earliest waves of immigration. According to his tri-hybrid theory the first colonisers of Australia were a short and slightly-built negrito people whose descendants can still be found on the Andaman Islands in the Indian Ocean and among Indigenous groups in Malaysia and the Philippines. Physical anthropologists are convinced that these groups represent the relic populations of a people who once lived throughout South-East Asia before being displaced by Asians from the north.[72] This also brings in a tenuous link with *Homo erectus*, because many Chinese today regard themselves as linear descendants of this hominid rather than archaic *Homo sapiens*.[73] Understandably this been disputed in some quarters, often by resurrecting an old argument that unique Asian physical features are merely the result of *Homo sapiens* adapting to harsher environmental conditions.[74] It can be contested on even firmer ground through genetics.[75] Be that as it may, there can be little doubt that the Indigenous peoples of South-East Asia were displaced by Asian invaders.

Birdsell labelled Australia's founding negrito people the Barrineans after Lake Barrine on the Atherton Tableland of North-East Queensland. He argued that these people were displaced by an influx of newcomers which he called the Murrayians, with the Barrineans only surviving in Tasmania and in small isolated populations in the dense rainforests of North-East Queensland.[76] Until comparatively recently the rainforest dwellers of the latter region were noted for their diminutive stature, and like the Tasmanian Aborigines they had short curly hair as opposed to the straight hair characteristic of most other Aboriginal people. The issue is not quite so straightforward, as early European settlers on the fringes of the North-East Queensland rainforest noted a considerable variation in height even within the same Aboriginal group.[77] Birdsell further contended that the language of the Queensland rainforest people was also markedly different from all other Aboriginal languages, an argument that can no longer be sustained. Robert Dixon, a linguist who specialises in the Indigenous languages of this region, has certainly detected a number of unusual features but considers them unmistakably part of the Pama-Nyungan Aboriginal language complex.[78] Notwithstanding that knowledge of Tasmanian Aboriginal languages is far from complete, it is known that they similarly fell within the same language group and shared close affinities with the Aboriginal languages of the south-eastern Australian mainland.[79] Environmental adaptation over time can also account for the diminutive stature of at least some of the North-East Queensland rainforest people.[80]

Birdsell linked his second wave of colonists, the Murrayians, to the Ainu people, who today inhabit the northernmost regions of Japan and eastern Siberia. The Ainu differ from all other Asian groups. They have fairer skins than their Japanese neighbours and are more sturdily built. They also have abundant body hair and males have a propensity to go bald – a rare trait among all other Asian people.[81] There is, however, no evidence to support the existence of either the Murrayians or their predecessors, the Barrineans, though it is a little different when it comes to Birdsell's third wave of colonisers, people he termed the Carpentarians. They were taller, thinner and less hairy than their predecessors and were possibly of Dravidian or related stock from the Indian sub-continent. According to Birdsell's theory these people predominated throughout northern Australia,[82] and this has been supported by mitochondrial DNA studies conducted among Aboriginal people in Arnhem Land, the Kimberleys and the Great Sandy Desert by the geneticists Alan Redd and Mark Stoneking. All three populations are genetically twelve times closer to Indians than they are to Papua New Guineans. The time of separation has been estimated at around 3,390 years BP, with a ninety-five per cent certainty that it occurred sometime between 1,686 and 5,093 years BP[83]. It is likely to have been these people who introduced

Colonisation Of Sahul: The Archaeological And Skeletal Evidence

the dingo into Australia, and when the archaeologist, Josephine Flood, attended a science congress in India and showed pictures of northern Australian Aboriginal people the local audience responded by declaring them to be unmistakably Dravidian. Birdsell thus appears to have been vindicated – but only in relation to his third wave of colonisers.[84]

Scholars overwhelmingly maintain that the Barrineans and Murrayians (whoever they may have really been) were part of a single founding population which physically diverged in response to differing environmental conditions across Australia.[85] The late palaeoanthropologist, Alan Thorne, was nevertheless among the minority who begged to differ. Thorne initially proposed that there had been two distinct waves of migration into Australia during the Pleistocene epoch, the first of which emanated from Java and were the direct descendants of *Homo erectus*. This group was distinguished by their extremely robust build, flatter receding forehead, projecting jaws and massive dentition. The second, and later immigrants, were far more gracile in build and originated in southern China.[86] The problem with Thorne's di-hybrid theory was that the gracile people from Lake Mungo proved to be older than the robust group from Kow Swamp.

In effect this was a complete reversal of human evolutionary theory as it applies elsewhere throughout the world, where robust people were succeeded by those of more gracile build.[87] To complicate the issue further, robust skeletons have since been located in the Willandra Lakes district, while more gracile skeletal material has been uncovered elsewhere. It is also known that Aboriginal people who lived in the Pleistocene were substantially larger than their Holocene descendants,[88] though why this was so is yet to be adequately explained. One argument is that a stockier build conserved more body heat during this cooler period, with body size diminishing as warmer conditions were ushered in by the Holocene,[89] but this fails to explain why Pleistocene Aborigines were also substantially taller than their Holocene successors. In the Murray River Valley of south-eastern Australia the average Pleistocene male stood 174 centimetres tall, while 2,000 years BP the average male height was 166 centimetres. Alternative arguments are that a reduction in physical size was linked to either climatic or dietary changes.[90] There is no direct evidence for the impact of climatic variations, and although the economy of the Willandra Lakes inhabitants certainly underwent a transition as these large bodies of fresh water slowly contracted before drying up completely 15,000 years BP,[91] in other regions of Australia the same resources appear to have been consumed during both epochs.

The physical characteristics of modern Aboriginal people also need to be kept in mind when investigating any supposed morphological transition. Aboriginal crania are long and narrow, with the wall constructed of very thick bone – thicker than most other contemporary humans. The brow ridges are also more prominent than is evident among any other people in the world, while the jaws and teeth are on average the largest known among *Homo sapiens*. There is a caveat: the size of Aboriginal teeth diminishes along a north to south gradient, with the desert dwellers possessing the smallest dentition of all Aborigines. While a reduction in the size of teeth has also marked human evolution generally, elsewhere it has been directly linked to the development of intensive agriculture – which was clearly not the case in Australia.[92]

Another significant factor in all this is the relative paucity of Pleistocene skeletal material. In Australia the bones from at least 120 individuals are suspected of being in excess of 9,000 years old, but only fifteen have been securely dated to the Pleistocene. The majority of the remains consist solely of crania, many of which are incomplete and some comprise just a few fragments.[93] Given increasing Aboriginal control of archaeological excavations it is unlikely that this situation will improve in the foreseeable future, and a considerable amount of ancient skeletal material has already been returned to modern Aboriginal groups. In some instances the fate of this material remains unknown. It is also rather unfortunate that while the crania can provide considerable information, much of the post-cranial material – the rest of the skeleton – has not received the same level of attention.[94] That was particularly applicable to the skeletal material recovered from Willandra Lakes and Kow Swamp, though more often than not it is only the crania which have survived the passage of time.

The so-called Talgai Skull was the first cranium discovered in Australia which tentatively dates from the Pleistocene. It was named after the pastoral property in southern Queensland where it was found protruding

Colonisation Of Sahul: The Archaeological And Skeletal Evidence

from a creek bank by a fencing contractor named William Naish. The year was probably 1886 (1884 is cited on occasion) and handed to the property owner who, in turn, passed it to his nephew-in-law, E.H.K. Crawford, a fellow pastoralist in New South Wales with a penchant for collecting 'curios'. Realising that it could have some value, Crawford attempted to sell the skull in 1896 but failed to attract a buyer.[95] He tried again in 1914, forwarding the skull to the distinguished geologist, Professor Edgeworth David at the University of Sydney, for valuation. This was only two years after the Piltdown hoax had been perpetrated in England, sparking an intense rivalry between British and Continental European scientists to find the oldest hominid remains on their home soil. The fragmented Talgai skull of obvious antiquity at the southern outpost of the British Empire suddenly assumed considerable importance, and it was accordingly purchased by the wealthy hotelier, racecourse-owner, newspaper proprietor and then Lord Mayor of Sydney, Sir James Joynton Smith, and presented as a gift to his city's university.[96]

The discovery of the Talgai skull was announced at the prestigious British Association for the Advancement of Science, which happened to be meeting at Sydney in August 1914. Largely due to the outbreak of the First World War, however, the skull was not thoroughly examined until 1918. That task fell to University of Sydney anatomist, Stewart Smith, whose London-based brother and fellow anatomist, Grafton Elliot Smith, was involved with Piltdown. Unlike Piltdown, the Talgai skull was undeniably genuine, and although Smith had no means of accurately dating the cranium he was convinced that it was from the Pleistocene. He reached that conclusion after comparing the Queensland find with hominid fossils from Europe, including the fake Piltdown cranium.[97] Despite this somewhat dubious methodology, time has since proved him right. The Talgai skull is now thought to have belonged to a youth who was killed by a violent blow to the head sometime between 9,000 and 11,000 years BP.[98] It could be of even greater antiquity, but what particularly distinguished the skull was its large size and prominent brow ridges and cheekbones.

Even then it was dwarfed by the second Pleistocene cranium discovered by a contractor excavating a channel on the edge of Kow

Swamp in northern Victoria in 1925. This skull lay just a short distance from the remains of at least eleven individuals who had been carefully interred in the distant past. Like the cranium from Talgai it had also been rolled along an ancient watercourse by floodwaters before finally coming to rest near the town of Cohuna. Lacking only the lower jaw, the Cohuna skull resembled Talgai in its general robustness, flat receding forehead, heavy brow ridges, forward-projecting upper jaw and exceptionally large teeth and palate.[99] As it was even more massive than the Talgai skull, the discovery had the effect of resurrecting speculation that hominids bearing the physical characteristics of *Homo erectus* had once inhabited Australia. The idea had first been advanced by German anatomist Hermann Klaatsch as early as 1907,[100] and it has continued in muted form to the present day. An unfortunate downside is that it has the potential for those on the extreme right to claim the Aborigines are somehow less 'human' than their white counterparts, and it certainly raises the question as to whether the Aborigines were actually the first Australians. These two issues have clouded the debate over Aboriginal origins. The majority of palaeoanthropologists consider that *Homo sapiens* evolved from *Homo erectus*, so whichever way it is portrayed there is no denying our common humanity.

Another Pleistocene skull was unearthed in 1940 near Keilor in southern Victoria, which has since been dated to 13,000 years BP. Unlike Talgai and Cohuna, the Keilor skull is essentially modern in appearance with a full and rounded forehead lacking prominent brow ridges.[101] Nor does the jaw project forward. The skeletal remains of far more robust people nevertheless continued to be unearthed, some of which are now known to have lived as recently as 5,000–6,000 years BP. In 1960 the robust Mossgiel skull with accompanying post-cranial remains was discovered near Booligal in south-western New South Wales,[102] followed by the Cossack skull 5,000 kilometres away in north-western Australia. The Cossack skull has been dated to 6,500 years BP, and is one of the largest skulls known. It shares many affinities with the Talgai and Cohuna crania, including an exceptionally long sloping forehead, and certainly bears no resemblance to any Aboriginal people currently living in this remote region of Australia.[103]

Colonisation Of Sahul: The Archaeological And Skeletal Evidence

In 1962 the discovery of yet another robust individual by the operator of a mechanical trench-digger at Kow Swamp in northern Victoria initially received little attention, with the remains quietly tucked away in a cardboard shirt-box lodged in the then National Museum of Victoria. They were neglected for five years before Alan Thorne was invited to Melbourne for the purpose of cataloguing the museum's skeletal material. Thorne was intrigued by the obviously archaic features of the fragments in the shirt-box and decided to track down the exact location where they had been found. All he had to go on was a label bearing the name of a police station, so he sifted through all the police records as far back as 1955. Thorne finally narrowed it down to six or seven possible sites, and as luck would have it he decided to conduct a preliminary excavation at Kow Swamp. This was indeed a fortuitous decision, because among the sixty-odd bones fragments uncovered by his team was one which fitted perfectly with a piece of bone from the shirt-box.[104]

By 1972 Thorne's archaeological team had uncovered the remains of around forty individuals in what was clearly an ancient burial ground. Some of the deceased had been encircled with white quartz, the nearest source of which was 100 kilometres away.[105] Radiocarbon dating suggested that the remains had been interred between 9,500 and 13,000 years BP, but more recent dating with OSL has pushed their age back to 19,000–22,000 years BP.[106] Thorne was convinced that these robust people were evidence of the continuance of *Homo erectus* physical characteristics in Australia, a line of reasoning that was reinforced by the Talgai, Cohuna, Mossgiel and Cossack skulls. He received little support as the majority of palaeoanthropologists insist that all ancient human skeletal material known from Australia falls within the extreme physical limits of *Homo sapiens*.[107]

Then came the discovery of Mungo I in 1969, the first gracile skeletal remains from the Willandra Lakes complex. Notwithstanding that the body had been cremated and the bones smashed before burial, Alan Thorne was able to reconstruct most of the remaining pieces, roughly twenty-five per cent of the entire skeleton. It was sufficient to identify the individual as a young female around nineteen years of age who was extremely short and delicately-built – indeed, she was so slight in stature that the marks of her musculature were barely perceptible on the bones. The skull was essentially modern in appearance, oval in shape with a rounded forehead, and she lacked the prominent brow ridges characterising the robust crania found elsewhere. 'Mungo Lady' easily fell within the physical range of modern Aboriginal people.[108] While Mungo II consisted of only thirty small bone fragments it is likely that this individual was of a similar gracile build.[109] So, too, was Mungo III. In this instance the bones belonged to a mature male estimated to have been around fifty years of age, who had chronic osteoarthritis in the right elbow during the final years of his life. The only distinguishing feature of Mungo III was the relatively large cranial vault and thick wall.[110]

While it appeared that this was a physically homogenous population, the situation altered with the discovery in 1980 of bone fragments known as Willandra Lakes Hominid 50 (WLH50). The top section of the skull and a number of post-cranial fragments were uncovered by archaeologists Jeanette Hope and Michael Macintyre on the ancient shoreline of Lake Garnpung, largest of the former lakes. Although undated they attest to considerable antiquity, and Alan Thorne suggested an age of perhaps 50,000 years BP. Unlike the first three individuals unearthed in this region, WLH50 was of robust build and the bone fragments share unmistakable affinities with *Homo erectus*. The frontal bone is extremely flat and the wall of the cranial vault reaches a maximum thickness of nineteen millimetres. This is particularly significant, for even though the cranial walls of modern Aboriginal skulls are among the thickest of any modern human group they rarely exceed eleven millimetres.[111] Steve Webb has contended that the extremely thick cranial wall of WLH50 could be the result of congenital anaemia, a pathological condition which affects the tissue in the spongy bone separating the inner and outer cranial walls. This can be genetically determined in regions where malaria is an endemic problem, and Indonesia is a particularly good example. If Webb is correct it could mean that WLH50 was one of the earliest hominid inhabitants of Australia,[112] and it may also mean that it is not Aboriginal.

The Keilor skull from southern Victoria is similar to the gracile crania of Willandra Lakes, so the proposition was advanced by Alan Thorne

Colonisation Of Sahul: The Archaeological And Skeletal Evidence

– and to a lesser extent Steve Webb – that there were two physically distinct groups of people living in Pleistocene Australia.[113] Others, including Colin Pardoe, have countered that it is simply a matter of sexual dimorphism, with the robust skeletal material representing males and the gracile remains females, with a range of body sizes between the genders.[114] There is also the possibility it is linked to cultural practises. Many of the skulls from the robust individuals have flattened foreheads which closely resemble *Homo erectus* and have therefore been used as evidence of a close link between the two. In 1975 Don Braithwaite from the Institute of Archaeology in London added a totally new dimension to the debate when he suggested that the flattened foreheads perhaps resulted from artificial deformation.[115]

The practice of producing flatter and more elongated heads by either binding or physically manipulating the tender skulls of infants for aesthetic purposes has been practised by numerous Indigenous groups around the world. It occurred among Melanesians immediately to Australia's north, including those of Mabuiag Island in Torres Strait, but there have only been two widely-separated accounts of artificial deformation being practised by the Australian Aborigines. On Cape York Peninsula mothers sometimes applied pressure with their hands to the forehead and back of the head to make the skulls of infants flatter.[116] In 1841 George Augustus Robinson observed a few Burrumbeet Aboriginal children in northern Victoria with artificially deformed skulls, though his notes make it clear that only a minority of children had been treated in this manner, and he did not record the technique that was used nor the reasoning behind it.[117] None of this, of course, precludes the possibility of artificial deformation having been more widespread during the Pleistocene.

In 1981 Peter Brown examined thirty-three complete crania from Coobool Creek, near Swan Hill in northern Victoria, which are believed to date from the early Holocene. Nine of the skulls were carefully reconstructed, and Brown was convinced that at least some of them showed evidence of artificial deformation. He reached the same conclusion after inspecting two of the Kow Swamp crania as well as the Cohuna skull, but he agreed that his findings did not entirely negate the argument that the size and characteristics of the robust Pleistocene skulls bore close affinities with those of *Homo erectus*.[118] No-one has yet examined the massive Cossack skull from north-western Australia for signs of artificial deformation, and there is no evidence that it was ever a cultural practice in this region. All that can be said is that two physically different groups of people *appear* to have occupied the continent during the Pleistocene. Whether that amounts to sexual dimorphism, a reversed evolutionary trend from gracility to robustness, or that the robust populations represent an entirely different species of hominid which disappeared in the mid-Holocene cannot be stated with any degree of certainty.

What can be said about the origins of the Aborigines, however, is that they were part of the early exodus of *Homo sapiens* from Africa and certainly had interaction with the mysterious Denisovans. Whether this was during their eastward migration or whether the ancient continent of Sahul was already occupied by another hominid is open to speculation. This is just one of the many mysteries of the ancient Aboriginal past, and that is why Australia is becoming increasingly important to global ideas of human evolution. Another conundrum which continues to perplex those who delve into the mists of Australian antiquity is the fate of the megafauna, the unique marsupials which had inhabited the continent for hundreds of thousands of years before the arrival of modern humans. The appearance of a new two-legged predator around 50,000 years BP coincided with their rapid slide into extinction, which is the focus of the following chapter.

DEMISE OF THE MEGAFAUNA

VI

When European mariners began visiting Australian shores from the seventeenth century they were fascinated by the unusual creatures which roamed the landscape. Animals resembling deer hopped on two legs rather than walked on all fours, and there was a beast reminiscent of a small rounded pig, with some early European settlers insisting that the wombat even tasted like pork. (Others, though, were less appreciative, describing the flesh as musky in flavour and full of sinews).[1] New discoveries included a sloth-like animal which slept for up to eighteen hours a day and lived only in certain eucalypts where it fed exclusively on the leaves. Possums filled an ecological niche occupied by squirrels in the northern hemisphere, and nothing prepared Europeans for the platypus, an animal resembling a mole, but aquatic and endowed with webbed feet and a duck-like bill. It was not until the latter half of the nineteenth century that they finally discovered it laid eggs like its prickly cousin, the echidna.[2] Then there was the flightless emu which could outpace the swiftest hunting dogs, along with a host of other furred and feathered creatures which tested their imagination to the full. Yet if these animals were bizarre they were nothing compared to the spectacular megafauna which confronted the Aborigines when they first stepped ashore on the ancient supercontinent of Sahul.

Among their ranks were the diprotodons, roughly the size of a modern rhinoceros, while the hippopotamus had its marsupial equivalent in the form of *Zygomaturus* sp., the largest of which was two metres in length and weighed in at a respectable 500 kilograms.[3] As with its placental counterparts in South-East Asia, the marsupial tapirs (*Palorchestes* sp.) appear to have been equipped with a prominent trunk, and their powerful forearms and claws were ideal for ripping bark from trees.

Animals familiar today had their own slightly larger ancestors, such as the extinct wombat (*Phascolonus gigas*), which reached a length of 1.8 metres and weighed 200 kilograms.[4] The ancestral koala (*Phascolarctus stirtonii*), was a third larger than its modern descendant, while the giant echidna (*Zaglossus Hackett*), weighed up to thirty kilograms, a far cry from the seven kilogram weight of existing species.[5] The largest macropods, kangaroos and wallabies, reached almost three metres in height, with the heaviest species, *Procoptodon goliah*, weighing in at 230 kilograms. Modern red kangaroos only average eighty kilograms in weight and stand up to 1.9 metres high.[6]

Avian fauna was no less impressive, and although the emu was present it was dwarfed by *Genyornis newtoni*, the heaviest bird that ever lived. *Genyornis* resembled a giant goose, stood just over two metres high and weighed up to 275 kilograms.[7] Given its proportionately short legs it is unlikely that this bird was anywhere near as swift as the emu, but any lack of mobility did not prevent the species from occupying virtually every available habitat. Both the mallee fowl and the coucal had ancestors twice their existing size,[8] though there were many other birds – like the emu – which co-existed with the megafauna and have remained unchanged to the present day.[9]

Keeping the populations of herbivores in check were the predators. Thylacines and Tasmanian devils were distributed throughout Sahul,[10] but the top mammalian carnivore, *Thylacoleo carnifax*, is only known from the more southern and eastern parts of Australia. Larger than a modern leopard, *Thylacoleo* was equipped with razor-sharp incisors and slicing premolars, formidable dentition reinforced by a strengthened jaw which gave the animal a massive bite.[11] There can be no doubt, however, that even *Thylacoleo* would have preferred to avoid confrontation with the top reptilian predators. The monitor lizard, *Megalania prisca*, is believed to have reached up to six metres in length, with teeth resembling huge steak knives. Along with a saltwater crocodile comparable in size to its modern descendant there was *Quinkana*, a three-metre-long crocodile which may have been terrestrial.[12] The more southerly areas of the continent were home to *Wonambi naracoortensis*, a five-metre-long python, which weighed up to fifty kilograms. Given that its head

Demise Of The Megafauna

was relatively small in proportion to its overall size, and that it may not have been able to fully disarticulate its jaws as in modern snakes, this large serpent probably subsisted on smaller-sized prey.[13] *Wonambi* is of particular interest because snakes rely on external heat absorbed through the skin to maintain their body temperature at a sufficiently high enough level to enable their bodies to function. Yet this species was able to survive comfortably in a climate much cooler than any existing constrictor could possibly tolerate.[14] So, too, did other less fearsome reptiles such as the giant horned land tortoises, *Meiolania* and *Ninjemys*, members of both genera as large as a small automobile.[15]

All of these animals, along with others we know little or nothing about, had roamed the supercontinent of Sahul for hundreds of thousands of years. During that immense span of time they had comfortably survived a host of climatic transitions, including sixteen Ice Ages and warmer, wetter or drier intervals.[16] At the time the bulk of the larger megafauna disappeared sometime between 46,000 and 50,000 years BP the Australian climate was relatively benign. Something extraordinary happened which triggered the extinction of all animals above 100 kilograms in weight as well as the majority of those which exceeded forty-four kilograms. After their lengthy reign at least fifty-five species of megafauna representing some twenty-eight different genera were wiped off the face of the earth.[17] It is likely that at least some of them found temporary refuge in the more inhospitable regions of the continent, including the then Tasmanian peninsula, but within a few thousand years they too were destined to die out. How many smaller species disappeared along with the megafauna can only be guessed, as the demise of the larger animals would have had a devastating rippling effect through the various ecosystems.[18]

At the time of the megafaunal extinctions on Sahul prevailing conditions were certainly cool, with temperatures up to 9° Celsius lower than today. It was also drier and in some areas extremely arid, with a desert landscape extending as far south as present north-west Tasmania,[19] but this had happened on many previous occasions without any dramatic impact on the megafauna. Moreover, it was 30,000 years before the peak of the Last Glacial Maximum which saw the continent become even colder and more arid. There is no evidence that this harsher period resulted in the widespread disappearance of the existing fauna.

From fortuitous fossil discoveries in South Australia's Naracoorte Caves, and especially from the Thylacoleo Caves discovered on the Nullarbor Plain in 2002, it is known that the ancient megafauna were well-adapted to living in arid conditions. The Thylacoleo Caves are sinkholes where animals have been plummeting twenty metres to their death over the last 500,000 years. It was there that palaeontologists found the first complete skeleton of the Marsupial Lion as well as a host of previously unknown species. Using sophisticated scientific techniques they were able to gain valuable information on the environments which existed at various periods of time, and one of the great surprises was that while the Nullarbor Plain was just as dry 50,000 years BP as it is today the vegetation was totally different. The region was covered with trees and succulent shrubs, and among the megafauna were two previously unknown species of tree kangaroo. Around that same time, however, the lush vegetation and its associated fauna mysteriously disappeared even though there had been no major climatic event.[20]

Although mass extinctions in the distant past are by no means unique to Australia, this continent shared with North America and the Pacific Islands some of the heaviest losses. They also occurred much earlier in Australia than anywhere else. In North America mammoths, camels, horses, giant ground sloths and sabre-toothed cats were among the megafauna which disappeared between 10,000 and 12,000 years BP. The total losses on that continent represented seventy-three percent of all mammals weighing in excess of forty-four kilograms.[21] The North American extinctions also seemingly coincided with the arrival of Amerindians, among them the so-called Clovis people, who may or may not have been the first human colonisers. It is known that these migratory people hunted mammoths, but until 2019 only fourteen kill sites had been identified, and there is no direct evidence that they exploited any of the other larger mammals.[22] The recent discovery of two pit-traps made by ancient humans at Tultepec, just north of Mexico City, around 14,000–15,000 years BP has only served to confirm this exclusive predation. All bones excavated from the pits belong solely to woolly mammoths, with cut-marks providing unequivocal evidence of butchering.[23]

This has led to speculation that it was climate change which drove the majority of large animals in North America to extinction. It could be relevant that it was the onset of warmer conditions which allowed modern humans to skirt the western side of the massive Laurentide ice sheet covering Canada and the northern United States and thus gain access to the American continent.[24] At the same time some of the megafaunal species may have been unable to adapt to warmer temperatures and its associated environmental transition. Conversely, however, American bison multiplied and if their later exploitation by Native American is any guide they were likely to have been hunted by the earliest human colonisers. It was not until the arrival of Europeans with their firearms that the continued existence of the bison was finally threatened. There was one major difference. Modern bison have evolved into their more energy-efficient form over the last 10,000 years, and are considerably smaller than their Pleistocene ancestors.[25]

In 1967 the American biogeographer, Paul Martin, argued that the majority of the North American megafauna had fallen victim to modern humans who had entered the continent in pursuit of large game animals and then followed them south.[26] Martin was not the first to raise that claim: during the nineteenth century scientists had postulated that human hunting might have wiped out the ancient megafauna of Europe, a belief that steadily lost favour as knowledge of climate change in the past increased.[27] Martin breathed new life into the 'blitzkrieg theory' when he contended there had been a whole series of localised extinctions which had been so rapid that no trace had been left in the archaeological record. Once the herbivores had been eliminated predators such as the sabre-toothed cat had succumbed to starvation. Martin believed the entire process had taken just 1,000 years to complete, drawing support for his rapid extermination theory from Oceania.[28]

On New Caledonia the ancient megafauna included a 1.7-metre high megapod resembling a brush turkey, a terrestrial crocodile, a large monitor lizard and a giant horned tortoise, all of which disappeared around 3,000 years BP when humans first arrived on the island.[29] An even more graphic example is provided by New Zealand, where the arrival of Polynesian voyagers directly led to the extinction of all eleven species of moa, some of which reached truly gigantic proportions. Deforestation, anthropogenic burning and the introduction of rats and dogs had the additional effect of exterminating at least twenty-five smaller vertebrates in New Zealand.[30] While it is a truism that insular populations are particularly vulnerable to new and highly-efficient predators, continents are another matter again.[31] That was particularly the case in Europe, Asia and Africa, where megafaunal extinctions followed inconsistent patterns.

It is known that both the Neanderthals and archaic *Homo sapiens* hunted a wide variety of the larger mammals in Europe.[32] Mammoths, woolly rhinoceros and horses were heavily targeted, while other animals were probably avoided. There is no evidence that the cave bear (*Ursus spelaeus*) was ever hunted for food, and yet unlike its close relative, the brown bear (*Ursus arctos*), this species became extinct – possibly through its highly-specialised herbivorous diet and limited distribution, or competition with humans for caves on which they were heavily dependent for hibernation.[33] Mammoths and woolly rhinoceros, on the other hand, were perfectly adapted to living in extremely cold conditions. With the advent of warmer temperatures at the end of the Pleistocene epoch both species apparently migrated from more southerly regions to find temporary sanctuary in the upper areas of Scandinavia and Siberia. They finally disappeared around 8,000 years BP, their extinction seemingly coinciding with the first appearance of modern humans into these inhospitable areas.[34]

The exception was Wrangel Island, which now lies 200 kilometres north of Siberia. Woolly mammoths ventured this far north along a land bridge which was inundated by rising seas some 12,000 years BP, trapping a sufficient number of animals to create a viable population. Wrangel had (and has) the most profuse vegetation of all the sub-Artic islands, but long-term isolation also resulted in the woolly mammoths evolving into a dwarf form. Whereas the typical woolly mammoth stood just over three metres high and weighed over six tonnes, the Wrangel Island animals were only 1.8 metres high and weighed a mere two

Demise Of The Megafauna

tonnes. They lived comfortably on their island home until 4,000 years BP, and although there is no evidence that these beasts were hunted by humans their disappearance strangely coincided with the earliest traces of the human presence.³⁵

Wild horses, on the other hand, were killed in substantial numbers by humans right across Europe and Asia. The sole remaining species, Przewalski's horse (*Equus przewalskii*), is today confined to the steppes of Mongolia and China.³⁶ Reindeer were another important prey species which disappeared from southern Europe between 11,000–12,000 years BP, but continue to flourish in more northerly latitudes today. Their transmigration was almost certainly a direct result of climate change rather than human predation.³⁷ Curiously, a number of large mammals which were obvious targets for human hunters followed a much slower path to extinction.

One of them was the giant deer (*Megaloceros giganteus*), otherwise known as the Irish elk, which flourished across Europe from Ireland in the west to central Siberia in the east. Standing up to two metres high at the shoulder with antlers spanning 3.6 metres, the giant deer was a truly formidable animal, a factor which may account for its survival until 8,000 years BP.³⁸ The auroch (*Bos primigenius*), giant ancestor of modern cattle, was extensively hunted for both its meat and pelt, yet it survived right up until the early seventeenth century. An aggressive beast, the auroch also stood two metres high at the shoulder and weighed in at a hefty 1,000 kilograms.³⁹ The European bison or wisent (*Bison bonasus*), comparable in size to its North American cousin, was hunted for its meat, hides and horns but somehow managed to survive in the wild until the 1920s when the last animals were shot by poachers. Like Przewalski's horse, however, sufficient stocks of European bison were held in zoos, with a highly-successful breeding program allowing its reintroduction into nature reserves.⁴⁰

It is clear from all this that while some of the European and Asian megafauna was extirpated through human hunting activities, others succumbed to climate change, and a few managed to survive – at least until historical times. The African continent differed again because very few large animals disappeared. The only plausible explanation which can account for their success is that they co-evolved with humans, thus providing sufficient time for adjustment to altering circumstances. It does need to be added, though, that such an outcome depended on the human population density remaining extremely low.[41] Elsewhere, the arrival of human predators was usually too sudden and their impact so great that the megafauna were quickly overwhelmed.

This leads us back to Australia where the rate of megafaunal extinctions was particularly catastrophic, an issue which is complicated by two unknown factors. One is the precise time that modern humans first arrived on the shores of Sahul; and, second, exactly when the megafauna began their inexorable slide into oblivion. Both occurrences lie just outside the maximum limits of radiocarbon dating, although more advanced scientific techniques have allowed a slightly clearer view of the overlap to emerge. That the megafauna were present when the Aboriginal people arrived can be readily accepted, even though a few sceptics still insist that Aboriginal tales of giant animals in the Dreaming, the Kadimakara, are based solely on the sighting of fossil remains.[42] There are quite a number of Aboriginal oral histories which mention these ancient creatures, some of which are almost certainly first-hand encounters with the huge flightless bird, *Genyornis newtoni*.[43] For example, in the 1840s Pemberton Hodgson, an early pastoralist on Queensland's Darling Downs, was told by local Aborigines that their ancestors had passed down stories of large emu-like birds capable of carrying two people. (They also related an account of an enormous animal in the distant past 'who tore up trees and spouted out streams of water').[44] Similarly, the so-called 'Callicum Bunyip' of the Ararat district in Victoria likely refers to *Genyornis newtoni*. Reputedly the size of a bullock, the creature had a head and neck like that of an emu.[45] In 2010 a painting of this member of the avian megafauna was identified during a survey of Aboriginal rock art in south-western Arnhem Land. It was initially believed to be a representation of an emu, but the distinctive beak persuaded a number of researchers that the bird is actually *Genyornis*.[46] However, this interpretation has been challenged by David Welch, who has argued that it is a stylised depiction of either an emu or a bustard (*Ardeotis australis*). Rather than a painting of great antiquity,

Demise Of The Megafauna

Welch insists the artwork is unlikely to be older than 8,000 years BP. He has also disputed a number of other interpretations of megafauna in Aboriginal art from both Arnhem Land and the Kimberley region of Western Australia,[47] so for the time being the validity of these depictions remains questionable.

The continental biomass is another elusive element in the Australian megafaunal debate. While *Genyornis* was abundant and widespread, that does not necessarily hold for the giant marsupials, some of which may have been scarce and possibly quite rare prior to the arrival of the Aborigines. Nature works in intriguing ways, and it often happens that large mammals maintain their numbers at an extremely low rate. They take longer to reach maturity and usually live to an advanced age. Females have a lengthy gestation period and produce few young, all of which makes them highly-susceptible to extinction through sudden change, whether natural or induced.[48]

Diprotodons are arguably the best-known example of the Australian megafauna, often portrayed as gregarious herd animals. The reality was something else, with fossil evidence suggesting they were probably solitary animals much like the modern rhinoceros. There are certainly fossil sites containing large quantities of diprotodon bones, but these are now understood to have accumulated over lengthy periods of time. An occasional death over hundreds of thousands of years at favourite watering places such as Lancefield Swamp in Victoria can provide the false impression that diprotodons were once common in the area.[49] Conversely, the giant macropods probably congregated in mobs like their modern counterparts and yet one of the most common genera, *Sthenurus*, disappeared completely while the red and grey kangaroos lived on. The various species of *Sthenurus* were more heavily built than existing kangaroos and only marginally taller. There is no anatomical evidence to suggest they were any less fleet than modern forms, so the key to their extinction could lie in a different feeding pattern. Red and grey kangaroos are grazers, while *Sthenurus* appears to have been a browser, largely feeding on succulent shrubs.[50] This brings us back to the giant flightless bird *Genyornis*, which is definitely known to have been a specialised browser.

Despite the ravages of time *Genyornis* eggshells litter vast areas of inland Australia along with those of ancient emus. They are distinguished by heavy dimpling, but it is the calcite they contain which has unlocked one of the mysteries of megafaunal extinctions. The calcite carbon is derived from blood, allowing scientists to determine what the birds were feeding on immediately before laying their eggs. In 2005 American scientist Gifford Miller and his Australian colleagues collected fragments of *Genyornis* eggshells from three widely-separated regions – Lake Eyre and Port Augusta in South Australia and the Willandra Lakes of south-western New South Wales. During the Pleistocene all three areas differed from each other just as much as they do today, and through amino acid and racemisation application to the organic matter and luminescence on the associated sand grains Miller and his team were able to provide an approximate date as to when the eggs were laid.[51]

They found that over 140,000 years *Genyornis newtoni* had been extremely abundant. Then, around 46,000–47,000 years BP, the species completely disappeared in all three regions. Analysis of the eggshells revealed that these giant birds had been almost totally dependent on drought-resistant succulent shrubs and nutritious grasses (C^3 vegetation) as a food source, whereas contemporary emus had a more broad-based diet which included less nutritious grasses (C^4 vegetation). After 46,000–47,000 years BP the diet of the emus switched almost entirely to C^4 vegetation, suggesting that the landscape had undergone a dramatic transformation from a mosaic of drought-resistant trees, shrubs and grasslands to fire-adapted grassland dominated by plants such as spinifex. Miller's team also examined carbon isotopes in the tooth enamel of fossil wombats and found that their diet had similarly changed to a heavy dependence on C^4 vegetation around the same time. Emus and wombats had therefore been able to adapt to a major environmental transition while *Genyornis* had not because of its more specialised feeding habits.[52] If this transformation had resulted from climate change it would have almost certainly impacted on New Zealand, the home of the moa. Yet there is no evidence that those giant birds were affected in any way, so the change in the Australian vegetation must have been triggered by something else. Miller and his colleagues argued

Demise Of The Megafauna

that it was caused by fire; not natural fire, but deliberate anthropogenic burning.[53]

Others have insisted that it could not have been human-induced as Aboriginal burning practises actually enhance the vegetation by releasing nutrients through carefully-controlled mosaic burns of limited scope.[54] That is the way it has probably been for thousands of years but not necessarily tens of thousands of years ago when the Aborigines arrived on the supercontinent of Sahul. The findings by Miller's team also provided valuable support for a wide-ranging survey carried out by Richard Roberts and Tim Flannery two years later. In 2001 the Roberts-Flannery team published their research on twenty-eight megafaunal sites across the Australian mainland. They used thorium uranium and luminescence to date sediments and quartz crystals immediately above and below the fossilised bones. Their date for extinction had been 50,000 years BP plus or minus 5,000 years, with a probability that it occurred 46,000 years BP.[55] That at least some of the megafauna had initially avoided extermination is clear, with the last remains in Tasmania dating from around 41,000 years BP – roughly the same time that Aborigines arrived in this more southerly region.[56]

For many years it was believed that Aboriginal stone tools associated with megafaunal bones at Lancefield Swamp and Spring Creek in Victoria provided unequivocal evidence of a protracted co-existence between humans and megafauna. It is now known that the fossil bones at Lancefield Swamp accumulated through the action of floodwaters, while those at Spring Creek predate the human presence.[57] More recently, Stephen Wroe and Judith Field argued that their excavations at Cuddie Springs, a pastoral property in north-western New South Wales, revealed an association between Aborigines and the megafauna extending over 10,000 years.[58] The findings were flawed. Although now usually dry, Cuddie Springs remains the terminal point for waters ebbing in from the local catchment area, which is why a well was sunk there in 1876. Like the Victorian sites, disarticulated bones have been carried in by the overflow, and apart from modern human activity the hooves of livestock have repeatedly broken through the crust, forcing the fossil bones and Aboriginal stone tools into lower sediment levels.[59]

Some of the artifacts include seed-grinding stones, which may not even date from the Pleistocene, and although it was reported that some of the bones bore cut marks from stone tools, all of them belonged to modern red kangaroos – not the extinct megafauna. The claim that bones had been dated was also incorrect. The protein had proved unsuitable so dates had been obtained from charcoal which could have come from anywhere.[60] Put simply, there is no firm evidence that the Aboriginal people and the megafauna co-existed for extended periods of time at Cuddie Springs, Lancefield Swamp or at any other location in Australia. While those sites are certainly of great importance to palaeontologists, they contribute nothing of substance to the megafaunal debate which now revolves around four possible scenarios.

One is that modern humans introduced some form of hyperdisease or virus which transferred to the megafauna with fatal results, an argument that has failed to gain any serious traction.[61] Evidence is entirely lacking, so at best it is an extremely remote possibility. Even though it is rapidly losing credibility the question of climate change continues to be raised. The fact of the matter is that the megafauna endured a host of Ice Ages and warmer interludes without any serious impact. Indeed, they survived the Anglian Glaciation of 400,000 years BP, probably the most severe Ice Age of all,[62] and yet the Australian megafauna disappeared when the climate was relatively stable and benign.

The third scenario is Paul Martin's 'blitzkrieg', which has been used by Tim Flannery in the Australian context. If the large herbivorous megafauna were long-lived animals with low reproductive rates it would certainly have made them vulnerable to overkill – however imperceptible that might have been. Extinction was even more likely if their numbers had already been at a low point, and simulations have shown that this could have been effected irrespective of whether juvenile or prime breeding animals had been targeted.[63] To counter this argument it has been pointed out that since water buffalo (*Babulus babulus*) were introduced into the Northern Territory in the 1820s the Aboriginal people have been ineffectual in containing their spread. Even today the Aborigines are reluctant to hunt these large animals unless armed with high-powered rifles and conveyed to their quarry in four-wheel-drive vehicles.[64] That is today, which is very different from the ancient past, and while the Aboriginal diet became more broad-based it was much more limited during the Pleistocene epoch. Right around the world hunter-gatherers ate fewer plant foods, relying instead on a heavy intake of lean meat. To prevent protein poisoning they also consumed large quantities of fat along with carbohydrates obtained from bone marrow. While modern nutritionists would condemn such a diet it was more than adequate to sustain a healthy lifestyle in the cooler conditions of the Pleistocene. Lower temperatures also meant that meat 'kept' better, thereby ensuring less wastage.[65] So it is quite possible that over-hunting, the 'blitzkrieg theory', could have exterminated the larger herbivorous megafauna, with the carnivores following suit through starvation.

As Gifford Miller's research has demonstrated, however, the ecosystems in at least three separate regions of Australia suddenly collapsed around the same time, an event which coincided with the disappearance of local megafauna. In the absence of any major climate change the landscape altered so radically and so abruptly that the only likely cause was fire, almost certainly anthropogenic. Whether it was intended to clear vegetation, as a deliberate hunting strategy, or entirely accidental must remain in the realm of supposition. It happened, even if the Aboriginal colonisers were unaware of the long-term consequences. Time would teach valuable lessons, perhaps forcing the Aborigines to become conservationists through necessity rather than choice. The Australian landscape was shaped by human agency, and it came at a very high price. While it is lamented that Australia's unique fauna and flora continues to disappear at an alarming rate, the deadliest blow of all appears to have fallen around 46,000–47,000 years BP. It was then that the continent lost its biggest, strangest and most ferocious wildlife along with a host of smaller creatures, some of which remain unknown to science.

PLEISTOCENE SAHUL: ADAPTATION AND INNOVATION

VII

With the demise of the megafauna the Aboriginal colonisers reigned supreme, but their adopted homeland was very different from the Australia of today. As noted in the previous chapter, temperatures were up to 9° Celsius lower than the present time. Glaciers covered much of southern and central Tasmania, the alpine regions of today's southeastern mainland, and the higher elevations of Papua New Guinea. Between 30,000–45,000 years BP there was greater precipitation and large permanent bodies of fresh water extended right across the continent. Lake Eye received considerable rainfall in the summer months, and it is suspected that rain continued to fall regularly throughout the winter. Monsoonal storms in the northern regions also delivered copious amounts of water into Lake Eyre and the other inland river systems.[1] Then, around 30,000 years BP, the first effects of the Last Glacial Maximum began to be felt, with the supercontinent of Sahul steadily becoming drier as ice was locked up in the polar regions. Sea levels fell to such an extent that the eastern coastline extended somewhere between forty and fifty kilometres further out than today. Many of Queensland's Great Barrier Reef islands are the summits of mountains which once studded an expansive coastal plain,[2] and of course Papua New Guinea, Tasmania and Kangaroo Island were extensions of the greater Australian landmass.

As the Last Glacial Maximum intensified the large permanent bodies of fresh water began to contract. Deserts which are still extant today became even more arid and desolate, while vegetation throughout the inland underwent a massive transformation. In eastern Sahul trees and shrubs in wide areas west of the Great Dividing Range disappeared to be replaced by dry grasslands.[3] Many districts previously occupied by

Pleistocene Sahul: Adaptation And Innovation

the Aboriginal people were abandoned, including the Lake Eyre Basin, the Strzelecki Desert and sections of the Nullarbor Plain. Archaeological excavations at Puritjarra rock shelter in the Cleland Range of Central Australia have shown that this location was occupied by the Aborigines as early as 39,000 years BP and temporarily vacated during the Last Glacial Maximum.[4] A similar situation unfolded at Kulpi Mara in the Levi Range which was occupied by Aborigines immediately prior to 30,000 years BP. The pattern thereafter became one of temporary occupation when conditions were favourable and withdrawal when they deteriorated.[5] It is quite possible that in some of the more marginal regions local Aboriginal populations became extinct as the peak of the Last Glacial Maximum was reached. Elsewhere, however, survival was assured through the presence of natural refuges such as Lawn Hill Gorge, just south of the Gulf of Carpentaria in north-west Queensland.

In 1989 Peter Hiscock conducted an excavation at Colless Creek Cave in Lawn Hill Gorge which provided a rare insight as to how the Aboriginal people coped during this particularly arid phase. The gorge remains today as a veritable oasis, one of Queensland's most spectacular national parks. The river is fed by sub-artesian water and provides the only permanent supply in an otherwise barren landscape where the dominant vegetation consists of spinifex and open eucalypt woodland. It flows through limestone gorges, with its fresh water pools supporting an array of fish, molluscs, freshwater turtles, crocodiles and even platypus. It was not all that dissimilar during the Pleistocene. The evidence suggests that the Aboriginal people were wholly restricted to the gorge system, where they manufactured tools from local stone and lived exclusively on the fauna and flora which were equally dependent on permanent water. No artifacts, ochre or butchered animal remains have been found outside the gorge which can be dated to the peak of the Last Glacial Maximum. It was not until the climate began to improve towards the end of the Pleistocene that exploitation of the wider surrounding area finally recommenced.[6]

The effect of extreme climatic conditions also had an important bearing on the Aboriginal colonisation and settlement of the continent. Sandra Bowdler's 'coastal colonisation' and the rival 'fast tracker' hypotheses have previously been discussed, but there is a third theory which is supported by archaeological evidence. In 1989 Peter Veth proposed his 'refuge, corridor and barrier' model to explain the Aboriginal occupation of Sahul during the Pleistocene. According to Veth the original colonisers had a broad-based and non-specialised economy, which meant they preferred the more mountainous and/or riverine environments which were easier to exploit for food. Those areas also contained permanent supplies of water when precipitation was either low or irregular. The refuges were connected by biogeographical corridors which at varying times provided at least sufficient food and water supplies to enable transient human passage. The true desert areas – barriers – were totally avoided, so in effect the Aboriginal colonisers exploited specific environments and there was no uniform settlement of the continent. The majority of the oldest Pleistocene sites are indeed located in Veth's refuges, while the rest are located in the corridors between them. Following this model through it means that it was not until the late Pleistocene that Aboriginal people could begin to exploit the most arid regions, and in some instances that might not have been fully accomplished until comparatively recently – perhaps only within the last few thousand years.[7]

If Veth's theory is accepted, the Aboriginal colonisers were general foragers who lacked specialised skills and technology. It also means they were highly-mobile, with settlement neither constant nor stable. There was thus little attachment to place, and the territoriality and finely-tuned adaptive strategies which are associated with the Aboriginal people today were therefore a relatively late development.[8] That said, it was the remarkable flexibility of the Pleistocene Aborigines which allowed them to settle so much of the continent, and to acquire the knowledge, social and economic strategies necessary for their descendants to spread into some of the harshest environments on earth. Not that this was anything new. The Pleistocene Aborigines were themselves descendants of people who had already expanded through a range of alien landscapes following their exodus from Africa.[9]

One region where people came and remained was Papua New Guinea, the most northerly part of Pleistocene Sahul. During the Last

Pleistocene Sahul: Adaptation And Innovation

Glacial Maximum glaciers formed on the highest peaks and sub-alpine grassland expanded to cover an area of 50,000 square kilometres. That grassland still exists, albeit, having shrunk to a mere 5,000 square kilometres. During the Pleistocene the tree-line lowered to around 2,000 metres, but below that was a host of mixed woodlands and extensive tracts of rainforest.[10] Papua New Guinea provides the earliest evidence of plant use on ancient Sahul, perhaps the most important of which was the pandanus palm with its edible seeds. At the village of Kosipe, which sits marginally below the 2,000-metre level, pollen cores from a swamp have revealed a large increase in charcoal deposits dating from around 30,000 years BP, suggestive of deliberate burning to increase pandanus palm yields. Archaeological evidence has also disclosed that between 15,000 and 26,000 years BP – at the very height of the Last Glacial Maximum – people continued to periodically visit the Kosipe area.[11]

A number of relatively small waisted axes, with flanges allowing handles to be fitted, have been recovered at Kosipe and other locations in the Papua New Guinea highlands.[12] Larger tools of this type, believed to date from 40,000 years BP, have also been excavated from deposits of volcanic ash on the Huon Peninsula. Their exact function remains unclear, though they may have been used to clear forest.[13] Given the assumed antiquity they could well have been manufactured by the first human colonisers of this region, and it is remarkable that similar waisted axes are known from only two other locations on Sahul, one of which is Kangaroo Island off the coast of present-day South Australia.

Roughly 145 kilometres long, sixty kilometres wide, and with a total area of some 4,400 square kilometres, Kangaroo Island is Australia's third largest island. At its closest point the island is separated from the mainland by 14.5 kilometres of turbulent water known as Backstairs Passage, and much of the original insular vegetation consisted of mallee scrub.[14] Today, the island has a very mild climate, but during the Pleistocene it was considerably cooler, drier and, of course, it was merely an extension of the continental landmass. It is not surprising, then, that this region was first colonised by people who shared close cultural affinities with others spread across an adjoining area of some 100,000 square kilometres – as far north as the Flinders Ranges and Lakes Frome and Torrens, now large salt lakes in extremely arid country.[15] Around 10,000 years BP Kangaroo Island was separated from the mainland by rising seas, and it was once thought that it had been abandoned by the local Aboriginal population just before they became totally isolated.[16]

There were certainly no human inhabitants when British navigator Matthew Flinders visited Kangaroo Island in March 1802, and judging by the extraordinarily tame kangaroos and seals Flinders surmised that humans had never previously set foot on the island.[17] This assumption altered dramatically four years later when European sealers and other colonial venturers began calling. A number of them established permanent camps, often cohabiting with Aboriginal women from the mainland and Tasmania. These new settlers killed the kangaroos and seals in great numbers as well as exterminating the endemic dwarf emu, a fate that was shared by its close relative on King Island in Bass Strait.[18]

Apart from these nineteenth-century Aboriginal women and their progeny there was no inkling that any other Aborigines had ever lived on Kangaroo Island until 1903, when geologist Walter Howchin came across a shell midden at The Brecknells on the south coast. Soon afterwards he collected eight hammerstones and a number of chipped quartz flakes in the vicinity of Murray's Lagoon, close to the centre of the island. Howchin recognised both the midden and stone tools as of Aboriginal origin and presumably of great antiquity, but at that stage the implements appeared to differ little from stone tools found elsewhere in Australia.[19] More stone tools were uncovered in the 1930s, prompting Norman Tindale from the South Australian Museum to conduct a detailed investigation of the area around Murray's Lagoon with his colleague, Harold Cooper. Tindale and Cooper discovered more hammerstones and some exceptionally large pebble tools, notably horsehoof cores, speculating they were of Pleistocene origin. Tindale identified similar stone artifacts on the adjacent mainland as far north as the Flinders Ranges which he collectively termed Kartan culture, the Ngarrindjeri Aboriginal name for Kangaroo Island which is generally held to mean either 'island of the dead' or 'hunting place of the dead'.[20] In the Kaurna (Adelaide) Aboriginal language, however, Karta meant 'female genitals', which has at least two possible interpretations.[21]

Pleistocene Sahul: Adaptation And Innovation

Before considering that double meaning, it needs to be said that Tindale began a major trend in Australian archaeology by attempting to show a close correlation between the stone tools from Kangaroo Island and those from South-East Asia. Cooper, on the other hand, continued surveying the island and between 1935 and 1937 located forty-seven ancient Aboriginal sites.[22] By 1958 that number had grown to 120, with the majority of implements comprising hammerstones, pebble choppers and horsehoof cores. They were made from quartzite obtained near Murray's Lagoon, with some of the tools located up to thirty-five kilometres from their source. All were of exceptional size.[23] Considerable emphasis has been placed on the horsehoof cores, which are simply a large pebble which has been placed on a striking platform, with flakes struck from around the circumference by a hammerstone to leave a distinctive shape resembling a horse's hoof. Apart from their large size, there is little to distinguish the Kangaroo Island horsehoof cores from others found throughout Australia. A number of archaeologists consider them to be a tool in their own right, possibly for removing bark from trees, but none of them display wear marks consistent with such use.[24] For all that, the important implements missing from the Kartan toolkit were small refined artifacts such as backed blades and flaked points, both of which characterise Aboriginal technological development within the last 5,000 years.[25] This led to the belief that the island must have been abandoned prior to separation from the mainland, a line of reasoning that was not seriously questioned until the 1970s when Ronald Lampert commenced his archaeological work. Yet, while Lampert became the indisputable authority on Kartan culture, his research actually raised more questions than it answered.

Lampert surveyed the entire island, and between 1971 and 1973 he excavated a limestone formation known as Seton Cave which now lies some eight kilometres from the coast. During the Pleistocene the sea was forty kilometres distant, and Lampert was able to demonstrate that people first visited the site around 16,000 years BP – the first time that any organic material from Kangaroo Island had been accurately dated. The problem was that the occupants were not the same people who had manufactured Kartan tools. Instead, they used small scrapers, mostly made from chert. Lampert uncovered 5,000 flakes at Seton Cave along with two implements made from the shinbone of a kangaroo, which he speculated were probably awls for working skins. Their diet included modern grey kangaroos, though the remains of *Sthenurus*, the extinct macropod, were found in the oldest deposits.[26] While there was no evidence that this member of the megafauna had fallen prey to human hunters, the real surprise was clearly the stone tools which also differed from those made by Aboriginal women living with European sealers in the early nineteenth century.

Between 11,000–16,000 years BP Seton Cave had only been used as a temporary campsite, with occupation intensifying at the beginning of the Holocene when warmer temperatures raised sea levels. It was then that molluscs began to figure in the diet of the inhabitants, although earlier middens could have long been submerged under the encroaching waters. Seton Cave was then abandoned, which appeared to accord well with the belief that total evacuation had been accomplished before the island was separated from the mainland. That idea was completely dispelled when Lampert began uncovering a series of small archaeological sites with even more sophisticated stone tools which post-dated the island's separation. Dates ranged from 4,300 to 5,200 years BP, and it is now accepted that people continued to occupy the island until at least 2,500 years BP.[27] They were not the same people as the original colonisers, so it is clear that two distinct groups occupied Kangaroo Island during the Pleistocene. The mystery of their identity deepened even further when an entirely different type of stone tool was discovered, albeit, with obvious links to Kartan technology.

They were twenty-four extremely large waisted axes with notched edges which had definitely been hafted. All were made from quartzite, and although two similar axes were known from the Flinders Ranges, the only other location where they have been recorded on the present Australian mainland is in the Mount Jukes-Seaforth district near Mackay in north-east Queensland. Lampert examined these axes and found that while they were manufactured from volcanic rock there was some resemblance to those from Kangaroo Island.[28] Kartan sites also reveal a degree of uniformity in their location, invariably situated on

Pleistocene Sahul: Adaptation And Innovation

northern slopes that offer protection from adverse weather conditions while maximising the warmth from the sun.[29]

The waisted axes from Papua New Guinea are a little different in that the waisting is about one-third of the way along, not roughly in the middle as are those from Kangaroo Island and North Queensland. Axes from Kosipe are also substantially smaller, and whether they were used for felling trees or, as others have suggested, pounding sago or some other hard foodstuff, remains unclear.[30] It is possible the waisted axes from the Mount Jukes-Seaforth district in the north could have served either of those purposes, but it seems improbable for Kangaroo Island. An alternative use was suggested by Norman Tindale, who noted that in more recent times the Aborigines in North Queensland killed animals caught in pitfall traps with large axes.[31] For the time being their exact purpose remains difficult to interpret, and nor is it known whether the waisted axes from Kangaroo Island and the Flinders Ranges were a local innovation or, alternatively, part of the toolkit of a people who had migrated south from Papua New Guinea. They could well be Australia's earliest stone tools.[32]

Given the large size of the Kartan stone technology, and their lack of sophistication when compared with the implements from Seton Cave and other locations on Kangaroo Island, Lampert was prompted to speculate whether these early colonisers had been 'heavily endowed with *Homo erectus* traits'.[33] It is unfortunate that no skeletal remains belonging to either group have yet been discovered, and the fate of the Kartan people remains a complete mystery. They could have fallen into extinction through an unknown cause; they could have been exterminated by their successors; or both groups could have intermixed. There could, in fact, be parallels with the disappearance of the Neanderthals on the opposite side of the world. The answer to this conundrum may also have a bearing on the Kaurna Aboriginal word Karta, which translates as 'female genitals'. Tindale suspected that it was of fairly recent origin, possibly referring to the abduction of Aboriginal women by European sealers residing on Kangaroo Island in the early nineteenth century.[34] There is another possibility. The word could very well be much older, perhaps a reference to the birth of the people or the first people. It is at least worth some reflection, and that brings us back to the fate of the Kartan successors.

After examining ethnographic accounts of Aboriginal population sizes on the neighbouring mainland, Lampert contended that the total population of Kangaroo Island at the time it was separated by rising seas would not have exceeded 440 individuals.[35] As a general rule any isolated population comprising fewer than 500 individuals cannot survive in the longer term owing to sex and age imbalance which ultimately leads to inbreeding. A small genetic pool is also particularly vulnerable to disease or natural catastrophe,[36] and it is known that Kangaroo Island experienced a significantly dry climatic phase between 2,000 and 5,000 years BP. Carbonised particles taken from a pollen core at Lashmars Lagoon may be evidence of anthropogenic burning as recently as 2,300 years BP.[37] If that assumption is correct it is the last evidence of the human presence on Kangaroo Island until the arrival of Matthew Flinders in 1802. It also begs the question as to whether the island was abandoned – or the population died out.

It is known that in the early nineteenth century a number of Aboriginal women abducted by European sealers attempted to swim back to the mainland across the Backstairs Passage, which is noted for its heavy swells and exceptionally strong currents. Only one is alleged to have succeeded, almost certainly an apocryphal tale for which there is no tangible proof.[38] Under the most ideal conditions it is possible that an exceptionally strong swimmer could succeed in reaching the mainland, but it is highly improbable that an entire group which included aged and young could make the crossing. Nor did the islanders have watercraft. There is no ethnographic evidence that Aboriginal people inhabiting the southern coast of Australia from the mouth of the Murray River west to Shark Bay in Western Australia ever used canoes or even log rafts in coastal waters.[39] The Ngarrindjeri people, whose territory stretches from Cape Jervis south to the Kingston district, certainly constructed canoes from the bark of the river red gum (*Eucalyptus camaldulensis*), but their use was entirely restricted to the quiet inland waterways; they were totally unsuited for crossing the rough waters of Backstairs Passage.[40] There is no evidence of physical contact between Aborigines on the island and

Pleistocene Sahul: Adaptation And Innovation

those on the mainland following its separation: neither the dingo nor any mainland technological developments such as the specialised 'small tool tradition' ever reached Kangaroo Island.[41] All the available evidence therefore leans towards the inhabitants becoming extinct, with their ultimate fate just as mysterious as that of the original Kartan colonisers.

Allowing for regional variations (including Kangaroo Island), stone technology during the Pleistocene was relatively uniform throughout Australia. Little is known about wooden implements and weapons as very few have survived, and knowledge of bone tools is only marginally better. Among the stone tools, flakes and scrapers in a myriad of shapes and sizes predominated. Many were retouched to sharpen their blunt edges, and they tended to be multi-functional for undertaking an array of tasks which included butchering animals, making skin coverings and shaping wooden weapons and implements. Distinctive thumbnail scrapers, so-named as they were roughly the size to a human thumbnail, appeared well before the closing phase of the Pleistocene and were widespread across ancient Sahul. Unlike most other stone tools, however, their exact purpose can only be conjectured.[42]

While they were substantially smaller than those of Kangaroo Island, hammerstones, horsehoof cores and pebble choppers were also widely used throughout the continent. Bifacially-flaked edge-ground hatchets appeared in northern Australia before 30,000 years BP, yet for some unknown reason they did not spread into more southerly areas until at least the mid-Holocene – around 4,500 years BP.[43] Quartz, chert and silcrete were favoured raw materials, though any suitable stone was utilised when necessary.[44] Rare minerals such as obsidian were especially prized. A natural volcanic glass, the edges of fractured obsidian are as sharp as a surgeon's scalpel. Large deposits occur in western New Britain which was never part of the Sahul landmass, but from around 20,000 years BP obsidian was traded extensively throughout the Bismarck Archipelago to the northern shores of Sahul and inland to the Papua New Guinea highlands.[45] Surprisingly enough, although an indigenous deposit of obsidian occurs on Cape York Peninsula and was widely utilised by local Aboriginal groups it did not become a major trade item.[46]

In the far south of the continent a meteorite strike 730,000 years BP at Mount Darwin, south-east of Queenstown in Tasmania, created natural glass that was of considerable importance to the Aboriginal people. Implements made from this material have been found up to 100 kilometres from the source.[47] Across a huge area of southern and central mainland Australia another form of natural glass – tektites – were similarly valued for their sharp fractured edges. Once believed to have been pieces of molten lava emanating from a lunar eruption and subsequently fused into glass as they passed through the earth's atmosphere,[48] tektites are now known to have been created from natural stone, often sedimentary rocks, following the hypervelocity impact of extraterrestrial objects.[49]

While some Pleistocene stone tools may have been hafted – and the waisted axes from Kangaroo Island, north-east Queensland and Papua New Guinea certainly were – the majority were hand-held and less sophisticated than succeeding Holocene technology.[50] There is disagreement whether grindstones were used during the Pleistocene. When dates from the archaeological excavation at Cuddie Springs in north-western New South Wales first gained acceptance it appeared that Pleistocene Aborigines had begun exploiting grass seeds as a major component of their diet.[51] Now those dates have largely been discredited there is no longer any degree of certainty. What is known is that the Aboriginal people of ancient Sahul carried out some of the earliest underground mining activity in the world.

Stone quarries where tools were manufactured can be found in all parts of Australia, but they are invariably surface outcrops. In more recent times the Aborigines avoided dark caves and subterranean recesses as they were regarded as the abodes of evil spirits and fearsome mythical creatures.[52] It was quite different 30,000 years BP, when Aboriginal toolmakers descended into deep underground caverns devoid of all natural light. Koonalda Cave on the Nullarbor Plain is one of those places, a natural sinkhole where the roof of a subterranean cavern has collapsed. It is just one of a number of others which can be found in this extremely arid region.[53] Koonalda Cave was first seriously investigated by Melbourne-based archaeologist Alexander Gallus in

Pleistocene Sahul: Adaptation And Innovation

1956, and what he found stunned the scientific community. Aboriginal people in the Pleistocene had regularly made their way down a dangerous and almost vertical slope to extract nodules of silica (chert) for making tools. Passageways which led off from the bottom of the descent to the major deposits extended up to 300 metres in total darkness, the miners finding their way with torches made from burning roots, the vestiges of which have been found along the floor of the passageways.[54] Silica is an excellent fine-grained stone which in more recent times was quarried from an exposed outcrop on the coast, twenty-two kilometres south of Koonalda Cave. During the Pleistocene this deposit was buried beneath massive sand dunes, leaving the only available source of this material lying deep underground.[55]

Radiocarbon dating has established that mining was carried out between 14,000 and 30,000 years BP, with the site also containing some of the oldest known examples of Aboriginal art. Known as finger flutings, they were made by drawing one or a number of fingers across the soft limestone – often in regular patterns.[56] Similar finger flutings are known from Palaeolithic caves in Europe, but this particular art form has continued in Australia to the present day, surely one of the oldest continuous art traditions in the world. A number of Aboriginal desert groups still make finger flutings as part of their sacred ceremonies. The Wardaman people, whose territory lies around the Victoria River to the east of Katherine in the Northern Territory, also make finger flutings on a large rock shelter which has important spiritual significance. The Wardaman claim that finger flutings release the supernatural power of the site,[57] so it is quite possible that at Koonalda Cave it was meant to ensure a continuous supply of the silica which was so vital to the local economy. Nor is this location unique; finger flutings are also known from a number of other localities in southern Australia as well as Papua New Guinea.[58]

Stone tools were just one component of the Aboriginal toolkit during the Pleistocene, and it can be safely assumed that they depended just as heavily on wooden implements and weapons as their Holocene descendants. The original colonisers would almost certainly have been equipped with wooden spears and digging sticks, but exactly when they invented spear-throwers and boomerangs is not clear. Arnhem Land rock art confirms their presence in the Pleistocene, and the fortuitous discovery of wooden tools and weapons in a South Australian peat bog known as Wyrie Swamp has unequivocally shown that returning boomerangs were in use prior to the advent of the Holocene.[59] It was a revolutionary invention, requiring an excellent understanding of both aerodynamics and torque. Bone tools, on the other hand, were either ground into points or perforated. Although many of them appear to have been used as awls for working skins, it is likely they served a number of purposes.[60]

Technology was just one dimension of the Pleistocene; how the Aboriginal people actually lived is another, and in virtually all cases the knowledge that we have is extremely limited. The Willandra Lakes complex of south-western New South Wales is a major exception. Though still far from complete, archaeologists have been able to construct a remarkable picture of human behaviour in the Pleistocene which, in at least a few instances, was little different from our own. As previously discussed, the first human remains uncovered from Lake Mungo were those of a gracile people not dissimilar from modern Aborigines. Later, of course, the remains of more robust individuals were uncovered elsewhere within the complex, though whether both groups co-existed or occupied the landscape at different times remains unclear. What is known from the cooking hearths is that their meat intake included scale-fish, molluscs, yabbies, frogs, reptiles and small unidentified mammals and birds. They also consumed emu eggs and undoubtedly harvested an array of vegetable foods, the only remaining evidence of the latter a few carbonated root tubes which have been dated to approximately 23,000 years BP.[61]

Around 24,000 years BP there was a dramatic infilling of the lake complex, with the waters of Lake Mungo rising five metres higher than on any previous occasion and temporarily connecting it to neighbouring Lake Leaghur. The in-flow also created an island in the northern section of the Mungo lunette, which Aboriginal people repeatedly visited to exploit stranded food resources. How they accessed the island remains a mystery. While there is no evidence of watercraft, it is possible they

Pleistocene Sahul: Adaptation And Innovation

resurrected ancient craft-building skills to accomplish multiple crossings. The alternative of swimming these deep waters laden with stone tools and other long-vanished weapons and utensils does not appear to have been a feasible option.[62]

It is also known that prior to drying up completely some 14,000–15,000 years BP Lake Mungo had clear water and a sandy bed, evidenced by the absence of catfish, freshwater turtles and shells of the freshwater mussel, *Alathyria jacksonii*, from cooking hearths. All these species prefer sluggish, muddy water, as does the Murray cod (*Maccullochella peelii*), the bones of which are very rare. None of the hearths contain any material from termite nests as was common in the succeeding epoch when termites became an important food item. That there were no termites in this region during the Pleistocene is confirmed by the absence of termite-eating animals such as the numbat, bilby and echidna.[63] Notwithstanding plant foods, we therefore have at least a partial understanding of what these Pleistocene people ate as well as what they did not.

The fish bones are of particular interest as the vast majority are from medium-sized golden perch (*Macquaria ambigua*), a consistency in size which suggests they were captured in nets, just as they were in more recent times by Aboriginal groups on the lower Darling River. If spears or lures had been used the size variation would have been greater. Golden perch breed in spring when floodwaters roll down from the highland catchment areas, so it is likely they were caught in late spring or early summer – once again corresponding with more recent practices. There is one conundrum. Golden perch only breed when water temperature rises above 23° Celsius, so presumably the water was warmed during its passage down the Lachlan River before entering the Willandra Lakes complex.[64]

Emus lay their eggs in winter, and as they were also targeted it is believed the ancient inhabitants arrived on the shores of Lake Mungo around this time, remaining through spring and summer. This correlates with nineteenth-century ethnographical observations. The Pleistocene people may have established a pattern followed by their later successors of moving away from permanent water sources in autumn and early winter when rain fell, thus allowing exploitation of the wider surrounding areas.[65] While all this seems quite plausible, caution still needs to be applied when comparing the limited archaeological evidence with more recent ethnographic accounts. They were not the same people even though their life-ways appear to have been remarkably similar. All that can be said with any degree of certainty is that many of the ancient food sources were seasonal, and the cooking hearths identified so far represent temporary camps where specific resources were targeted for brief periods of time. While they possibly used nets for fishing, knowledge of the general technology remains limited. Stone tools were mainly flakes and scrapers, the majority made from silcrete quarried fifteen kilometres to the south-west of Lake Mungo.[66] A few horsehoof cores have also been found, and the commonly-used archaeological term 'core tool and scraper tradition' was named after the Lake Mungo toolkit. Since the early 1970s it has been applied to Pleistocene sites right across Australia.[67]

Despite what might appear to have been a lack of technical sophistication, the ancient inhabitants of Lake Mungo and surrounds displayed aspects of human behaviour little different from today. The skeletal remains of Mungo I and Mungo III revealed that these people practised both cremation and inhumation. Mungo I, the gracile female discovered by Jim Bowler in 1968, was cremated soon after death, but the heat from the funeral pyre was not sufficiently intense to completely incinerate the body: the vertebrae and neck bones were merely scorched. After cremation the bones were pulverised, with the fragments and ash then gathered up and buried in a shallow hole either directly below the funeral pyre or immediately adjacent to it. Ochre was sprinkled over the remains before they were covered, an act which has been interpreted as a mark of respect for the deceased female.[68] On the other hand, this could just as easily indicate something other than reverential treatment.

The bones of Mungo III, the male discovered in 1974, were also sprinkled with ochre before burial. Instead of cremation, however, the body was carefully laid out in a shallow grave with the hands clasped together.[69] The ochre used for both burials came from the Barrier Ranges, 200 kilometres north-west of Lake Mungo,[70] though whether the source

Pleistocene Sahul: Adaptation And Innovation

was within the extended territory of these people or an imported trade item cannot be known. It was obviously considered valuable and, as evidenced by the spread of obsidian from New Britain, exchange networks were certainly a feature of the Pleistocene, a development that reached its zenith in Australia during the following epoch when they criss-crossed the entire continent.[71] Respect for the dead was certainly observed by the robust Kow Swamp people some 19,000–22,000 years BP. All the bodies had been buried with great care, face upwards with limbs extended. Some had also been encircled with white quartz obtained from 100 kilometres away. Like the ochre at Lake Mungo, the quartz clearly had special significance, and encircling the bodies in this manner may have been ritualistic.[72] Whether either group believed in the afterlife is another matter again.

A remarkable discovery in the Willandra Lakes complex in 2003 provided a profoundly intimate view of Pleistocene life. Sets of human footprints on what had once been an ephemeral soak between Lakes Garnpung and Leaghur were dated using optically stimulated luminescence to between 19,000–23,000 years BP. One hundred and twenty-three prints of both adults and juveniles were initially detected, but after careful investigation the number quickly rose to more than 750. One of the tracks was thought to have been made by an individual kneeling in a canoe, propelling the craft forward in the shallow waters with one leg. In fact, it proved to something entirely different. To fully understand the track-ways three experienced Pintupi trackers were brought down from the Northern Territory in 2006, and they identified the supposed canoe track as the mark of a one-legged man. He had supported himself with a pole, the impressions of which were detected in the ancient dried mud.[73] Despite this serious physical handicap the individual does not appear to have been a burden on the group, perhaps an indicator of their general affluence.

Another set of prints possibly represent a family group who travelled east across the soak. At one point a young child around four or five years of age turned back in the opposite direction before suddenly stopping – perhaps called back by one of the adults or an older sibling. After skimming a finger in the mud the child had scurried around in an arc to hurriedly rejoin the group, a personal insight into ancient human behaviour that is extremely rare in the archaeological record anywhere in the world. Just a day or two later yet another group passed across the soak in pursuit of game. Some of them ran parallel to their quarry in a bid to intercept it, and the Pintupi trackers were able to show where a spear had been hurled at the animal, only to miss its mark and ricochet off the mud, leaving a distinctive skid-mark.[74] The majority of these prints had been made by a tall well-built people, distinctly different from the earlier gracile inhabitants exemplified by Mungo I and Mungo III. They appear to have had robust features, and their physical remains have been found on the ancient shoreline of Lake Garnpung.[75] So once again there is evidence of two very different people, but in this instance there is a display of behaviour among the robust group that is distinctly modern in its dynamics.

Further insights into Pleistocene life have also been gained through art, particularly the rock paintings of Arnhem Land. It is here that succeeding sequences of what has been termed the Pre-Estuarine Period document changes in tools and weapons, plants and animals as well as human society more generally from perhaps 50,000 years BP down to the early Holocene. Although dating has proved somewhat problematic, those held to be of the greatest antiquity portray extinct long-beaked echidnas, thylacines and Tasmanian devils. As previously noted, some of them may (or may not) depict the ancient megafauna.

The Dynamic Phase followed with its distinctively-shaped human-like figures, many wearing elaborate headdresses. They are equipped with an array of weapons, including barbed spears, boomerangs and possibly a spear-thrower. Boomerangs and spear-throwers disappeared from the Aboriginal toolkit in this region long before the advent of the Holocene, when open landscapes gave way to dense forests. As well as headdresses, many of the figures also wear belts and armbands, and although it is not clear whether they represent real people or perhaps supernatural beings, the armaments and clothing were probably part of the actual social fabric. Paintings show individuals and entire groups, often engaged in specific activities. Some are having sex, others are killing animals or people. The scenes of inter-personal conflict are at times quite graphic. Figures hurl spears or boomerangs at their opponents, while the intended victims are either avoiding the projectiles or being delivered the *coup de grace* after being struck. The major difference between the earlier and later scenes is that the combatants in the former are fewer in number. Towards the end of this art phase they are much more common, possibly indicating a substantive alteration in social life. This may reflect population growth and a dramatic increase in conflict, with violence becoming the norm. At the very least it can be said that the Pleistocene artists of Arnhem Land were familiar with the concept of organised warfare.[76]

Other paintings could depict rituals. Their full meaning is unclear, and its needs to be said that there is a common trend in archaeology to lump anything not fully understood into the ritual basket. The paintings could, in fact, mean virtually anything at all, and that is no less apparent than with the anthropomorphic creatures known as therianthropes, believed to date from around 20,000 years BP. Some are portrayed watching real people or running alongside them. Others are attacking and killing people.[77] Notwithstanding the high degree of violence, Pre-Estuarine Period art also reveals an appreciation of personal ornamentation which, in turn, may have relied on extensive exchange networks.

Personal ornamentation, especially in the form of beads and pendants, is a common hallmark of modern human behaviour and has been around for a very long time indeed. The oldest beads known, all made from mollusc shells, are from Africa. In Europe archaic *Homo sapiens*, the Cro-Magnons, similarly made beads from mollusc shells, but they extended the range of raw materials to include ivory, bone and steatite (otherwise known as soapstone). In France, Germany and Russia beads were also made from fox canines, while in what is now the Czech Republic the preferred material was beaver incisors. In a great many instances the raw material for making beads was exotic, often coming from a considerable distance away. Marine shell beads in France were worn up to 250 kilometres from the coast, and throughout Europe the shells used for this purpose were restricted to only a dozen or so species, with periwinkles, dogwinkles, turret and elephant tusk shells dominating. All were small, substantially smaller than the mollusc species gathered for food, and particular shapes were favoured for their aestheticism.[78]

Importantly, beads and other personal ornamentation have a social meaning. As a form of non-verbal communication they signify difference or status. They can indicate membership of a specific group, marital status or marriage availability, or even grief. One way or another it all relates to identity, and it has been suggested that when personal ornamentation rose to prominence in Europe during the Palaeolithic Period – the Pleistocene epoch in Australia – it may have been linked to population growth.[79] It was definitely associated with increased communication between groups who often lived far apart. In Australia some of the best evidence of body ornamentation, modern human behaviour, and possibly exchange relationships during the Pleistocene, comes from the far west of the continent.

Mandu Mandu rock shelter is located midway along the Western Australian coast, with deposits dating back to 32,000 years BP. In 1989, twenty-two small cone shells belonging to a single species, *Conus dorrensis*, were excavated at the site. All of them had been modified as beads, a very exacting process given that they are a very small shell. The apex was first removed by rubbing it on an abrasive surface, after which the internal structure was destroyed by inserting a sharp stick into the aperture and continually twisting it, an action that eventually pierced the end of the shell. The shells were then threaded together on a string, the rub marks of which were detected under high magnification.[80]

Further north in the Kimberleys ancient beads made from elephant tusk shells were excavated at Riwi rock shelter. They were associated with material radiocarbon dated to 30,000 years BP. This rock shelter is now situated 300 kilometres from the coast, but 30,000 years BP the sea was 500 kilometres away. If these shells were traded inland from the coast it was a lengthy route, and it is interesting that Aboriginal people living along the Kimberley coast today still make beads from elephant tusk shells.[81] They clearly held special significance for the people of Riwi, as freshwater mussels featured in their diet and land snails were (and are) common in the area. In other parts of Australia mussel and

Pleistocene Sahul: Adaptation And Innovation

snail shells were sometimes modified for personal decoration, but there is no indication that they were used for that purpose at Riwi. The shell beads from both Riwi and Mandu Mandu represent non-edible species which were deliberately selected for either their decorative qualities or, in the case of the elephant tusk shells, the relative ease of perforation and threading. As with the ochre from Lake Mungo, it is not entirely clear whether the elephant tusk shells were part of an exchange network or directly obtained by the wearers themselves. Many archaeologists favour the former because it is known that pearl-shell was being exchanged throughout the Kimberleys by at least 19,000 years BP.[82]

At Devil's Lair in the far south-west, the Aboriginal people also made beads for personal ornamentation – possibly as early as 32,000 years BP. Unlike their northern counterparts, however, these people used bone rather than shells, and they are quite exquisite.[83] This site has also yielded an array of bone tools, notably bone points which are all quite small, revealing the dexterity of their makers. Stone tools, on the other hand, were all made from imported material, particularly quartz and chert.[84] These are mostly flakes, but among other human debris was a perforated piece of marl (calcium carbonate or mudstone) which could well have been worn as a pendant. Three pieces of limestone have also been recovered, all bearing scratch marks made by a pointed instrument, but what these 'engraved plaques' represent is yet another mystery of the Pleistocene.[85]

Devil's Lair was never a permanent occupation site, with small groups probably camping there for only a few days or perhaps a few weeks every year. The economy of these transient people was broad-based, their diet consisting largely of mammals, birds, reptiles and frogs hunted in the surrounding forests and heaths. They also gathered freshwater mussels in the swamps and molluscs on the coast, with the bulk of the food prepared within this large limestone cave. Like the people of Lake Mungo on the opposite side of the continent they also consumed emu eggs, the charred shells indicating that Devil's Lair was probably a winter refuge.[86] It continued to be used in this manner until around 6,000 years BP, when rubble and a sheet of flowstone blocked further entry.[87] This site is in many ways typical of others during the

Pleistocene, where the inhabitants had a broad-based economy requiring little specialist knowledge.

The major exception was in south-west Tasmania, where the Aboriginal colonisers specifically targeted the red-necked wallaby (*Macropus rufogriseus*) as their primary food source. Wombats were the main secondary prey. Although the Aborigines who arrived in this region as early as 35,000 years BP almost certainly balanced their dietary intake with some plant foods, at least eighty percent of their meat intake was provided by these two species. The wallabies were a particularly reliable food source as they are solitary animals which spend their entire lives tethered to limited areas of open grassland. Archaeologists have also been able to determine that the hunters concentrated on the exploitation of either young or aged animals, thereby having minimal impact on reproduction rates.[88] This is arguably the earliest evidence of a conservation strategy aimed squarely at ensuring the long-term sustainability of a crucial resource. The wallabies also provided fur cloaks essential for people who at that time were further south than anyone else on earth, and based on the presence of the emu eggshells it is believed they hunted in this region during late winter and early spring. Their movements throughout the remainder of the year are not known.[89] The exploitation of red-necked wallabies in the south-west continued until the late Pleistocene, when warmer temperatures encouraged the growth of temperate rainforest and the Aborigines seemingly abandoned the region.[90]

While it is unlikely that a complete picture of Pleistocene Australia will ever be gained, it is significant that the innovations and adaptations of this epoch provided the foundations for what was to follow. Aboriginal people entered and colonised almost an entire continent, avoiding only those areas which were either too arid or too cold to sustain an adequate living. Their success was heavily dependent on mobility and broad-based economies, and it was left for their descendants to acquire the specialist skills necessary to finalise the conquest of Australia. Notwithstanding their obvious limitations, the people of the Pleistocene successfully occupied wide areas of the inland and penetrated as far south as the lower areas of the then Tasmanian peninsula – at least on a seasonal

Pleistocene Sahul: Adaptation And Innovation

basis. Their greatest test came with the Last Glacial Maximum between 15,000 and 25,000 years BP. Many groups were forced into refuges such as Lawn Hill Gorge, and although these extreme conditions may have resulted in some localised extinctions the majority survived.

Virtually nothing is known of the plant foods exploited during the Pleistocene except in the case of Papua New Guinea, where the seeds of the pandanus palm appear to have become an important component of the diet by 30,000 years BP. The early inhabitants of that most northerly region of Sahul, particularly those living around the present-day Huon Peninsula, also used large hafted axes, possibly to clear forests, which itself may have been a precursor to intensive agriculture. A real conundrum is the appearance of similar axes at only two other widely-separated locations on the continent – Mount Jukes in north-east Queensland and Kangaroo Island, which now lies off the coast of South Australia. It was on that island and adjacent areas that the distinctive Kartan culture has been recognised. There is a general consensus that those people could well have been among the earliest colonists, though their actual identity remains elusive as no physical remains have yet been uncovered. They suddenly disappeared from the archaeological record, as did their successors who left behind evidence of their own distinctive presence.

Taken as a whole, the Pleistocene exhibits a limited range of technological development, with the so-called 'core tool and scraper tradition' long-lasting and widespread. Apart from the waisted axes, innovative types of stone tools included edge-ground hatchets and thumbnail scrapers, both of which only appeared towards the latter end of the epoch. Stone tools were manufactured from a range of raw material, though chert and quartz were clearly the most favoured. In the far north imported obsidian was highly-prized – so much so that it became a major trade item by 20,000 years BP. Yet strangely enough, an indigenous outcrop of obsidian on Cape York had little impact throughout the wider region. In the far south Darwin glass was also relatively restricted in its distribution, while across a wide swathe of southern and central Australia tektites were readily utilised when available.

Although a greater sense of conservatism appears to have pervaded the Pleistocene compared to the following epoch there was certainly an element of innovation. For one thing, the inhabitants of the Nullarbor Plain pioneered underground mining in Australia 30,000 years BP. Koonalda Cave also features finger flutings in the soft limestone, a form of artistic expression which continues to be practised among some Aboriginal groups to the present day. It could well be the oldest continuous artistic tradition in the world. While the full range of wooden implements and weapons is unknown, the invention of the returning boomerang and the spear-thrower during the Pleistocene were revolutionary. The returning boomerang is of particular interest as it is hardly the hallmark of an ultra-conservative people.

Perhaps the best glimpses of Pleistocene life have been obtained from the archaeological sites in the Willandra Lakes complex of south-western New South Wales. Cooking hearths have allowed the reconstruction of an ancient broad-based economy which included mammals, birds, reptiles and amphibians, yabbies and scale-fish, the latter presumably caught by nets. These ancient people practised both cremation and inhumation, and they decorated their dead with ochre prior to burial. The presence of ochre also hints at long-distance exchange networks, though it is equally possible that the people of the Pleistocene were much more mobile than their descendants, who developed a profound sense of place. At first glance it might appear to be insignificant, but much has been learnt from their feet. Interpretation of the Willandra Lakes track-ways has provided a remarkable view of human behaviour which differs little from our own.

Elsewhere in Australia further insights have been gained from art, particularly the rock art of Arnhem Land. They document social change across an immense span of time, and although not all of it is particularly positive it appears to reflect dramatic demographic growth, which is something usually associated with the mid-Holocene. The violence and warfare portrayed in the Arnhem Land paintings also has remarkable parallels in the present, two of the most disturbing aspects of modern human behaviour. Further instances of modern behaviour in the Pleistocene can be found in personal ornamentation, which at times required considerable technical dexterity.

Pleistocene Sahul: Adaptation And Innovation

They were like us but so unlike us. Their achievement was the colonisation of an entire continent during a particularly harsh period of human history. How much the Aboriginal colonisers altered the Australian environment can only be conjectured, but the landscape certainly felt their heavy impact. The evidence also points strongly towards their having a hand in the extinction of the larger megafauna. At the very least the demise of these unique creatures strangely coincided with the arrival of modern humans, a correlation that cannot be dismissed lightly. On the other hand, the Pleistocene Aborigines bequeathed to their descendants the knowledge and ability that would be honed to an extraordinarily high pitch during the succeeding Holocene epoch. It is to that period where we next direct our attention.

HOLOCENE AUSTRALIA
AND REGIONAL CASE STUDIES

VIII

The Holocene epoch which was marked by warmer temperatures and rising seas commenced around 11,700 years BP and continues to this very day. Unlike the Pleistocene, where there was some degree of stability and uniformity, the last 10,000 years – and particularly the last 5,000 – witnessed considerable change and increasing complexity. It was during the Holocene that Aboriginal people formed their close affinity to land and territory which is so familiar today. There is evidence from a number of widespread regions that local Aboriginal groups were also becoming more sedentary, though whether they would have eventually become totally so is another matter again. Moreover, it was within the last 10,000 years that the Aborigines completed their conquest of the continent, settling in the most inhospitable regions which had previously been avoided. While this was due in part to more favourable climatic factors, population growth and social imperatives were equally important. All were intrinsically linked.

Right across Australia there were major transformations within the Aboriginal economies, with new resources targeted that required specialist skills and knowledge. New and improved technologies ranging from tools and weapons to large-scale engineering projects appeared. The development of watercraft permitted coastal groups to colonise or at least exploit islands which had previously been beyond their reach. During this epoch art, ceremonies and exchange relationships reached unprecedented heights. Exchange networks not only extended into all corners of the continent, but also across the seas. Aboriginal goods were exported, while other commodities and ideas flowed in from the wider world. The full extent of these international links still await a

Holocene Australia And Regional Case Studies

more detailed analysis as it is still unclear whether some of the more recent technological developments were introduced or the result of local initiatives. The appearance of the boomerang and spear-thrower in the Pleistocene had already made it abundantly clear that the Aboriginal people possessed their own special genius. Although it can be argued that Aboriginal societies continued to be characterised by a degree of conservatism they were certainly not averse to change. It was just that their acceptance of imports was highly-selective. The dingo, for instance, was deemed beneficial, while bows and arrows as well as agricultural practices were not. Australia is the only populated continent on earth where bows and arrows were never part of the toolkit at some point in human history.[1]

Before investigating these complex threads it is necessary to outline the climatic and environmental elements which had their own bearing on Aboriginal Australia during the Holocene. Increasingly warmer temperatures from the end of the Pleistocene led to a melt-down of the polar icecaps and rising seas around the globe. Papua New Guinea was severed from the Australian landmass around 12,000 years BP, followed by Tasmania and Kangaroo Island some two millennia later. Henceforth the Aboriginal populations of both southern islands were totally isolated, with only the Tasmanians destined to survive. Overall, approximately twenty per cent of the Australian landmass was inundated until conditions finally began to stabilise around 6,000 years BP.[2] There can be little doubt that this massive loss of land created severe problems for Aboriginal coastal groups, with retreat inland the only available option. Encroachment on the territory of others would inevitably have created conflict, and this is perhaps reflected in a number of Aboriginal oral histories from around Australia.

One example is the Aboriginal 'legend' of Glass House Mountains, a spectacular series of trachyte peaks lying just to the north of Brisbane in south-east Queensland. They are the hard inner cores of extinct volcanoes, the outer matrix of which have long since eroded away. To the local Kabi Kabi (or Gubbi Gubbi) people the peaks represent individuals of a large single family. The highest, Mount Beerwah to the west, is the mother who stands heavy with child. Closer to the coast, the second-largest peak is Tibrogargan, the father. The remaining peaks are their children, with the eldest son, Coonowrin, roughly in the centre. All were living happily until one day Tibrogargan noticed the seas beginning to rise and called on his eldest son to assist his mother to safety. Coonowrin panicked. As he attempted to make his own escape a club wielded by his angry father dislocated his neck which is still evident today: Coonowrin roughly translates as 'crooked neck'. Disgusted by his son's cowardice, Tibrogargan turned his back to keep watch on the rising sea, just as he continues to do.[3] Like the majority of Aboriginal oral histories there are multiple layers of meaning, and there is certainly a moral dimension to this particular 'legend'. The rising seas are nevertheless an indicator of great antiquity, and it is plausible that the conflict between father and son is a metaphorical account of a violent clash between displaced coastal people and those into whose territory they encroached.

Apart from warmer temperatures, precipitation also increased during the Holocene, though there were sporadic climatic fluctuations. Around 5,000 years BP intensification of the El Nino Southern Oscillation system (ENSO) ushered in an acute dry phase across southern Australia, with sand dunes forming in the lower parts of Victoria and northern Tasmania. This brief period of aridity was periodically broken by flooding rains, but from around 2,000 years BP conditions became reasonably stable, and they have remained more or less static over the last 1,000 years.[4] Climatic fluctuations in the mid-Holocene may have contributed to the diffusion of technology, as it was then that edge-ground axes which had been predominant in northern Australia began to be widely manufactured across the southern half of the continent. Unifacial and bifacial points also became far more common across wide areas of Australia.[5] Among a number of other implements comprising the 'small tool tradition' were backed blades, small flakes up to five centimetres in length. One edge was sharpened while the other was purposely blunt. The archaeologist, Josephine Flood, has compared these tools to modern-day penknives, and they were used for a wide variety of tasks. The presence of adhesive gum on some of them could also signify their use as barbs on 'death spears', lethal weapons that could not be withdrawn from the victim. The only way to extract a

Holocene Australia And Regional Case Studies

spear barbed with such blades was to push it through the body, an act which invariably had fatal consequences.[6]

The multi-functionalism of small tools was the key to their widespread adoption. Although backed blades are known from the Pleistocene, they too were restricted to the more northerly areas of Australia; after 5,000 years BP they began to be made across wide areas of southern Australia including the desert regions. Backed blades remained an important component of the toolkit until 2,000–3,000 years BP, and although their dominance faded, they were still in use until a few centuries ago.[7] There certainly appears to have been a correlation between the spread of small multi-functional tools and the intensification of ENSO, which itself posed enormous risks for hunter-gatherer societies. Food sources became less dependable, and it made sense to be able to manufacture large numbers of these tools from limited quantities of suitable stone.[8] The extreme risk factors also paved the way for new food management strategies which, in turn, may have led to population growth and concomitant expansion into areas which had previously been avoided owing to their limited resources.

These push-pull factors have been at the heart of one of the major debates in Australian archaeology. Until the 1980s it was widely accepted that any new development in Aboriginal Australia had invariably been a survival response to climatic and environmental conditions. In other words, the Aborigines had been passive agents in a process largely beyond their control. In the 1980s, however, Harry Lourandos was at the forefront of a cadre of younger archaeologists who began to seriously question this passive response. Lourandos, in particular, argued that the Aborigines had been motivated by social and cultural imperatives and were active agents who knowingly manipulated the environment to meet their specific needs.[9] To support his 'intensification' hypothesis, Lourandos drew heavily on ethnographic and archaeological work in south-western Victoria, where an extensive eel fishery had been developed around Toolondo, Mount William and Lake Condah. Yet, while these 'eel farms' are certainly one of the more unusual aspects of Holocene Aboriginal Australia, it still remains unclear whether they arose as a direct consequence of environmental *or* cultural factors. It may well have been a convergence of both.

The landscape of south-western Victoria is largely open plain and savannah woodland interspersed by small perennial rivers. The last eruption of Mount Eccles around 30,000 years BP resulted in an extensive basalt lava flow that blocked some of the natural drainage systems, thereby creating a myriad of swamps and marshlands which overflow during the wetter months of autumn and winter.[10] They provided an ideal habitat for a host of mammals, waterbirds and fish, one of the latter becoming a major staple of the Gunditjmara Aboriginal people and related groups. The population of this region increased substantially in the mid-Holocene, though this may have been due to the rich natural resources *and* the specialised aquaculture systems. Whatever the precise reason, it is known that the Aboriginal people began to alter their environment around 4,500 years BP, with pollen samples showing a dramatic transition in the vegetation towards water-tolerant she-oaks. Water was suddenly overly-abundant, a good indicator of the emergence of an unusual inland fishery primarily focusing on the short-finned eel (*Anguilla australis*).[11]

This species reaches a length of one metre and is found throughout the Pacific as far east as Tahiti. In Australia short-finned eels inhabit coastal waterways, lakes and swamps from the Albert River in south-east Queensland south to Tasmania and as far west as the Mount Gambier district of South Australia. A few have also been reported from the Murray-Darling River system. Short-finned eels are omnivorous, feeding on aquatic plants, insects, crustaceans, frogs and fish until they reach maturity at roughly fourteen years of age for males and up to twenty-four years for females depending on environmental conditions. With the coming of the rainy season the mature eels migrate to the sea and commence a lengthy journey to their spawning grounds off New Caledonia. Following spawning the larvae drift with the ocean currents until they reach coastal waterways and undergo a metamorphosis into elvers which swim upstream to repeat the lifecycle.[12] In south-western Victorian migration to the sea occurs in March and April, and although the hydrological works built by the Aboriginal people took full advantage of the migratory routes, the various systems also ensured that a regular supply of eels was available all year round.[13]

Holocene Australia And Regional Case Studies

On the southern margin of Lake Condah the Aborigines constructed an interconnected labyrinth of canals and traps which linked this standing body of water with Darlots Creek, a tributary of the Fitzroy River. More canals and races were built between shallow outlying depressions surrounding Lake Condah, thus enlarging the habitat of the eels.[14] This was particularly important, as these fish are strongly territorial with home ranges extending up to 400 metres. Too many eels crowded together means fewer eels owing to their cannibalistic tendencies. The canals were either dug out of the earth or constructed with volcanic rocks up to a metre in height. In a few instances the Aborigines had to dig out the hard basalt bedrock to maintain a smooth flow of water in either direction, allowing mature eels to migrate downstream while providing the elvers with access to the complex. Some of these canals were up to 300 metres in length.[15]

No more than eight traps, or dead-end canals which were possibly closed off with wooden trapdoors, operated at any one time. V-shaped nets with a wide opening were made from plaited vegetable fibre and strategically placed to secure the eels (and other fish), which were then quickly killed by biting the back of the head. The system was so carefully constructed that traps were able to function at different times depending on the flood level, and although the entire complex required a considerable amount of organised labour to complete, it could be operated by fewer than twenty people.[16] Outside the wet season, eels could also be caught using spears or nets, with any surplus exchanged with other Aboriginal groups.[17].

Archaeologist Heather Builth examined nearby trees with heart-shaped cavities which are referred to by the modern Aboriginal community as 'cooking trees'. They certainly were. Builth found traces of eel oil within the cavities, indicating their use as hearths where the fish were smoke-dried for long-term preservation.[18] This was not unique. The Ngarrindjeri people from Lake Alexandrina and the Coorong in South Australia also smoked fish (including eels), which were exchanged for external commodities. Unlike their Victorian counterparts, however, the Ngarrindjeri used spears, nets, lines and hooks to catch their prey.[19] Smoke-drying fish was a complicated and exacting process. The Ngarrindjeri technique was to cut larger fish into manageable sizes and gut the smaller ones. They were then placed on glowing embers and regularly turned to ensure that both sides were equally roasted. All bones were then carefully extracted and the fish checked to make sure they were completely free of moisture. The heads were then removed, the bodies completely opened and placed on a mound of grass surrounded by small fires. When all was in readiness samphire and fig bush was piled on the fires to produce dense clouds of smoke, and when the entire process had been completed the fish were wrapped in grass and hung in reed baskets. It was well worth the effort, as smoke-dried fish remained edible for up to eight months.[20]

The hydrological works at Lake Condah are truly fascinating, but even these were overshadowed in scope by the complexes at Mount William and Toolondo, the latter lying at the foot of the Great Dividing Range in one of the driest districts of south-western Victoria. The landscape is relatively flat and subject to drought, with the small watercourses often reduced to a series of shallow swamps.[21] The Aboriginal people began by linking the shallow depressions with a number of channels similar to those at Lake Condah, but they went further by connecting Budgeongutte Swamp, which had a natural connection to the coastal river system, with Clear Swamp almost three kilometres away. A patch of elevated ground separated the two swamps, so it was necessary to construct a channel more than a metre deep and 2.5 metres wide.[22] Approximately 3,000 cubic metres of soil was removed during this process, which substantially increased the available habitat of the eels. When the rains came in autumn and winter mature eels were flushed into canals equipped with built-in traps.[23] Importantly, at all three locations – Toolondo, Mount William and Lake Condah – these complex system were also designed to retain water during the severe droughts which strike the region roughly every decade.[24]

As well as eels the Aborigines of south-western Victoria could also draw on a wide range of other natural resources. Vegetable foods, especially the daisy yam (*Microseris lanceolata*), were vital staples. Tubers were available all year round, and although they acquire a bitter taste during the colder months, the Aborigines had an ideal substitute at this

Holocene Australia And Regional Case Studies

time of year with *Convolvulus*. Other plant foods included bulrushes, orchid tubers, sedge and bracken fern roots, the various species of which were heavily exploited across a wide area of south-eastern Australia. The root was roasted to extract the starch and then baked into a form of bread. The carbohydrate content is higher than the English potato,[25] and it needs to be noted that the Aborigines placed far greater emphasis on plant foods during the Holocene than their Pleistocene predecessors. Increasing dependence on vegetables would surely have required a considerable degree of experimentation, not all of which could have been successful, as a number of the plants used by the Aborigines contain some of the most lethal toxins known to modern science.

In south-western Victoria fire was used to eliminate competing plants on the yam beds and to expose the tubers. This had the additional effects of increasing the size of the beds as well as productivity. Tubers store starch as a survival mechanism, with regular burning increasing the quantity. Women using digging sticks for the harvest simultaneously aerated the soil and thinned out thick clumps of tubers. Taken together, this was a highly-refined horticultural practice which bordered on farming, and with the wetlands providing abundant animal foods the Aborigines had a nutritious and well-balanced diet.[26] It is possible they could have chosen to adopt a sedentary lifestyle; instead, they relocated to the coast in late spring and remained there during the summer months. This provided a welcome change of diet and prevented the over-exploitation of inland resources.[27] There was nevertheless an air of permanency when it came to the matter of housing at Lake Condah.

Unlike the temporary shelters frequently depicted in ethnographic literature, the eel-harvesters of Lake Condah built substantial dwellings. These were of circular design with a stone base up to one metre in height. The huts were around three metres in diameter, 1.8 metres high in their entirety, and capable of accommodating up to a dozen people. They also featured a low doorway that could be closed off at night with a sheet of bark. Above the base the dwellings consisted of a wooden framework roofed over with rushes or bark and covered with mud to provide waterproofing and insulation. A small aperture at the top allowed smoke from the cooking hearth to escape, and in wet weather this, too, could be closed off with a sod of earth. Many of these huts had common dividing walls.[28]

In the Lake Condah district and throughout south-western Victoria more generally, the Aboriginal people also built mounds of earth. Some are small; others are up to two metres high and thirty metres in diameter. In some instances huts were erected on top, though most were open occupation sites with cooking hearths.[29] While they may have been an efficient means of keeping the inhabitants above the floodplains during the wetter months, at least some of them also appear to have been used as garden beds, particularly for daisy yams.[30] Importantly, manipulation of the natural resources – particularly eels – served to strengthen social networks through marriage, ceremonies and exchange. In the south-western districts and elsewhere in Victoria where resources were plentiful and the Aboriginal population relatively dense, societies were undergoing an unusual transition at the time of European contact. Clan leaders had emerged, men endowed with considerable prestige and authority.[31] A similar situation arose in Tasmania,[32] and it could be that these groups were slowly heading towards social stratification akin to that of Polynesian and Melanesian societies in the Pacific.

A sedentary, or even a semi-sedentary lifestyle, can nevertheless come at a cost. Physical anthropologist Steve Webb analysed Aboriginal skeletal material from a number of regions in Australia for evidence of health problems that may have existed in the past. At the time of European contact one of the densest Aboriginal populations existed in the central Murray River district of northern Victoria and southern New South Wales.[33] These people were even more sedentary than the eel harvesters of south-western Victoria, and Webb discovered that an exceptionally high number of the skeletons bore Harris Lines. During times of seasonal stress the long bones reduce in thickness, but when conditions improve new bone is laid down to leave an intricate network of fine lines. In the central Murray seventy-nine per cent of the skeletons had Harris Lines.[34] While the general health of the population remained unaffected, it was clear they differed from other Aboriginal groups in Australia. Webb's investigation confirmed that these people were largely sedentary and lived in close proximity to each other. They also shared

Holocene Australia And Regional Case Studies

abundant but overly-exploited resources. When a seasonal shortage occurred it placed enormous stress on the population,[35] something which had largely been avoided by the eel harvesters of south-western Victoria.

There are other parallels with the eel harvesters of Victoria's south-west. At Swan Hill in northern Victoria local Aboriginal people constructed canals with built-in traps to catch fish when the Murray River was in flood.[36] Even more significant was the complex on the Barwon River at Brewarrina in north-western New South Wales, where a huge maze of stone-walled fish-traps extended up to 500 metres. Stone wings guided the fish into the traps which were sealed off when sufficient numbers had entered. They were then speared or caught by hand. Although the entire complex was collectively-owned, families laid claim to their own traps, and the fishing season was a time to invite neighbouring groups to share in the spoils and to fulfil social imperatives. Ceremonies were held, marriages arranged, disputes settled, goods and intellectual ideas exchanged. Times of plenty had more significant ramifications than merely satisfying appetites.[37] Aboriginal stone fish-traps – some many times larger than the inland complex at Brewarrina – can be found right around the Australian coast.[38] Again, this appears to have been a late Holocene development, and it may have been only within the last 1,000 years or so that coastal Aborigines began to make fish-hooks from shells. Whether this was a local innovation or an external introduction remains unclear.[39]

Innovation was certainly evident in the lifestyle of one coastal group of Aborigines. Off the north-west coast of Australia in the Buccaneer Archipelago lies High Cliffy Island, a tiny speck just one kilometre in length and 300 metres wide. It was here that Aborigines built a series of huts approximately three metres in diameter with low stone bases remarkably similar to the dwellings at Lake Condah on the opposite side of the continent. In fact, these people used the very same construction technique, the huts are virtually the same size, and they are clustered together in much the same way. Rather than eels, intensification on High Cliffy Island was made possible through the surrounding coral reef with its abundant seafoods. The main drawback was the absence of a permanent supply of fresh water, a problem overcome by digging soaks on the neighbouring Montgomery Islands, which were part of the wider foraging area.[40] Although rich natural resources allowed for a sedentary existence, people cannot survive indefinitely in splendid isolation. The success of all Aboriginal societies during the Holocene was heavily dependent on the development and maintenance of broad social networks, and in the case of the islanders off the north-west coast it was made possible through an outcrop of high-quality chert, found nowhere else in the archipelago nor on the adjacent mainland. This was the medium through which exchange, marriage and ceremonies connected the islanders with their mainland neighbours.[41]

The more conducive climatic patterns of the Holocene also made possible the final conquest of the arid interior. Reactivation of the southeast Asian monsoon brought periodic heavy falls of rain over much of the inland, resulting in the movement of people from the core range areas where permanent water was available, down the inland river systems to the lower catchments. From there they could temporarily occupy the arid plains. Curiously, though, a sharp increase in the number of inland occupation sites does not become apparent until around 4,000 years BP, precisely when there was another dry phase. Why this should have happened is problematic,[42] but the process was undoubtedly assisted through acquired knowledge and the multi-functional implements of the 'small tool tradition', particularly backed blades and tula adzes, which are retouched flakes generally made from chert or silcrete and hafted onto a wooden handle with resin.[43] The real key to the permanent settlement of the inland, however, was through a radical change in the economy. While seed-grinding during the Pleistocene remains highly questionable, there is no doubt that it was widely practiced within the last 5,000 years.

While Australia lacked cereal crops such as wheat and barley which triggered the 'agricultural revolution' in the Near East around 10,000 years BP, it does possess two species of wild millet similar to the cultivated Asian species that were later taken to Europe. *Panicum decompositum* and *Panicum australianse* are found in the interior of all the Australian mainland States where the annual rainfall does not exceed 300 millimetres.[44] Wild millet seeds unevenly during the summer months

Holocene Australia And Regional Case Studies

between December and March, and only small quantities of grain could be harvested at any one time. To overcome this problem the Aborigines harvested the seed when it was full and the grass still green, piling it into stacks and threshing the entire larder when it had completely dried. Those stacks were occasionally of considerable size, with European explorers comparing them to the hayricks of the British countryside.[45]

Women ground the seed into flour using a millstone, and after winnowing to remove the husks it was mixed with water to make a paste which could be eaten raw, but was usually baked in hot ashes.[46] Sometimes the women chose to make small cakes, colloquially known in more recent times as 'johnny cakes', or larger loaves familiarly known to modern Australians as damper. Yet, even with the adoption of cereal crops, long-term survival in the dry interior still depended on strategies developed during the Pleistocene. In times of severe drought the Aboriginal people withdrew to reliable water sources, only venturing out again after rain had fallen. Mobility remained essential, and there is linguistic evidence that in the last few hundred years there was a steady movement of people from the Hamersley Range into the Western Desert and progressively east, with the concomitant displacement of Aboriginal groups in their path. That process was still underway when European settlers arrived in the nineteenth century.[47]

Aboriginal settlement of the arid lands was, of course, highly-dependent on the availability of water, and serious attempts were made to conserve this vital resource which, in turn, allowed wider social networks to be maintained. In 1889 the European explorer, Ernest Giles, recorded three clay dams in the heart of the Great Victoria Desert, the largest of which had a 1.5 metre-high wall and was eighteen metres in length. It was a circular enclosure with an entrance through which water entered after infrequent downpours across the drainage system. This particular dam was estimated to be capable of temporarily holding between 6,000–7,000 litres of water, and numerous other water conservation projects have since been identified throughout the interior. They were invariably built in clay-pans among sandhills to take full advantage of any run-off, with the clay banks often reinforced with mulga wood to reduce erosion.[48]

One dam near Tibooburra in far north-western New South Wales illustrates how the system worked in practice. It was dependent on the overflow from the Bulloo River, which usually only happened once in a decade. An earth bank almost six metres high was constructed around a clay lake bed, extending in a curve for roughly 100 metres. It required the removal of some 150 cubic metres of earth, but the reward more than justified the effort. When full the dam would have held up to 300,000 litres of water, and allowing for evaporation and seepage this would have provided sufficient water to sustain a reasonably large group of people for months at a time. Nearby stone arrangements suggest that when the dam was in use important ceremonies were held, with various groups coming together to re-establish their wider social network.[49] In other parts of Australia, though, these social imperatives could be fulfilled without having to manipulate the environment. All that was required was the periodic super-abundance of a single natural resource.

One of Australia's most ancient conifers, the bunya pine (*Araucaria bidwillii*), is found in south-east Queensland. Growing to a height of around forty-five metres, these trees fruit every year, but ever third year they produce an exceptionally heavy crop of seeds which are full of complex carbohydrates encased within large soft-shelled cones.[50] This was the time for Aboriginal groups to converge on the Bunya Mountains near Dalby, west of Brisbane, or the Blackall Range just to Brisbane's north. The triennial harvest attracted people from as far as Bundaberg and Mount Perry to the north and as far south as the Richmond and Clarence River districts in northern New South Wales. Nineteenth century European observers recorded up to 700 Aborigines coming together at any one time to share in the bunya feasts, which were hosted by local clans and thereby fulfilled social imperatives across a huge geographical area. An unusual aspect was private ownership, with initiated men belonging to the local clan claiming exclusive rights to two or three trees. Ownership also conferred responsibility, with the initiate expected to ascend their own trees with a vine to knock down the cones and share the seeds with relatives and guests. Those exclusive rights were passed down from father to son.[51]

Although bunya nuts can be eaten raw, they were usually ground into a paste and baked in hot ashes. With their nutritive value largely

Holocene Australia And Regional Case Studies

limited to carbohydrates, it was still necessary to exploit the surrounding scrublands which were rich in supplementary foods such as paddymelons and possums, scrub turkey eggs, reptiles, insects, yams and figs.[52] Without the bunya nuts, though, these large and lengthy gatherings would not have been possible. In this instance there was no need to alter the environment, with custodianship and inheritance important ways of ensuring the long-term sustainability of this crucial resource. Nor was it necessary to manipulate the environment far to the south, where the annual appearance of a small brown moth provided the Aborigines with the means to permanently occupy the Australian alpine region.

Every summer between October and February bogong moths (*Agrotis infusa*) from the western plains of New South Wales and Queensland avoid the fierce heat of the inland by aestivating on the highest peaks of the Australian and Victorian Alps. Aestivation is simply the summer equivalent of hibernation, and there can be as many as 17,000 of these small insects crammed into just one square metre of rock crevice. They briefly leave their retreats at dawn and dusk before returning to shelter, where they are totally at the mercy of predators.[53] In the past their main threat came from the Aboriginal people. Three separate Aboriginal groups moved into the alpine region during the Holocene. The Ngarigo occupied the eastern half of the Snowy Mountains and the Monaro high plains. To their immediate west were the Walgalu, whose territory extended towards Tumut and roughly south to a line between Kiandra in New South Wales and the Bogong Mountains in Victoria. Further south again were the Jaimathang, whose territory encompassed the Victorian Alps. All three groups were comprised of numerous bands, generally extended kin, all of whom shared close cultural affinities – perhaps not surprising in a region which is relatively resource-deficient when compared to lower surrounding areas.[54]

This also meant the mountain dwellers were far more mobile, their toolkit limited to easily-transportable weapons and implements, including the formidable 'death spears' carried by initiated men. At the opposite end of the scale was the most useful instrument of all, the digging sticks carried by women in their search for small game and vegetable foods such as the daisy yam.[55] For much of the year these three alpine groups were heavily dependent on plant foods, supplemented by marsupials and monotremes, birds, reptiles and amphibians (including the tiny corroboree frogs), fish and yabbies.[56] Like many other Aboriginal people in the cooler climes of southern mainland Australia the alpine dwellers made warm, waterproof cloaks from possum skins, a single cloak requiring anywhere from fifty to more than eighty individual pelts to complete.[57]

In winter the various bands constructed sturdy weather-proof huts of stringybark in the largely frost-free river valleys. Owing to the limited natural resources and the necessity of frequent movement large communal gatherings to meet social imperatives would not have been possible without the annual migration of the bogong moths.[58] The arrival of these insects was the main event on the social calendar which brought people together from wide areas of the alpine region. Only initiated men were permitted to climb the higher peaks to gather the moths, the harvest taking place after carefully-prescribed rituals had been observed. They were scraped into fine mesh nets, with smoke used to flush out those in the deeper crevices.[59]

The moths were either lightly-grilled on a pre-heated stone or carefully roasted on hot ashes which shrivelled the body to roughly the size of a grain of wheat. Stirring separated wings and legs, and after winnowing the entire mix only the head and body remained. Despite their minute size they comprise around twenty per cent fat and twenty-seven per cent protein. This is a high-energy food, with just half a kilogram of moths per day providing 1,500 calories or 6,300 kilojoules. The Aboriginal people regularly consumed far greater amounts, and although the moths can be eaten raw, roasted or grilled, they were usually ground into a paste using a stone pestle and baked into small cakes which kept for up to a week. Smoking preserved the cakes even longer, a process carried out by the initiated harvesters before they rejoined the others waiting below.[60] In their absence the women and children gathered vegetable foods and small game, a necessary activity given that the annual feasts (like the triennial bunya harvest in south-east Queensland) attracted up to 700 people at any one location. Campsites were formally arranged with strict divisions between families, single men and visitors.[61]

The annual migration of the moths from the inland probably commenced several thousand years ago, but archaeological evidence

Holocene Australia And Regional Case Studies

suggests that the alpine harvest only dates back to around 1,000 years BP.[62] So it was a relatively recent phenomenon, and notwithstanding that it was only a seasonal resource, the bogong moths proved to be the key to long-term settlement in this particularly harsh environment. In other areas of Australia natural resources had to be carefully managed to ensure their long-term sustainability, though it was a little different in those areas where cycads were present. There are four genera of cycads in Australia, ancient plants which bear a superficial resemblance to palms. All are extremely slow-growing, with a number of species living for centuries under optimum conditions. Cycads are distributed in Australia from southern New South Wales to Queensland and across the north to the Kimberley region of Western Australia. They also occur in the far south-west of the continent, and one species, *Macrozamia macdonnellii*, is found in a few upland areas of central Australia.[63] These plants were widely utilised by the Aboriginal people, but this was one resource that required expert knowledge and extremely careful preparation.

All cycads produce a fruit which sometimes resembles a pineapple, and as they mature they generally turn bright red – which is often a warning signal in Nature. So it should be with the cycad, as the seeds of these plants contain some of the most lethal toxins known to modern science. Some of them also possess carcinogenic properties.[64] While seed which has lain on the ground for prolonged periods can be eaten raw or cooked with little risk, the Aboriginal people had a number of different methods for preparing fresh seed as food, mostly involving leaching or roasting – often a combination of both.[65] Owing to the inherent risk, preparation required considerable knowledge and skill, but the end result more than justified the effort. Cycads are exceptionally nutritious, containing forty-three per cent carbohydrates and five per cent protein. Loaves of cycad bread could also be stored in shallow trenches after being carefully wrapped in bark or other vegetable matter. Many species produce large quantities of seed and these plants can yield more food per hectare than the majority of modern cultivated crops. The Aborigines also extended the size of cycad stands by eliminating competing vegetation with fire, and in well-watered areas with fertile soil regular burning substantially increased seed production.[66] Like the bunya and bogong moth harvests, large-scale preparation of cycad seeds was the time for communal gatherings, once again fulfilling social imperatives.

Cycad seeds have long been an important food resource in other parts of the world, so it is possible that knowledge to prepare them safely was introduced into Australia during the mid-Holocene. Until 1996 there was no indication in the archaeological record of cycad exploitation earlier than 4,500 years BP, but that all changed when an ancient pit containing cycad seeds and lined with the residue of grass tree leaves was discovered at Cheetup Cave in south-western Australia. Charcoal from a layer of charred wood returned a radiocarbon date of 15,240–16,120 years BP, which is now recognised as evidence of cycad detoxification from the Pleistocene.[67]

The reason why they only became a significant food source in the mid-Holocene could be linked to climate change and/or complex social developments. Through the appearance of the dingo there was also contact with outsiders around this time – possibly the last wave of pre-European migrants into the antipodes. The earliest trace of the dingo in the archaeological record is from Madura Cave on the Nullarbor Plain, where the remains have been dated to 3,500 years BP. Other dates beyond the 3,000-year barrier come from the north coast of New South Wales and Fromm's Landing in South Australia. The dingo almost certainly spread rapidly throughout mainland Australia, perhaps within a century. After the fox was liberated in Victoria in the 1870s it took just sixty years to reach north-western Australia.[68]

The original home of the dingo was once believed to have been the Indian sub-continent, and as the last pre-European migration into Australia apparently involved Dravidian people it was assumed the dingo was closely related to the Indian pariah dog (which it superficially resembles).[69] Mitochondrial DNA has since shown the dingo's closest living relative to be the New Guinea singing dog, another introduced canine, both genetically linked to wild dog populations in southern China.[70] Dingoes were probably brought to Australia for hunting and as pets, but they were also useful alarms when enemies were near and warm blankets on cold nights. They were much more than an economic auxiliary, and given the animal's propensity to return to the wild when it reaches maturity it is not surprising that they occupy a significant place in Aboriginal ritual and mythology. The introduction of the dingo also coincided with the disappearance of the thylacine and Tasmanian devil on mainland Australia, presumably through their inability to compete with this new advanced predator.[71] It is not entirely unreasonable to suspect that the people who introduced the dingo also brought with them new technological, economic and intellectual knowledge as part of their cultural baggage. Notwithstanding the example from south-west Australia, this could have included refined techniques for the detoxification of cycad seeds. The dingo was also introduced onto the islands of Torres Strait,[72] and for the last 2,000 years this region has provided an important connection between the Australian Aborigines and the wider world.

Many of the islands in the east and west of Torres Strait are the peaks of submerged mountains, and the islands of Mer, Erub and Ugar in the east are the summits of extinct volcanoes. This accounts for the rich red fertile soils of those islands, where agriculture plays a significant role in the economy. There are relatively few good patches of soil in the west and very little on the central islands, most of which are sandy cays created by wind and wave action following the inundation of the land bridge between Australia and Papua New Guinea around 12,000 years BP. Only seventeen of the islands are permanently inhabited, and to varying degrees all the islanders rely heavily on maritime resources such as fish, lobsters, dugong, molluscs and turtle.[73]

The earliest evidence of humans in Torres Strait comes from a rock-shelter on Badu Island in the western group, where occupation has been dated to around 9,000 years BP.[74] Over the following millennia, however, there was a considerable movement of people throughout Torres Strait and Badu was not permanently inhabited until 3,500 years BP. By 2,500 years BP the major islands had been settled by Melanesian seafarers, who remain as Australia's second indigenous people.[75] Two cultural traits shared by all the islanders were warfare and trade. Insular people with limited resources and subject to population pressure are often aggressive, and this was no less so in Torres Strait. The islanders developed a brisk trade in human heads, skulls bestowing status as well as being used for divination and ancestral worship. They were incorporated into religious practices, notably the powerful Malo-Bomai cult of the eastern islanders, and ritual anthropophagy – cannibalism – was a regular feature of life.[76]

Warfare in Torres Strait differed from their neighbours to the north and south. In Papua New Guinea payback was common, often formalised into set-piece battles between opposing sides. Conflict resolution among the Australian Aborigines was also governed by strict procedures,[77] but excepting the most densely populated regions it was far less violent with fewer fatalities. The one anomaly was in the far south-west of the continent, where a system of payback emerged that was remarkably similar to the Papua New Guinean concept.[78] Warfare in Torres Strait, on the other hand, was characterised by deadly surprise raids and tactical advantage. There were no set-piece battles, and the main weapons consisted of bows and arrows as well as wood and stone clubs. Heads were severed with razor-sharp bamboo knives.[79]

While violence was one dimension of Torres Strait islander life, there was another which was equally important. Owing to their geographical location between Australia and Papua New Guinea the islanders forged a complex exchange network in which they were the suppliers, recipients and middle-men. The Aboriginal people of Cape York supplied red ochre, spears and spear-throwers. While all three commodities were widely used within Torres Strait, they were also in great demand in Papua New Guinea and regularly traded north. Shells such as cowries, trochus, bailer and especially gold-lipped pearl-shell, were supplied directly from Torres Strait. They were the universal currency throughout the islands and in Papua New Guinea, used for purchasing goods, paying the family of an intended bride, and to compensate an aggrieved party.[80]

From Papua New Guinea came agricultural products such as sago, a starchy cereal made from the sago palm, the fronds of which were also exported to Torres Strait where they were woven into grass skirts. Other Papua New Guinean goods included cassowary feathers and bird of paradise plumes for making elaborate headdresses.[81] Prior to the arrival of Europeans, pigs were a restricted import because of their propensity to escape and go feral, thereby posing a serious risk to cultivated crops and human life.[82] The most important commodities imported from Papua New Guinea, however, were the timber hulls for the sea-going

Holocene Australia And Regional Case Studies

canoes on which the islanders were totally dependent. There were no trees on the islands large enough to make canoes, some of which were up to twenty metres in length and equipped with outriggers and sails.[83]

There is circumstantial evidence that the Torres Strait islanders were beginning to establish settlements on Cape York Peninsula just prior to the arrival of Europeans.[84] Their influence is certainly apparent in Aboriginal costumes, the outrigger canoes used by Aboriginal coastal dwellers as far south as the Whitsunday Islands, and the bamboo platforms – neets – which were erected for spearing dugong in shallow waters.[85] The Aborigines nevertheless rejected bows and arrows, the primary weapon of their northern neighbours. Nor were they greatly influenced by agricultural practises in Torres Strait and Papua New Guinea.

While the Australian Aborigines engaged in numerous horticultural activities during the Holocene, systematic farming was another matter again. As already mentioned, fire was used to increase the production of cycad seeds and yams. Across the continent the tops of tubers were intentionally left attached to the tendril after harvesting to ensure a new crop. Yams were also transported to offshore islands to provide a reliable food supply, and fruit seeds were deliberately spat into camp refuse containing organic matter to encourage the growth of more trees.[86] In the inland regions the Aboriginal people harvested and processed wild millet and more than seventy-nine examples of food storage have also been recorded.[87] An even more relevant example came in November 1971, when W.C. Dix and M.E. Lofgren recorded an Aboriginal site in Western Australia's north-eastern goldfields region. At this location were two stone arrangements associated with a clay pan that was one of the few natural storage basins in an area where large salt lakes dominated. Local Aborigines called the site *Kurumi*, also the name of a seed-producing food plant (poss. *Tecticornia arborea*) and the seed itself. Informants demonstrated how the seed was ground and baked into a damper and pointed out withered specimens of the plant in the dry bed of the claypan, adding that seeds were carefully scattered in cracks so that when heavy rain finally fell they could harvest bountiful crops. Dix and Lofgren suggested that this practice could amount to 'incipient agriculture' which,[88] although limited in scope, is remarkably close to early European farming techniques. So in spite of a recent claim to the contrary, the question must be asked why these semi-agricultural practices were not taken a step further, particularly in more fertile regions of the continent?

Josephine Flood has argued that hunting and gathering reflected an affluent lifestyle, and there was no need to increase the production of vegetable foods.[89] It was a little more complex than that, and it is also necessary to avoid falling into the trap of associating agriculture with 'progress'.[90] Despite their success as farmers, many coastal people in Europe suddenly abandoned agriculture between 4,000–5,000 years BP and turned their attention to the sea, particularly the exploitation of seals. This dramatic transformation of coastal economies appears to have been linked to climate change which significantly increased the productivity of the North Sea,[91] an example which clearly illustrates that agriculture is not necessarily the be all and end all even when conditions are favourable. They seldom were in Australia.

Tim Flannery has advanced the interesting proposition that Aboriginal people fully grasped the implications of ENSO, which ushered in the warm, dry climatic phase of the mid-Holocene. Just as it remains today, ENSO was extremely variable, with alternating patterns of drought and flooding rains occurring in roughly two to eight-year cycles. It simply did not pay to rely too heavily on one or a number of plant resources when failure could easily spell disaster. Hunting and gathering at least ensured both short- and long-term survival, with the added benefit of providing a well-balanced diet. Flannery elaborated further by suggesting that the variability of ENSO in the mid-Holocene, coupled with the relative poverty of many Australian ecosystems, forced the Aboriginal people to cap population growth. To guarantee an adequate gene pool, and to gain access to resources in neighbouring areas in times of need, social networks were strengthened through out-marriage.[92]

This could explain why the bunya and bogong moth harvests were relatively recent phenomena. It might also account for the more intense exploitation of cycads within the last 5,000 years. Out-marriage and the strengthening of social networks were of primary importance at all of these communal gatherings. Another instance can be shown with greenstone from a quarry at Mount William in southern Victoria, which

Holocene Australia And Regional Case Studies

was highly-prized for making hatchet heads across a wide area of south-eastern Australia. Close examination of their distribution nonetheless reveals that it parallels linguistic boundaries and social networks. Exchange in this instance was driven by social imperatives rather than merely supply and demand.[93]

It also needs to be borne in mind that it was only during the Holocene that exchange networks conveying both material goods and intellectual ideas were extended right throughout the continent. This effectively prevented the isolation of any Aboriginal group irrespective of its geographical location.[94] Indeed, exchange systems and social affiliations were arguably the most valued resources of the Aboriginal people.[95] Agriculture was not, although Bill Gammage has raised the point that the refinement of Aboriginal fire regimes resulted in the Australian landscape being so carefully managed that it can rightly be regarded as constituting one huge farm.[96]

The Aborigines used fire for a multitude of purposes, not the least of which was to maintain biodiversity and ensure the sustainability of exploitable resources. Fire was a means of signalling and to keep track of people as they moved across country. It was essential for clearing pathways that wound their way through territories and interconnected widely-separated regions of Australia.[97] Fire was a device for hunting animals and to regenerate plants. It was utilised for destroying vermin around campsites, to harden wooden tools and weapons, and to melt the resin used in their manufacture. Fire was an aspect of cleansing and healing, for light during nocturnal ceremonies, for warmth and, in some parts of Australia, to cremate the dead.[98] As European settlers found, the Aborigines could also use fire as an effective weapon of war.[99] Above all, fire linked together a grid pattern of managed landscapes across the entire continent, the control mechanism of the grasslands and the Indigenous fauna. Kangaroos, for example, prefer to feed on green grass and shun the brown. So mosaics were created where patches of green grass alternated with brown, the belts of timber or brush separating them providing the animals with safe havens. By this means the Aboriginal people knew where kangaroos and other prey animals could be found at any time.[100] This was clearly a form of animal husbandry which differed from European-style farms only through the absence of artificial fences.[101]

Land management with fire was also built on knowledge of the seasons. In spring, cooler fires were used to burn the margins of swamps and belts of timber, often when rain was pending. More intense fires in autumn cleared undergrowth and thickets, but this pattern varied according to the need for regenerating fire-dependent plants. Some areas were burnt every six months, or once a year, or every few years depending on their requirements.[102] Aboriginal land management practices ensured that trees grew on poor soils and grass on the rich where it could flourish,[103] and it was the open parklands they created which early European settlers found ideal for grazing introduced sheep and cattle. Kangaroos and other marsupials were managed virtually the same way by the Aborigines. Firebreaks prevented sacred sites or groves of fruit trees from being damaged or destroyed, a protective measure greatly assisted by their expert knowledge of wind shifts.[104] All this was a far cry from the use of fire perhaps 50,000 years earlier, when it may have contributed to the extinction of the megafauna and undoubtedly transformed the landscape of Australia. During the Holocene the entire continent became one huge cultural artifact, a managed land where diverse people formed strong attachments to place. It was through their complex social interactions that each group was intrinsically linked to others beyond their own immediate purview. This was the zenith of Aboriginal colonisation, and the island of Tasmania further serves to show just how well the Aboriginal people overcame all their formidable obstacles. In this instance the difficulties were compounded by 10,000 years of isolation.

Charles Darwin in 1854 when he was working on his revolutionary theory of evolution. The publication of *On the Origin of Species* five years later allowed the discipline of archaeology to be placed on a firm footing

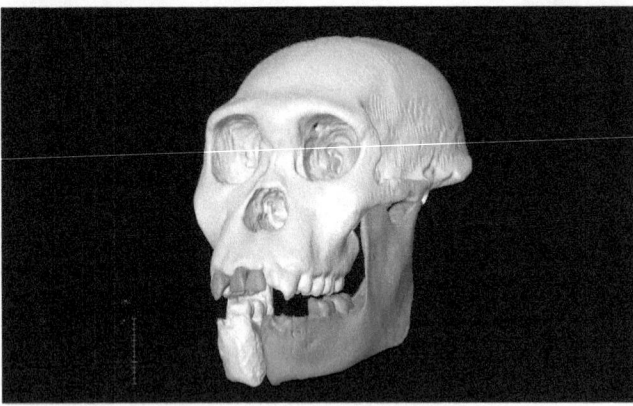

Top: Paul Dirks with a cast of a female *Australopithecus sediba* skull
Bottom: Reconstruction of *Australopithecus sediba*, the most recently discovered hominid
Opposite top: Modified reconstruction of a Neanderthal child from Gibraltar, the last stronghold of this hominid. It was once believed to have been a lumbering dim-witted brute but there is an increasing trend towards humanising this contemporary of *Homo sapiens*
Opposite: Skull of *Homo floresiensis*, the diminutive 'Hobbit' that inhabited the Indonesian island of Flores until at least 13,000 years BP

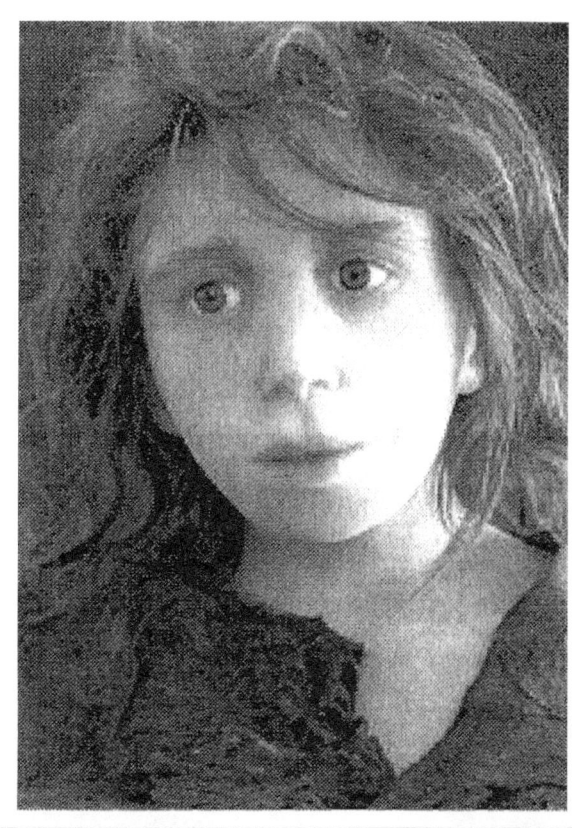

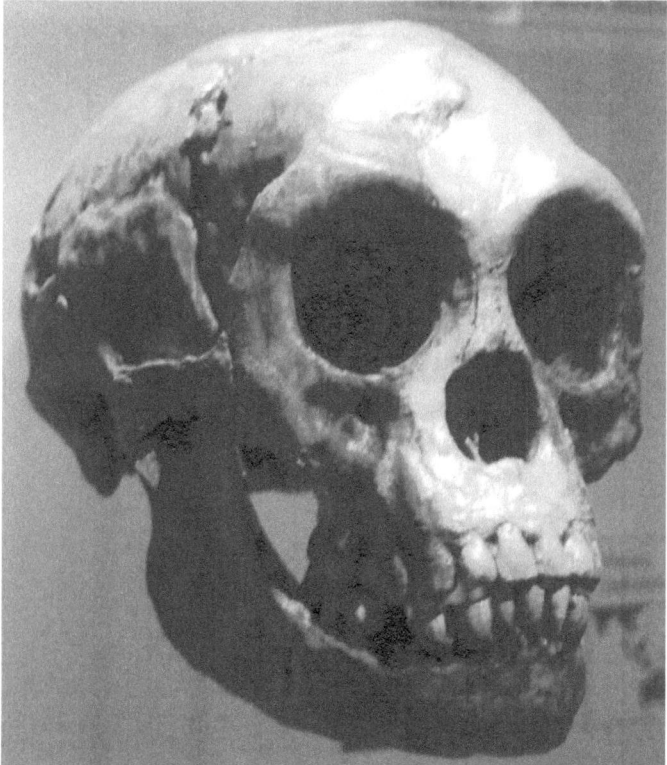

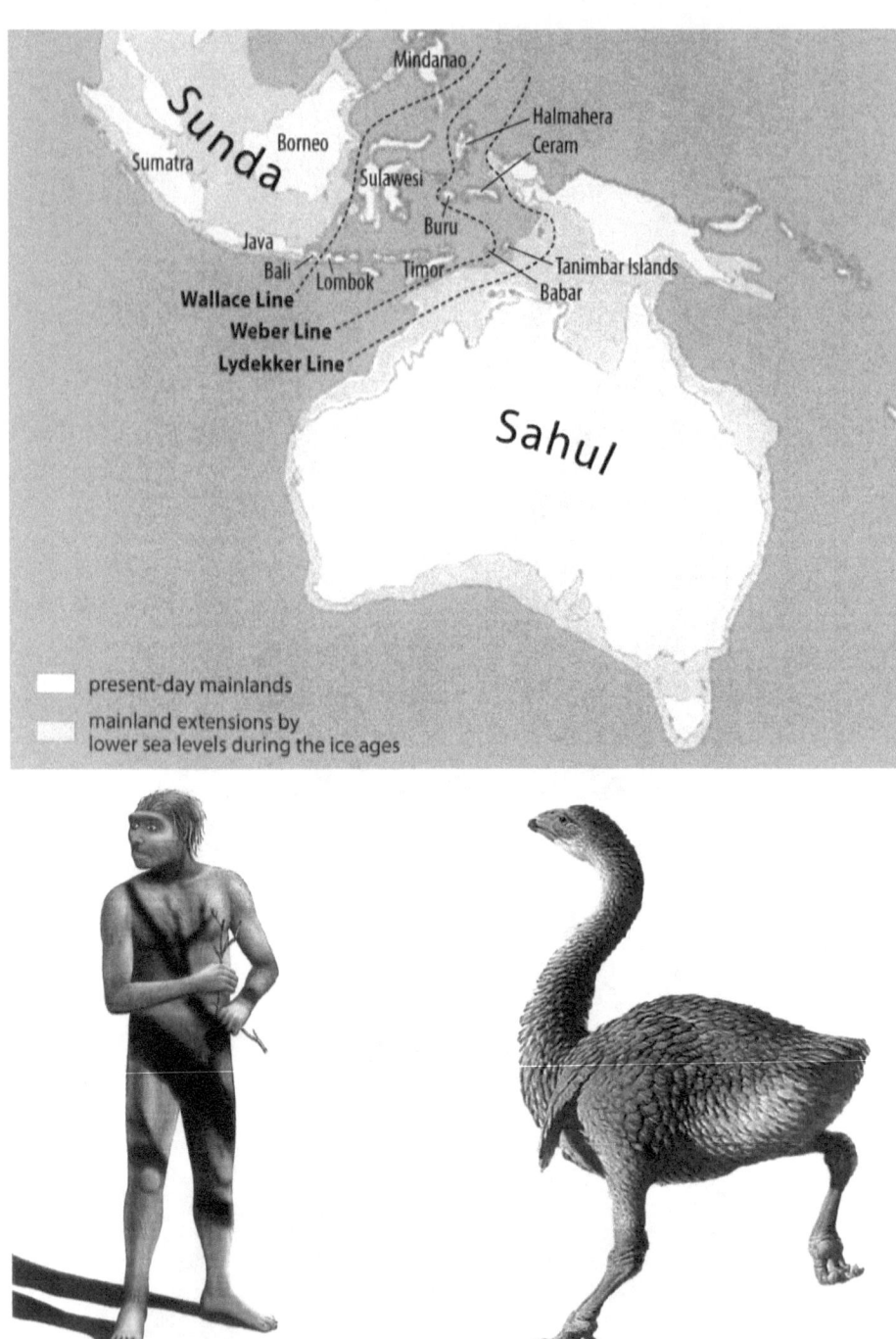

Top: At all times in human history the ancient super-continent of Sahul was only accessible via a sea-crossing from Sunda
Left: A reconstruction of *Homo erectus*, the first hominid known to have been capable of crossing formidable water barriers
Right: Australia's giant extinct bird, *Genyornis newtoni*, stood just over two metres tall and weighed up to 275 kilograms

Marsupial tapirs, *Palorchestes sp.*, were among the more unusual examples of Australia's giant megafauna

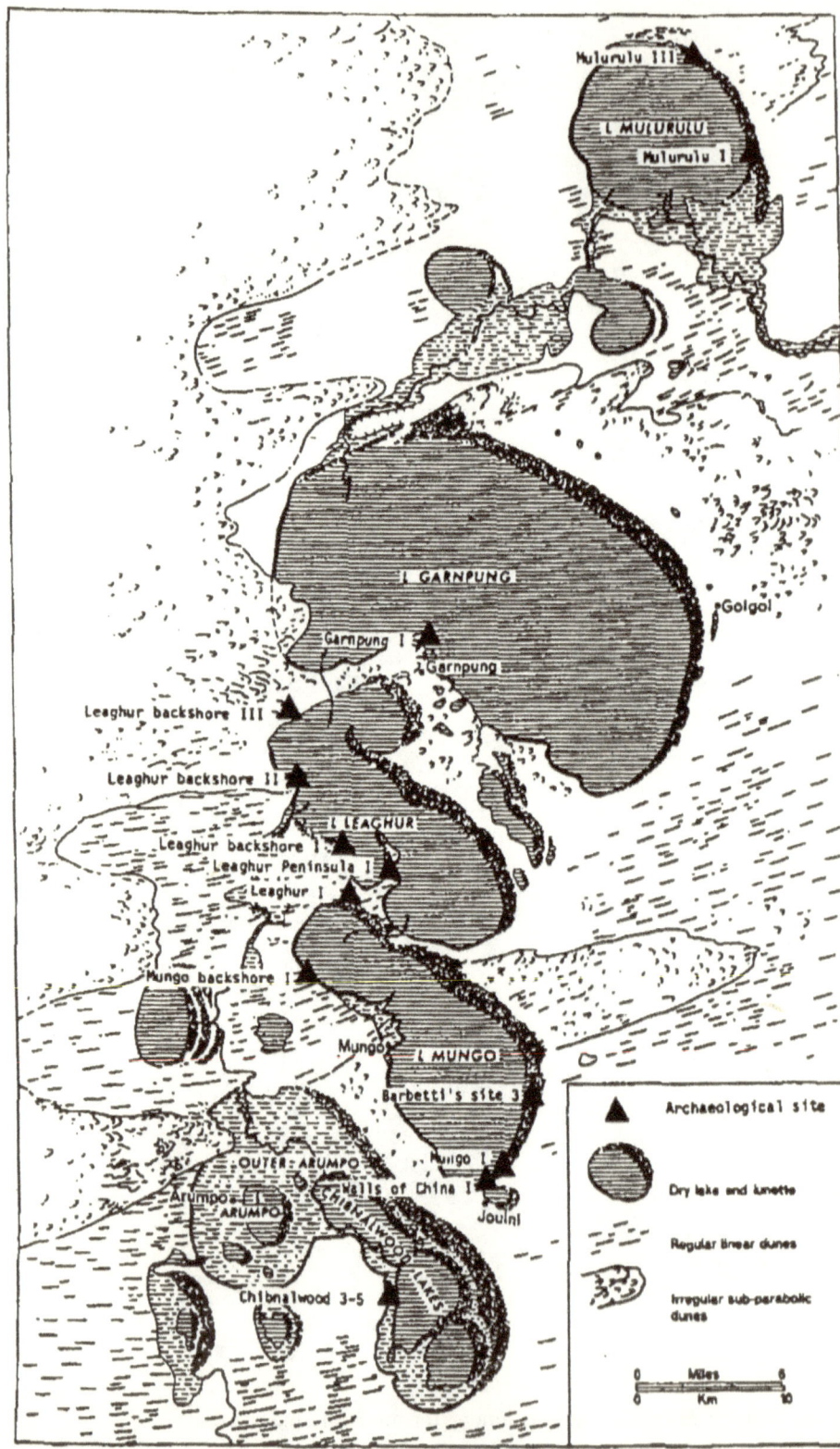

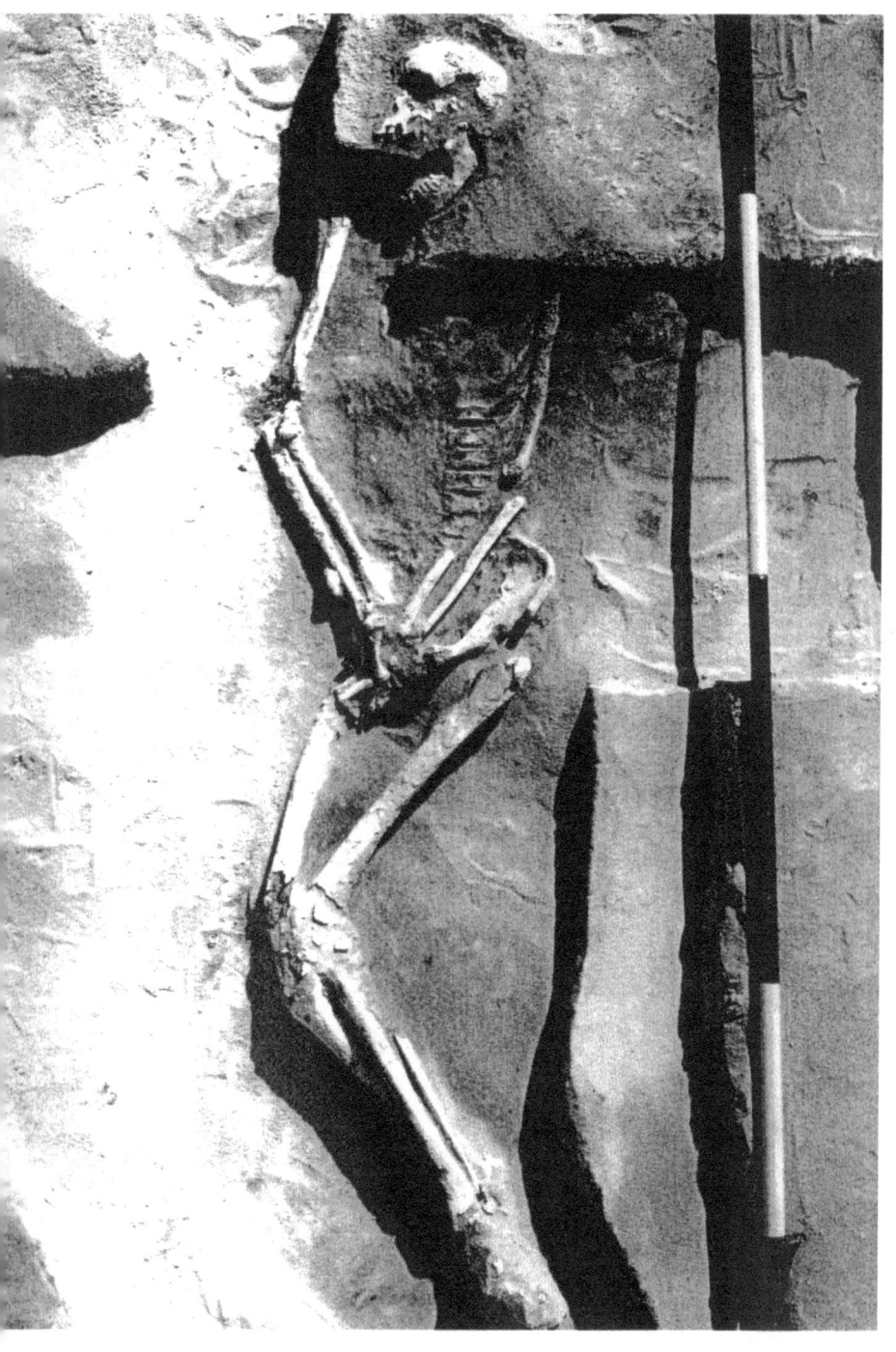

he skeletal remains of Mungo III date from around 42,000 years BP
opposite: Willandra Lakes archaeological sites in south-western New South Wales
rry Allen, 'Reinterpreting the 1969–1972 Willandra Lakes archaeological surveys', *Archaeology in Oceania*, .33, No.3, October 1998, 208

Undated photograph of a hunter in the Fraser Range of Western Australia

Although Truganini (c.1812–76) was definitely not the last of the Tasmanian Aboriginal people, she witnessed the destruction of customary society in the wake of European colonisation

TASMANIA:
AN ISOLATED TRAJECTORY

IX

Owing to the presumed physical and cultural differences between the Tasmanian Aborigines and their mainland counterparts, it is perhaps not surprising that an array of theories supporting a separate origin were widely canvassed during the nineteenth and early twentieth centuries. Their pigmentation, generally short stature, woolly hair and less sophisticated material culture were all seized on by European theorists in a perverse bid to portray the Tasmanians as one of the most 'primitive' people on earth. Thomas Huxley, assistant surgeon and naturalist on HMS *Rattlesnake* which voyaged around the world between 1846–1850 charting little-known waters, later argued that the Tasmanians were Asiatic negritos closely related to the Indigenous people of New Caledonia. Huxley never visited Tasmania, as the Australian leg of *Rattlesnake*'s voyage was confined to the tropical waters of north-east Queensland and Torres Strait. In 1868 Huxley nevertheless contended that the Tasmanians had migrated south from New Caledonia along a chain of islands in the Tasman Sea which had long since disappeared.[1] There was no geological evidence that such islands ever existed, and Huxley's contention was based solely on his premise that a direct oceanic voyage was beyond the realm of probability. Strangely, this mythical migratory route was the only point seized on by Huxley's critics, who countered that a direct journey by sea was actually more likely.

In 1908 Sir William Turner's examination of crania suggested to him that a negrito people had migrated across the Australian mainland to Tasmania rather than through any island chain,[2] while in 1935 the distinguished Professor of Anatomy at the University of Melbourne, Frederic Wood-Jones, reasoned that the Tasmanians would have been quite capable of making a direct voyage from New Caledonia.[3] It was left unsaid by all these theorists why the Tasmanians would have wanted to leave the tropics for cooler southern climes. Yet, there were even more bizarre theories which directly linked the Tasmanians to the African continent.

Commenting on Francis Allen's argument in 1879 that the Tasmanians came from Africa, Hyde Clarke drew attention to a language remarkably similar to that of the Tasmanians which was to be found among the 'Nyam-Nyam people' of the 'African Lake regions'.[4] Allen's theory was that the Tasmanians migrated from Africa around the existing coastline before dispersing south. He disagreed with another contemporary, Professor Harry Govier, who insisted the migrants had taken a much shorter route across a long-submerged land bridge extending through Madagascar and the Seychelles all the way to Borneo before reaching the Australian mainland.[5] Even more extraordinary was the theory that the origins of the Tasmanians actually lay in the very opposite direction – Patagonia in South America. From there the Tasmanians had voyaged west, skirting the Antarctic ice-sheet, before turning north to a landfall in Tasmania. Through a distinct lack of evidence this particular theory was soon dismissed, as was the suggestion that the Tasmanians were autochthonous.[6] In 1870 historian James Bonwick insisted that the Tasmanians were one of a number of negrito peoples who had originated on a long-lost continent,[7] another imaginative hypothesis that was also consigned to the dustbin of wishful thinking.

Then there were the tri-hybrid theories. As mentioned previously, John Mathew argued in 1899 that the Tasmanians were of Papuan stock who had been the first people to colonise the continent, crossing into Tasmania via a land bridge which had subsequently been submerged by rising seas.[8] He was at least right about the land bridge, even though Mathew had no way of proving it at the time. In fact, Mathew was well ahead of his time, as well into the 1930s anthropologists and other-like minded thinkers were still attempting to explain how the Tasmanians could have accomplished a successful crossing of Bass Strait. In 1936, for instance, Archibald Meston, a self-proclaimed authority on the Tasmanian Aborigines, speculated they had crossed by canoe from

Tasmania: An Isolated Trajectory

Wilson's Promontory into north-east Tasmania via the Kent and Furneaux Islands or, alternatively, from Cape Otway into the north-west via King Island.[9]

The common denominator in all these varied ideas was that the Tasmanians were a negrito people quite distinct from the Aborigines of the Australian mainland. A slight variant as late as the 1960s came from the pen of archaeologist Rhys Jones, who proposed that the Tasmanians arrived on the north-west coast of Australia from Indonesia after the continent had already been occupied by the Aborigines. In their search for vacant land they had travelled down to the south-west before turning east to eventually find the uninhabited Tasmanian Peninsula.[10]

The Tasmanians also spoke Pama-Nyungan, the dominant language group throughout Australia prior to the arrival of Europeans.[11] Although only fragments of the Tasmanian languages have survived, it was sufficient for linguist John Taylor to identify the regional origins of the Tasmanians on the mainland. According to Taylor there were at least three, possibly four, waves of migration into Tasmania, the first of which crossed the Bassian Plain around 40,000 years BP. Entry into the then Tasmanian Peninsula prior to that time would have been difficult owing to the extreme aridity and cold, as well as a lack of food resources on the plain itself. Increasing precipitation from around 40,000 years BP provided the first real opportunity for the Aboriginal people to penetrate the southernmost extremity of the Sahul landmass.[12]

According to Taylor's hypothesis the initial colonisers of Tasmania came from the Murray River basin, entering the then peninsula across the western side of the Bassian Plain, which included the higher ground that is now King Island. Having reached Tasmania proper they spread down the west coast, and inland along the river valleys. Archaeological excavations have confirmed the presence of the Aboriginal people in south-west Tasmania as early as 35,000 years BP. This first wave of colonisers also spread east along northern Tasmania, but further expansion southwards on the east coast was blocked by the harsh prevailing conditions.[13]

Towards the end of the Last Glacial Maximum, perhaps as early as 15,000 years BP when conditions were slowly beginning to improve, the eastern section of the Bassian Plain was crossed by a second wave of colonisers from what is today south-eastern Victoria. They either displaced, or merged with, the existing population in north-east Tasmania before expanding on two fronts. One group moved west and then south, reaching its southernmost limit at present-day Macquarie Harbour. The second group penetrated the central districts as far south as today's southern Midlands.[14] Taylor believed that around this same time another wave of colonisers from south-west Victoria and the south-eastern districts of South Australia occupied the western side of the Bassian Plain. They remained there until around 10,000 years BP when rising seas forced an evacuation south into north-west Tasmania where they merged with the resident population. An internal migration followed, with some of these people moving east and then south to permanently occupy the Derwent estuary around 6,000 years BP.[15] While Taylor's argument is based entirely on linguistics, it does have a great deal of merit. If accepted, it also means that the Tasmanian Aborigines only coalesced into nine relatively distinct but loose-knit socio-political entities within the last 10,000 years. It is known that a number of quite different regional languages were spoken by the Aboriginal Tasmanians.

From Taylor's model it is clear that permanent settlement of south-east Tasmania was a relatively late phenomenon. That did not prevent the modern Tasmanian Aboriginal community from claiming in 2010 that an occupation site on the Jordan River dated from at least 40,000 years BP.[16] Unfortunately, both the archaeology and the sensational press announcements were seriously flawed. A peer-review of the interim archaeological report in August 2010 made it clear that artifacts uncovered at this location had not been accurately dated. Sections of the sediments certainly had been, but that is an entirely different matter.[17] In fact, there is no evidence of the Aboriginal presence in south-eastern Tasmania before 8,000 years BP, and no indication of intensive settlement until the mid-Holocene.[18] Indeed, the only part of southern Tasmania that could have been occupied during the Pleistocene – at least on a temporary basis – were the river valleys of the south-west. Even then, survival depended on both seasonal and altitudinal movement.

A fortuitous discovery in Fraser Cave by geomorphologist Kevin Kiernan in 1977 provided the first indication of the Aboriginal presence

Tasmania: An Isolated Trajectory

in this region, though at that time no-one suspected just how far back it extended. In 1981 Kiernan and a number of archaeologists, including Rhys Jones, returned to Fraser Cave to conduct a thorough investigation.[19] Now known as Kutikina, this important archaeological site was to play a major role in the protest against the Gordon-below-Franklin Dam, an issue that led to much of Tasmania's south-west being protected by World Heritage legislation. Kutikina proved to be just one of a number of caves which have provided valuable insights into the world of the ancient Tasmanians. In 1981 the Aboriginal presence in this region was dated to 20,000 years BP;[20] further discoveries have now shown that the Aborigines were living and hunting in south-west Tasmania as early as 34,000 years BP.[21] Kutikina itself was a temporary base camp for a group of perhaps twenty or thirty people. They returned from foraging trips to butcher and cook their prey, with just one cubic metre of the cave floor containing almost a quarter of a million fragments of animal bone. The bulk of it came from a single species – the red-necked wallaby (*Macropus rufogriseus*).

Along with the bones were thousands of stone artifacts manufactured from chert, quartz, quartzite and Darwin glass,[22] the natural glass formed by the meteorite impact at Mount Darwin 730,000 years BP. Darwin glass varies in colour from white to black or from light to dark green, and is found across 410 square kilometres north, south and west of the impact site. It is rare in the crater itself,[23] and this was one form of stone material that could not be quarried. Fragments were (and are) collected on the ground or among the roots of upturned trees.[24] Excavations at Kutikina have shown that both quartz and Darwin glass tended to be used more widely after the Last Glacial Maximum. Stone tools were largely scrapers, including the thumbnail type, some of which had been retouched to maintain their cutting edge. Bone points made from the fibulae of red-necked wallabies were also common in the deposits; some of them may have been awls for making fur cloaks.[25]

The discovery of Kutikina provided the impetus to conduct a more thorough archaeological survey of south-west Tasmania, a task greatly assisted by the Southern Forests Archaeological Project initiated by Melbourne's La Trobe University in 1988. Kutikina is a large cave, the main chamber almost twenty metres long and more than twelve metres wide. The roof is five metres high, but this is just one of more than twenty caves in the south-west that have been identified as Aboriginal occupation sites since the survey began. All but one of them had been abandoned by 11,000 years BP, when warmer and wetter conditions resulted in the widespread encroachment of unproductive temperate rainforest. Prior to that time the landscape was predominantly tundra-like grassland interspersed with alpine shrubs,[26] ideal habitat for red-necked wallabies. Large quantities of animal bone have been found at all these sites, ninety per cent of it belonging to this one species. Many of the bones from the hind legs and feet had also been split longitudinally to extract the marrow, the carbohydrates essential for the metabolism of a high-protein diet.[27] This would have been even more important if plant foods had been relatively scarce.

Unlike larger macropods, red-necked wallabies are both solitary and sedentary. Their home range is limited to between fifteen and twenty hectares, expanding around thirty hectares every two or three years. As a grazing and browsing animal they are practically tethered to patches of grassland bordered by thick shrubs which provide shelter during the day.[28] While they were the main target of Aboriginal hunters, other animals also featured in the diet. Wombat bones, for instance, are reasonably plentiful in the cave deposits, and it appears the Pleistocene Aborigines particularly favoured the brain of this species. Other animal foods included ringtail and brush tail possums, pademelon, eastern grey kangaroo and quolls. The remains of birds have also been found in the deposits, especially the Tasmanian native hen and the extinct Tasmanian emu, whose eggs were apparently consumed at Nunumira Cave in the Florentine River valley.[29] The consumption of emu eggs suggests that this site was occupied in late winter and early spring.[30] Evidence from the other caves reveal a fairly regular seasonal movement along the river valleys as well as movement from lower to higher altitudes, the highest caves only being accessed during the warmer summer months.[31]

A number of caves provided the first solid evidence of Tasmanian Aboriginal rock paintings. Although hand stencils were previously known from three sandstone rock-shelters in south-eastern Tasmania

Tasmania: An Isolated Trajectory

they were thought to have been the work of Aborigines brought from New South Wales in the late 1820s–early 1830s to assist in rounding up the Tasmanians for forced removal to the Bass Strait islands. The stencils appeared to be relatively recent and all three rock-shelters were located near European settlements.[32] Then, in January 1986, hand stencils were discovered in the remote Maxwell River Valley. They are known from three caves – Ballawinne, Weld and Mina – with radiocarbon dating of human blood that had been mixed with the ochre returning an age of just under 11,000 years BP.[33] The paintings were apparently produced just before these sites were permanently abandoned, but the art tradition itself is now known to have survived on the east coast until at least the mid-Holocene. While recording archaeological sites in eastern Tasmania in 1987, Steve Brown from the University of Sydney noticed red colouring on an exposed rock shelter at Fisheries Creek in Freycinet National Park. Initially thinking they were faded hand stencils, Brown dismissed the idea on later reflection, but his first thought was actually correct. It was only through the application of the Decorrelation Stretch (DStretch) technique in 2013, however, that their existence was finally confirmed. Importantly, six new hand stencils at Fisheries Creek were identified at the same time, all of which date from around 3,400 years BP.[34] Further west it was a very different matter and that particularly relates to occupation during the Pleistocene.

The only cave where the Aboriginal presence has been shown to extend into and through the Holocene is Parmerpar Meethaner in the Forth Valley, slightly to the north of the Maxwell River Valley. The oldest deposits have been dated to 34,000 years BP; the youngest to 780 years BP. Even at the height of the Last Glacial Maximum the Forth Valley remained ice-free, which explains why occupation was able to continue.[35] For all that, there are a few other anomalies which set Parmerpar Meethaner apart from the caves further south. Raw materials for making stone tools were all sourced locally, and prior to 18,000 years BP quartzite flakes dominated. Between 10,000–15,000 years BP quartz artifacts became more common, at which time they were superseded by those made from hornfels, a hard metamorphic rock which continued to be favoured until 3,500 years BP. Surprisingly, while thumbnail scrapers made from Darwin glass are common in Mackintosh Cave just thirty-five kilometres to the west, no artifacts made from this material are present at Parmerpar Meethaner. Mackintosh Cave marks the northernmost limit of Darwin glass implements, while Nunamira Cave in the Florentine Valley marks their easternmost distribution.[36]

The occupants of Parmerpar Meethaner also had a different economy to their southern neighbours. Here the remains of red-necked wallaby are completely absent, and even wombats appear to have been hunted irregularly. The main emphasis was on the exploitation of small to medium-sized animals such as ringtail possum, pademelon and potoroo. Bluetongue lizards, fish and possibly birds also featured in the diet.[37] Parmerpar Meethaner was apparently occupied by people from the north who were culturally distinct from their southern neighbours, and there is a possibility that it was elements of this group who also occupied Warragarra rock-shelter in the Upper Mersey Valley, where the economy was very similar. Warragarra was temporarily abandoned in the mid-Holocene before being reoccupied around 3,400 years BP.[38] Both sites are also poignant reminders that the Tasmanian Aborigines cannot be simply grouped together as a single entity sharing a monoculture. On the contrary, there were a number of different cultures, which reinforces Taylor's argument that Tasmania was colonised by at least three separate groups of Aboriginal people. They did have one thing in common: ancient skeletal remains uncovered at Nanwoon Cave in the Florentine Valley and on King Island suggest that the Pleistocene Tasmanians were of gracile build, closely resembling the Aboriginal people who lived around Keilor in southern Victoria and Lake Mungo in south-western New South Wales 40,000 years ago.[39]

King Island is of particular interest as it was once suspected that a relict population may have been stranded there after the flooding of the Bassian Plain.[40] The general consensus today is that King Island was abandoned prior to being severed from the Tasmanian mainland around 10,000 years BP, but it still holds its mysteries. Twenty-two Aboriginal sites have been recorded on the island, all but two of which date from the Pleistocene. The exceptions are Cataraqui Point, where a small midden dates from 1,980 years BP, and another at Quarantine

Tasmania: An Isolated Trajectory

Bay, which is even more recent at around 1,100 years BP. Both sites were occupied only briefly, with molluscs comprising at least part of the diet. Stone tools made from spongolite, a form of chert, have also been found at both locations. While it is possible that deposits of spongolite may now lie beneath the waters of Bass Strait, the only source known today is an old Aboriginal quarry at Rebecca Creek in north-western Tasmania. The presence of these stone tools has led to speculation that Aboriginal watercraft may have been driven by winds and currents to King Island from either the Tasmanian mainland or Hunter Island, which was regularly being visited by the Aborigines from around 2,500 years BP.[41] It is a plausible explanation, but it was also a virtual death sentence for the castaways, whose chances of returning home were virtually nil.

A very different picture emerges on Flinders Island at the opposite end of Bass Strait. Shell middens provide mute evidence that a relict population did indeed remain on the island long after it was severed by rising seas from the Tasmanian mainland. By 4,500 years BP, however, they had disappeared, their fate just as mysterious as the (possible) King Island castaways. While there may have been sufficient food resources to sustain a small population, the availability of fresh water would have presented serious problems. Flinders Island was – and still is – subject to drought in the summer months, with Pats River the only reliable source of fresh water. The disappearance of the Flinders Islanders coincided with an arid climatic phase, so it is quite within the realm of possibility that it was during this time that Pats River temporarily dried up. If the population had already been below the sustainable threshold of 500 individuals (which appears likely) they were already under serious threat of extinction.[42] Nor was the wholesale abandonment of the island an option. Watercraft only appeared in Tasmania within the last few thousand years, and their use was restricted to the south and north-west coasts of Tasmania. In the east they were found no further north than Maria Island,[43] so on the balance of probabilities the population of Flinders Island almost certainly slid into extinction.

It was anything but oblivion on the Tasmanian mainland, where the Aboriginal people coalesced into nine socio-political entities with different cultures and language during the Holocene.⁴⁴ While they are often referred to in the literature as 'tribes', these groups were far more loose-knit than any formal tribal division. In turn, they comprised two smaller social units. At the most basic level was the nuclear and extended family of anywhere from two to a dozen or more individuals. A number of these families periodically came together to form bands, perhaps as many as eighty to 100 people at any one time. The boundaries of their combined territory was delineated by topographical features such as rivers and ranges, and varied in extent from 500 to 750 square kilometres. As in the more densely-populated areas of southern Victoria, bands were led by mature men who had distinguished themselves in various ways, particularly through hunting and/or fighting.⁴⁵

How many bands existed in Tasmania prior to the arrival of Europeans has been the subject of considerable debate. Using the journals of George Augustus Robinson, who travelled the length and breadth of Tasmania in the late 1820s and 1830s 'conciliating' the Aboriginal people, Brian Plomley surmised there were probably around forty-six bands in existence. Rhys Jones, on the other hand, considered this figure too conservative, insisting there may have been as many as seventy to eighty-five bands scattered throughout Tasmania.⁴⁶ This could be a more realistic figure, as Robinson was informed by his Aboriginal assistants that a number of bands had disappeared prior to permanent British settlement in 1803 – possibly as a consequence of deadly infectious diseases unwittingly introduced by early European mariners.⁴⁷ This, of course, makes it extremely difficult to estimate the total pre-contact Aboriginal population. Archaeological evidence has also suggested that the population increased substantially within the last two or three thousand years, the Tasmanian Aborigines expanding their social universe to exploit new environments, including offshore islands.⁴⁸ For all the uncertainty, it is generally agreed that the Aboriginal population probably numbered somewhere between 4,000 and 5,000 by the late eighteenth century.⁴⁹ This was a density comparable to the richest coastal and riverine environments of mainland Australia's south-east.⁵⁰

Tasmanian Aboriginal society was strictly patriarchal, and with only rare exceptions marriage was monogamous. Partners generally married in their late teens from outside their own band, and although the custom was for wives to take up residence with the husband, it was not unusual for a man to join his intended bride's band in order to gain the consent of her parents. In some instances they remained with the wife's band after marriage.[51] Both men and women were scarified with cicatrices to signify the band to which they belonged. The outer skin of the neck, torso and upper limbs was cut with a sharp instrument, and ochre, fat and wood ash rubbed into the wounds to leave permanently raised scars, the pattern replicated on both sides of the body.[52] Unlike their mainland counterparts, there is no record of the Tasmanians having practised tooth avulsion, circumcision or sub-incision.[53] Nor did the Tasmanian Aborigines clothe themselves with warm possum-skin cloaks as on mainland Australia. Tasmanian wearing apparel was limited to a kangaroo or wallaby skin cape draped over the shoulder, a basic covering more commonly used by women.[54] In some instances kangaroo and wallaby skin covers were also used to protect injured feet.[55] In coastal areas both men and women adorned themselves with shell necklaces,[56] and they often smeared their bodies with powdered charcoal, ochre and seal fat. This was only partly decorative, as it had the added effect of insulating their bodies against the cold.[57] Hairstyles were gender-based. Women had short cropped hair, while the men usually wore their hair long, often wound into ringlets and coated with ochre.[58]

The dwellings of the Tasmanian Aborigines differed on a regional basis, with basic shelters and windbreaks often sufficient in the milder climate of the east coast. In the south and south-east semi-permanent huts were built during adverse weather conditions, while in the west and north-west sophisticated beehive-like structures were constructed as protection against the harsher climatic elements. Some of these dwellings were up to five metres in diameter and two metres in height, and capable of accommodating up to a dozen people. The walls consisted of three layers of material. Wooden hoops were first thatched with rushes and covered with grass packing, with the outer layer consisting of peppermint bark. A narrow entrance, usually only a metre or so in height, could be closed off with a bark door, and the floors were frequently excavated to protect resting occupants from any draughts.[59] A touch of aestheticism was often present in the form of bark paintings depicting animals, humans and cosmic bodies, the skill in execution impressing early European observers.[60]

Although the painting of cave walls and rock-shelters may not have been a particularly common activity, the Tasmanian Aborigines were adept at inscribing intricate patterns in tree trunks.[61] Dendroglyphs, however, are more commonly associated with the Aboriginal people of New South Wales and south-east Queensland. Not so inscriptions in stone, with petroglyphs found across wide areas of the Australian mainland as well as Tasmania, where they are largely restricted to the north and north-west. Only a few are known from the east coast. Some of the Tasmanian petroglyphs feature lines, although the majority of those in the north-west consist of concentric circles and may have been linked to religious practises.[62]

Tasmanian Aboriginal cosmology is poorly understood, much of it recorded by European catechists who were attempting to replace Aboriginal spiritual beliefs with their own Christian doctrine.[63] While a number of creation myths are known, only one has been documented in any detail. This relates to the creation of the first man, Parlevar, by an ancestral being named Moihernee. Unfortunately, Parlevar lacked joints in his legs and was equipped with a tail, imperfections that were rectified by Droemerdeen, another ancestral being, who later fought in the heavens with Moihernee. The latter was defeated and fell to earth, where he lived at Cox's Bight in south-west Tasmania. He was followed down by his wife who lived in the adjacent sea, and when Moihernee died he turned into stone. Julia Clark noted how this myth draws together ancestral beings, people and land.[64] Moihernee's victorious combatant, Droemerdeen is known to have been associated with the star Canopus, and many other stars had a connection with people and animals. The Aborigines at Cape Portland in north-eastern Tasmania believed that certain stars in the Milky Way created rivers, while others produced fire. Earth's lunar satellite also featured prominently in a number of ceremonies, which only took place during the phase of the full moon.[65]

Unlike mainland Australia there is no record of initiation ceremonies, but nor can it be assumed that many Tasmanian ceremonies were merely

Tasmania: An Isolated Trajectory

leisure activities as the Tasmanian historian, Brian Plomley, believed. George Augustus Robinson documented a dance performed by women which appears to have paid homage to fire spirits,[66] while the meaning behind numerous others was no doubt beyond the comprehension of European observers. That said, quite a number of songs and dances performed at night celebrated natural phenomena, known examples including the kangaroo and emu dances and, in the post-contact period, the horse dance.[67] Although both sexes participated in dances, it was women who provided most of the vocal accompaniment, with the musical arrangement consisting of beating two sticks in time or on rolled kangaroo skins.[68] Song and dance were also political devices. They were often used to express defiance as a prelude to armed aggression or, alternatively, to re-establish cordial relations following a violent confrontation between groups. Composers of songs and dances were accorded high status, a ranking which also applied to gifted storytellers, some of whom could keep their audience enthralled for hours. Wooraddy and Eumarrah exerted considerable influence over their respective bands, and it could be relevant that both men were renowned storytellers.[69]

Death was marked by long periods of grieving during which dirges were sung in the mornings. In southern Tasmania the spirits of the dead were believed to return to the heavens, while in the north they were held to live on the islands of Bass Strait.[70] Although there have been unsubstantiated reports that the Tasmanian Aborigines buried their dead in the ground or lodged their remains in hollow trees, the usual practice was cremation. Bones and ashes were frequently kept by relatives to ward off evil spirits and for healing,[71] though there are known burial grounds – including one near Ross in the Midlands – where the cremated remains were later interred.[72]

In life the Tasmanians certainly had a less sophisticated toolkit than mainland Aborigines, but this should not be seen as evidence of cultural regression. Notwithstanding their appearance on mainland Australia before the flooding of the Bassian Plain, there is no evidence that boomerangs or spear-throwers were ever used in Tasmania. Despite this absence the Tasmanian toolkit was more than sufficient to cater for daily sustenance. Stone flakes and hand-held hatchets continued to be used right throughout the Holocene, though they diminished in size when superior raw material was used in their manufacture. The best stone tools were made from spongolite, which was quarried in the north-west and exchanged down the west coast and across part of northern Tasmania.[73] Hornfels was the most easily-accessible material in south-eastern Tasmania.[74] High-quality stone tools were treated with the greatest care, often sheathed with bark and carried in specially-woven baskets. It has also been noted that there were slight regional differences in the shape and cutting edges of stone tools regardless of the material used to make them.[75]

The existence of stone-and-mortar implements hint at the possibility of seed-grinding, particularly as these items were quite distinct from the ballwattener stones used to grind ochre.[76] Just as on mainland Australia, ochre – haematite – was held in high regard by the Tasmanians and extensively exchanged throughout the island.[77] As could only be expected, wooden utensils and weapons were an essential part of the toolkit. The most lethal were the fighting and hunting spears of the men, some of which were up to three metres in length. Made from either tea-tree or dogwood, they were hard and flexible, with the point sharpened with a chert tool and then fire-hardened. The shafts were straightened by alternately heating them over a fire and bending between clenched teeth. Although thrown by hand they were extremely accurate up to sixty metres, with a maximum range in the order of ninety metres. Spears were launched at the centre of gravity which, given the unequal diameter of the shaft, was around one-third of the way behind the sharpened point.[78] These formidable weapons were more than a match for European muskets during the frontier conflict of the early nineteenth century.[79]

Another important wooden implement used by men for both hunting and fighting was a waddy around sixty centimetres in length. The handle was roughened to provide a good grip, while the heavier end was worked into a bulging point. Sometimes held in the hand to strike an opponent, the waddy was also thrown with a rotary motion, often to down flying birds. Stones were regularly thrown with accuracy when

Tasmania: An Isolated Trajectory

hunting or fighting, and wooden stakes similarly served a dual purpose. After being charred to resist decay, the shafts were buried in the ground with their sharpened ends projecting up to sixty centimetres to wound kangaroos and wallabies – or human enemies.[80]

George Augustus Robinson recorded two ingenious traps consisting of small grass blinds. They were erected beside a flat rock on which was placed a fish weighted down with a stone. As crows landed for a tempting feast they were seized and killed by the concealed hunter, a fate shared by ducks when worms were the proffered bait.[81] Hunting large game was the preserve of men, while women and children collected plant foods, insects and smaller animals. Unlike mainland Australia, it was the women who ascended trees with grass ropes to procure possums.[82] On the coast women also harvested most of the marine resources, including seals. A small group of women would swim out to a colony and patiently imitate the seals before suddenly rising and clubbing a number of animals to death. When diving for molluscs such as abalone the women equipped themselves with a spatula to prise the shells from the rocks. This implement was between twenty and thirty centimetres long with a chisel-shaped end, and on land it was useful for stripping bark and digging ochre. Women made two different types of baskets from vegetable fibre, one having a close-knit weave, the other larger mesh.[83] While abalone shells sufficed for drinking water, women also fashioned water carriers from the fronds of kelp, and it was they who did most of the cooking.[84]

Not surprisingly, Tasmanian women were adept swimmers, and it appears to have been only within the last 3,000 years that the Tasmanian Aborigines invented their own style of watercraft to reoccupy or exploit offshore islands. As mentioned previously, however, these craft were restricted in their distribution. They consisted of either reed or bark bundles bound with vegetable fibre, the central bundle providing much of the buoyancy, with one or two outer bundles acting as stabilisers. Up to three metres in length and bearing an upturned bow and stern, the largest of these craft were capable of carrying up to ten passengers. They were propelled by a long pole rather than paddles, and in deeper water the pole was pushed through the water or the canoe was pulled along by swimmers on either side. By this means the Tasmanian Aborigines were able to cross considerable stretches of water, regularly visiting the remote Maatsuyker Island off the south-west coast to exploit seals and muttonbirds.[85]

On land the most valuable asset of the Aborigines was fire. Like their mainland counterparts, the Tasmanians developed strategic fire regimes for a variety of purposes. As well as hunting, fire was also essential for warmth. It was used for cooking, as a means of communication, to regenerate grasslands, and to clear vegetation around campsites, along pathways and the surrounds of foraging areas.[86] Much of the Tasmanian landscape was radically altered by anthropogenic burning, and early European mariners seldom failed to comment on the extensive tracts of coastal land they saw ablaze.[87] Yet strangely, a long-held myth was that the Tasmanians were incapable of producing fire themselves, relying instead on lightning strikes and other natural phenomena. This served to explain why the Aborigines were seldom without smouldering fire-sticks of rotten wood or twists of bark.[88] The genesis of the myth probably lies in the writings of George Augustus Robinson, who on one occasion was informed by his Aboriginal guides that extinguishment of their fire-sticks would force them to subsist on raw food until they encountered other Aborigines who would share this vital resource.[89] Not for the first time Robinson appears to have been the victim of deception and the fact that corpses were usually cremated should have warned against this fallacious belief. Yet it was not until 1973 that it was first seriously challenged by Gisela Volger.

Examining the journals of early French mariners, Volger noticed their frequent references to flint-like stone and tinder in woven baskets at Aboriginal campsites. Both had been carefully wrapped in grass and soft bark to keep them dry, and the Frenchmen were in no doubt that the Tasmanians used them for making fire through the percussion method. Chert, rather than flint, was not the only available material, as quartz is equally effective for striking sparks.[90] Conversely, later claims that the Tasmanians may have also used wooden fire-drills or saws to create fire remain highly-questionable.[91] Given the generally damp climate of Tasmania it is not surprising that the Aborigines relied heavily on

Tasmania: An Isolated Trajectory

firesticks as a matter of convenience. It does need to be said, however, that during prolonged periods of wet weather the loss of a fire source would have had serious consequences – at least on a temporary basis.

This raises the question of food, which underlay much of the seasonal movement of the Aboriginal people. It has often been assumed that the majority of the Tasmanians wintered on the coast, but this, too, has proved somewhat contentious. Betty Hiatt's detailed study of Tasmanian Aboriginal economies has shown that many inland resources were exploited throughout the year according to their availability. Movement inland irrespective of the season may also have been triggered by important social imperatives such as ceremonies and the exchange of commodities.[92] Archaeological evidence has confirmed that at least one group – the Ben Lomond people – spent the greater part of the year in the forests of Tasmania's north-east.[93] So while many probably did congregate on the coast during the winter months, others did not.

Combing through early European accounts, Hiatt catalogued an extensive range of animal foods. Kangaroos, wallabies, bandicoots, possums, wombats, native rodents and platypus were all part of the Aboriginal diet. So, too, were echidnas and eastern quolls,[94] but there is no record of any of Tasmania's three largest carnivores – the thylacine, Tasmanian devil and tiger quoll, being targeted as a food source. The problem is compounded by the writings of George Augustus Robinson, whose Aboriginal guides claimed 'they had speared plenty' of thylacines without explicitly stating whether they ate them.[95] While in pursuit of the Big River people in November 1831, however, Robinson and his guides stumbled on a thylacine lair. While the female escaped, her three pups were killed and 'Umarrah and his wife carried away the carcases of those animals and purposed eating them'.[96] No mention is made of the Tasmanian devil or tiger quoll.

On the coast seals and beached whales were certainly important components of the Aboriginal larder, as were muttonbirds, penguins and pelicans. Other avian fauna targeted by Aboriginal hunters included swans, ducks, crows, native hens, pigeons and the extinct Tasmanian emu. In addition to seagulls, the eggs of all these birds were gathered when available,[97] but with the exception of bluetongue lizards the

Tasmanians refrained from hunting reptiles and amphibians.[98] Molluscs, on the other hand, became a very significant resource. Harvesting was limited to inter-tidal species, crabs and barnacles until around 3,700 years BP, at which point in time the exploitation of sub-littoral species began. This systemic change in the coastal economies also embraced lobsters (crayfish),[99] though whether scale-fish continued to feature in the Tasmanian diet has been the subject of considerable discussion.

In 1965 Rhys Jones began excavating two caves at Rocky Cape on the north-west coast of Tasmania. The lowest levels dating back to 8,000 years BP contained a large quantity of fish bones representing thirty-one different species, all of which were (and still are) most effectively caught using baited box-traps with funnel-shaped entrances. Neither spears, nets, line and hook would have been useful for catching any of the species found in the Aboriginal middens. From the amount of bones Jones concluded that scale-fish had been an extremely significant component of the coastal economy, but between 3,400–3,800 years BP the percentage of fish bones steadily dwindled before disappearing altogether.[100] That reduction was paralleled by bone tools, suggesting a correlation between the two. Later archaeological excavations elsewhere also served to demonstrate that the disappearance of fish bones and bone tools at Rocky Cape was not simply a regional phenomenon; it occurred at many other sites around the Tasmanian coast at roughly the same time.[101] While the abandonment of bone tools still awaits an adequate explanation, the apparent loss of scale-fish from the Aboriginal diet has given rise to a number of interesting hypotheses.

Coupled with their reduced toolkit, Jones questioned whether lengthy isolation had led to cultural regression, dooming the Tasmanian Aborigines to 'a slow strangulation of the mind?'[102] Other archaeologists were not so sure. Both David Horton and Sandra Bowdler queried the significance of scale-fish as a food source,[103] a line of reasoning resurrected more recently by Peter Hiscock, who argued that scale-fish probably only constituted between five and ten per cent of the coastal diet.[104] Both Harry Allen and, later, Josephine Flood, took a different tack, insisting that the abandonment of scale-fish had been a sensible decision when the climate briefly cooled and the pursuit of high-energy foods such as seals and seabirds became essential.[105] A novel approach was taken by Tim Flannery, who suggested the disappearance of scale-fish may have been due to mass-poisoning caused by the dinoflagellate bloom known as 'red tide'. Mass poisonings from this source are certainly not unknown, but it is difficult to see how this could have taken place at such widely-separated locations at roughly the same time. To link this with the disappearance of bone tools, Flannery insisted that specialist toolmakers could have been among the many victims.[106] For all its originality, this line of reasoning does tend to stretch the bounds of credibility a little too far.

To provide support for his original abandonment theory, Rhys Jones drew heavily on ethnographic accounts by early Europeans. In 1777 William Anderson, a member of James Cook's third and final expedition to the Pacific, had been surprised to see the Bruny Islanders recoil in horror when offered elephant fish. Cook himself mentioned that the Aboriginal people of Adventure Bay refused scale-fish presented to them as a gift, but it could be relevant that they declined everything else, including bread, iron and fishhooks. In 1792 William Bligh examined Aboriginal middens at Adventure Bay and found the remains of shells and crayfish, but no fish bones or scales. The following year members of Tobias D'Entrecasteaux's expedition similarly found 'no debris of fishes' at any Aboriginal campsites they inspected. In 1802 the Tasmanians made signs to Nicolas Baudin they did not eat scale-fish, although they willingly accepted a stingray from Emmanuel Hamelin, captain of one of Baudin's two vessels. The following day the stingray was found on a beach minus its liver, and Hamelin recalled that the liver of these cartilaginous fish had also been relished by the Aborigines at Shark Bay in Western Australia.[107] After embarking on a fishing expedition of their own one calm night, some of Baudin's crew observed the Aborigines 'fishing' along the shore with torches. Unfortunately, they were unable to see exactly what the Aborigines were after. While torchlight certainly attracts scale-fish, and is used in conjunction with spears to catch flounder in Tasmania today,[108] it also lures edible invertebrates such as squid. But there was at least one early mariner who made a contrary observation. In 1792 Lieutenant Le Dez, an officer on Marion Dufresne's expedition visiting Marion and North Bays in southern Tasmania, recorded fish bones and burnt shells at Aboriginal camps. An experienced mariner, it is unlikely that Le Dez confused fish bones with the remains of crayfish or any other animal among the camp detritus.[109]

Later European observers were mixed in their assessment as to whether or not the Tasmanian Aborigines consumed scale-fish. In May 1833 George Augustus Robinson recorded in his journal that while Aboriginal women accompanying the 'Friendly Mission' enjoyed fishing with hook and line they did not eat the catch; they gave it to Robinson and his son instead.[110] On the other hand, Robinson's nephew, James Young, stated that Aboriginal people exiled on Flinders Island regularly caught wrasse and bluefish with fishing tackle and, importantly, ate what they caught. In 1832 the Ordinance Office in Hobart regularly supplied fishing tackle to the Aboriginal settlement.[111]

Examining the papers of Ernest Westlake, an English collector of Aboriginal artifacts who toured Tasmania in 1908–1909, Rebe Taylor uncovered a number of references from old settlers and their descendants who were adamant the Aborigines included scale-fish in their diet. Perhaps the telling point is that two of them informed Westlake that while the Aborigines had no hesitation consuming scale-fish caught by themselves, they refused to accept any from Europeans, believing it might be harmful.[112] While it could be that the capture of scale-fish followed carefully-prescribed rituals, this belief can also account for the rejection of scale-fish offered by early European mariners. The descendants of the Aborigines who remained on the Bass Strait islands and formed a distinct community also ate scale-fish on a regular basis, though whether this can be accepted as evidence of cultural continuity as Taylor insists, or an aspect of their European heritage, is somewhat problematic.[113]

Ian McFarlane has identified stone fish traps in north-western Tasmania which appear to be of Aboriginal origin, and he has suggested a number of possibilities to account for the absence of fish bones from Aboriginal middens since 3,500 years BP. They could, for instance, have been destroyed by fire, dispersed by scavenging seabirds and Tasmanian devils, or it could even be that the Aborigines had simply begun cooking

Tasmania: An Isolated Trajectory

their catch elsewhere. For example, food preparation sites below the high-tide level would have eliminated all trace of any meals.[114]

It nonetheless seems to have been more than a coincidence that fish bones disappeared from coastal middens at the very time the Aborigines commenced exploiting sub-tidal molluscs and crustaceans. This obvious systemic change in coastal economies was not reflected on land, where vegetable foods were probably less significant in the Tasmanian Aboriginal diet when compared with most regions on the Australian mainland. Despite that, it does need to be borne in mind that while Tasmania is relatively depauperate in edible plant foods, there is a distinct lack of information regarding Aboriginal ethnobotany. The estimation that vegetable foods comprised barely eight per cent of the total diet in eastern Tasmania, rising to twenty per cent in the west, can only remain conjectural at best,[115] and given the colder, wetter conditions of the west coast as opposed to the more moderate eastern districts it could be expected that this trend would be quite the reverse.

Notwithstanding the paucity of ethnographic accounts, impressive lists of plant foods known to have been utilised by the Tasmanians have been compiled by researchers. They included roots, seeds, fruits, vegetables and such other produce as grass tree shoots, seaweed and fungi.[116] A heavy reliance on fatty animal foods still required at least some plant foods for a well-balanced diet and general well-being. Sweeteners were also available in the form of banksia nectar and manna gum sap, and it is known that the Big River people (and probably other groups) accessed the Central Plateau to drink the fermented sap of the cider gum (*Eucalyptus gunnii*), the only alcoholic beverage known to any Australian Aborigines before the arrival of Europeans.[117] That the Tasmanians ate well is supported by an apparent absence of serious endemic illnesses until contact with Europeans.

Early mariners and British settlers did record of number of maladies among the Tasmanian Aborigines, including ulceration of the legs, which might have been the bacterial infection known as yaws. Interestingly, yaws offers some protection from syphilis, and although gonorrhoea caused a high rate of infertility among Aboriginal women in the post-contact period, the incidence of other sexually-transmitted diseases was comparatively low in Tasmania.[118] Other documented medical disorders were a cancerous sore on an elderly woman, a young girl afflicted with spasms, an adolescent girl with an undeveloped left breast, and another whose lameness was possibly due to a congenital dislocation of the hip. There was a single case of cataracts.[119] In 1777 members of James Cook's expedition were entertained by a red-haired hunchback who had probably been born with a defective vertebral column. Noted for his wit and humour, this man was still living happily eleven years later when William Bligh returned to Adventure Bay.[120] Red hair is an extremely rare mutation among Tasmanian Aborigines – so rare, in fact, that only one other case is known.[121]

So while the Tasmanians were in generally good health at the time of contact with outsiders, the same cannot be said for the post-contact period. As can only be expected of a virgin soil population, introduced diseases had a particularly devastating impact and, as mentioned earlier, at least some Tasmanian bands disappeared soon after the arrival of early European mariners. There can be little doubt they fell victim to a deadly epidemic which had been unwittingly brought ashore. Unfortunately, that was just the beginning of a series of catastrophic events which were replicated on the mainland of Australia. Disease, colonisation, dispossession and violence on the frontier were to irrevocably shatter the Indigenous antipodean societies forever.

BIBLIOGRAPHY

BOOKS

Berndt, R. and C. Berndt with J. Stanton, *A World That Was: The Yaraldi of the Murray River and the Lakes, South Australia* (Melbourne: Miegunyah Press, 1993).
Berndt, R. and C. Berndt, *The World of the First Australians: Aboriginal Traditional Life Past and Present* (Canberra: Aboriginal Studies Press, 1999).
Brimfield, B., *Long Trek South: A Search for the History of the Palaeolithic Tasmanians* (Mowbray, Tas: Self-published, 2010).
Brown, A., *Ill-Starred Captains: Flinders and Baudin* (Fremantle, WA: Fremantle Arts Centre Press, 2004).
Bryson, B., *A Short History of Nearly Everything* (London: Doubleday, 2003).
Butlin, N., *Economics of the Dreamtime: A Hypothetical History* (Cambridge: Cambridge University Press, 1993).
Calder, G., *Levee, Line and Martial Law: A History of the Dispossession of the Mairremmener People of Van Diemen's Land 1803–1832* (Launceston, Tas: Fullers Bookshop, 2010).
Celoria, F., *Archaeology* (New York: Grosset & Dunlap, 1973).
Chaloupka, G., *Journey in Time: The World's Longest Continuous Art Tradition* (Chatswood, NSW: Reed, 1993).
Clode, D., *Prehistoric giants: the megafauna of Australia* (Melbourne: Museum Victoria, 2009).
Constable, G. et. al, *The Neanderthals* (New York: Time-Life, 1973).
Day, D., *The Doomsday Book of Animals: A Natural History of Vanished Species* (New York: Viking Press, 1981).
Dortch, C.E., *Devils Lair: A search for Ancient Man in Western Australia* (Perth: Western Australian Museum Press, 1976).
Dortch, C.E., *Devil's Lair: a study in prehistory* (Perth: Western Australian Museum, 1984).
du Cross, H., *Much More than Stones and Bones: Australian Archaeology in the Late Twentieth Century* (Carlton South, Vic: Melbourne University Press, 2002).
El Mallakh, K. and A. Brackman, *The Gold of Tutankhamen* (New York: Newsweek Books, 1978).
Flannery, T., *The Future Eaters: An ecological history of the Australasian lands and people* (Sydney: Reed New Holland, 1999).
Flood, J., *The Moth Hunters: Aboriginal Prehistory of the Australian Alps* (Canberra: Australian Institute of Aboriginal Studies, 1980).
Flood, J., *Archaeology of the Dreamtime: the story of prehistoric Australia and its people* (Sydney: Collins Australia, 1989).

Flood, J., *The Riches of Ancient Australia: A Journey into Prehistory* (St Lucia, Qld: University of Queensland Press, 1990).
Flood, J., *Archaeology of the Dreamtime: The story of prehistoric Australia and its people* (Pymble, NSW: Angus & Robertson, 1992).
Flood, J., *Rock Art of the Dreamtime: Images of Ancient Australia* (Pymble, NSW: Angus & Robertson, 1997).
Flood, J., *Archaeology of the Dreamtime: the story of prehistoric Australia and its people* (Marleston, SA: J.B. Publishing, 2004).
Flood, J., *The Original Australians* (Crows Nest, NSW: Allen & Unwin, 2006).
Gammage, B., *The Biggest Estate on Earth: How Aborigines Made Australia* (Crows Nest, NSW: Allen & Unwin, 2011).
Gere, C., *Knossos and the Prophets of Modernism* (Chicago: University of Chicago Press, 2009).
Heizer, R. (ed.), *The Archaeologist at Work: A Source Book in Archaeological Method and Interpretation* (New York: Harper and Brothers, 1959).
Hiscock, P., *The Archaeology of Ancient Australia* (London: Routledge, 2008).
Historical Records of Australia, Vol.1, Ser.1.
Holdaway, S. and N. Stern, *A Record in Stone: The Study of Australia's Flaked Stone Artefacts* (Melbourne: Museum Victoria and Aboriginal Studies Press, 2008).
Holden, R. and N. Holden, *Bunyips: Australia's folklore of fear* (Canberra: National Library of Australia, 2001).
Horton, D., *Recovering the Tracks: The Story of Australian Archaeology* (Canberra: Aboriginal Studies Press, 1991).
Isaacs, J., *Bush Food: Aboriginal Food and Herbal Medicine* (Sydney: Ure Smith, 1991).
Jenkin, G., *Conquest of the Ngarrindjeri* (Adelaide: Rigby, 1985).
Johanson, D. and J. Shreeve, *Lucy's Child: The Discovery of a Human Ancestor* (London: Penguin, 1991).
Johnson, M. and I. McFarlane, *Van Diemen's Land: An Aboriginal History* (Sydney: New South Wales University Press, 2015).
Kamp, W., *Charles Darwin and the Origin of Species* (London: Cassell, 1968).
Leakey, L.S.B., *By the Evidence: Memoirs, 1903–1972* (New York: Harcourt Brace Jovanovich, 1974).
Leakey, R., *The Making of Mankind* (London: Michael Joseph, 1981).
Lewin, R., *Human Evolution: An Illustrated Introduction* (New York: W.H. Freedman and Company, 1985).
Lewin, R., *Bones of Contention: Controversies in the Search for Human Origins* (New York: Simon & Schuster, 1987).
Long, J. et. al., *Prehistoric Mammals of Australia and New Guinea: One Hundred Million Years of Evolution* (Sydney: University of New South Wales Press, 2002).
Lourandos, H., *Continent of Hunter-Gatherers: New Perspectives in Australian Prehistory* (Cambridge: Cambridge University Press, 1997).
Mathew, J., *Eaglehawk and Crow: A study of the Australian Aborigines including an inquiry into their origin and a survey of Australian languages* (London: David Nutt, 1899).
McFarlane, I., *Beyond Awakening: The Aboriginal Tribes of North West Tasmania – A History* (Launceston, Tas: Fullers Bookshop, 2008).
Memmott, P., *Gunyah Goondie + Wurley: The Aboriginal Architecture of*

Bibliography

Australia (St Lucia, Qld: University of Queensland Press, 2007).
Merrick, J. and G. Schmida, *Australian Freshwater Fishes: Biology and Management* (North Ryde, NSW: School of Biological Sciences, Macquarie University, 1984).
Moorehead, A., *Darwin and the Beagle* (New York: Harper & Row, 1970).
Moorehead, A., *The Fatal Impact: The Invasion of the South Pacific 1767–1840* (Sydney: Mead and Beckett, 1987).
Morwood, M. and P. van Oosterzee, *The Discovery of the Hobbit: The Scientific Breakthrough that Changed the Face of Human History* (Milsons Point, NSW: Random House, 2007).
Mulvaney, D.J., *Encounters in Place: Outsiders and Aboriginal Australians 1606–1985* (St Lucia, Qld: University of Queensland Press, 1989).
Mulvaney, J. and J. Kamminga, *Prehistory of Australia* (St Leonards, NSW: Allen & Unwin, 1999).
Mulvaney, J., *Digging Up A Past* (Sydney: University of New South Wales Press, 2011).
Palmer, D. (ed.), *The Marshall Illustrated Encyclopedia of Dinosaurs and Prehistoric Animals* (London: Marshall Editions, 1999).
Petrie, C., *Tom Petrie's Reminiscences of Early Queensland* (Brisbane: Watson, Ferguson & Co., 1904).
Piggott, S., *Approach to Archaeology* (London: Adam & Charles Black, 1960).
Plomley, N.J.B., *The Baudin Expedition and the Tasmanian Aborigines 1802* (Hobart: Blubber Head Press, 1983).
Plomley, N.J.B., *Jorgen Jorgenson and the Aborigines of Van Diemen's Land: being a reconstruction of his 'lost' book on their customs and habits, and on his role in the Roving Parties and the Black Line* (Hobart: Blubber Head Press, 1991).
Plomley, B [N.J.B.], *The Tasmanian Aborigines* (Launceston, Tas: Plomley Foundation, 1993).
Plomley, N.J.B. (ed.), *Friendly Mission: The Tasmanian Journals and Papers of George Augustus Robinson 1829–1834* (Launceston, Tas: Queen Victorian Museum and Art Gallery and Quintus Publishing, 2008).
Poirer, F. and J. McKee, *Understanding Human Evolution* (Upper Saddle River, NJ: Prentice Hall, 1999).
Relethford, J., *The Human Species: An Introduction to Biological Anthropology* (Mountain View, Cal: Mayfield Publishing Company, 1997).
Renfrew, C. and P. Bahn, *Archaeology: Theories, Methods, and Practice* (London: Thomas and Hudson, 1996).
Reynolds, H., *The Other Side of the Frontier: Aboriginal resistance to the European invasion of Australia* (Ringwood, Vic: Penguin, 1995).
Roberts, A., *The Incredible Human Journey: The Story of How We Colonised the Planet* (London: Bloomsbury Publishing, 2009).
Rolls, M. and M. Johnson, *Historical Dictionary of Australian Aborigines* (Lanham, MD: Rowman and Littlefield, 2019).
Roth, H. Ling, *The Aborigines of Tasmania* (Halifax, UK: F. King & Sons, 1899).
Roughley, T.C., *Fish and Fisheries of Australia* (Sydney: Angus and Robertson, 1966).
Ryan, L., *The Aboriginal Tasmanians* (Crows Nest, NSW: Allen & Unwin, 1996).
Schmida, G., *Australian Freshwater Fishes: Biology and Management* (North

Ryde, NSW: School of Biological Sciences, Macquarie University, 1984).
Shackley, M., *Neanderthal Man* (London: Gerald Duckworth & Co., 1980).
Shipman, P., *The Man Who Found the Missing Link: Eugene Dubois and His Lifelong Quest to Prove Darwin Right* (New York: Simon & Schuster, 2001).
Singe, J., *The Torres Strait: People and History* (St Lucia, Qld: University of Queensland Press, 1989).
Stanbury, P. and G. Phipps, *Australia's Animals Discovered* (Sydney: Pergamon Press, 1980).
Stringer, C. and C. Gamble, *In Search of the Neanderthals: solving the puzzle of human origins* (London: Thomas Hudson, 1993).
Tattersall, I., *The Strange Case of the Rickety Cossack and Other Cautionary Tales from Human Evolution* (New York: Palgrave Macmillan, 2015).
Tonkinson, R., *The Mardu Aborigines: Living the Dream in Australia's Desert* (Fort Worth, TX: Holt, Rinehart and Winston, 1991).
Trigger, B., *A History of Archaeological Thought* (Cambridge: Cambridge University Press, 1990).
Troughton, E., *Furred Animals of Australia* (Sydney: Angus & Robertson, 1967).
Tudge, C., *The Link: Uncovering Our Earliest Ancestor* (London: Little, Brown, 2009).
Tuniz, C., R. Gillespie and C. Jones, *The Bone Readers: Atoms, genes and the politics of Australia's deep past* (Crows Nest, NSW: Allen & Unwin, 2009).
Tutt, S. (ed.), *Pioneer Days: Stories and Photographs of European Settlement Between the Pine and the Noosa Rivers, Queensland* (Caboolture, Qld: Caboolture Historical Society, 1974.
Voigt, A. and N. Drury, *Wisdom From The Earth: The Living Legacy of the Aboriginal Dreamtime* (East Roseville, NSW: Simon & Schuster, 1997).
Von Daniken, E., *In Search of Ancient Gods: My Pictorial Evidence for the Impossible* (London: Corgi Books, 1975).
Walsh, J.E., *Unravelling Piltdown: The Science Fraud of the Century and Its Solution* (New York: The Softback Preview, 1997).
Warren, P., *The Making of the Past: The Aegean Civilizations* (Oxford: Elsevier-Phaidon, 1975).
Webb, S., *The Willandra Lakes Hominids* (Canberra: Department of Prehistory, Research School of Pacific Studies, Australian National University, 1989).
Wendt, H. (trans. R. Winston and C. Winston), *Before the Deluge: The Story of Palaeontology* (London: Victor Gollancz, 1968).
White, J.P. and J.F. O'Connell, *A Prehistory of Australia, New Guinea and Sahul* (North Ryde, NSW: Academic Press, 1982).
White, M. and J. Gribbin, *Darwin: A Life in Science* (London: Simon & Schuster, 1995).
Woodford, J., *The Wollemi Pine: The incredible discovery of a living fossil from the age of dinosaurs* (Melbourne: Text Publishing, 2004).

MONOGRAPHS

Allen, J., 'Peer Review of the Draft Final Archaeological Report and Test Excavation of the Jordan River Levee Site Southern Tasmania', J. Allen

Bibliography

Archaeological Consultancies, 22 October 2010.
Balouet, J.C. and S.L. Olson, 'Fossil Birds from Late Quarternary Deposits in New Caledonia', *Smithsonian Contributions to Zoology*, No.469 (1989).
Coutts, P., R. Frank and P. Hughes, 'Aboriginal Engineers of the Western District, Victoria', *Records of the Victorian Archaeological Survey*, No.7 (June 1978).
Gammage, B., 'Australia Under Aboriginal Management', 15th Barry Andrews Memorial Lecture, Australian Defence Force Academy, Canberra, 31 October 2002.
Lampert, R., *The Great Kartan Mystery: Terra Australis 5* (Canberra: Department of Prehistory, Research School of Pacific Studies, Australian National University, 1981).
Plomley, B. and M. Cameron, 'Plant Foods of the Tasmanian Aborigines', *Records of the Queen Victoria Museum, Launceston*, No.101 (1993).

CHAPTERS

Allen, J. and J.F. O'Connell, 'Getting from Sunda to Sahul', in G. Clark, F. Leach and S. O'Connor (eds), *Islands of Inquiry: Colonisation, Seafaring and the Archaeology of Maritime Landscapes* (Canberra: ANU E Press, 2008), pp.31–46.
Baird, R.F., '*Centropus*: The Giant Coucal', in P.V. Rich and G.F. van Tets (eds), *Kadimakara: Extinct Vertebrates of Australia* (Lilydale, Vic: Pioneer Design Studio, 1985), pp.205–208.
Birdsell, J., 'The Recalibration of a Paradigm for the First Peopling of Greater Australia', in J. Allen, J. Golson and R. Jones (eds), *Sunda and Sahul: Prehistoric Studies in Southeast Asia, Melanesia and Australia* (London: Academic Press, 1977), pp.113–167.
Bowdler, S., 'The Coastal Colonisation of Australia', in J. Allen, J. Golson and R. Jones (eds), *Sunda and Sahul: Prehistoric Studies in Southeast Asia, Melanesia and Australia* (London: Academic Press, 1977), pp.205–246.
Bowdler, S., 'Harry Lourandos' life and work: An Australian archaeological odyssey', in B. David, B. Barker and I. McNiven (eds), *The Social Archaeology of Australian Indigenous Societies* (Canberra: Aboriginal Studies Press, 2006), pp.40–49.
Bulmer, S., 'Waisted blades and axes: A functional interpretation of some early stone tools from Papua New Guinea', in R.V.S. Wright (ed.), *Stone tools as cultural markers: change, evolution and complexity* (Canberra: Australian Institute of Aboriginal Studies, 1977), pp.40–59.
Carter, M., 'North of the Cape and south of the Fly: discovering the archaeology of social complexity in Torres Strait', in D. Bruno, B. Barker and I. McNiven (eds), *The Social Archaeology of Australian Indigenous Societies* (Canberra: Aboriginal Studies Press, 2006), pp.287–303.
Clark, J., 'Devils and Horses: Religion and Creative Life in Tasmanian Aboriginal Society', in M. Roe (ed.), *The Flow of Culture: Tasmanian Studies* (Canberra: Australian Academy of the Humanities, 1987), pp.50–72.
Collett, D., 'Endangered space and Aboriginal settlement on the coast of Tasmania', in S. Sullivan, S. Bockwell and A. Webb (eds), *Archaeology in*

the North: Proceedings of the 1993 Australian Archaeological Association Conference (Darwin: North Australia Research Unit, Australian National University, 1994), pp.341–357.

Dixon, R.M.W., 'Tribes, languages and other boundaries in northeast Queensland', in N. Peterson (ed.), *Tribes and Boundaries in Australia* (Canberra: Australian Institute of Aboriginal Studies, 1976), pp.207–238.

Flood, J., 'Moth Hunters of the Southeastern Highlands', in D.J. Mulvaney and J.P. White (eds), *Australians to 1788* (Broadway, NSW: Fairfax, Syme and Weldon Associates, 1987), pp.275–291.

Guiler, E., 'Tasmanian Devil', in R. Strahan (ed.), *The Australian Museum Book of Australian Mammals* (Sydney: Angus & Robertson, 1983), pp.27–28.

Horton, D., 'Bunya Nuts', in D. Horton (ed.), *The Encyclopaedia of Aboriginal Australia: Vol.1* (Canberra: Aboriginal Studies Press, 1994), pp.165–166.

Horton, D., 'Colonisation', in D. Horton (ed.), *The Encyclopaedia of Aboriginal Australia: Vol.1* (Canberra: Aboriginal Studies Press, 1994), p.212–213.

Jelinek, A., 'Man's Role in the Extinction of Pleistocene Faunas', in P. Martin and H. Wright Jnr (eds), *Pleistocene Extinctions: The Search for a Cause* (New Haven, Conn: Yale University Press, 1967), pp.193–200.

Johnson, M., '"A modified form of whaling": The Moreton Bay dugong fishery 1846–1920', in M. Johnson (ed.), *Moreton Bay Matters* (Brisbane: Brisbane History Group, 2002), pp.27–38.

Jones, R., 'Tasmanian Tribes', Appendix in N. Tindale, *Aboriginal Tribes of Australia: Their Terrain, Environmental Controls, Distribution, Limits, and Proper Names* (Canberra: Australian National University Press, 1974), pp.319–354.

Jones, R., 'The Tasmanian paradox', in R.V.S. Wright (ed.), *Stone tools as cultural markers: change, evolution and complexity* (Canberra: Australian Institute of Aboriginal Studies, 1977), pp.189–204.

Jones, R., 'Hunting Forbears', in M. Roe (ed.), *The Flow of Culture: Tasmanian Studies* (Canberra: Australian Academy of the Humanities, 1987), pp.14–49.

Jones, R., 'The Coming of the Aborigines – A Pleistocene Perspective', in J. Hardy and A. Frost (eds), *Studies from Terra Australis to Australia: No.6* (Canberra: Highland Press in association with the Australian Academy of Humanities, 1989), pp.11–24.

Kowalski, K., 'The Pleistocene Extinction of Mammals in Europe', in P. Martin and H. Wright Jnr (eds), *Pleistocene Extinctions: The Search for a Cause* (New Haven, Conn: Yale University Press, 1967), pp.349–364.

Lampert, R., 'Kangaroo Island and the antiquity of Australians', in R.V.S. Wright (ed.), *Stone tools as cultural markers: change, evolution and complexity* (Canberra: Australian Institute of Aboriginal Studies, 1977), pp.213–218.

Lourandos, H., 'Swamp Managers of Southwestern Victoria', in D.J. Mulvaney and J.P. White (eds), *Australians to 1788* (Broadway, NSW: Fairfax, Syme & Weldon Associates, 1987), pp.293–307.

McDowell, R. and J. Beumer, 'Freshwater Eels', in R. McDowell (ed.), *Freshwater Fishes of South-Eastern Australia* (Terrey Hills, NSW: Reed, 1980), pp.44–47.

McNiven, I., B. David and B. Barker, 'The social archaeology of Indigenous Australia', in B. David, B. Barker and I. McNiven (eds), *The Social*

Bibliography

Archaeology of Australian Indigenous Societies (Canberra: Aboriginal Studies Press, 2006), pp.2–19.
Morwood, M., 'Early hominid occupation of Flores, East Indonesia, and its wider significance', in I. Metcalf, J. Smith, M. Morwood and I. Davidson, *Faunal and Floral Migrations and Evolution in SE Asia-Australia* (Lisse: A.A. Balkema Publishers, 2001), pp.387–398.
Moser, S., 'Building the discipline of Australian archaeology: Fred McCarthy at the Australian Institute of Aboriginal Studies', in M. Sullivan, S. Brockwell and A. Webb (eds), *Archaeology in the North: Proceedings of the 1993 Australian Archaeological Association Conference* (Darwin: North Australia Research Unit, Australian National University, 1994), pp.17–29.
Mulvaney, D.J., 'The End of the Beginning: 6000 years ago to 1788', in D.J. Mulvaney and J.P. White (eds), *Australians to 1788* (Broadway, NSW: Fairfax, Syme & Weldon Associates, 1987), pp.75–113.
Pardoe, C., 'The Pleistocene is still with us: Analytical constraints and possibilities for the study of ancient human remains in archaeology', in M. Smith, M. Spriggs and B. Fankhauser (eds), *Sahul in Review: Pleistocene Archaeology in Australia, New Guinea and Island Melanesia* (Canberra: Department of Prehistory, Research School of Pacific Studies, Australian National University, 1993), pp.81–94.
Senut, B., 'The Earliest Putative Hominids', in W. Henke and I. Tattersall (eds), *Handbook of Paleoanthropology* (New York: Springer-Verlag, 2007), pp.1519–1538.
Shoemaker, A., 'Ancient and modern footprints: music and the mysteries of Lake Mungo', in A. Chan and A. Noble (eds), *Sounds of Translation: Intersections of Music, Technology and Society* (Acton, ACT: ANU E Press, 2009), pp.79–90.
Sim, R., 'Prehistoric human occupation in the King and Furneaux Island regions, Bass Strait', in M. Sullivan, S. Brockwell and A. Webb (eds), *Archaeology in the North: Proceedings of the 1993 Australian Archaeological Association Conference* (Darwin: North Australia Research Unit, Australian National University, 1994), pp.358–374.
Smith, M.J., '*Wonambi naracoortensis* The Giant Australian Python', in P.V. Rich and G.F. van Tets (eds), *Kadimakara: Extinct Vertebrates of Australia* (Lilydale, Vic: Pioneer Design Studio, 1985), pp.156–159.
Taylor, J., 'Aboriginal Languages', in A. Alexander (ed.), *The Companion to Tasmanian History* (Hobart: Centre for Tasmanian Historical Studies, University of Tasmania, 2005), p.3.
Taylor, J., 'Aboriginal Language of Health and Well-being in Van Diemen's Land: Palawa (Tasmanian Aboriginal) Health and Nutrition', in P. Richards, B. Valentine and T. Dunning (eds), *Effecting a Cure: Aspects of Health and Medicine in Launceston* (Launceston, Tas: Myola House of Publishing, 2006), pp.3–18.
Tets, G.F. van, '*Progura gallinacea*: The Australian Giant Megapode', in P.V. Rich and G.F. van Tets (eds), *Kadimakara: Extinct Vertebrates of Australia* (Lilydale, Vic: Pioneer Design Studio, 1985), pp.195–199.
Williams, E., 'Earth mounds in south-west Victoria: What were they used for and how do we know they were cultural features?', in M. Sullivan, S. Brockwell and A. Webb (eds), *Archaeology in the North: Proceedings of the 1993 Australian Archaeological Association Conference* (Darwin:

North Australian Research Unit, Australian National University, 1994), pp.162–166.
Wood, B.A., 'Evolution of australopithecines', in S. Jones, R. Martin and D. Pilbeam (eds), *The Cambridge Encyclopedia of Human Evolution* (Cambridge: Cambridge University Press, 1992), pp.231–240.

ARTICLES

Abdel-Salam, G. and A. Czeizel, 'A Case-Control Etiologic Study of Microcephaly', *Epidemiology*, Vol.11, No.5 (September 2000), pp.571–575.
Aiello, L., 'Five Years of *Homo floresiensis*', *American Journal of Physical Anthropology*, Vol.142, No.2 (June 2010), pp.1–13.
Allen, F.A., 'The Original Range of the Papuan and Negrito Races', *Journal of the Anthropological Institute of Great Britain and Ireland*, Vol.8 (1879), pp.38–50.
Allen, H., 'Reinterpreting the 1969–1972 Willandra Lakes archaeological surveys', *Archaeology in Oceania*, Vol.33, No.3 (October 1998), pp.207–220.
Allen, J., 'Johann Winckelmann: Classicist', *Metropolitan Museum of Art Bulletin*, Vol.17, No.8 (April 1949), pp.228–232.
Allen, J., 'Aspects of V. Gordon Childe', *Labour History*, No.12 (May 1967), pp.52–59.
Alroy, J., 'A Multispecies Overkill Simulation of the End-Pleistocene Megafaunal Mass Extinction', *Science*, Vol.292, No.5523 (8 June 2001), pp.1893–1896.
Altmann, S., 'Baboons, Space, Time, and Energy', *American Zoologist*, Vol.14, No.1 (Winter 1974), pp.221–248.
Anderson, A., 'Faunal collapse, landscape change and settlement history in remote Oceania', *World Archaeology*, Vol.33, No.3 (January 2002), pp.375–390.
Anon, 'The Piltdown Skull', *British Medical Journal*, Vol.2, No.2751 (20 September 1913), p.762.
Anon, 'Prehistoric Man: Skull found in Victoria', *Queenslander* (Brisbane), 1 May 1926, p.11.
Anon, 'Wombat Ham: Pioneers Enjoyed It', *Gippsland Times* (Sale), 16 July 1934, p.4.
Anon, 'The Leakey Footprints: An Uncertain Path', *Science News*, Vol.115, No.13 (31 March 1979), pp.196–197.
Anon, 'The Mossgiel Man', *Australian Archaeology*, No.21 (December 1985), pp.133–138.
Anon, 'A "New" Jaw Reopens Some Old Questions', *National Geographic*, Vol.193, No.4 (April 1998), n.p.
Anon, 'A Miss for Moderns And Neanderthals', *Science*, Vol.300, No.5621 (9 May 2003), pp.893–894.
Anon, 'Dental exam shows Neanderthals cooked veges', *Australian* (Sydney), 29 December 2010, p.3.
Anon, 'Boning up on ancient man's skills', *Courier-Mail* (Brisbane), 17 August 2013, p.43.
Anon., 'Cavemen beat humans in race to feed on birds', *Weekend Australian*

Bibliography

(Sydney), 9–10 August 2014, p.13.
Anon, 'Inland seafarers or good swimmers?', *Koori Mail* (Lismore), 1 July 2015, p.31.
Anon, 'Ancient ape clue to tall story', *Herald Sun* (Melbourne), 8 November 2019, p.27.
Anon, 'Mammoth discovery', *Herald Sun* (Melbourne), 8 November 2019, p.28.
Antón, S.C., W.R. Leonard and M.L. Robertson, 'An ecomorphological model of the initial hominid dispersal from Africa', *Journal of Human Evolution*, Vol.43, No.6 (December 2002), pp.773–785.
Antón, S., 'All who wander are not lost: New hominin cranial fossils highlight the early exploits of *Homo erectus*', *Science*, Vol.368, No.6486 (3 April 2020), pp.34–35.
Appenzeller, T., 'Europe's first artists were Neanderthals: Spanish cave paintings date to before modern humans arrived in region', *Science*, Vol.359, No.6378 (23 February 2018), pp.852–853.
Argue, D. et. al., 'The affinities of *Homo floresiensis* based on phylogenetic analyses of cranial, dental, and postcranial characters', *Journal of Human Evolution*, Vol.107 (June 2017),107–133.
Asmussen, B., '"There is likewise a nut …": A Comparative Ethnohistory of Aboriginal Processing Methods and Consumption of Australian *Bowenia*, *Cycas*, *Lepidozamia* and *Macrozamia* species', *Technical Reports of the Australian Museum*, No.23 (2010), pp.147–163.
Ayala, F., 'The Myth of Eve: Molecular Biology and Human Origins', *Science*, Vol.270, No.5244 (22 December 1995), pp.1930–1936.
Bahn, P., '50,000-year-old Americans of Pedra Furada', *Nature*, Vol.362, No.6416 (11 March 1993), pp.114–115.
Baldry, H.C., 'Who Invented the Golden Age?', *Classical Quarterly*, Vol.2, Nos.1–2 (January–April 1952), pp.83–92.
Balme, J., 'Excavations revealing 40,000 years of occupation at Mimi Caves, south central Kimberley, Western Australia', *Australian Archaeology*, No.51 (December 2000), pp.1–5.
Balme, J. and K. Morse, 'Shell beads and social behaviour in Pleistocene Australia', *Antiquity*, Vol.80, No.310 (December 2006), pp.799–811.
Balter, M., 'Paleoanthropologist Now Rides High On a New Fossil Tide', *Science*, Vol.333, No.6048 (9 September 2011), pp.1373–1375.
Barker, E.R., 'Past Excavations at Herculaneum', *Burlington Magazine for Connoisseurs*, Vol.11, No.51 (June 1907), pp.144–156.
Barlow, N., 'Erasmus Darwin, F.R.S. (1731–1802)', *Notes and Records of the Royal Society of London*, Vol.14, No.1 (June 1959), pp.85–98.
Barr, J., 'Pre-scientific Chronology: The Bible and the Origin of the World', *Proceedings of the American Philosophical Society*, Vol.143, No.3 (September 1999), pp.379–387.
Barton, R.N.E., et. al., 'Gibraltar Neanderthals and results of recent excavations in Gorham's, Vanguard and Ibex Caves', *Antiquity*, Vol.73, No.279 (March 1999), pp.13–23.
Barwick, D., 'Mapping the Past: An Atlas of Victorian Clans 1835–1904 – Part 1', *Aboriginal History*, Vol.8 (1984), pp.100–131.
Bednarik, R., 'Cave Use by Australian Pleistocene Man', *Proceedings of the University of Bristol Spelaeological (Caving) Society*, Vol.17, No.3 (1986), pp.227–245.

Bednarik, R., 'The Initial Peopling of Wallacea and Sahul', *Anthropos*, BD92, H4/6 (1997), pp.355–367.
Begun, D., '*Sivapithecus* is east and *Dryopithecus* is west, and never the twain shall meet', *Anthropological Science*, Vol.113, No.1 (2005), pp.53–64.
Berger, L., *et. al.*, 'Small-Bodied Humans from Palau, Micronesia', *Public Library of Science One*, Vol.3, No.3 (12 March 2008), pp.1–11.
Berger, T. and E. Trinkaus, 'Patterns of Trauma among the Neanderthals', *Journal of Archaeological Science*, Vol.22, No.6 (November 1995), pp.841–852.
Bermudez De Castro, J., *et al.*, 'The Atapuerca Sites and Their Contribution to the Knowledge of Human Evolution in Europe', *Evolutionary Anthropology*, Vol.13, No.1 (15 February 2004), pp.25–41.
Bickel, L., 'Ancient man in Kow Swamp', *Science News*, Vol.97, No.10 (7 March 1970), pp.254–255.
Bielicki, T., 'On "Homo habilis"', *Current Anthropology*, Vol.7, No.5 (December 1966), pp.576–580.
Binford, L. and C. Todd, 'On Arguments for the "Butchering" of Giant Geladas', *Current Anthropology*, Vol.23, No.1 (February 1982), pp.108–111.
Black, L., 'Aboriginal Fisheries of Brewarrina', *South African Archaeological Bulletin*, Vol.2, No.5 (March 1947), pp.15–16.
Blake, T., '"This Noble Tree": J.C. Bidwill and the Naming of the Bunya Pine', *Queensland Review*, Vol.9, No.2 (November 2002), pp.39–46.
Blasco, R. *et. al.*, 'The earliest pigeon fanciers', *Scientific Reports*, Vol.4, No.5971 (7 August 2014), pp.1–7.
Blench, R., 'The Languages of the Tasmanians and Their Relation to the Peopling of Australia: Sensible and Wild Theories', *Australian Archaeology*, No.67 (December 2008), pp.13–18.
Bonwick, J., 'On the Origin of the Tasmanians Geologically considered', *Journal of the Ethnological Society of London*, Vol.2, No.2 (1870), pp.121–131.
Bowdler, S., 'Fish and Culture: A Tasmanian Polemic', *Mankind*, Vol.12, No.4 (December 1980), pp.334–340.
Bower, B., 'Erectus Unhinged', *Science News*, Vol.141, No.25 (20 June 1992), pp.408–409 and 411.
Bower, B., '"Dwarf" mammoths outlived last ice age', *Science News*, Vol.143, No.13 (27 March 1993), p.197.
Bower, B., 'Spanish fossils enter human ancestry fray', *Science News*, Vol.151, No.22 (31 May 1997), p.333.
Bower, B., 'European Roots: Human ancestors go back in time in Spanish cave', *Science News*, Vol.173, No.13 (29 March 2008), pp.196–197.
Bowler, J. *et. al.*, 'Pleistocene human remains from Australia: a living site and human cremation from Lake Mungo, western New South Wales', *World Archaeology*, Vol.2, No.1 (June 1970), pp.39–59.
Braidwood, R., 'Vere Gordon Childe 1892–1957', *American Anthropologist*, Vol.60, No.4 (August 1958), pp.733–736.
Brain, C.K., 'The Probable Role of Leopards as Predators of the Swartkrans Australopithecines', *South African Archaeological Bulletin*, Vol.24, Nos.95–96 (November 1969), pp.170–171.
Brasil, L., 'The Emu of King Island', *Emu*, Vol.14, No.2 (October 1914), pp.88–97.
Braun, D., 'Australopithecine Butchers', *Nature*, Vol.466, No.7308 (12 August 2010), p.828.

Bibliography

Breen, S., 'Tasmanian Aborigines - Making Fire', *Tasmanian Historical Research Association Papers and Proceedings*, Vol.39, No.1 (March 1992), pp.40–43.
Bridge, M., 'Science rings changes about history', *Weekend Australian* (Sydney), 21-22 March 2020, p.15.
Brook, B. and D. Bowman, 'The uncertain blitzkrieg of Pleistocene megafauna', *Journal of Biogeography*, Vol.31, No.4 (April 2004), pp.517–523.
Brook, B., R. Gillespie and P. Martin, 'Megafauna Mix-Up', *Australasian Science*, Vol.27, No.5 (June 2006), pp.35–37.
Brown, D., 'Bypass finds date to 40,000 years', *Mercury* (Hobart), 27 April 2010, p.3.
Brown, P., 'Artificial Cranial Deformation: a component in the variation in Pleistocene Australian Aboriginal crania', *Archaeology in Oceania*, Vol.16 (1981), pp.156–167.
Brown, P. and M. Morwood, 'Comments from Peter Brown and Mike Morwood', *Before Farming*, Vol.4 (2004), pp.5–7.
Brumm, A., et. al., 'Early stone technology on Flores and its implications for *Homo floresiensis*', *Nature*, Vol.441, No.7093 (1 June 2006), pp.624–628.
Brumm, A. et. al., 'Age and context of the oldest known hominin fossils from Flores', *Nature*, Vol.534, No.7606 (9 June 2016), pp.249–253.
Builth, H. et. al., 'Environmental and cultural change on the Mt Eccles lava-flow landscapes of southwest Victoria, Australia', *Holocene*, Vol.18, No.3 (May 2008), pp.413–424.
Callaway, E., 'Fossil genome reveals ancestral link', *Nature*, Vol.468, No.7327 (23 December 2010), p.1012.
Callaway, E., 'Hobbit relatives hint at family tree', *Nature*, Vol.534, No.7606 (9 June 2016), pp.164–165.
Campbell, B., 'Conceptual Progress in Physical Anthropology: Fossil Man', *Annual Review of Anthropology*, Vol.1 (1972), pp.27–54.
Carbonell, E., et al., 'The first hominin of Europe', *Nature*, Vol.452, No.7186 (27 March 2008), pp.465–469.
Chan, E. et. al., 'Human origins in a southern African palaeo-wetland and first migrations', *Nature*, Vol.575No.7781 (7 November 2019), pp.185–189.
Clarke, R. and K. Kuman, 'The skull of StW 573, a 3.67 Ma *Australopithecus Prometheus* skeleton from Sterkfontein Caves, South Africa', *Journal of Human Evolution*, Vol.134 (September 2019), pp.1–31.
Clarkson, C. et. al., 'Human occupation of northern Australia by 65,000 years ago, *Nature*, Vol.547, No.7663 (20 July 2017), pp.306–310.
Collette, J., 'Hermann Klaatsch's Views on the Significance of the Australian Aborigines', *Aboriginal History*, Vol.11 (1987), pp.98–99.
Cooper, A. and C.B. Stringer, 'Did the Denisovans Cross Wallace's Line?', *Science*, Vol.342, No.6156 (18 October 2013), pp.321–323.
Cooper, H.M., 'Large Stone Implements from South Australia', *Records of the South Australian Museum*, Vol.7 (1943), pp.343–369.
Cosgrove, R., 'Thirty Thousand Years of Human Colonization in Tasmania: New Pleistocene Dates', *Science*, Vol.243, No.4899 (31 March 1989), pp.1706–1708.
Cosgrove, R., 'Late Pleistocene behavioural variation and time trends: the case from Tasmania', *Archaeology in Oceania*, Vol.30, No.3 (October 1995), pp.83–104.

Cosgrove, R., 'Forty-Two Degrees South: The Archaeology of Late Pleistocene Tasmania', *Journal of World Prehistory*, Vol.13, No.4 (December 1999), pp.357–402.
Couture, P. 'Sir Henry Creswicke Rawlinson: Pioneer Cuneiformist', *Biblical Archaeology*, Vol.47, No.3 (September 1984), pp.143–145.
Culotta, E., 'Neanderthals Were Cannibals, Bones Show', *Science*, Vol.286, No.5437 (1 October 1999), pp.18–19.
Culotta, E., 'Discoverers Charge Damage to "Hobbit" Specimens', *Science*, Vol.307, No.5717 (25 March 2005), p.1848.
Culotta, E., 'The Fellowship of the Hobbit', *Science*, Vol.317, No.5839 (10 August 2007), pp.740–742.
Culotta, E., 'When Hobbits (Slowly) Walked the Earth', *Science*, Vol.320, No.5875 (25 April 2008), pp.433–435.
Dalton, R., 'Little lady of Flores forces rethink of human evolution', *Nature*, Vol.431, No.7012 (28 October 2004), p.1029.
Dalton, R., 'Ancient DNA set to rewrite human history', *Nature*, Vol.465, No.7295 (13 May 2010), pp.148–149.
David, B. et. al., 'Badu 15 and the Papuan-Austronesian settlement of Torres Strait', *Archaeology in Oceania*, Vol.39, No.2 (July 2004), pp.65–78.
Davis, E., 'King Nabonidus and the Missing Link City', *Journal of Egyptian Archaeology*, Vol.37 (December 1951), pp.54–55 and 58.
Davis, L. et. al., 'Late Upper Paleolithic occupation at Cooper's Ferry, Idaho, USA ~ 16,000 years ago', *Science*, Vol.365, No.6456 (30 August 2019), pp.891–897.
Dayton, L., 'Mass Extinctions Pinned on Ice Age Hunters', *Science*, Vol.292, No.5523 (8 June 2001), p.1819.
Dayton, L., 'Magic and mystery of an Ice Age couple', *Weekend Australian* (Sydney), 12–13 June 2004, p.5.
Dayton, L., 'Research to go on without "hobbit"', *Weekend Australian* (Sydney), 8–9 January 2005), p.4.
Dayton, L., 'Hobbits "deformed"', *Weekend Australian* (Sydney), 20–21 May 2006, p.5.
Dayton, L., 'Beasts hounded to extinction', *Weekend Australian* (Sydney), 27–28 January 2007, p.28.
Dayton, L., 'Mungo Man has rival to title of oldest Australian', *Australian* (Sydney), 8 December 2009, p.3.
Dayton, L., 'DNA shows there's a caveman inside us all', *Australian* (Sydney), 7 May 2010), p.8.
Dayton, L. and L. Hall, 'Big bird rocks art', *Australian* (Sydney), 1 June 2010, p.3.
Dayton, L., 'Fossils force rethink on tools', *Australian* (Sydney), 12 August 2010, p.11.
Dayton, L., 'Long time here but dingoes were another China export', *Australian* (Sydney), 8 September 2011, p.3.
Defleur, A. et.al., 'Neanderthal Cannibalism at Moula-Guercy, Ardèche, France', *Science*, Vol.286, No.5437 (1 October 1999), pp.128–131.
Derrincourt, R., 'Getting "Out of Africa": Sea Crossings and Culture in Hominin Migrations', *Journal of World Prehistory*, Vol.19, No.2 (June 2005), pp.119–132.
Détroit, F. et. al., 'A new species of *Homo* from the Late Pleistocene of the

Bibliography

Philippines', *Nature*, Vol.568, No.7751 (11 April 2019), pp.181–186.
Diamond, J., 'The Astonishing Micropygmies', *Science*, Vol.306, No.5704 (17 December 2004), pp.2047–2048.
Dix, S., 'New Aboriginal hand stencil discoveries at the Freycinet National Park, Tasmania', *Australian Archaeology*, Vol.82, No.1 (2016), pp.76–79.
Dix, W.C. and M.E. Lofgren, 'Kurumi: Possible Aboriginal Incipient Agriculture Associated with a Stone Arrangement', *Records of the Western Australian Museum*, Vol.3, Pt.1 (1974–1975), pp.73–77.
Donlon, D., 'Aboriginal skeletal collections and research in physical anthropology: an historical perspective', *Australian Archaeology*, No.39 (1994), pp.73–82.
Dortch, C.E., 'Devil's Lair, an Example of Prolonged Cave Use in South-Western Australia', *World Archaeology*, Vol.10, No.3 (February 1979), pp.258–279.
Douglas, K., 'Skeletons in the cabinet: popular palaeontology and the Pleistocene extinction debate in historical perspective', *Alcheringa*, Vol.30, Supp.1 (2006), pp.115–128.
Dunn, M. 'Our origins 200,000 years older: Ancient skull reveals new timeline', *Herald Sun* (Melbourne), 3 April 2020, p.23.
Earle, T. and R. Preucel, 'Processual Archaeology and the Radical Critique', *Current Anthropology*, Vol.28, No.4 (August-October 1987), pp.501–538.
Easton, D.F., 'Heinrich Schliemann: Hero or Fraud?', *Classical World*, Vol.91, No.5 (May-June 1998), pp.335–343.
Edwards, Z., 'Bypass site set for human history claim', *Examiner* (Launceston), 11 March 2010, p.7.
Eiseley, L., 'Neanderthal Man and the Dawn of Human Paleontology', *Quarterly Review of Biology*, Vol.32, No.4 (December 1957), pp.323–329.
Falk, D., *et. al.*, 'The Brain of LB1, *Homo floresiensis*', *Science*, Vol.308, No.5719 (8 April 2005), pp.242–245.
Fargo, V., 'Sir Flinders Petrie', *Biblical Archaeologist*, Vol.47, No.4 (December 1984), pp.220–223.
Field, J., 'Trampling Through the Pleistocene: Does Taphonomy Matter at Cuddie Springs?', *Australian Archaeology*, No.63 (December 2006), pp.9–20.
Finlayson, C., 'Biogeography and evolution of the genus *Homo*', *Trends in Ecology and Evolution*, Vol.20, No.8 (August 2008), pp.457–463.
Fischman, J., 'Hard Evidence', *Discover*, Vol.13, No.2 (February 1992), pp.44–51.
Fitzsimmons, K. *et. al.*, 'The Mungo Mega-Lake Event, Semi-Arid Australia: Non-Linear Descent into the Last Ice Age, Implications for Human Behaviour', *Public Library of Science One*, Vol.10, No.6 (17 June 2015), pp.1–19.
Flannery, T., 'Debating Extinction', *Science*, Vol.283, No.5399 (8 January 1999), pp.182–183.
Fletcher, R., 'The Evolution of Human Behaviour', *Australian Natural History*, Supp. No.2 (1988), pp.47–51.
Flood, J., 'Copying the Dreamtime: Anthropic Marks in Early Aboriginal Australia', *Rock Art Research*, Vol.23, No.2 (November 2006), pp.239–246.

Forster, P. and S. Matsumara, 'Did Early Humans Go North or South?', *Science*, Vol.308, No.5724 (13 May 2005), pp.965–966.

Forth, G., 'Flores after floresiensis: Implications of local reaction to recent palaeoanthropological discoveries on an east Indonesian island', *Bijdragen tot de Taal –, Land-en Volkenkunde*, Vol.162, Nos.2–3 (2006), pp.336–349.

Forth, G., 'Hominids, hairy hominoids and the science of humanity', *Anthropology Today*, Vol.21, No.3 (June 2008), pp.13–17.

Franklin, N. and P. Habgood, 'Modern Human Behaviour and Pleistocene Sahul in Review', *Australian Archaeology*, No.65 (December 2007), pp.1–16.

French, M., 'What Fate Awaits? The Indigenous Peoples of the Darling Downs in 1851–52', *Queensland Review*, Vol.9, No.1 (May 2002), pp.23–33.

Fudali, R. and R. Ford, 'Darwin Glass and Darwin Crater: A Progress Report', *Meteoritics*, Vol.14 (September 1979), pp.283–296.

Gammage, B., '"...far more happier than we Europeans": Aborigines and farmers', *London Papers in Australian Studies*, No.12 (2005), pp.1–27.

Garvey, J., 'Preliminary zooarchaeological interpretations from Kutikina Cave, south-west Tasmania', *Australian Aboriginal Studies*, No.1 (2006), pp.57–62.

Garvey, J., 'Surviving an Ice Age: The Zooarchaeological Record from Southwestern Tasmania', *Palaios*, Vol.22, No.6 (November 2007), pp.583–585.

Gerritsen, R., 'Evidence for Indigenous Australian Agriculture', *Australasian Science*, Vol.31, No.6 (July-August 2010), pp.35–37.

Gibbons, A., '*Homo erectus* in Java: A 250,000–Year Anachronism', *Science*, Vol.274, No.5294 (13 December 1996), pp.1841–1842.

Gibbons, A., 'Ancient Island Tools Suggest *Homo erectus* Was a Seafarer', *Science*, Vol.279, No.5357 (13 March 1998), pp.1635–1637.

Gibbons, A., 'Millennium Ancestor Gets Its Walking Papers', *Science*, Vol.319, No.5870 (21 March 2008), pp.1599 and 1601.

Gibbons, A., 'A New Kind of Ancestor: *Ardipithecus* Unveiled', *Science*, Vol.326, No.5949 (2 October 2009), pp.36–40.

Gibbons, A., '*Ardipithecus ramidus*, *Science*', Vol.326, No.5960 (18 December 2009), pp.1598–1599.

Gibbons, A., 'Aboriginal Genome Shows Two-Wave Settlement of Asia', *Science*, Vol.333, No.6050 (23 September 2011), pp.1689 and 1691.

Gillespie, R. and B. David, 'The Importance, or Impotence, of Cuddie Springs', *Australasian Science*, Vol.22, No.9 (October 2001), pp.42–43.

Glazko, G., et al, 'Eighty percent of proteins are different between humans and chimpanzees', *Gene*, Vol.346 (2005), pp.215–219.

Goebel, T., M. Wayrers and D. O'Rourke, 'The Late Pleistocene Dispersal of Modern Humans in the Americas', *Science*, Vol.319, No.1497 (14 March 2008), pp.1497–1502.

Gome, L., 'Obituary', *Folklore*, Vol.11, No.2 (June 1900), pp.185–187.

Gómez-Robles, A., 'The dawn of *Homo floresiensis*', *Nature*, Vol.534, No.7606 (9 June 2016), pp.188–189.

Goodrum, M., 'Prolegomenon to a History of Paleoanthropology: The Study of Human Origins as a Scientific Enterprise: Part 1: Antiquity to the Eighteenth Century', *Evolutionary Anthropology*, Vol.13, No.5 (October 2004), pp.172–180.

Bibliography

Goodrum, M., 'Prolegomenon to a History of Paleoanthropology: The Study of Human Origins as a Scientific Enterprise: Part 2: Eighteenth to Twentieth Century', *Evolutionary Anthropology*, Vol.13, No.6 (December 2004), pp.224–233.
Gore, R., 'Neanderthals: The Dawn of Humans', *National Geographic*, Vol.189, No.1 (January 1996), pp.2–35.
Gould, S., 'The Origin and Function of "Bizarre" Structure: Antler Size and Skull Size in the "Irish Elk," *Megaloceros giganteus*', *Evolution*, Vol.28, No.2 (June 1974), pp.191–220.
Grayson, D., 'The Archaeological Record of Human Impacts on Animal Populations', *Journal of World Prehistory*, Vol.15, No.1 (March 2001), pp.1–68.
Grayson, D. and D. Meltzer, 'A requiem for North American overkill', *Journal of Archaeological Science*, Vol.30, No.5 (May 2003), pp.585–593.
Griffith, F.L.L., 'The Decipherment of the Hieroglyphics', *Journal of Egyptian Archaeology*, Vol.37 (December 1951), pp.38–46.
Griffiths, J.G., 'Did Hesiod Invent the "Golden Age"?', *Journal of the History of Ideas*, Vol.19, No.1 (January 1958), pp.91–93.
Gruber, J., 'The Neanderthal Controversy: Nineteenth-Century Version', *Scientific Monthly*, Vol.67, No.6 (December 1948), pp.436–439.
Hall, S., 'Last of the Neanderthals', *National Geographic*, Vol.214, No.4 (October 2008), pp.34–59.
Hammond, P., 'Step back to the Ice Age', *Courier-Mail* (Brisbane), 7–8 April 2007, pp.26–27.
Harris, A., D. Ranson and S. Brown, 'Maxwell River Archaeological Survey 1986', *Australian Archaeology*, No.27 (1988), pp.89–97.
Haynes, G., 'The catastrophic extinction of North American mammoths and mastodons', *World Archaeology*, Vol.33, No.3 (February 2002), pp.391–416.
Heizer, R., 'The Background of Thomsen's Three-Age System', *Technology and Culture*, Vol.3, No.3 (Summer 1962), pp.259–266.
Henneberg, M. and A. Thorne, 'Flores may be pathological *Homo sapiens*', *Before Farming*, Vol.4 (2004), pp.2–4.
Henneberg, M. et. al., 'Evolved developmental homeostasis disturbed in LB1 from Flores, Indonesia, denotes Down syndrome and not diagnostic traits of the invalid species *Homo floresiensis*', *Proceedings of the National Academy of the United States of America*, Vol.111, No.33 (19 August 2014), pp.11967–11972.
Herries, A. et. al., 'Contemporaneity of *Australopithecus*, *Paranthropus*, and early *Homo erectus* in South Africa', *Science*, Vol.368, No.6486 (3 April 2020), pp.47–66.
Hershkovitz, I., L. Kornreich and Z. Laron, 'Comparative Skeletal Features Between *Homo floresiensis* and Patients with Primary Growth Hormone Insensitivity (Laron Syndrome)', *American Journal of Physical Anthropology*, Vol.134, No.2 (October 2007), pp.198–208.
Hiatt, B., 'The Food Quest and the Economy of the Tasmanian Aborigines [Part 1]', *Oceania*, Vol.38, No.2 (December 1967), pp.99–133.
Hiatt, B., 'The Food Quest and the Economy of the Tasmanian Aborigines [Part 2]', *Oceania*, Vol.38, No.3 (March 1968), pp.190–219.
Hiscock, P., 'Technological Responses to Risk in Holocene Australia', *Journal of*

World Prehistory, Vol.8, No.3 (September 1994), pp.267–292.
Hiscock, P., 'The New Age of alternative archaeology in Australia', Archaeology in Oceania, Vol.31, No.3 (October 1996), pp.152–164.
Hobbs, W., 'James Hutton, The Pioneer of Modern Geology', Science, Vol.64, No.1655 (17 September 1926), pp.261–265.
Hoffmann, D.L. et. al., 'U-Th dating of carbonate crusts reveals Neanderthal origin of Iberian cave art', Science, Vol.359, No.6378 (23 February 2018), pp.912–915.
Howchin, W., 'Further Notes on the Geology of Kangaroo Island', Transactions of the Royal Society of South Australia, Vol.27 (1903), pp.75–90.
Hrdlicka, A., 'Dr. Eugene Dubois, 1858–1940', Scientific Monthly, Vol.52, No.6 (June 1941), pp.578–580.
Hudjashou, G. et. al., 'Revealing the prehistoric settlement of Australia by Y chromosome and mtDNA analysis', Proceedings of the National Academy of Sciences of the United States of America, Vol.104, No.21 (22 May 2007), pp.8725–8730.
Hulse, F., 'Race as an Evolutionary Episode', American Anthropologist, Vol.64, No.5 (October 1962), pp.929–945.
Jacob, T., et. al., 'Pygmoid Australomelanesian Homo sapiens skeletal remains from Liang Bua, Flores: Population affinities and pathological abnormalities', Proceedings of the National Academy of Sciences of the United States of America, Vol.103, No.36 (5 September 2006), pp.13421–13426.
Jaroff, L., 'The Neanderthal Mystery', Time (New York), 14 March 1994, pp.60–61.
Johnson, C.N., 'Determinants of loss of mammal species during the Late Quarternary "megafauna" extinctions: life history and ecology, but not body size', Proceedings of the Royal Society of London: Series B, Vol.269, No.1506 (7 November 2002), pp.2221–2227.
Johnson, M., '"Cranial connections": Queensland's "Talgai Skull" debate of 1918 and custodianship of the past', Aboriginal History, Vol.24 (2000), pp.117–131.
Johnston, H. and P. Clark, 'Willandra Lakes Archaeological Investigations, 1968–98', Archaeology in Oceania, Vol.33, No.3 (October 1998), pp.105–119.
Jones, C., 'Hobbit species may not have been human', Australian (Sydney), 30 September 2009, pp.23 and 26.
Jones, P., 'Going to pieces over human jigsaw', 'Australian Literary Review', in Australian (Sydney), 4 June 2008, p.9.
Jones, R., 'Firestick Farming', Australian Natural History, Vol.16, No.7 (15 September 1969), pp.224–228.
Jones, R., 'Australia Felix – The Discovery of a Pleistocene Prehistory', Journal of Human Evolution, Vol.6, No.4 (May 1977), pp.353–361.
Jones, R., 'The Fifth Continent: Problems Concerning the Human Colonization of Australia', Annual Review of Anthropology, Vol.8 (1979), pp.445–466.
Jones, R., 'Ice-Age Hunters of the Tasmanian Wilderness', Australian Geographic, No.8 (October-December 1987), pp.26–45.
Jones, R., 'Tasmanian Archaeology: Establishing the Sequences', Annual Review of Anthropology, Vol.24 (October 1995), pp.423–446.
Joyner, G., 'The meaning of yahoo and dulugal: European and Aboriginal

perspectives of the so-called "Australian gorilla"', *Canberra Historical Journal*, No.3 (March 1994), pp.27–34.
Judge, J., 'Minoans and Mycenaeans: Greece's Brilliant Bronze Age', *National Geographic*, Vol.153, No.2 (February 1978), pp.142–185.
Jungers, W., 'Hobbit nay-sayers fail to overturn theories', 'Weekend Australian Magazine', in *Weekend Australian* (Sydney), 26–27 July 2008, pp.12–13.
Kimbel, W. et. al., '*Ardipithecus ramidus* and the evolution of the human cranial base', *Proceedings of the National Academy of the United States of America*, Vol.111, No.3 (21 January 2014), pp.948–953.
King, E., 'The Origin of Tektites: A Brief Overview', *American Scientist*, Vol.65, No.2 (March–April 1977), pp.212–218.
Kirtley, B., 'Unknown Hominids and New World Legends', *Western Folklore*, Vol.23, No.2 (April 1964), pp.77–90.
Klein, R., 'Anatomy, Behavior, and Modern Human Origins', *Journal of World Prehistory*, Vol.9, No.2 (June 1995), pp.167–198.
Lahr, M. and R. Foley, 'Human evolution writ small', *Nature*, Vol.431, No.7012 (28 October 2004), pp.1043–1044.
Lalueza-Fox, C. et. al., 'A Melanocortin 1 Receptor Allele Suggests Varying Pigmentation Among Neanderthals', *Science*, Vol.318, No.1453 (30 November 2007), pp.1453–1455.
Lampert, R., 'Waisted Blades in Australia?', *Records of the Australian Museum*, Vol.35, No.4 (1983), pp.145–151.
Lampert, R. and P. Hughes, 'Early Human Occupation of the Flinders Ranges', *Records of the South Australian Museum*, Vol.22 (1988), pp.139–168.
Laurie, V., 'Secrets unearthed: humankind just got a little older', *Weekend Australian* (Sydney), 28–29 November 2015, p.3.
Lawrence, D., 'Customary exchange in Torres Strait', *Australian Aboriginal Studies*, No.2 (1998), pp.13–25.
Leake, J., 'Did we have sex with the Neanderthals?', *Australian* (Sydney), 26 October 2009, p.3.
Leake, J., 'Modern man cleared: interbreeding led to the fall of the Neanderthals', *Australian* (Sydney), 12 November 2018, p.8.
Leakey, M. and R. Hay, 'Pliocene footprints in the Laetoli Beds at Laetoli, Tanzania', *Nature*, Vol.278 (22 March 1979), pp.317–323.
Lee-Thorp, J., J.F. Thackeray and N. van der Merwe, 'The hunters and the hunted revisited', *Journal of Human Evolution*, Vol.39, No.6 (December 2000), pp.565–576.
Lemonick, M., 'How Man Began', *Time* (14 March 1994), pp.55–60.
Lemonick, M. and A. Dorfman, 'Father of Us All?', *Time*, No.28 (22 July 2002), pp.36–43.
Lewin, R., 'The Taung Baby Reaches Sixty', *Science*, Vol.227, No.4691 (8 March 1985), pp.1188–1190.
Lewin, R., 'Human origins: the challenge of Java's skulls', *New Scientist*, No.1924 (7 May 1994), pp.36–40.
Line, P., '"Giants" in the land: an assessment of *Gigantopithecus* and *Meganthropus*', *Journal of Creation*, Vol.20, No.1 (2006), pp.105–108.
Lister, A.M., 'Mammoths in miniature', *Nature*, Vol.362, No.6418 (25 March 1993), pp.288–289.
Lister, A.M. et. al., 'The phylogenetic position of the "giant deer" *Megaloceros giganteus*', *Nature*, Vol.438, No.7069 (8 December 2005), pp.850–853.

Long, G., 'Marsupial Baby Killer or Aussie Big "Cat"?', *Australasian Science*, Vol.24, No.9 (October 2003), pp.31–32.
Long, G., 'Megafauna Theory Faces Extinction', *Australasian Science*, Vol.28, No.2 (March 2007), pp.18–19.
Lord, C., 'A Note on the Burial Customs of the Tasmanian Aborigines', *Papers and Proceedings of the Royal Society of Tasmania for the Year 1923*, pp.45–46.
Lourandos, H., 'Change or stability?: hydraulics, hunter-gatherers and population in temperate Australia', *World Archaeology*, Vol.11, No.3 (February 1980), pp.245–264.
Lovejoy, C.O., 'The Origin of Man', *Science*, Vol.211, No.4480 (23 January 1981), pp.341–350.
Macintosh, N.W.G., 'The Cohuna Cranium: Physiography and Chemical Analysis', *Oceania*, Vol.23, No.4 (June 1953), pp.277–296.
Manning, S. *et. al.*, 'Mediterranean radiocarbon offsets and calendar dates for prehistory', *Science Advances*, Vol.6, No.12 (18 March 2020), pp.1–13.
Marean, C., 'Early human use of marine resources and pigment in South Africa during the Middle Pleistocene', *Nature*, Vol.449, No.7164 (18 October 2007), pp.905–909.
Martin, P., 'The Discovery of America', *Science*, Vol.179, No.4077 (9 March 1973), pp.969–974.
Massimo, L., *et. al.*, 'Chicken-pox and Chromosome Aberrations', *British Medical Journal*, Vol.2, No.5454 (17 July 1965), p.172.
McBrearty, S. and C. Stringer, 'The coast in colour', *Nature*, Vol.449, No.7164 (18 October 2007), pp.793–794.
McBryde, I., 'Kulin greenstone quarries: the social contexts of production and distribution for the Mt William site', *World Archaeology*, Vol.16, No.2 (October 1984), pp.267–285.
McConnell, K. and S. O'Connor, '40,000 Year record of food plants in the Southern Kimberley Ranges, Western Australia', *Australian Archaeology*, No.45 (1997), pp.20–31.
McDougall, I., 'Dating Human Evolution', *Australian Natural History*, Supplement 2 (1988), pp.43–45.
McFarlane, I., 'Pevay: A Casualty of War', *Tasmanian Historical Research Association Papers and Proceedings*, Vol.48, No.4 (December 2001), pp.280–305.
McFarlane, I., 'Adolphus Schayer: Van Diemen's Land and the Berlin Papers', *Tasmanian Historical Research Association Papers and Proceedings*, Vol.57, No.2 (August 2010), pp.105–118.
McNiven, I., 'Tula Adzes and Bifacial Points on the East Coast of Australia', *Australian Archaeology*, No.36 (1993), pp.22–33.
McNiven, I., 'Inclusions, exclusions and transitions: Torres Strait Islander constructed landscapes over the past 4000 years, northeast Australia', *Holocene*, Vol.18, No.3 (May 2008), pp.449–462.
McNiven, I. and D. Bell, 'Fishers and Farmers: historicising the Gunditjmara freshwater fishery, western Victoria', *La Trobe Journal*, No.85 (May 2010), pp.83–105.
Megalogenis, G., 'Rethinking the Noble Savage', *Weekend Australian* (Sydney), 3–4 August 2002, pp.19 and 22.
Meijer, H. and R.A. Due, 'A new species of giant marabou stork (Aves:

Ciconiiformes) from the Pleistocene of Liang Bua, Flores (Indonesia)', *Zoological Journal of the Linnean Society*, Vol.160, No.4 (December 2010), pp.707–724.
Mellars, P., 'Neanderthals and the modern human colonization of Europe', *Nature*, Vol.432, No.7016 (25 November 2004), pp.461–465.
Mellars, P. and J. French, 'Tenfold Population Increase in Western Europe at the Neanderthal-to-Modern Human Transition', *Science*, Vol.333, No.6042 (29 July 2011), pp.623–627.
Mijares, A.S., *et. al.*, 'New evidence for a 67,000-year-old human presence at Callao Cave, Luzon, Philippines', *Journal of Human Evolution*, Vol.59, No.1 (July 2010), pp.123–132.
Miller, G., *et al*, 'Pleistocene Extinction of *Genyornis newtoni*: Human Impact on Australian Megafauna', *Science*, Vol.283, No.5399 (8 January 1999), pp.205–208.
Miller, G. *et. al.*, 'Ecosystem Collapse in Pleistocene Australia and a Human Role in Megafaunal Extinction', *Science*, Vol.309, No.5732 (8 July 2005), pp.287–290.
Miller, G. *et. al.*, 'Detecting human impacts on the flora, fauna, and summer monsoon of Pleistocene Australia', *Climate of the Past*, Vol.3, No.3 (July 2007), pp.463–473.
Miranda, C., 'The First Supper', *Courier-Mail* (Brisbane), 27–28 October 2007, pp.36–37.
Morgan, A. and J. Sutton, 'A Critical Description of Some Recently Discovered Bones of the Extinct Kangaroo Island Emu (*Dromaius diemenianus*)', *Emu*, Vol.28, No.1 (July 1928), pp.1–19.
Morwood, M. and P. Trezise, 'Edge-Ground Axes in Pleistocene Greater Australia: New Evidence from S.E. Cape York Peninsula', *Queensland Archaeological Research*, Vol.7 (1990), pp.77–90.
Morwood, M., *et. al.*, 'Stone artefacts from the 1994 excavation at Mata Menge, West Central Flores, Indonesia', *Australian Archaeology*, No.44 (June 1997), pp.26–34.
Morwood, M., T. Sutikina and R. Roberts, 'The People Time Forgot', *National Geographic*, Vol.207, No.4 (April 2005), pp.5–15.
Morwood, M., *et. al.*, 'Preface: research at Liang Bua, Flores, Indonesia', *Journal of Human Evolution*, Vol.57, No.5 (November 2009), pp.437–449.
Mounier, A., F. Marchal and S. Confemi, 'Is *Homo heidelbergensis* a distinct species? New insight on the Mauer mandible', *Journal of Human Evolution*, Vol.56, No.3 (March 2009), pp.219–246.
Mountford, C. and R. Edwards, 'Aboriginal Rock Engravings of Extinct Creatures in South Australia', *Man*, Vol.62 (July 1922), pp.97–99.
Murray, T. and J.P. White, 'Cambridge in the bush? Archaeology in Australia and New Guinea', *World Archaeology*, Vol.13, No.2 (October 1981), pp.255–263.
Mysterud, A. *et. al.*, 'Population ecology and conservation of endangered megafauna: the case of the European bison in Bialowieza Primeval Forest, Poland', *Animal Conservation*, Vol.10, No.1 (February 2007), pp.77–87.
Nelson, M., 'The mummy's curse: historical cohort study', *British Medical Journal*, Vol.325, No.7378 (21–28 December 2002), pp.1482–1484.
Nicklin, L., 'The prehistory cowboy strikes again', *Bulletin* (Sydney), 12 June 1990, pp.92–93.

Noetling, F., 'A Native Burial Ground on Charlton Estate, Near Ross', *Papers and Proceedings of the Royal Society of Tasmania for the Year 1908*, pp.36–43.
Obendorf, P., C. Oxnard and B. Kefford, 'Are the small human-like fossils found on Flores human endemic cretins?', *Proceedings of the Royal Society B*, Vol.275, No.1640 (7 June 2008), pp.1287–1296.
O'Connell, J.F. and J. Allen, 'When Did Humans First Arrive in Greater Australia and Why Is It Important to Know?', *Evolutionary Anthropology*, Vol.6, No.4 (1998), pp.132–146.
O'Connell, J.F. and J. Allen, 'Dating the Colonization of Sahul (Pleistocene Australia-New Guinea): a review of recent research', *Journal of Archaeological Research*, Vol.31, No.6 (June 2004), pp.835–853.
O'Connell, J.F., K. Hawkes and N.G. Blurton Jones, 'Grandmothering and the evolution of *Homo erectus*', *Journal of Human Evolution*, Vol.36, No.5 (May 1999), pp.461–485.
O'Connor, S., 'The Stone House Structures of High Cliffy Island, North West Kimberley, WA', *Australian Archaeology*, No.25 (December 1987), pp.30–39.
O'Connor, S., M. Spriggs and P. Veth, 'Excavation at Lene Hara Cave establishes occupation in East Timor at least 30,000–35,000 years ago', *Antiquity*, Vol.76, No.291 (March 2002), pp.45–49.
O'Connor, S., 'New evidence from East Timor contributes to our understanding of earliest human colonisation east of the Sunda Shelf', *Antiquity*, Vol.81, No.313 (September 2007), pp.523–535.
O'Dea, K., 'Traditional diet and food preferences of Australian Aboriginal hunter-gatherers', *Philosophical Transactions: Biological Sciences*, Vol.334, No.1270 (29 November 1991), pp.233–241.
O'Keefe, B., 'Hobbit "had been to dentist for a filling"', *Weekend Australian* (Sydney), 19–20 April 2008, p.3.
O'Keefe, 'The tooth, and nothing but', *Weekend Australian* (Sydney), 19–20 April 2008, p.24.
O'Rourke, J.E., 'A Comparison of James Hutton's *Principles of Knowledge* and *Theory of the Earth*', *Isis*, Vol.69, No.1 (March 1978), pp.5–20.
Padian, K., 'Ten Myths about Charles Darwin', *Bioscience*, Vol.59, No.9 (October 2009), pp.800–804.
Page, L., 'James Hutton: Uniformitarianism Versus Evolution', *Proceedings of the Oklahoma Academy of Science for 1959*, Vol.40 (1960), pp.103–105.
Patou-Mathis, M., 'Neanderthal Subsistence Behaviours in Europe', *International Journal of Osteoarchaeology*, Vol.10, No.5 (September-October 2000), pp.379–395.
Peers, C., 'The Beginnings of Prehistoric Studies in Britain', *Man*, Vol.32 (September 1932), p.202.
Penniman, T.K., 'General Pitt Rivers', *Man*, Vol.46 (July-August 1946), pp.73–74.
Peterson, R., 'William Stukeley: an eighteenth-century phenomenologist?', *Antiquity*, Vol.77, No.296 (June 2003), pp.394–400.
Pickering, R. et. al., '*Australopithecus sediba* at 1.977 Ma and Implications for the Origins of the Genus *Homo*', *Science*, Vol.333, No.6048 (9 September 2011), pp.1421–1423.
Piggott, S., 'Robert Eric Mortimer Wheeler: 10 September 1890–22 July 1976',

Bibliography

Biographical Memoirs of Fellows of the Royal Society, Vol.23 (November 1977), pp.623–642.
Pike-Tay, A., R. Cosgrove and J. Garvey, 'Systematic seasonal land use by late Pleistocene Tasmanian Aborigines', *Journal of Archaeological Science*, Vol.35, No.9 (September 2008), pp.2532–2544.
Pitt, E., 'Hobbit finder dies of cancer', *Australian* (Sydney), 24 July 2013, p.30.
Prentis, M., 'From Lemuria to Kow Swamp: The Rise and Fall of Tri-hybrid Theories of Aboriginal Origins', *Journal of Australian Studies*, No.45 (June 1995), pp.79–91.
Price, M., 'Stirring skull shakes human tree', *Science*, Vol.365, No.6456 (30 August 2019), p.850.
Prideaux, G., *et. al.*, 'An arid-adapted middle Pleistocene vertebrate fauna from south-central Australia', *Nature*, Vol.445, No.7126 (25 January 2007), pp.422–425.
Raichlen, D., H. Pontzer and M. Sockol, 'The Laetoli footprints and early hominin locomotor kinematics', *Journal of Human Evolution*, Vol.54, No.1 (January 2008), pp.112–117.
Raichlen, D., *et al.*, 'Laetoli Footprints Preserve Earliest Direct Evidence of Human-Like Bipedal Biomechanics', *Public Library of Science One*, Vol.5, No.3 (March 2010), pp.1–6.
Ramage, N., 'Goods, Graves, and Scholars: 18th-Century Archaeologists in Britain and Italy', *American Journal of Archaeology*, Vol.96, No.4 (October 1992), pp.653–661.
Redd, A. and M. Stoneking, 'Peopling of Sahul: Mtdna Variation in Aboriginal Australian and Papua New Guinean Populations', *American Journal of Human Genetics*, Vol.65, No.3 (September 1999), pp.808–828.
Reich, D., *et al.*, 'Genetic history of an archaic hominin group from Denisova Cave in Siberia', *Nature*, Vol.468, No.7327 (23 December 2010), pp.1053–1060.
Reynolds, T.E.G., 'Revolution or resolution? The archaeology of modern human origins', *World Archaeology*, Vol.23, No.2 (October 1991), pp.155–166.
Rice, D., 'Not all clubs and red meat. Signs are that Neanderthals knew how to fish', *Sun-Herald* (Sydney), 29 March 2020, p.21.
Richards, G., 'Genetic, physiologic and ecogeographical factors contributing to variation in *Homo sapiens*: *Homo floresiensis* reconsidered', *Journal of Evolutionary Biology*, Vol.19, No.6 (November 2006), pp.1744–1767.
Rightmire, G.P., 'Patterns in the evolution of *Homo erectus*', *Paleobiology*, Vol.7, No.2 (Spring 1981), pp.241–246.
Rightmire, G.P., 'The Dispersal of *Homo erectus* from Africa and the Emergence of More Modern Humans', *Journal of Anthropological Research*, Vol.47, No.2 (Summer 1991), pp.177–191.
Rightmire, G.P., 'Human Evolution in the Middle Pleistocene: The Role of *Homo heidelbergensis*', *Evolutionary Anthropology*, Vol.6, No.6 (December 1998), pp.218–227.
Ritchie, A., 'Mary Leakey and the Laetoli Tracks', *Australian Natural History*, Supplement No.2 (1988), pp.26–27.
Roberts, R. *et. al.*, 'Optical and radiocarbon dating at Jinmium rock shelter in northern Australia', *Nature*, Vol.393, No.6683 (28 May 1998), pp.358–362.
Roberts, R. *et. al.*, 'New Ages for the Last Australian Megafauna: Continent-

Wide Extinction About 46,000 Years Ago', *Science*, Vol.292, No.5523 (8 June 2001), pp.1888–1892.
Roberts, R. *et. al.*, 'The Last Australian Megafauna', *Australasian Science*, Vol.22, No.9 (October 2001), pp.40–41.
Roebroeks, W., 'Hominid behaviour and the earliest occupation of Europe: an exploration', *Journal of Human Evolution*, Vol.41, No.5 (November 2001), pp.437–461.
Rose, M., 'Dear Mary', *BioScience*, Vol.35, No.6 (June 1985), pp.374–375.
Ross, J., '"Hobbit" had Down syndrome', *Australian* (Sydney), 24 July 2013, p.5.
Ross, J., 'Flores Hobbits out of Africa', *Weekend Australian* (Sydney), 22–23 April 2017, p.10.
Rothwell, N., 'Politics etched in stone', *Australian* (Sydney), 23 September 1996, pp.1 and 5.
Rothwell, N., 'In search of the Little People', 'Weekend Australian Review', in *Weekend Australian* (Sydney), 3–4 May 2014, pp.8–10.
Rowlands, R.J. and J.M. Rowlands, 'An Aboriginal Dam in Northwestern New South Wales', *Mankind*, Vol.7, No.2 (December 1969), pp.132–136.
Ruse, M., 'Charles Darwin and the "Beagle"', *Wilson Quarterly*, Vol.6, No.1 (Winter 1982), pp.164–175.
Ryder, O., 'Przewalski's Horse: Prospects for Reintroduction into the Wild', *Conservation Biology*, Vol.7, No.1 (March 1933), pp.13–15.
Savolainen, P. *et. al.*, 'A detailed picture of the origin of the Australian dingo obtained from the study of mitochondrial DNA', *Proceedings of the National Academy of Sciences of the United States of America*, Vol.101, No.33 (17 August 2004), pp.12387–12390.
Sayre, G., 'The Mound Builders and the Imagination of American Antiquity in Jefferson, Bartram, and Chateaubriand', *Early American Literature*, Vol.33, No.3 (1998), pp.225–249.
Schmitz, R. *et. al.*, 'The Neanderthal type site revisited: Interdisciplinary investigations of skeletal remains from the Neander Valley, Germany', *Proceedings of the National Academy of Sciences of the United States of America*, Vol.99, No.20 (1 October 2002), pp.13342–13347.
Schrire, C., 'An Analysis of Human Behaviour and Animal Extinctions in South Africa and Australia in Late Pleistocene Times', *South African Archaeological Bulletin*, Vol.35, No.131 (June 1980), pp.3–12.
Schulz, D., 'Backdating the clock', *Bulletin* (Sydney), 25 July 1995, pp.36–37.
Schulz, D., 'Little Big Man', 'Weekend Australian Magazine', in *Weekend Australian* (Sydney), 11–12 December 2004, pp.56–57, 59 and 61.
Seth, P., N. Manjunath and S. Balaya, 'Rubella Infection: The Indian Scene', *Reviews of Infectious Diseases*, Vol.7, Supp.1 (March–April 1985), pp.564–567.
Schwartz, J. and I. Tattersall, 'Significance of some previously unrecognized apomorphies in the nasal region of *Homo neanderthalensis*', *Proceedings of the National Academy of Sciences of the United States of America*, Vol.93, No.20 (1 October 1996), pp.10852–10854.
Schwimmer, E.G., 'Warfare of the Maori', *Te Ao Hou The New World*, No.36 (September 1961), pp.51–54.
Sherratt, A., 'V. Gordon Childe: Archaeology and Intellectual History', *Past and Present*, No.125 (November 1989), pp.151–185.

Bibliography

Shipman, P., W. Bosler and K. Davis, 'Butchering of Giant Geladas at an Acheulian Site', *Current Anthropology*, Vol.22, No.3 (June 1981), pp.257–268.
Sigurdsson, S., S. Cashdollar and S. Sparks, 'The Eruption of Vesuvius in A.D.79: Reconstruction from Historical and Vulcanological Evidence', *American Journal of Archaeology*, Vol.86, No.1 (January 1982), pp.39–51.
Sim, R., 'Prehistoric Sites on King Island in the Bass Strait: Results of Archaeological Survey', *Australian Archaeology*, No.31 (December 1990), pp.34–43.
Simon, C., 'Preserved bones reveal fiery death at Herculaneum', *Science News*, Vol.122, No.21 (November 1982), p.327.
Singh, G. and E. Geissler, 'Late Cainozoic History of Vegetation, Fire, Lake Levels and Climate, at Lake George, New South Wales, Australia', *Philosophical Transactions of the Royal Society of London: Series B*, Vol.311, No.1151 (3 December 1985), pp.379–447.
Smith, C., 'Why caution is the best technique', *Australian* (Sydney), 24 September 1996, p.13.
Smith, D., 'Young Mungo theory raises desert storm', 'Insight', in *Age* (Melbourne), 22 February 2002, p.5.
Smith, D., 'When Hobbits hunted pygmy elephants', *Sydney Morning Herald* (Sydney), 28 October 2004, p.4.
Smith, G. Elliott, 'Sinanthropus – Peking Man: its discovery and significance', *Scientific Monthly*, Vol.33, No.3 (September 1931), pp.193–211.
Smith, M.A., '"The Opening Chapter of the Romance of Excavation in Australia": Reflections on Norman Tindale's Archaeology', *Historical Records of Australian Science*, Vol.13, No.2 (September 2000), pp.151–160.
Smith, M. and J. Ross, 'What happened at 1500–1000 cal. BP in Central Australia? Timing, impact and archaeological signatures', *Holocene*, Vol.18, No.3 (2008), pp.379–388.
Smith, R., 'Alfred Russel Wallace: Philosophy of Nature and Man', *British Journal for the History of Science*, Vol.6, No.2 (December 1972), pp.177–199.
Smith, S.A., 'The Fossil Human Skull Found at Talgai, Queensland', *Philosophical Transactions of the Royal Society of London: Series B*, Vol.28 (1918), pp.351–387
Smith, S., 'William Matthew Flinders Petrie 1853–1942', *Obituary Notices of Fellows of the Royal Society*, Vol.5, No.14 (November 1945), pp.3–16.
Specht, J. et. al., 'Prehistoric Obsidian Exchange in Melanesia: A Perspective from the Talasea Sources', *Australian Archaeology*, No.27 (December 1987), pp.3–16.
Sponheimer, M., et al., 'Isotopic Evidence for Dietary Variability in the Early Hominin *Paranthropus robustus*', *Science*, Vol.314, No.5801 (10 November 2006), pp.980–982.
Spooner, N.A., 'Human occupation at Jinmium, northern Australia: 116,000 years or much less?', *Antiquity*, Vol.72, No.275 (March 1998), pp.173–178.
Stiller, M. et. al., 'Withering Away – 25,000 Years of Genetic Decline Preceded Cave Bear Extinction', *Molecular Biology and Evolution*, Vol.27, No.5 (May 2010), pp.975–978.
Stone, T. and M. Cupper, 'Last Glacial Maximum ages for robust humans at

Kow Swamp, southern Australia', *Journal of Human Evolution*, Vol.45, No.2 (August 2003), pp.99–111.
Straus, W., 'The Great Piltdown Hoax', *Science*, Vol.119, No.3087 (26 February 1954), pp.265–269.
Stringer, C., 'Coasting out of Africa', *Nature*, Vol.405, No.6782 (4 May 2000), pp.24–27.
Stuart, A.J. *et. al.*, 'Pleistocene to Holocene extinction dynamics in giant deer and woolly mammoth', *Nature*, Vol.431, No.7009 (7 October 2004), pp.684–689.
Sutikna, T. *et. al.*, 'Revised stratigraphy and chronology for *Homo floresiensis* at Liang Bua in Indonesia', *Nature*, Vol.532, No.7599 (21 April 2016), pp.366–369.
Suwa, G., 'The *Ardipithecus ramidus* skull and its implications for hominid origins', *Science*, Vol.326, No.5949 (2 October 2009), pp.68e1–68e7.
Suwa, G., *et al.*, 'Paleobiological Implications of the *Ardipithecus ramidus* Dentition', *Science*, Vol.326, No.5949 (2 October 2009), pp.9499.
Swisher, C.C. III., *et al.*, 'Age of the Earliest Known Hominids in Java, Indonesia', *Science*, Vol.263, No.5150 (25 February 1994), pp.1118–1121.
Swisher, C.C. III., *et al*, 'Latest *Homo erectus* of Java: Potential Contemporaneity with *Homo sapiens* in Southeast Asia', *Science*, Vol.274, No.5294 (13 December 1996), pp.1870–1874.
Tattersall, I. and J. Schwartz, 'Hominids and hybrids: The place of Neanderthals in human evolution', *Proceedings of the National Academy of Sciences of the United States of America*, Vol.96, No.13 (22 June 1999), pp.7117–7119.
Taylor, J., 'The Tasmanian Languages', *Launceston Historical Society Papers and Proceedings*, Vol.11 (1999), pp.44–54.
Taylor, J., 'The Aboriginal Discovery and Colonisation of Tasmania', *Tasmanian Historical Research Association Papers and Proceedings*, Vol.50, No.4 (December 2003), pp.216–224.
Taylor, R., 'The polemics of eating fish in Tasmania: the historical evidence revisited', *Aboriginal History*, Vol.31 (2007), pp.1–26.
Thompson, J., 'Covered cave deposits hide mysteries of past', *Sunday Tasmanian* (Hobart), 2 April 1995, p.63.
Thorley, P., 'Pleistocene settlement in the Australian arid zone: occupation of an inland riverine landscape in the central Australian ranges', *Antiquity*, Vol.72, No.275 (March 1998), pp.34–45.
Thorley, P., 'Rock-art and the archaeological record of Indigenous settlement in Central Australia', *Australian Aboriginal Studies*, No.1 (2004), pp.79–88.
Thorne, A. and R. Sim, 'The Gracile Male Skeleton from Late Pleistocene King Island, Australia', *Australian Archaeology*, No.38 (1994), pp.8–10.
Tindale, N. and B. Maegraith, 'Traces of an Extinct Aboriginal Population on Kangaroo Island', *Records of the South Australian Museum*, Vol.4, No.3 (1931), pp.275–289.
Tindale, N., 'Relationship of the Extinct Kangaroo Island Culture with Cultures of Australia, Tasmania and Malaya', *Records of the South Australian Museum*, Vol.6 (1937), pp.39–60.
Tobias, P., 'Cranial Capacity of Zinjanthropus and Other Australopithecines', *Current Anthropology*, Vol.6, No.4 (October 1965), pp.414–417.
Tobias, P., 'Louis Seymour Bazett Leakey 1903–1972', *South African Archaeological Bulletin*, Vol.28, Nos.109–110 (June 1973), pp.3–7.

Bibliography

Tobias, P., 'Piltdown: An Appraisal of the Case against Sir Arthur Keith', *Current Anthropology*, Vol.33, No.3 (June 1992), pp.243-293.
Tobias, P., 'Ape-like *Australopithecus* After Seventy Years: Was It A Hominid?', *Journal of the Royal Anthropological Institute*, Vol.4, No.2 (June 1998), pp.283-308.
Tocheri, M., et. al., 'The Primitive Wrist of *Homo floresiensis* and Its Implications for Hominin Evolution', *Science*, Vol.317, No.5845 (21 September 2007), pp.1743-1745.
Traill, D., 'Schliemann's "Dream of Troy": The Making of a Legend', *Classical Journal*, Vol.81, No.1 (October-November 1985), pp.13-24.
Tringham, R., 'V. Gordon Childe 25 Years After: His Relevance for the Archaeology of the Eighties', *Journal of Field Archaeology*, Vol.10, No.1 (Spring 1983), pp.85-100.
Trinkaus, E. and W. Howells, 'The Neanderthals', *Scientific American*, Vol.241, No.6 (December 1979), pp.118-133.
Turney, C. et. al., 'Early Human Occupation at Devil's Lair, Southwestern Australia 50,000 Years Ago', *Quarternary Research*, Vol.55, No.1 (January 2001), pp.3-13.
Turney, C. et. al., 'Late-surviving megafauna in Tasmania, Australia, implicate human involvement in their extinction', *Proceedings of the National Academy of Sciences of the United States of America*, Vol.105, No.34 (26 August 2008), pp.12150-12153.
Urry, J., 'Old Questions: New Answers? Some Thoughts on the Origin and Antiquity of Man in Australia', *Aboriginal History*, Vol.2, Pt.2 (1978), pp.149-16.
van den Bergh, G.D., et. al., 'The Liang Bua faunal remains: a 95 k.y.r. sequence from Flores, East Indonesia', *Journal of Human Evolution*, Vol.57, No.5 (November 2009), pp.527-537.
van den Bergh, G.D. et. al., '*Homo floresiensis*-like fossils from the early Middle Pleistocene of Flores', *Nature*, Vol.534, No.7606 (9 June 2016), pp.245-248.
Vernes, K. and A. Dennis, 'Mammalian Diet and Broad Hunting Strategy of the Dingo (*Canis familiaris dingo*) in the Wet Tropical Rain Forests of Northeastern Australia', *Biotropica*, Vol.33, No.2 (June 2001), pp.339-345.
Veth, P. et. al., 'Excavations at Parnkupirti, Lake Gregory, Great Sandy Desert: OSL ages for occupation before the Last Glacial Maximum', *Australian Archaeology*, No.69 (December 2009), pp.1-10.
Veth, P. et. al., 'Minjiwarra: archaeological evidence of human occupation of Australia's northern Kimberley by 50,000 BP', *Australian Archaeology*, Vol.85, No.2 (2019), pp.115-125.
Volger, G., 'Making Fire by Percussion in Tasmania', *Oceania*, Vol.44, No.1 (September 1973), pp.58-63.
Wade, N., 'Voice from the Dead Names New Suspect for Piltdown Hoax', *Science*, Vol.202, No.4372 (8 December 1978), p.1062.
Walker, A., 'Diet and Teeth: Dietary hypotheses and human evolution', *Philosophical Transactions of the Royal Society of London*, Vol.292, No.1057 (8 May 1981), pp.57-64.
Walker, A., M. Zimmermann and R. Leakey, 'A possible case of hypervitaminosis A in *Homo erectus*', *Nature*, Vol.296, No.5854 (18 March 1982), pp.248-250.
Webb, R.E., 'Megamarsupial extinction: the carrying capacity argument',

Antiquity, Vol.72, No.275 (March 1998), pp.46–55.
Webb, S., 'Intensification, Population and Social Change in Southeastern Australia: The Skeletal Evidence', Aboriginal History, Vol.8 (1984), pp.154–172.
Webb, S., 'Cranial Thickening in an Australian Hominid as a Possible Palaeoepidemiological Indicator', American Journal of Physical Anthropology, Vol.82, No.4 (August 1990), pp.403–411.
Webb, S. M. Cupper and R. Robins, 'Pleistocene human footprints from the Willandra Lakes, southeastern Australia', Journal of Human Evolution, Vol.50, No.4 (April 2006), pp.405–413.
Weisburd, S., 'Creatures of the Dreamtime: A new exhibit digs into Australia's strange past lives', Science News, Vol.133, No.16 (16 April 1988), pp.248–250.
Weisburd, S., 'Australia's animals of the past: A museum exhibit brings some of Australia's ancient and strange creatures to light', Bioscience, Vol.38, No.8 (September 1988), pp.528–532.
Welch, D., 'Thy *Thylacoleo* is a thylacine', Australian Archaeology, Vol.80, No.1 (2015), pp.40–47.
Welch, D., 'That Bird is not *Genyornis*', Australian Archaeology, Vol.82, No.2 (2016), pp.184–191.
Wenner, A., 'Communication with Queen Honey Bees by Substrate Sound', Science, Vol.138, No.3538 (19 October 1962), pp.446–448.
Westaway, M., 'Footprints of the First Australians', Australasian Science, Vol.31, No.2 (March 2010), pp.14–18.
White, J.P. and J.F. O'Connell, 'Australian Prehistory: New Aspects of Antiquity', Science, Vol.203, No.4375 (5 January 1979), pp.21–28.
White, T., 'Evolutionary Implications of Pliocene Hominid Footprints', Science, Vol.208, No.4440 (11 April 1980), pp.175–176.
Wilhelm, J., 'Heinrich Schliemann's Sacramento Connection', California History, Vol.63, No.3 (Summer 1984), pp.224–229.
Williams, E., 'Documentation and Archaeological Investigation of an Aboriginal "Village" Site in South Western Victoria', Aboriginal History, Vol.8 (1984), pp.173–188.
Will, M., 'Neanderthal surf and turf', Science, Vol.367, No.6485 (27 March 2020), pp.1422–1423.
Wills, C., 'When Did Eve Live? An Evolutionary Detective Story', Evolution, Vol.49, No.4 (August 1995), pp.593–607.
Windschuttle, K. and T. Gillin, 'The extinction of the Australian Pygmies', Quadrant, Vol.46, No.6 (June 2002), pp.7–18.
Wolpoff, M., 'Evolution in *Homo erectus*: the question of stasis', Paleobiology, Vol.10, No.4 (Autumn 1984), pp.389–406.
Wolpoff, M. et. al., 'Why *not* the Neanderthals', World Archaeology, Vol.36, No.4 (December 2004), pp.527–546.
Wood, B., 'Origin and evolution and the genus *Homo*', Nature, Vol.355, No.6363 (27 February 1992), pp.783–790.
Wood, B., 'Hominid revelations from Chad', Nature, Vol.418, No.6894 (11 July 2002), pp.133–135.
Woodward, D., 'Diet in Tasmania over a Thousand Generations: A Preliminary History', Tasmanian Historical Studies, Vol.3, No.1 (1990–1991), pp.139–149.

Bibliography

Woolston, F.P. and F.S. Colliver, 'The Wildsoet Interview – Some Recollections of the Aborigines of the Tully Area', *Queensland Heritage*, Vol.3, No.3 (November 1975), pp.3–14.
Wroe, S., 'A review of terrestrial mammalian and reptilian carnivore ecology in Australian fossil faunas, and factors influencing their diversity: the myth of reptilian domination and its broader ramifications', *Australian Journal of Zoology*, Vol.50, No.1 (2002), pp.1–24.
Wroe, S., J. Field and D. Grayson, 'Megafaunal extinction: climate, humans and assumptions', *Trends in Ecology and Evolution*, Vol.21, No.2 (February 2006), pp.61–62.
Wunderly, J., 'The Origin of the Tasmanian Race', *Man*, Vol.38 (December 1938), pp.198–203.
Xing, G. and W. Chunxue, 'In Search of the Ancestors of Chinese People', *Paleoanthropology*, Vol.24, No.2 (2010), pp.111–114.
Yravedra, J. and L. Cobo-Sánchez, 'Neanderthal exploitation of ibex and chamois in southwestern Europe', *Journal of Human Evolution*, Vol.78 (January 2015), pp.12–32.
Zalmout, I.S., et al., 'New Oligocene primate from Saudi Arabia and the divergence of apes and Old World monkeys', *Nature*, Vol.466, No.7304 (15 July 2010), pp.360–364.
Zhang, J-F. and R. Dennell, 'The last of Asia conquered by *Homo sapiens*', *Science*, Vol.362, No.6418 (30 November 2018), pp.992–993.
Zhang, Y. and T. Harrison, '*Gigantopithecus blacki*: a giant ape from the Pleistocene of Asia revisited', *American Journal of Physical Anthropology*, Vol.162, No. S63 (January 2017), pp.153–177.
Zilhão, J. et. al., 'Last Interglacial Iberian Neanderthals as fisher-hunter-gatherers', *Science*, Vol.367, No.6485 (27 March 2020), pp.367–380.

THESES
McFarlane, I., 'Aboriginal Society in North West Tasmania: Dispossession and Genocide' (unpublished PhD thesis, University of Tasmania, 2002).
Taylor, J., 'The Palawa (Tasmanian Aboriginal) Languages' (unpublished MA thesis, University of Tasmania, 2004).

WEBSITES
>http://australian museum.net.au/Orrorin-tugenensis< (accessed 9 February 2011).
>http://drpeterjdadamo.com.wiki.pl/Blood_Groups_Races_and_People< (accessed 10 February 2010).
Kivell, T., 'Fossil ape hints at how bipedal walking evolved', *Nature Online* >doi:10.1038/s41586-019-1731-0< (accessed 6 November 2019).
Rathje, W.L., 'The Garbage Project & "The Archaeology of Us" >http://traumwerk.stanford.edu:3455/17/174< (accessed 24 February 2010).
Salleh, A., 'Is the hobbit just a dwarf cretin?', >www.abc.net.au/science/articles/2008/03/05/2181122.htm< (accessed 29 March 2010).
>www.historyonthenet.com/Historical_People/howard_carter.htm< (accessed 20 December 2010).
>www.mnsu.edu/emuseum/information/biography/klmno/leakey_mary.html< (accessed 22 December 2010).

NOTES

INTRODUCTION

1. A. Voight and N. Drury, *Wisdom From The Earth: The Living Legacy of the Aboriginal Dreamtime* (East Roseville, NSW: Simon & Schuster, 1997), p.23.
2. R. Smith, 'Alfred Russel Wallace: Philosophy of Nature and Man', *British Journal for the History of Science*, Vol.6, No.2 (December 1972), p.177.
3. J. Flood, *Archaeology of the Dreamtime: The story of prehistoric Australia and its people* (Pymble, NSW: Angus & Robertson, 1992), pp.29–30 [Hereafter: Flood, *Archaeology of the Dreamtime* (1992 ed.)].
4. Voigt and Drury, *Wisdom From The Earth*, p.24.
5. G. Joyner, 'The meaning of *yahoo* and *dulugal*: European and Aboriginal perspectives of the so-called "Australian gorilla"', *Canberra Historical Journal*, No.33 (March 1994), p.27.
6. Anon, 'A "New" Jaw Reopens Old Questions', *National Geographic*, Vol.193, No.4 (April 1998), n.p.
7. J. Woodford, *The Wollemi Pine: The incredible discovery of a living fossil from the age of dinosaurs* (Melbourne: Text Publishing, 2004), p.119.
8. G. Glazko *et. al.*, 'Eighty percent of proteins are different between humans and chimpanzees', *Gene*, Vol.346 (2005), p.215.
9. M. Lemonick and A. Dorfman, 'Father of Us All?', *Time*, No.28 (22 July 2002), pp.42–43.
10. C. Marean, 'Early human use of water resources and pigment in South Africa during the Middle Pleistocene', *Nature*, Vol.449, No.7164 (18 October 2007), p.905.
11. B. Bower, 'Erectus Unhinged', *Science News*, Vol.141, No.25 (20 June 1992), p.408.
12. C.C. Swisher III *et. al.*, 'Latest *Homo erectus* of Java: Potential Contemporaneity with *Homo sapiens* in Southeast Asia', *Science*, Vol.274, No.5294 (13 December 1996), p.1870.
13. E. Callaway, 'Fossil genome reveals ancestral link', *Nature*, Vol.468, No.7327 (23 December 2010), p.1012; D. Reich *et. al.*, 'Genetic history of an archaic hominin group from Denisova Cave in Siberia', *Nature*, Vol.468, No.7327 (23 December 2010), p.1053.
14. A. Cooper and A.B. Stringer, 'Did the Denisovans Cross Wallace's Line?', *Science*, Vol.324, No.6156 (18 October 2013), p.321.
15. R. Leakey, *The Making of Mankind* (London: Michael Joseph, 1981), pp.36–37.
16. C.O. Lovejoy, 'The Origin of Man', *Science*, Vol.211, No.4480 (23 January 1981), p.342.
17. Leakey, *The Making of Mankind*, p.131.
18. P. Tobias, 'Cranial Capacity of Zinjanthropus and Other Australopithecines', *Current Anthropology*, Vol.6, No.4 (October 1965), p.414.
19. G.P. Rightmire, 'Patterns in the evolution of *Homo erectus*', *Paleobiology*, Vol.7, No.2 (Spring 1981), p.243.

Notes

20   R. Lewin, *Bones of Contention: Controversies in the Search for Human Origins* (New York: Simon & Schuster, 1987), pp.66–67.
21   Leakey, *The Making of Mankind*, p.18.
22   R. Lewin, *Human Evolution: An Illustrated Introduction* (New York: W.H. Freedman and Company, 1985), p.22.
23   Leakey, *The Making of Mankind*, p.18.
24   *Ibid.*, pp.20–21.
25   M.A. Smith, '"The Opening Chapter of the Romance of Excavation in Australia": Reflections on Norman Tindale's Archaeology', *Historical Records of Australian Science*, Vol.13, No.2 (September 2000), p.151.
26   H. du Cros, *Much More than Stones and Bones: Australian Archaeology in the Late Twentieth Century* (Carlton South, Vic: Melbourne University Press, 2002), p.22.
27   R. Lewin, 'Human origins: the challenge of Java's skulls', *New Scientist*, No.1924 (7 May 1994), pp.39–40.
28   J. Urry, 'Old Questions: New Answers? Some Thoughts on the Origin and Antiquity of Man in Australia', *Aboriginal History*, Vol.2, Pt.2 (1978), p.157.
29   >http://drpeterjdadamo.com.wiki/wiki.pl/Blood_Groups,_Races_and_People< (accessed 10 February 2010).
30   S. O'Connor, M. Spriggs and P. Veth, 'Excavation at Lene Hara Cave establishes occupation in East Timor at least 30,000–35,000 years ago', *Antiquity*, Vol.76, No.291 (March 2002), p.45.
31   R. Jones, 'The Coming of the Aborigines – A Pleistocene Perspective', in J. Hardy and A. Frost (eds), *Studies from Terra Australis to Australia* (Canberra: Highland Press in association with the Australian Academy of Humanities, 1989), p.16.
32   P. Hiscock, *The Archaeology of Ancient Australia* (London: Routledge, 2008), pp.45–46.
33   R. Cosgrove, 'Thirty Thousand Years of Human Colonization in Tasmania: New Pleistocene Dates', *Science*, Vol.243, No.4899 (31 March 1989), pp.1706–1708; R. Cosgrove, 'Late Pleistocene behavioural variation and trends: the case from Tasmania', *Archaeology in Oceania*, Vol.30, No.3 (October 1995), p.83.
34   Hiscock, *The Archaeology of Ancient Australia*, pp.91–92.
35   Jones, 'The Coming of the Aborigines', p.18.
36   D. Clode, *Prehistoric giants: the megafauna of Australia* (Melbourne: Museum Victoria, 2009), pp.6–8 and 32.
37   G. Miller *et. al.*, 'Pleistocene Extinction of *Genyornis newtoni*: Human Impact on Australian Megafauna', *Science*, Vol.283, No.5399 (8 January 1999), p.83.
38   J. Singe, *The Torres Strait: People and History* (St Lucia, Qld: University of Queensland Press, 1989), pp.2–4.
39   L. Ryan, *The Aboriginal Tasmanians* (Crows Nest, NSW: Allen & Unwin, 1996), p.14.
40   B. Plomley, *The Tasmanian Aborigines* (Launceston, Tas: Brian Plomley, 1993), p.29.
41   S. Bowdler, 'Fish and Culture: A Tasmanian Polemic', *Mankind*, Vol.12, No.4 (December 1980), p.334.
42   S. Breen, 'Tasmanian Aborigines – Making Fire', *Tasmanian Historical Research Association Papers and Proceedings*, Vol.39, No.1 (March 1992), p.40.

I ARCHAEOLOGY AND ARCHAEOLOGICAL ENDEAVOUR

1   C. Renfrew and P. Bahn, *Archaeology: Theories, Methods, and Practice* (London: Thomas and Hudson, 1996), p.11.

2   Ibid., p.12.
3   J. Mulvaney and J. Kamminga, *Prehistory of Australia* (St Leonards, NSW: Allen & Unwin, 1999), p.121.
4   S. Piggott, *Approach to Archaeology* (London: Adam & Charles Black, 1960), pp.2–3.
5   Renfrew and Bahn, *Archaeology*, p.12.
6   F.L.L. Griffith, 'The Decipherrment of the Hieroglyphics', *Journal of Egyptian Archaeology*, Vol.137 (December 1951), pp.39 and 42.
7   P. Couture, ''Sir Henry Creswicke Rawlinson: Pioneer Cuneiformist', *Biblical Archaeology*, Vol.47, No.3 (September 1984), pp.143–144.
8   H.C. Baldry, 'Who Invented the Golden Age?', *Classical Quarterly*, Vol.2, Nos.1–2 (January–April 1952), p.91; J.G. Griffiths, 'Did Hesiod Invent the "Golden Age"?', *Journal of the History of Ideas*, Vol.19, No.1 (January 1958), p.91.
9   E. Davis, 'King Nabonidus and the Missing Link City', *Journal of Egyptian Archaeology*, Vol.37 (December 1951), pp.54–55.
10 Renfrew and Bahn, *Archaeology*, p.20.
11 R. Peterson, 'William Stukeley: an eighteenth-century phenomenologist?', *Antiquity*, Vol.77, No.296 (June 2003), pp.394–395.
12 G. Sayre, 'The Mound Builders and the Imagination of American Antiquity in Jefferson, Bartram, and Chateaubriand', *Early American Literature*, Vol.33, No.3 (1998), pp.225–226.
13 R. Heizer (ed.), *The Archaeologist at Work: A Source Book in Archaeological Method and Interpretation* (New York: Harper & Brothers, 1959), pp.218–221.
14 C. Peers, 'The Beginnings of Prehistoric Studies in Britain', *Man*, Vol.32 (September 1932), p.202.
15 B. Trigger, *A History of Archaeological Thought* (Cambridge: Cambridge University Press, 1990), p.90.
16 J. Barr, 'Pre-Scientific Chronology: The Bible and the Origin of the World', *Proceedings of the American Philosophical Society*, Vol.143, No.3 (September 1999), p.380.
17 H. Wendt (trans. R. Winston and C. Winston), *Before the Deluge: The Story of Palaeontology* (London: Victor Gollancz, 1968), pp.97–98.
18 L. Page, 'James Hutton: Uniformitarianism Versus Evolution', *Proceedings of the Oklahoma Academy of Science for 1959*, Vol.40 (1960), pp.103–104; J.E. O'Rourke, 'A Comparison of James Hutton's *Principles of Knowledge and Theory of the Earth*', *Isis*, Vol.69, No.1 (March 1978), p.5.
19 W. Hobbs, 'James Hutton, The Pioneer of Modern Geology', *Science*, Vol.64, No.1655 (17 September 1926), p.264.
20 M. Goodrum, 'Prolegomenon to a History of Paleoanthropology: The Study of Human Origins as a Scientific Enterprise Part 2: Eighteenth to Twentieth Century', *Evolutionary Anthropology*, Vol.13, No.6 (December 2004), pp.227–229.
21 R. Heizer, 'The Background of Thomsen's Three-Age System', *Technology and Culture*, Vol.3, No.3 (Summer 1962), p.259.
22 Ibid., p.264.
23 A. Sherratt, 'V. Gordon Childe: Archaeology and Intellectual History', *Past and Present*, No.125 (November 1989), p.168.
24 N. Barlow, 'Erasmus Darwin, F.R.S. (1731–1802)', *Notes and Records of the Royal Society of London*, Vol.14, No.1 (June 1959), pp.93–94.
25 Leakey, *The Making of Mankind*, pp.24–25.
26 K. Padian, 'Ten Myths about Charles Darwin', *Bioscience*, Vol.59, No.9 (October 2009), p.801; A. Moorehead, *Darwin and the Beagle* (New York: Harper & Row, 1970), pp.26–30.

Notes

27   M. Ruse, 'Charles Darwin and the "Beagle"', *Wilson Quarterly*, Vol.6, No.1 (Winter 1982), pp.166–169.
28   Padian, 'Ten Myths about Charles Darwin', p.803.
29   M. White and J. Gribbin, *Darwin: A Life in Science* (London: Simon & Schuster, 1995), pp.209–210.
30   Leakey, *The Making of Mankind*, p.26.
31   *Ibid.*
32   W. Kamp, *Charles Darwin and the Origin of Species* (London: Cassell, 1968), pp.82–83.
33   Renfrew and Bahn, *Archaeology*, p.26.
34   H. Sigurdsson, S. Cashdollar and S. Sparks, 'The Eruption of Vesuvius in A.D. 79: Reconstruction from Historical and Vulcanological Evidence', *American Journal of Archaeology*, Vol.86, No.1 (January 1982), pp.39 and 49–50; C. Simon, 'Preserved bones reveal fiery death at Herculaneum', *Science News*, Vol.122, No.21 (November 1982), p.327.
35   E.R. Barker, 'Past Excavations at Herculaneum', *Burlington Magazine for Connoisseurs*, Vol.11, No.51 (June 1907), p.144.
36   N. Ramage, 'Goods, Graves, and Scholars: 18th-Century Archaeologists in Britain and Italy', *American Journal of Archaeology*, Vol.96, No.4 (October 1992), p.654; J.L. Allen, 'Johann Winckelmann: Classicist', *Metropolitan Museum of Art Bulletin*, Vol.7, No.8 (April 1949), pp.228–230.
37   Renfrew and Bahn, *Archaeology*, pp.22–23.
38   See for example: P. Warren, *The Making of the Past: The Aegean Civilizations* (Oxford: Elsevier-Phaidon, 1975), p.12.
39   J. Wilhelm, 'Heinrich Schliemann's Sacramento Connection', *California History*, Vol.63, No.3 (Summer 1984), pp.224–226.
40   D. Traill, 'Schliemann's 'Dream of Troy': The Making of a Legend', *Classical Journal*, Vol.81, No.1 (October-November 1985), p.13.
41   Wilhelm, 'Heinrich Schliemann's Sacramento Connection', pp.226 and 229.
42   D.F. Easton, 'Heinrich Schliemann: Hero or Fraud?', *Classical World*, Vol.91, No.5 (May-June 1998), pp.341–342.
43   *Ibid.*, p.342.
44   J. Judge, 'Minoans and Mycenaens: Greece's Brilliant Bronze Age', *National Geographic*, Vol.153, No.2 (February 1978), p.148.
45   C. Gere, *Knossos and the Prophets of Modernism* (Chicago: University of Chicago Press, 2009), p.111.
46   L. Gomme, 'Obituary', *Folklore*, Vol.11, No.2 (June 1900), pp.185–186; T.K. Penniman, 'General Pitt Rivers', *Man*, Vol.46 (July-August 1946), p.73; Trigger, *A History of Archaeological Thought*, p.197.
47   S. Smith, 'William Matthew Flinders Petrie 1853–1942', *Obituary Notices of the Royal Society*, Vol.5, No.14 (November 1945), p.3.
48   V. Fargo, 'Sir Flinders Petrie', *Biblical Archaeologist*, Vol.47, No.4 (December 1984), pp.220–222.
49   K. El Mallakh and A. Brackman, *The Gold of Tutankhamen* (New York: Newsweek Books, 1978), pp.27, 75 and 79–82.
50   M. Nelson, 'The mummy's curse: historical cohort study', *British Medical Journal*, Vol.325, No.7378 (21–28 December 2002), pp.1482–1484.
51   >www.historyonthenet.com/Historical_People/howard_carter.htm< (accessed 20 December 2010).
52   S. Piggott, 'Robert Eric Mortimer Wheeler: 10 September 1890–22 July 1976', *Biographical Memoirs of Fellows of the Royal Society*, Vol.23 (November 1977), pp.626–627, 631–632 and 640.
53   R. Braidwood, 'Vere Gordon Childe 1892–1957', *American Anthropologist*, Vol.60, No.4 (August 1958), p.735; J. Allen, 'Aspects of V. Gordon Childe',

Labour History, No.12 (May 1967), pp.53–56.
54   R. Tringham, 'V. Gordon Childe 25 Years After: His Relevance for the Archaeology of the Eighties', *Journal of Field Archaeology*, Vol.10, No.1 (Spring 1983), p.87.
55   P. Tobias, 'Louis Seymour Bazett Leakey 1903–1972', *South African Archaeological Bulletin*, Vol.28, Nos.109–110 (June 1973), p.3.
56   L.S.B. Leakey, *By the Evidence: Memoirs, 1903–1972* (New York: Harcourt Brace Jovanovich, 1974), pp.15, 42 and 76.
57   Tobias, 'Louis Seymour Bazett Leakey 1903–1972', p.5; M. Rose, 'Dear Mary', *BioScience*, Vol.35, No.6 (June 1985), p.375.
58   >www.mnsu.edu/museum/information/biography/klmno/leakey_mary.html< (accessed 22 December 2010).
59   Lewin, *Bones of Contention*, pp.133–134; Trigger, *A History of Archaeological Thought*, p.136.
60   R. Berndt and C. Berndt, *The World of the First Australians: Aboriginal Traditional Life Past and Present* (Canberra: Aboriginal Studies Press, 1999), pp.6–7.
61   Governor Phillip to Lord Sydney, 15 May 1788, *Historical Records of Australia*, Vol.1, Ser.1, pp.28–29; J.P. White and J.F. O'Connell, *A Prehistory of Australia, New Guinea and Sahul* (North Ryde, NSW: Academic Press, 1982), p.22.
62   A. Moorehead, *The Fatal Impact: The Invasion of the South Pacific 1767–1840* (Sydney: Mead and Beckett, 1987), pp.171–173.
63   White and O'Connell, *A Prehistory of Australia, New Guinea and Sahul*, p.24.
64   M. Johnson, '"A Modified Form of Whaling": The Moreton Bay dugong fishery 1846–1920', in M. Johnson (ed.), *Moreton Bay Matters* (Brisbane: Brisbane History Group, 2002), pp.36–37.
65   White and O'Connell, *A Prehistory of Australia, New Guinea and Sahul*, pp.24–25.
66   Hiscock, *The Archaeology of Ancient Australia*, p.145.
67   Smith, '"The Opening Chapter of the Romance of Excavation in Australia"', pp.151–153. See also: D. Horton, *Recovering the Tracks: The Story of Australian Archaeology* (Canberra: Aboriginal Studies Press, 1991), p.170.
68   Horton, *Recovering the Tracks*, pp.153 and 166.
69   Smith, '"The Opening Chapter of the Romance of Excavation in Australia"', pp.152 and 157–158.
70   *Ibid.*, p.152.
71   Horton, *Recovering the Tracks*, pp.154 and 176.
72   S. Moser, 'Building the discipline of Australian archaeology: Fred McCarthy at the Australian Institute of Aboriginal Studies', in M. Sullivan, S. Brockwell and A. Webb (eds), *Archaeology in the North: Proceedings of the 1993 Australian Archaeological Association Conference* (Darwin: North Australia Research Unit, Australian National University, 1994), p.20.
73   *Ibid.*, pp.21–22.
74   T. Murray and J.P. White, 'Cambridge in the bush? Archaeology in Australia and New Guinea', *World Archaeology*, Vol.13, No.2 (October 1981), p.20.
75   Horton, *Recovering the Tracks*, p.155.
76   *Ibid.*
77   Flood, *Archaeology of the Dreamtime* (1992 ed.), p.97.
78   Murray and White, 'Cambridge in the bush?', pp.257–258.
79   V. Laurie, 'Secrets unearthed: humankind just got a little older', *Weekend Australian* (Sydney), 28–29 November 2015, p.3.
80   C. Clarkson *et. al.*, 'Human occupation of northern Australia by 65,000 years ago', *Nature*, Vol.547, No.7663 (20 July 2017), p.306.
81   White and O'Connell, *A Prehistory of Australia, New Guinea and Sahul*, p.29.

Notes

82   Trigger, *A History of Archaeological Thought*, pp.295–296.
83   I. McNiven, B. David and B. Barker, 'The social archaeology of Indigenous Australia', in B. David, B. Barker and I. McNiven (eds), *The Social Archaeology of Australian Indigenous Societies* (Canberra: Aboriginal Studies Press, 2006), pp.7–9. See also: Flood, *Archaeology of the Dreamtime* (1992 ed.), p.181.
84   McNiven, David and Barker, 'The social archaeology of Indigenous Australia', p.9. See also: H. Lourandos, 'Change or stability? Hydraulics, hunter-gatherers and population in temperate Australia', *World Archaeology*, Vol.11, No.3 (February 1980), p.246.
85   S. Bowdler, 'Harry Lourandos' life and work: an Australian archaeological odyssey', in David, Barker and McNiven, *The Social Archaeology of Australian Indigenous Societies*, pp.43–44.
86   T. Earle and R. Preucel, 'Processual Archaeology and the Radical critique', *Current Anthropology*, Vol.28, No.4 (August-October 1987), p.510; Renfrew and Bahn, *Archaeology*, p.43.
87   E. von Daniken, *In Search of Ancient Gods: My Pictorial Evidence for the Impossible* (London: Corgi Books, 1975), pp.183–189.
88   P. Hiscock, 'The New Age of alternative archaeology in Australia', *Archaeology in Oceania*, Vol.31, No.3 (October 1996), pp.158–159.
89   Wendt, *Before the Deluge*, pp.317–318.
90   M. Goodrum, 'Prolegomenon to a History of Paleoanthropology, The Study of Human Origins as a Scientific Enterprise Part 1: Antiquity to the Eighteenth Century', *Evolutionary Archaeology*, Vol.13, No.5 (October 2004), p.173.
91   Renfrew and Bahn, *Archaeology*, pp.111–112.
92   *Ibid.*, p.132.
93   C. Tuniz, R. Gillespie and C. Jones, *The Bone Readers: Atoms, genes and the politics of Australia's deep past* (Crows Nest, NSW: Allen & Unwin, 2009), pp.32–33.
94   Renfrew and Bahn, *Archaeology*, p.134.
95   Tuniz, Gillespie and Jones, *The Bone Readers*, p.33.
96   S. Manning *et. al.*, 'Mediterranean radiocarbon offsets and calendar dates for prehistory', *Science Advances*, Vol.6, No.12 (18 March 2020), p.1; M. Bridge, 'Science rings changes about history', *Weekend Australian* (Sydney), 21–22 March 2020, p.15.
97   Tuniz, Gillespie and Jones, *The Bone Readers*, pp.44-45.
98   *Ibid.*, pp.38–39.
99   F. Celoria, *Archaeology* (New York: Grosset & Dunlap, 1973), p.143.
100 Renfrew and Bahn, *Archaeology*, pp.145–147; N.A. Spooner, 'Human occupation at Jinmium, northern Australia: 116,000 years or much less?', *Antiquity*, Vol.72, No.275 (March 1998), p.173.
101 Mulvaney and Kamminga, *Prehistory of Australia*, p.52.
102 I. McDougall, 'Dating Human Evolution', *Australian Natural History*, Supplement 2 (1988), pp.43–44.
103 Tuniz, Gillespie and Jones, *The Bone Readers*, p.41.
104 W.L. Rathje, 'The Garbage Project & "The Archaeology of Us"', >http://traumwerk.stanford.edu:3455/17/174< (accessed 24 February 2010).

II HUMAN ORIGINS, EVOLUTION AND GLOBAL DISPERSAL

1   C. Tudge, *The Link: Uncovering Our Earliest Ancestor* (London: Little, Brown, 2009), pp.25–27.
2   I.S. Zalmout *et. al.*, 'New Oligocene primate from Saudi Arabia and the divergence of apes and Old World monkeys', *Nature*, Vol.466, No.7304 (15 July

2010), pp.360–363.
3   J. Relethford, *The Human Species: An Introduction to Biological Anthropology* (Mountain View, CA: Mayfield Publishing Company, 1997), p.245.
4   Y. Zhang and T. Harrison, '*Gigantopithecus blacki*: a giant ape from the Pleistocene of Asia revisited', *American Journal of Physical Anthropology*, Vol.162, No.S63 (January 2017), p.153.
5   P. Line, '"Giants" in the land: an assessment of *Gigantopithecus* and *Meganthropus*', *Journal of Creation*, Vol.20, No.1 (2006), p.105.
6   Zhang and Harrison, '*Gigantopithecus blacki*', pp.168–169; F. Poirer and J. McKee, *Understanding Human Evolution* (Upper Saddle River, NJ: Prentice Hall, 1999), p.119.
7   Zhang and Harrison, '*Gigantopithecus blacki*', p.157.
8   Leakey, *The Making of Mankind*, p.48.
9   *Ibid.*, p.89.
10 *Ibid.*, p.45.
11 D. Begun, '*Sivapithecus* is east and *Dryopithecus* is west, and never the twain shall meet', *Anthropological Science*, Vol.113, No.1 (2005), p.55.
12 D. Palmer (ed.), *The Marshall Illustrated Encyclopedia of Dinosaurs and Prehistoric Animals* (London: Marshall Editions, 1999), p.292.
13 Leakey, *The Making of Mankind*, p.45.
14 T. Kivell, 'Fossil ape hints at how bipedal walking evolved', *Nature Online* doi:10.1038/s41586-019-1731-0 (accessed 6 November 2019); Anon, 'Ancient ape clue to tall story', *Herald Sun* (Melbourne), 8 November 2019, p.27.
15 *Ibid.*, pp.45–48.
16 Lemonick and Dorfman, 'Father of Us All?', pp.37–40.
17 B. Wood, 'Hominid revelations from Chad', *Nature*, Vol.418, No.6894 (11 July 2002), p.134.
18 A. Gibbons, 'Millennium Ancestor Gets Its Walking Papers', *Science*, Vol.319, No.5870 (21 March 2008), pp.1599–1601.
19 B. Senut, 'The Earliest Putative Hominids', in W. Henke and I. Tattersall (eds), *Handbook of Paleoanthropology: Vol.3* (New York: Springer Verlag, 2007), p.1529.
20 >http://australianmuseum.net.au/Orrorin-tugenensis< (accessed 9 February 2011).
21 A. Gibbons, 'A New Kind of Ancestor: *Ardipithecus* Unveiled', *Science*, Vol.326, No.5949 (2 October 2009), pp.36–39.
22 G. Suwa, 'The *Ardipithecus ramidus* skull and its implications for hominid origins', *Science*, Vol.326. No.5949 (2 October 2009), p.68.
23 G. Suwa *et. al.*, 'Paleobiological Implications of the *Ardipithecus ramidus* Dentition', *Science*, Vol.326, No.5949 (2 October 2009), pp.98–99.
24 W. Kimbel *et.al.*, '*Ardipithecus ramidus* and the evolution of the human cranial base', *Proceedings of the National Academy of the United States of America*, Vol.111, No.3 (21 January 2014), p.948.
25 A. Gibbons, '*Ardipithecus ramidus*', *Science*, Vol.326, No.5960 (18 December 2009), pp.1598–1599.
26 Lemonick and Dorfman, 'Father of Us All?', p.43.
27 S. Altmann, 'Baboons, Space, Time, and Energy', *American Zoologist*, Vol.14, No.1 (Winter 1974), pp.228–230.
28 M. Lemonick, 'How Man Began', *Time* (14 March 1994), p.56.
29 P. Tobias, 'Ape-like *Australopithecus* After Seventy Years: Was It A Hominid?', *Journal of the Royal Anthropological Institute*, Vol.4, No.2 (June 1998), pp.284–286.
30 R. Lewin, 'The Taung Baby Reaches Sixty', *Science*, Vol.227, No.4691 (8 March 1985), pp.1188–1189.

Notes

31   M. Price, 'Stunning skull shakes human family tree', *Science*, Vol.365, No.6456 (30 August 2019), p.850.
32   D. Johanson and J. Shreeve, *Lucy's Child: The Discovery of a Human Ancestor* (London: Penguin, 1991), p.19.
33   R. Clarke and K. Kuman, 'The skull of StW 573, a 3.67 Ma *Australopithecus prometheus* skeleton from Sterkfontein Caves, South Africa', *Journal of Human Evolution*, Vol.134 (September 2019), p.1.
34   R. Pickering *et.al.*, '*Australopithecus sediba* at 1.977 Ma and Implications for the Origins of the Genus *Homo*', *Science*, Vol.333, No.6048 (9 September 2011), p.1421.
35   A. Herries *et. al.*, 'Contemporaneity of *Australopithecus*, *Paranthropus*, and early *Homo erectus* in South Africa', *Science*, Vol.368, No.6486 (3 April 2020), p.48.
36   B.A. Wood, 'Evolution of australopithecines', in S. Jones, R. Martin and D. Pilbeam (eds), *The Cambridge Encyclopedia of Human Evolution* (Cambridge: Cambridge University Press, 1992), p.239.
37   Leakey, *The Making of Mankind*, p.70.
38   A. Ritchie, 'Mary Leakey and the Laetoli Tracks', *Australian Natural History*, Supp. No.2 (1988), p.27.
39   *Ibid.*; M. Leakey and R. Hay, 'Pliocene footprints in the Laetoli Beds at Laetoli, Tanzania', *Nature*, Vol.278, No.5702 (22 March 1979), pp.317–318.
40   Anon., 'The Leakey Footprints: An Uncertain Path', *Science News*, Vol.115, No.13 (31 March 1979), p.196.
41   T. White, 'Evolutionary Implications of Pliocene Hominid Footprints', *Science*, Vol.208, No.4440 (11 April 1980), p.175.
42   D. Raichlen *et. al.*, 'Laetoli Footprints Preserve Earliest Direct Evidence of Human-Like Bipedal Biomechanics', *Public Library of Science One*, Vol.5, No.3 (March 2010), p.3.
43   Tobias, 'Ape-Like Australopithecus After Seventy Years', p.299.
44   D. Raichlen, H. Pontzer and M. Sockol, 'The Laetoli footprints and early hominin locomotor kinematics', *Journal of Human Evolution*, Vol.54, No.1 (January 2008), p.113.
45   Leakey, *The Making of Mankind*, p.74.
46   C.K. Brain, 'The Probable Role of Leopards as Predators of the Swartkrans Australopithecines', *South African Archaeological Bulletin*, Vol.24, Nos.95–96 (November 1969), pp.170–171.
47   M. Sponheimer *et. al.*, 'Isotopic Evidence for Dietary Variability in the Early Hominin *Paranthropus robustus*', *Science*, Vol.314, No.5801 (10 November 2006), pp.980–981.
48   B. Wood, 'Origin and evolution of the genus *Homo*', *Nature*, Vol.355, No.6363 (27 February 1992), p.783; Relethford, *The Human Species*, p.276.
49   D. Braun, 'Australopithecine butchers', *Nature*, Vol.466, No.7308 (12 August 2010), p.828.
50   Lemonick, 'How Man Began', p.58.
51   T. Bielicki, 'On "Homo habilis"', *Current Anthropology*, Vol.7, No.5 (December 1966), pp.576–577.
52   Lewin, *Bones of Contention*, pp.146–147.
53   R. Klein, 'Anatomy, Behavior, and Modern Human Origins', *Journal of World Prehistory*, Vol.9, No.2 (June 1995), p.172.
54   D. Argue *et. al.*, 'The affinities of *Homo floresiensis* based on phylogenetic analyses of cranial, dental, and postcranial characters', *Journal of Human Evolution*, Vol.107 (June 2017), pp.107–108 and 130; J. Ross, 'Flores Hobbits out of Africa', *Weekend Australian* (Sydney), 22–23 April 2017, p.10.
55   F. Détroit *et. al.*, 'A new species of Homo from the Late Pleistocene of the

Philippines', *Nature*, Vol.568, No.7751 (11 April 2019), p.181
56 A. Gómez-Robles, 'The dawn of *Homo floresiensis*', *Nature*, Vol.534, No.7606 (9 June 2016), p.189.
57 Relethford, *The Human Species*, p.182.
58 Leakey, *The Making of Mankind*, p.89.
59 *Ibid.*, p.92.
60 W. Roebroeks, 'Hominid behavior and the earliest occupation of Europe: an exploration', *Journal of Human Evolution*, Vol.41, No.5 (November 2001), p.448.
61 Leakey, *The Making of Mankind*, p.93.
62 Relethford, *The Human Species*, pp.281–282.
63 Wood, 'Origin and evolution of the genus *Homo*', p.783.
64 *Ibid.*, pp.279–280.
65 Leakey, *The Making of Mankind*, p.131.
66 *Ibid.*
67 *Ibid.*, pp.131–133.
68 *Ibid.*
69 Relethford, *The Human Species*, p.344.
70 K. Vernes and A. Dennis, 'Mammalian Diet and Broad Hunting Strategy of the Dingo (*Canis familiaris dingo*) in the Wet Tropical Rain Forests of Northeastern Australia', *Biotropica*, Vol.33, No.2 (June 2001), p.340.
71 Leakey, *The Making of Mankind*, p.108.
72 A. Wenner, 'Communication with Queen Honey Bees by Substrate Sound', *Science*, Vol.138, No.3538 (19 October 1962), pp.446–447.
73 L. Dayton, 'Fossils force rethink on tools', *Australian* (Sydney), 12 August 2010, p.11.
74 Leakey, *The Making of Mankind*, pp.83–84.
75 J. Lee-Thorp, J.F. Thackeray and N. van der Merwe, 'The hunters and the hunted revisited', *Journal of Human Evolution*, Vol.39, No.6 (December 2000), p.572.
76 G.P. Rightmire, 'The Dispersal of *Homo erectus* from Africa and the Emergence of More Modern Humans', *Journal of Anthropological Research*, Vol.47, No.2 (Summer 1991), p.183; Bower, 'Erectus Unhinged', p.408; A. Gibbons, '*Homo erectus* in Java: A 250,000-Year Anachronism', *Science*, Vol.274, No.5294 (13 December 1996), p.1841.
77 J.F. O'Connell, K. Hawkes and N.G. Blurton Jones, 'Grandmothering and the evolution of *Homo erectus*', *Journal of Human Evolution*, Vol.36, No.5 (May 1999), p.462.
78 Gibbons, '*Homo erectus* in Java, p.1841; S. Antón, 'All who wander are not lost: New hominin cranial fossils highlight the early exploits of *Homo erectus*', *Science*, Vol.368, No.6486 (3 April 2020), p.35.
79 C.C. Swisher III *et. al.*, 'Latest *Homo erectus* of Java: Potential Contemporaneity with *Homo sapiens* in Southeast Asia', *Science*, Vol.274, No.5294 (13 December 1996), pp.1870 and 1873.
80 M. Dunn, 'Our origins 200,000 years older: Ancient skull reveals new timeline', *Herald Sun* (Melbourne), 3 April 2020, p.23.
81 Lewin, *Human Evolution*, p.53.
82 Leakey, *The Making of Mankind*, pp.116–117.
83 Herries *et. al.*, 'Contemporaneity of *Australopithecus, Paranthropus*, and early *Homo erectus* in South Africa', p.47.
84 *Ibid.*, p.112.
85 A. Hrdlicka, 'Dr. Eugene Dubois, 1858–1940', *Scientific Monthly*, Vol.52, No.6 (June 1941), pp.578–579.
86 P. Shipman, *The Man Who Found the Missing Link: Eugene Dubois and His*

Lifelong Quest to Prove Darwin Right (New York: Simon & Schuster, 2001), pp.159–162 and 171.
87   B. Bryson, *A Short History of Nearly Everything* (London: Doubleday, 2003), pp.388–389.
88   G. Elliott Smith, 'Sinanthropus – Peking Man: its discovery and significance', *Scientific Monthly*, Vol.33, No.3 (September 1931), pp.200–203.
89   I. Tattersall, *The Strange Case of the Rickety Cossack and Other Cautionary Tales from Human Evolution* (New York: Palgrave Macmillan, 2015), p.54.
90   M. Wolpoff, 'Evolution in *Homo erectus*: the question of stasis', *Paleobiology*, Vol.10, No.4 (Autumn 1984), p.390.
91   Bower, 'Erectus Unhinged', p.408.
92   Relethford, *The Human Species*, p.307.
93   Bryson, *A Short History of Nearly Everything*, pp.401–402.
94   C.C. Swisher III *et. al.*, 'Age of the Earliest Known Hominids in Java, Indonesia', *Science*, Vol.263, No.5150 (25 February 1994), p.1119.
95   Lemonick, 'How Man Began', p.59.
96   S.C. Anton, W.R. Leonard and M.L. Robertson, 'An ecomorphological model of the initial hominid dispersal from Africa', *Journal of Human Evolution*, Vol.43, No.6 (December 2002), p.781; Tuniz, Gillespie and Jones, *The Bone Readers*, pp.159–160.
97   Roebroeks, 'Hominid behaviour and the earliest occupation of Europe', p.448.
98   Lewin, 'Human origins', p.39.
99   Lemonick, 'How Man Began', pp.59–61.
100 L. Aiello, 'Five Years of *Homo floresiensis*', *American Journal of Physical Anthropology*, Vol.142, No.2 (June 2010), p.10.
101 Lewin, 'Human origins', pp.38–39.
102 O'Connell, Hawkes and Blurton Jones, 'Grandmothering and the evolution of *Homo erectus*', p.473.
103 A. Walker, 'Diet and Teeth: Dietary Hypotheses and human evolution', *Philosophical Transactions of the Royal Society of London*, Vol.292, No.1057 (8 May 1981), pp.62–63; A. Walker, M. Zimmermann and R. Leakey, 'A possible case of hypervitaminosis A in *Homo erectus*', *Nature*, Vol.296, No.5854 (18 March 1982), pp.248–250.
104 Leakey, *The Making of Mankind*, p.118.
105 P. Shipman, W. Bosler and K. Davis, 'Butchering of Giant Geladas at an Acheulian Site', *Current Anthropology*, Vol.22, No.3 (June 1981), pp.257, 260 and 263–264.
106 For a rebuttal of this hypothesis see: L. Binford and C. Todd, 'On Arguments for the "Butchering" of Giant Geladas', *Current Anthropology*, Vol.23, No.1 (February 1982), pp.108–110.
107 Leakey, *The Making of Mankind*, p.121.
108 *Ibid.*, pp.123–124.
109 *Ibid.*, pp.124–125.
110 J. Bermudez De Castro *et. al.*, 'The Atapuerca Sites and Their Contribution to the Knowledge of Human Evolution in Europe', *Evolutionary Anthropology*, Vol.13, No.1 (15 February 2004), p.29; E. Carbonell *et. al.*, 'The first hominin of Europe', *Nature*, Vol.452, No.7186 (27 March 2008), p.465; B. Bower, 'European Roots: Human ancestors go back in time in Spanish cave', *Science News*, Vol.173, No.13 (29 March 2008), p.196.
111 B. Bower, 'Spanish fossils enter human ancestry fray', *Science News*, Vol.151, No.22 (31 May 1997), p.333.
112 G.P. Rightmire, 'Human Evolution in the Middle Pleistocene: The Role of *Homo heidelbergensis*', *Evolutionary Anthropology*, Vol.6, No.6 (December 1998), pp.220–223.

113   B. Campbell, 'Conceptual Progress in Physical Anthropology: Fossil Man', *Annual Review of Anthropology*, Vol.1 (1972), p.47; A. Mounier, F. Marchal and S. Confemi, 'Is *Homo heidelbergensis* a distinct species? New insight on the Mauer mandible', *Journal of Human Evolution*, Vol.56, No.3 (March 2009), p.221.
114   S. McBrearty and C. Stringer, 'The coast in colour', *Nature*, Vol.449, No.7164 (18 October 2007), p.793.
115   Marean *et. al.*, 'Early human use of marine resources and pigment in South Africa during the Middle Pleistocene', pp.905–907; C. Miranda, 'The First Supper', *Courier-Mail* (Brisbane), 27–28 October 2007, pp.36–37.
116   E. Chan *et. al.*, 'Human origins in a southern African palaeo-wetland and first migrations', *Nature*, Vol.575, No.7781 (7 November 2019), p.185.
117   F. Ayala, 'The Myth of Eve: Molecular Biology and Human Origins', *Science*, Vol.270, No.5244 (22 December 1995), pp.1933–1936; Tuniz, Gillespie and Jones, *The Bone Readers*, pp.193–195.
118   C. Wills, 'When Did Eve Live? An Evolutionary Detective Story', *Evolution*, Vol.49, No.4 (August 1995), p.606.
119   R. Derrincourt, 'Getting "Out of Africa": Sea Crossings and Culture in Hominin Migrations', *Journal of World Prehistory*, Vol.19, No.2 (June 2005), pp.126–128; P. Forster and S. Matsumura, 'Did Early Humans Go North or South?', *Science*, Vol.308, No.5724 (13 May 2005), pp.965–966.
120   C. Stringer, 'Coasting out of Africa', *Nature*, Vol.405, No.6782 (4 May 2000), pp.24–26; C. Finlayson, 'Biogeography and evolution of the genus *Homo*', *Trends in Ecology and Evolution*, Vol.20, No.8 (August 2005), p.460.
121   Forster and Matsumura, 'Did Early Humans Go North or South?', pp.965–966; T.E.G. Reynolds, 'Revolution or resolution? The archaeology of modern human origins', *World Archaeology*, Vol.23, No.2 (October 1991), p.160.
122   Zhang, J-F and R. Dennell, 'The last of Asia conquered by *Homo sapiens*', *Science*, Vol.362, No.6418 (30 November 2018), pp.992–993.
123   P. Mellars, 'Neanderthals and the modern human colonization of Europe', *Nature*, Vol.432, No.7016 (25 November 2004), p.461.
124   C. Stringer, 'Coasting out of Africa', *Nature*, Vol.405, No.6782 (4 May 2000), pp.24–26; Finlayson, 'Biogeography and evolution of the genus *Homo*', p.460.
125   L. Davis *et. al.*, 'Late Upper Paleolithic occupation at Cooper's Ferry, Idaho, USA, ~ 16,000 years ago', *Science*, Vol.365, No.6456 (30 August 2019), p.891.
126   P. Bahn, '50,000-year-old Americans of Pedra Furada', *Nature*, Vol.362, No.6416 (11 March 1993), pp.114–115.
127   T. Appenzeller, 'Europe's first artists were Neanderthals: Spanish cave paintings date to before modern humans arrived in region', *Science*, Vol.359, No.6378 (23 February 2018), pp.852–853; D.L. Hoffmann *et. al.*, 'U-Th dating of carbonate crusts reveals Neanderthal origin of Iberian cave art', *Ibid.*, pp.912–915.
128   R. Fletcher, 'The Evolution of Human Behaviour', *Australian Natural History*, Supplement 2 (1988), pp.49 and 51.
129   Anon, 'The Piltdown Skull', *British Medical Journal*, Vol.2, No.2751 (20 September 1913), p.762; W. Straus, 'The Great Piltdown Hoax', *Science*, Vol.119, No.3087 (26 February 1954), p.265.
130   N. Wade, 'Voice from the Dead Names New Suspect for Piltdown Hoax', *Science*, Vol.202, No.4372 (8 December 1978), p.1062.
131   Tattersall, *The Strange Case of the Rickety Cossack and Other Cautionary Tales from Human Evolution*, p.45.
132   P. Tobias, 'Piltdown: An Appraisal of the Case against Sir Arthur Keith', *Current Anthropology*, Vol.33, No.3 (June 1992), pp.246–249.
133   *Ibid.*, p.259.

Notes

134 J.E. Walsh, *Unravelling Piltdown: The Science Fraud of the Century and Its Solution* (New York: The Softback Preview, 1997), pp.192–193.

III THE NEANDERTHAL ANOMALY

1   E. Trinkaus and W. Howells, 'The Neanderthals', *Scientific American*, Vol.241, No.6 (December 1979), pp.122 and 128.
2   S. Hall, 'Last of the Neanderthals', *National Geographic*, Vol.214, No.4 (October 2008), p.58.
3   Mellars, 'Neanderthals and the modern human colonization of Europe', p.461.
4   Leakey, *The Making of Mankind*, p.148.
5   C. Stringer and C. Gamble, *In Search of the Neanderthals: solving the puzzle of human origins* (London: Thomas and Hudson, 1993), pp.91–92.
6   C. Lalueza-Fox *et. al.*, 'A Melanocortin 1 Receptor Allele Suggests Varying Pigmentation Among Neanderthals', *Science*, Vol.318, No.1453 (30 November 2007), pp.1453–1454.
7   Trinkaus and Howells, 'The Neanderthals', p.126.
8   Relethford, *The Human Species*, p.318.
9   Lewin, *Human Evolution*, p.72.
10 R. Gore, 'Neanderthals: The Dawn of Humans', *National Geographic*, Vol.189. No.1 (January 1996), p.10.
11 J. Schwartz and I. Tattersall, 'Significance of some previously unrecognized apomorphies in the nasal region of *Homo neanderthalensis*', *Proceedings of the National Academy of Sciences of the United States of America*, Vol.93, No.20 (1 October 1996), pp.10853–10854.
12 J. Fischman, 'Hard Evidence', *Discover*, Vol.13, No.2 (February 1992), p.47.
13 Stringer and Gamble, *In Search of the Neanderthals*, p.93.
14 Fischman, 'Hard Evidence', pp.47–48.
15 Gore, 'Neanderthals', p.30.
16 M. Wolpoff *et. al.*, 'Why *not* the Neanderthals?', *World Archaeology*, Vol.36, No.4 (December 2004), p.535; Tuniz, Gillespie and Jones, *The Bone Readers*, p.185.
17 Hall, 'Last of the Neanderthals', p.38.
18 Anon, 'A Miss for Moderns and Neanderthals', *Science*, Vol.300, No.5621 (9 May 2003), pp.893–894.
19 G. Constable *et. al.*, *The Neanderthals* (New York: Time-Life, 1973), p.10.
20 R. Schmitz *et. al.*, 'The Neanderthal type site revisited: Interdisciplinary investigations of skeletal remains from the Neander Valley, Germany', *Proceedings of the National Academy of the United States of America*, Vol.99, No.20 (1 October 2002), p.13342; Leakey, *The Making of Mankind*, pp.145–146.
21 Constable *et. al.*, *The Neanderthals*, p.15.
22 L. Eiseley, 'Neanderthal Man and the Dawn of Human Paleontology', *Quarterly Review of Biology*, Vol.32, No.4 (December 1957), p.325.
23 J. Gruber, 'The Neanderthal Controversy: Nineteenth-Century Version', *Scientific Monthly*, Vol.67, No.6 (December 1948), p.439.
24 Constable *et. al.*, *The Neanderthals*, p.15.
25 L. Jaroff, 'The Neanderthal Mystery', *Time* (New York), 14 March 1994, p.60.
26 Gore, 'Neanderthals', p.8.
27 Constable *et. al.*, *The Neanderthals*, p.19; Jaroff, 'The Neanderthal Mystery', pp.60–61.
28 *Ibid.*, p.27.

29   Anon, 'Dental exam shows Neanderthals cooked veges', *Australian* (Sydney), 29 December 2010, p.3.
30   J. Zilhão et. al., 'Last Interglacial Iberian Neandertals as fisher-hunter-gatherers', *Science*, Vol.367, No.6485 (27 March 2020), pp.367 and 372–373; M. Will, 'Neanderthal surf and turf', *Ibid.*, pp.1422–1423; D. Rice, 'Not all clubs and red meat. Signs are that Neanderthals knew how to fish', *Sun-Herald* (Sydney), 29 March 2020, p.21.
31   Constable et. al., *The Neanderthals*, p.29; S. Gould, 'The Origin and Function of "Bizarre" Structure: Antler Size and Skull Size in the "Irish Elk", *Megaloceros giganteus*', *Evolution*, Vol.28, No.2 (June 1974), pp.191 and 193; Gore, 'Neanderthals', pp.9 and 21; J. Yravedra and L. Cobo-Sánchez, 'Neanderthal exploitation of ibex and chamois in southwestern Europe', *Journal of Human Evolution*, Vol.78 (January 2015), pp.12–13.
32   Hall, Last of the Neanderthals', p.40.
33   D. Day, *The Doomsday Book of Animals: A Natural History of Vanished Species* (New York: Viking Press, 1981), pp.188–189.
34   T. Berger and E. Trinkaus, 'Patterns of Trauma among the Neanderthals', *Journal of Archaeological Science*, Vol.22, No.6 (November 1995), pp.848–850; Hall, 'Last of the Neanderthals', p.53.
35   Gore, 'Neanderthals', p.22.
36   *Ibid.*, pp.22 and 25.
37   E.G. Schwimmer, 'Warfare of the Maori', *Te Ao Hou The New World*, No.36 (September 1961), p.51.
38   Gore, 'Neanderthals', p.22.
39   Berger and Trinkaus, 'Patterns of trauma among the Neanderthals', pp.843 and 848.
40   Gore, 'Neanderthals', pp.23 and 27.
41   Leakey, *The Making of Mankind*, pp.152–153.
42   *Ibid.*, p.153.
43   A. Defleur et. al., 'Neanderthal Cannibalism at Moula-Guercy, Ardèche, France', *Science*, Vol.286, No.5437 (1 October 1999), pp.128–131.
44   E. Culotta, 'Neanderthals Were Cannibals, Bones Show', *Science*, Vol.286, No.5437 (1 October 1999), pp.18–19.
45   *Ibid.*, p.19.
46   Tuniz, Gillespie and Jones, *The Bone Readers*, p.184.
47   M. Shackley, *Neanderthal Man* (London: Gerald Duckworth & Co., 1980), pp.35–36.
48   Gore, 'Neanderthals', p.28.
49   *Ibid.*, p.22.
50   Anon, 'Boning up on ancient man's skills', *Courier-Mail* (Brisbane), 17 August 2013, p.43.
51   Gore, 'Neanderthals', p.19.
52   Appenzeller, 'Europe's first artists were Neanderthals: Spanish cave paintings date to before modern humans arrived in region', pp.852–853; Hoffmann et. al., 'U-Th dating of carbonate crusts reveals Neanderthal origin of Iberian cave art', pp.912–915.
53   Trinkaus and Howells, 'The Neanderthals', p.118.
54   M. Patou-Mathis, 'Neanderthal Subsistence Behaviours in Europe', *International Journal of Osteoarchaeology*, Vol.10, No.5 (September-October 2000), pp.380–381.
55   Gore, 'Neanderthals', p.28.
56   Leakey, *The Making of Mankind*, p.150.
57   Gore, 'Neanderthals', p.28.
58   *Ibid.*, p.34.

Notes

59 Hall, 'Last of the Neanderthals', pp.54–55; P. Mellars and J. French, 'Tenfold Population Increase in Western Europe at the Neanderthal-to-Modern Human Transition', *Science*, Vol.333, No.6042 (29 July 2011), p.627.
60 Stringer and Gamble, *In Search of the Neanderthals*, pp.183 and 193.
61 I. Tattersall and J. Schwartz, 'Hominids and hybrids: The place of Neanderthals in human evolution', *Proceedings of the National Academy of Sciences of the United States of America*, Vol.96, No.13 (22 June 1999), p.7117; J. Leake, 'Did we have sex with Neanderthals?', *Australian* (Sydney), 26 October 2009, p.3.
62 R. Dalton, 'Ancient DNA set to rewrite human history', *Nature*, Vol.465, No.7295 (13 May 2010), p.148.
63 L. Dayton, 'DNA shows there's a caveman inside us all', *Australian* (Sydney), 7 May 2010, p.8; J. Leake, 'Modern man cleared: inbreeding led to the fall of Neanderthals', *Australian* (Sydney), 12 November 2018, p.8.
64 Hall, 'Last of the Neanderthals', p.58.
65 R. Barton *et. al.*, 'Gibraltar Neanderthals and results of recent excavations in Gorham's, Vanguard and Ibex Caves', *Antiquity*, Vol.73, No.279 (March 1999), p.21.
66 R. Blasco *et. al.*, 'The earliest pigeon fanciers', *Scientific Reports*, Vol.4, No.5971 (7 August 2014), pp.1 and 6; Anon, 'Cavemen beat humans in race to feed on birds', *Weekend Australian* (Sydney), 9–10 August 2014, p.13.

IV THE HOBBIT ENIGMA

1 M. Morwood and P. van Oosterzee, *The Discovery of the Hobbit: The Scientific Breakthrough that Changed the Face of Human History* (Milsons Point, NSW: Random House, 2007), pp.6–7.
2 Tuniz, Gillespie and Jones, *The Bone Readers*, pp.166–167.
3 Morwood and van Oosterzee, *The Discovery of the Hobbit*, p.295.
4 T. Sutikna *et. al.*, 'Revised stratigraphy and chronology for *Homo floresiensis* at Liang Bua in Indonesia', *Nature*, Vol.532, No.7599 (21 April 2016), p.366.
5 C. Jones, 'Hobbit species may not have been human', *Australian* (Sydney), 30 September 2009, pp.23 and 26.
6 Aielio, 'Five Years of *Homo floresiensis*', p.3.
7 L. Dayton, 'Hobbits "deformed"', *Weekend Australian* (Sydney), 20–21 May 2006, p.5; Tuniz, Gillespie and Jones, *The Bone Readers*, p.166.
8 S. O'Connor, 'New evidence from East Timor contributes to our understanding of earliest human colonisation east of the Sunda Shelf', *Antiquity*, Vol.81, No.313 (September 2007), p.523.
9 A. Brumm *et. al.*, 'Early stone technology on Flores and its implications for *Homo floresiensis*', *Nature*, Vol.441, No.7093 (1 June 2006), p.628; G.D. van den Bergh *et. al.*, 'The Liang Bua faunal remains: a 95 k.y.r. sequence from Flores, East Indonesia', *Journal of Human Evolution*, Vol.57, No.5 (November 2009), p.533.
10 M. Morwood, 'Early hominid occupation of Flores, East Indonesia, and its wider significance', in I. Metcalf, J. Smith, M. Morwood and I. Davidson, *Faunal and Floral Migrations and Evolution in SE Asia-Australia* (Lisse: A.A. Balkema Publishers, 2001), p.388.
11 M. Morwood *et. al.*, 'Preface: research at Liang Bua, Flores, Indonesia', *Journal of Human Evolution*, Vol.57, No.5 (November 2009), pp.439–440.
12 Morwood and van Oosterzee, *The Discovery of the Hobbit*, pp.12–13.
13 A. Gibbons, 'Ancient Island Tools Suggest *Homo erectus* Was a Seafarer', *Science*, Vol.279, No.5357 (13 March 1998), p.1636.
14 D. Shulz, 'Little Big Man', 'Weekend Australian Magazine', in *Weekend*

Australian (Sydney), 11–12 December 2004, p.59.
15 Morwood and van Oosterzee, *The Discovery of the Hobbit*, pp.16–17.
16 M. Morwood et. al., 'Stone artefacts from the 1994 excavation at Mata Menge, West Central Flores, Indonesia', *Australian Archaeology*, No.44 (June 1997), p.31.
17 Ibid.
18 Schulz, 'Little Big Man', p.59.
19 J. Diamond, 'The Astonishing Micropygmies', *Science*, Vol.306, No.5704 (17 December 2004), p.2047.
20 M. Lahr and R. Foley, 'Human evolution writ small', *Nature*, Vol.431, No.7012 (28 October 2004), p.1044.
21 van den Bergh et. al., 'The Liang Bua faunal remains', p.530.
22 Ibid., p.528.
23 H. Meijer and R.A. Due, 'A new species of giant marabou stork (Aves: Ciconiiformes) from the Pleistocene of Liang Bua, Flores (Indonesia)', *Zoological Journal of the Linnean Society*, Vol.160, No.4 (December 2010), pp.716 and 719.
24 Aiello, 'Five Years of *Homo floresiensis*', p.9.
25 van den Bergh et. al., 'The Liang Bua faunal remains', p.534.
26 Morwood, 'Early hominid occupation of Flores', p.396.
27 van den Bergh, 'The Liang Bua faunal remains', p.533.
28 Ibid; E. Culotta, 'The Fellowship of the Hobbit', *Science*, Vol.317, No.5839 (10 August 2007), p.741.
29 Morwood et. al., 'Preface', pp.438–440.
30 Schulz, 'Little Big Man', p.59.
31 R. Dalton, 'Little lady of Flores forces rethink of human evolution', *Nature*, Vol.431, No.7012 (28 October 2004), p.1029.
32 Culotta, 'The Fellowship Of the Hobbit', p.742.
33 Tuniz, Gillespie and Jones, *The Bone Readers*, p.169.
34 M. Morwood, T. Sutikina and R. Roberts, 'The People Time Forgot', *National Geographic*, Vol.207, No.4 (April 2005), p.12; Culotta, 'The Fellowship Of the Hobbit', p.741.
35 Brumm et. al., 'Early stone technology on Flores and its implications for *Homo floresiensis*', p.624.
36 G.D. van den Bergh et. al., '*Homo floresiensis*-like fossils from the early Middle Pleistocene of Flores', *Nature*, Vol.534, No.7606 (9 June 2016), p.245; A. Brumm et. al., 'Age and context of the oldest known hominin fossils from Flores', *Nature*, Vol.534, No.7606 (9 June 2016), p.249.
37 E. Callaway, 'Hobbit relatives hint at family tree', *Nature*, Vol.534, No.7606 (9 June 2016), pp.164–165; Gómez-Robles, 'The dawn of *Homo floresiensis*', p.189.
38 van den Bergh et. al., 'The Liang Bua faunal remains', p.532.
39 Schulz, 'Little Big Man', p.59.
40 Tuniz, Gillespie and Jones, *The Bone Readers*, p.169.
41 G. Forth, 'Hominids, hairy hominoids and the science of humanity', *Anthropology Today*, Vol.21, No.3 (June 2008), p.13.
42 L. Dayton, 'Research to go on without "hobbit"', *Weekend Australian* (Sydney), 8–9 January 2005, p.4.
43 Tuniz, Gillespie and Jones, *The Bone Readers*, p.172.
44 L. Massimo et. al., 'Chicken-pox and Chromosome Aberrations', *British Medical Journal*, Vol.2, No.5454 (17 July 1965), p.172; P. Seth, N. Manjunath and S. Balaya, 'Rubella Infection: The Indian Scene', *Reviews of Infectious Diseases*, Vol.7, Supp.1 (March–April 1985), p.866; G. Abdel-Salam and A. Czeizel, 'A Case-Control Etiologic Study of Microcephaly', *Epidemiology*,

Notes

Vol.11, No.5 (September 2000), p.571.
45 Tuniz, Gillespie and Jones, *The Bone Readers*, p.172.
46 *Ibid.*
47 M. Henneberg and A. Thorne, 'Flores may be pathological *Homo sapiens*', *Before Farming*, Vol.4 (2004), p.3.
48 P. Brown and M. Morwood, 'Comments from Peter Brown and Mike Morwood', *Before Farming*, Vol.4 (2004), pp.5–7.
49 D. Falk *et. al.*, 'The Brain of LB1, *Homo floresiensis*', *Science*, Vol.308, No.5719 (8 April 2005), pp.242–245.
50 T. Jacob *et. al.*, 'Pygmoid Australomelanesian *Homo sapiens* skeletal remains from Liang Bua, Flores: Population affinities and pathological abnormalities', *Proceedings of the National Academy of Sciences of the United States of America*, Vol.103, No.36 (5 September 2006), p.13426.
51 G. Richards, 'Genetic, physiologic and ecogeographical factors contributing to variation in *Homo sapiens*: *Homo floresiensis* reconsidered', *Journal of Evolutionary Biology*, Vol.19, No.6 (November 2006), p.1762.
52 I. Hershkovitz, L. Kornreich and Z. Laron, 'Comparative Skeletal Features Between *Homo floresiensis* and Patients With Primary Growth Hormone Insensitivity (Laron Syndrome)', *American Journal of Physical Anthropology*, Vol.134, No.2 (October 2007), pp.206–207.
53 A. Salleh, 'Is the hobbit just a dwarf cretin?', www.abc.net.au/science/articles/2008/03/05/2181122.htm (29 March 2010).
54 E. Culotta, 'Discoverers Charge Damage to "Hobbit" Specimens', *Science*, Vol.307, No.5717 (25 March 2005), p.1848.
55 Tuniz, Gillespie and Jones, *The Bone Readers*, p.175.
56 *Ibid.*, p.174.
57 B. O'Keefe, 'Hobbit "had been to dentist for a filling"', *Weekend Australian* (Sydney), 19–20 April 2008, p.3.
58 B. O'Keefe, 'The tooth, and nothing but', *Weekend Australian* (Sydney), 19–20 April 2008, p.24.
59 P. Jones, 'Going to pieces over human jigsaw', 'Australian Literary Review', in *Australian* (Sydney), 4 June 2008, p.9.
60 W. Jungers, 'Hobbit nay-sayers fail to overturn theories', 'Weekend Australian Review', in *Weekend Australian* (Sydney), 26–27 July 2008, pp.12–13.
61 M. Henneberg *et. al.*, 'Evolved developmental homeostasis disturbed in LB1 from Flores, Indonesia, denotes Down syndrome and not diagnostic traits of the invalid species *Homo floresiensis*', *Proceedings of the National Academy of the United States of America*, Vol.111, No.33 (19 August 2014), p.11967. J. Ross, '"Hobbit" had Down syndrome', *Australian* (Sydney), 5 August 2014, p.5.
62 E. Pitt, 'Hobbit finder dies of cancer', *Australian* (Sydney), 24 July 2013, p.30.
63 P. Obendorf, C. Oxnard and B. Kefford, 'Are the small human-like fossils found on Flores human endemic cretins?', *Proceedings of the Royal Society B*, Vol.275, No.1640 (7 June 2008), p.1294.
64 M. Tocheri *et. al.*, 'The Primitive Wrist of *Homo floresiensis* and Its Implications for Hominin Evolution', *Science*, Vol.317, No.5845 (21 September 2007), pp.1743–1744; Jones, 'Going to pieces over human jigsaw', p.9.
65 E. Culotta, 'When Hobbits (Slowly) Walked the Earth', *Science*, Vol.320, No.5875 (25 April 2008), pp.433–434.
66 Culotta, 'The Fellowship of the Hobbit', p.742.
67 L. Berger *et. al.*, 'Small-Bodied Humans from Palau, Micronesia', *Public Library of Science One*, Vol.3, No.3 (12 March 2008), p.1.
68 M. Balter, 'Paleoanthropologist Now Rides High On a New Fossil Tide', *Science*, Vol.333, No.6048 (9 September 2011), p.1375.
69 A.S. Mijares *et. al.*, 'New evidence for a 67,000-year-old human presence at

Callao Cave, Luzon, Philippines', *Journal of Human Evolution*, Vol.59, No.1 (July 2010), pp.123 and 131.
70   *Ibid.*, p.131; Détroit *et. al.*, 'A new species of *Homo* from the Late Pleistocene of the Philippines', pp.181 and 185.
71   Argue *et. al.*, 'The affinities of *Homo floresiensis* based on phylogenetic analyses of cranial, dental, and postcranial characters', pp.107 and 130.
72   Ross, 'Flores Hobbits out of Africa', p.10.
73   Gómez-Robles, 'The dawn of *Homo floresiensis'*, p.189.
74   Forth, 'Hominids, hairy hominoids and the science of humanity', pp.14–15.
75   B. Kirtley, 'Unknown Hominids and New World Legends', *Western Folklore*, Vol.23, No.2 (April 1964), p.82; G. Forth, 'Flores after floriensis: Implications of local reaction to recent palaeoanthropological discoveries on an east Indonesian island', *Bijdragen tot de Taal –, Land-en Volkenkunde*, Vol.162, Nos.2–3 (2006), pp.346–347.
76   N. Rothwell, 'In search of the Little People', 'Weekend Australian Review', in *Weekend Australian* (Sydney), 3–4 May 2014, pp.8–10.
77   M. Rolls and M. Johnson, *Historical Dictionary of Australian Aborigines* (Lanham, MD: Rowman & Littlefield, 2019), pp.74–75.

V   COLONISATION OF SAHUL: THE ARCHAEOLOGICAL AND SKELETAL EVIDENCE

1   Morwood and van Oosterzee, *The Discovery of the Hobbit*, pp.208–209.
2   G. Hudjashou *et. al.*, 'Revealing the prehistoric settlement of Australia by Y chromosome and mtDNA analysis', *Proceedings of the National Academy of Sciences of the United States of America*, Vol.104, No.21 (22 May 2007), pp.8726–8727.
3   Cooper and Stringer, 'Did the Denisovans Cross Wallace's Line?', p.321.
4   Mulvaney and Kamminga, *Prehistory of Australia*, pp.105–107; Flood, *Archaeology of the Dreamtime: the story of prehistoric Australia and its people* (Marleston, SA: J.B. Publishing, 2004), p.32 [hereafter Flood, *Archaeology of the Dreamtime* (2004 ed.)].
5   Mulvaney and Kamminga, *Prehistory of Australia*, p.223.
6   Flood, *Archaeology of the Dreamtime* (2004 ed.), p.31.
7   G. Miller *et. al.*, 'Detecting human impacts on the flora, fauna, and summer monsoon of Pleistocene Australia', *Climate of the Past*, Vol.3, No.3 (July 2007), p.463.
8   R. Bednarik, 'The Initial Peopling of Wallacea and Sahul', *Anthropos*, BD92, H4/6 (1997), p.361.
9   N. Butlin, *Economics of the Dreamtime: A Hypothetical History* (Cambridge: Cambridge University Press, 1993), pp.33–34.
10 J. Allen and J.F. O'Connell, 'Getting from Sunda to Sahul', in G. Clark, F. Leach and S. O'Connor (eds), *Islands of Inquiry: Colonisation, Seafaring and the Archaeology of Maritime Landscapes* (Canberra: ANU E Press, 2008), p.37.
11 Mulvaney and Kamminga, *Prehistory of Australia*, p.107.
12 White and O'Connell, *A Prehistory of Australia, New Guinea and Sahul*, p.47.
13 J. Birdsell, 'The Recalibration of a Paradigm for the First Peopling of Greater Australia', in J. Allen, J. Golson and R. Jones (eds), *Sunda and Sahul: Prehistoric Studies in Southeast Asia, Melanesia and Australia* (London: Academic Press, 1977), pp.121–128.
14 O'Connor, Spriggs and Veth, 'Excavation at Lene Hara Cave establishes occupation in East Timor at least 30,000–35,000 years ago', pp.33–34.

Notes

15 N. Franklin and P. Habgood, 'Modern Human Behaviour and Pleistocene Sahul in Review', *Australian Archaeology*, No.65 (December 2007), p.8.
16 Mulvaney and Kamminga, *Prehistory of Australia*, pp.174–175.
17 J.P. White and J.F. O'Connell, 'Australian Prehistory: New Aspects of Antiquity', *Science*, Vol.203, No.4375 (5 January 1979), p.25.
18 O'Connor, 'New evidence from East Timor contributes to our understanding of earliest human colonisation east of the Sunda Shelf', p.531.
19 White and O'Connell, *A Prehistory of Australia, New Guinea and Sahul*, p.45.
20 Mulvaney and Kamminga, *Prehistory of Australia*, p.109.
21 Jones, 'The Coming of the Aborigines', p.21.
22 Flood, *Archaeology of the Dreamtime* (2004 ed.), p.82.
23 V. Laurie, 'Secrets unearthed: humankind just got a little older', *Weekend Australian* (Sydney), 28–29 November 2015, p.3.
24 P. Veth et. al., 'Excavations at Parnkupirti, Lake Gregory, Great Sandy Desert: OSL ages for occupation before the Last Glacial Maximum', *Australian Archaeology*, No.69 (December 2009), p.9; L. Dayton, 'Mungo Man has rival to title of oldest Australian', *Australian* (Sydney), 8 December 2009, p.3.
25 P. Veth *et.al.*, 'Minjiwarra: archaeological evidence of human occupation of Australia's northern Kimberley by 50,000 BP', *Australian Archaeology*, Vol.85, No.2 (2019), pp.115 and 124.
26 K. McConnell and S. O'Connor, '40,000 Year record of food plants in the Southern Kimberley Ranges, Western Australia', *Australian Archaeology*, No.45 (1997), pp.20–21.
27 J. Balme, 'Excavations revealing 40,000 years of occupation at Mimi Caves, south central Kimberley, Western Australia', *Australian Archaeology*, No.51 (December 2000), p.2.
28 J.F. O'Connell and J. Allen, 'Dating the Colonization of Sahul (Pleistocene Australia-New Guinea): a review of recent research', *Journal of Archaeological Research*, Vol.31, No.6 (June 2004), p.838.
29 D. Horton, 'Colonisation', in D. Horton (ed.), *The Encyclopaedia of Aboriginal Australia: Vol.1* (Canberra: Aboriginal Studies Press, 1994), p.212.
30 S. Bowdler, 'The Coastal Colonisation of Australia', in Allen, Golson and Jones, *Sunda and Sahul*, pp.221–223.
31 White and O'Connell, *A Prehistory of Australia, New Guinea and Sahul*, pp.50–51.
32 Mulvaney and Kamminga, *Prehistory of Australia*, pp.132–133.
33 C. Turney et. al., 'Early Human Occupation at Devil's Lair, Southwestern Australia 50,000 Years Ago', *Quarternary Research*, Vol.55, No.1 (January 2001), p.11.
34 J. Flood, *Rock Art of the Dreamtime: Images of Ancient Australia* (Pymble, NSW: Angus & Robertson, 1997), p.228.
35 Hiscock, *The Archaeology of Ancient Australia*, pp.55–56.
36 C. Mountford and R. Edwards, 'Aboriginal Rock Engravings of Extinct Creatures in South Australia', *Man*, Vol.62 (July 1922), pp.97–99.
37 White and O'Connell, *A Prehistory of Australia, New Guinea and Sahul*, p.53.
38 C.N. Johnson, 'Determinants of loss of mammal species during the Late Quarternary "megafauna" extinctions: life history and ecology, but not body size', *Proceedings of the Royal Society of London: Series B*, Vol.269, No.1506 (7 November 2002), p.2221.
39 J. Alroy, 'A Multispecies Overkill Simulation of the End-Pleistocene Megafaunal Mass Extinction', *Science*, Vol.292, No.5523 (8 June 2001), p.1893.
40 J.F. O'Connell and J. Allen, 'When Did Humans First Arrive in Greater Australia and Why Is It Important to Know?', *Evolutionary Anthropology*, Vol.6, No.4 (1998), p.134.

41 Ibid., pp.138–139.
42 Mulvaney and Kamminga, *Prehistory of Australia*, p.134.
43 R. Jones, 'Australia Felix – The Discovery of a Pleistocene Prehistory', *Journal of Human Evolution*, Vol.6, No.4 (May 1977), p.354.
44 R. Jones, 'The Fifth Continent: Problems Concerning the Human Colonization of Australia', *Annual Review of Anthropology*, Vol.8 (1979), p.445.
45 O'Connell and Allen, 'Dating the Colonization of Sahul (Pleistocene Australia-New Guinea)', p.836.
46 White and O'Connell, *A Prehistory of Australia, New Guinea and Sahul*, p.42.
47 Urry, 'Old Questions: New Answers?', p.150.
48 Flood, *Archaeology of the Dreamtime: The story of prehistoric Australia and its people* (Sydney: Collins Australia, 1989), p.41. [Hereafter: Flood, *Archaeology of the Dreamtime* (1989 ed.)].
49 H. Johnston and P. Clark, 'Willandra Lakes Archaeological Investigations, 1968–98', *Archaeology in Oceania*, Vol.33, No.3 (October 1998), p.107.
50 Tuniz, Gillespie and Jones, *The Bone Readers*, p.29; J. Mulvaney, *Digging Up A Past* (Sydney: University of New South Wales Press, 2011), p.151
51 Johnston and Clark, 'Willandra Lakes Archaeological Investigations, 1968–98', p.107.
52 L. Dayton, 'Magic and mystery of an Ice Age couple', *Weekend Australian* (Sydney), 12–13 June 2004, p.5.
53 C.E. Dortch, *Devil's Lair: A search for Ancient Man in Western Australia* (Perth: Western Australian Museum Press, 1976), p.5.
54 T. Flannery, *The Future Eaters: An ecological history of the Australasian lands and people* (Sydney: Reed New Holland, 1999), pp.275–276 and 295–296.
55 Flood, *Archaeology of the Dreamtime* (1989 ed.), p.90.
56 Mulvaney and Kamminga, *Prehistory of Australia*, pp.182 and 189.
57 D. Schulz, 'Backdating the clock', *Bulletin* (Sydney), 25 July 1995, p.36.
58 Ibid.; L. Nicklin, 'The prehistory cowboy strikes again', *Bulletin* (Sydney), 12 June 1990, pp.92–93.
59 Hiscock, *The Archaeology of Ancient Australia*, pp. 37 and 43.
60 C. Clarkson *et. al.*, 'Human occupation of northern Australia by 65,000 years ago', *Nature*, Vol.547, No.7663 (20 July 2017), pp.306 and 309.
61 N. Rothwell, 'Politics etched in stone', *Australian* (Sydney), 23 September 1996, pp.1 and 5.
62 C. Smith, 'Why caution is the best technique', *Australian* (Sydney), 24 September 1996, p.13.
63 R. Roberts *et. al.*, 'Optical and radiocarbon dating at Jinmium rock shelter in northern Australia', *Nature*, Vol.393, No.6683 (28 May 1998), p.358.
64 Tuniz, Gillespie and Jones, *The Bone Readers*, pp.97–98.
65 G. Singh and E. Geissler, 'Late Cainozoic History of Vegetation, Fire, Lake Levels and Climate, at Lake George, New South Wales, Australia', *Philosophical Transactions of the Royal Society of London: Series B*, Vol.311, No.1151 (3 December 1985), pp.380 and 439–442.
66 H. Lourandos, *Continent of Hunter-Gatherers: New Perspectives in Australian Prehistory* (Cambridge: Cambridge University Press, 1997), p.88.
67 M. Prentis, 'From Lemuria to Kow Swamp: The Rise and Fall of Tri-hybrid Theories of Aboriginal Origins', *Journal of Australian Studies*, No.45 (June 1995), p.83.
68 Ibid.
69 Ibid.
70 K. Douglas, 'Skeletons in the cabinet: popular palaeontology and the Pleistocene extinction debate in historical perspective', *Alcheringa*, Vol.30, Supp.1 (2006), pp.122–123.

Notes

71 Ibid., p.85; Mulvaney and Kamminga, *Prehistory of Australia*, pp.153–154.
72 Mulvaney and Kamminga, *Prehistory of Australia*, p.154.
73 A. Roberts, *The Incredible Human Journey: The Story of How We Colonised the Planet* (London: Bloomsbury Publishing, 2009), p.180; G. Xing and W. Chunxue, 'In Search of the Ancestors of Chinese People', *Paleoanthropology*, Vol.24, No.2 (2010), pp.112–113.
74 F. Hulse, 'Race as an Evolutionary Episode', *American Anthropologist*, Vol.64, No.5 (October 1962), pp.940–941.
75 Roberts, *The Incredible Human Journey*, p.194.
76 Prentis, 'From Lemuria to Kow Swamp', p.85.
77 F.P. Woolston and F.S. Colliver, 'The Wildsoet Interview – Some Recollections of the Aborigines of the Tully Area', *Queensland Heritage*, Vol.3, No.3 (November 1975), pp.7–8.
78 R.M.W. Dixon, 'Tribes, languages and other boundaries in northeast Queensland', in N. Peterson (ed.), *Tribes and Boundaries in Australia* (Canberra: Australian Institute of Aboriginal Studies, 1976), pp.222–223.
79 J. Taylor, 'The Tasmanian Languages', *Launceston Historical Society Papers and Proceedings*, Vol.11 (1999), p.54; J. Taylor, 'Aboriginal Languages', in A. Alexander (ed.), *The Companion to Tasmanian History* (Hobart: Centre for Tasmanian Historical Studies, University of Tasmania, 2005), p.3.
80 K. Windschuttle and T. Gillin, 'The Extinction of the Australian Pygmies', *Quadrant*, Vol.46, No.6 (June 2002), p.17.
81 Mulvaney and Kamminga, *Prehistory of Australia*, p.154.
82 *Ibid.*
83 A. Redd and M. Stoneking, 'Peopling of Sahul: mtDNA Variation in Aboriginal Australian and Papua New Guinean Populations', *American Journal of Human Genetics*, Vol.65, No.3 (September 1999), pp.821–822; J. Flood, *The Original Australians* (Crows Nest, NSW: Allen & Unwin, 2006), pp.185 and 188.
84 Flood, *The Original Australians*, p.188.
85 Flood, *Archaeology of the Dreamtime* (2004 Ed.), pp.73–74.
86 Mulvaney and Kamminga, *Prehistory of Australia*, p.162; Tuniz, Gillespie and Jones, *The Bone Readers*, p.145.
87 Flood, *Archaeology of the Dreamtime* (1989 Ed.), p.68.
88 Hiscock, *The Archaeology of Ancient Australia*, p.99.
89 A. Thorne and R. Sim, 'The Gracile Male Skeleton from Late Pleistocene King Island, Australia', *Australian Archaeology*, No.38 (1994), p.9.
90 Mulvaney and Kamminga, *Prehistory of Australia*, p.168.
91 D. Smith, 'Young Mungo theory raises desert storm', 'Insight' in *Age* (Melbourne), 22 February 2002, p.5.
92 Mulvaney and Kamminga, *Prehistory of Australia*, pp.152 and 168.
93 C. Pardoe, 'The Pleistocene is still with us: Analytical constraints and possibilities for the study of ancient human remains in archaeology', in M. Smith, M. Spriggs and B. Fankhauser (eds), *Sahul in Review: Pleistocene Archaeology in Australia, New Guinea and Island Melanesia* (Canberra: Department of Prehistory, Research School of Pacific Studies, Australian National University, 1993), p.81.
94 D. Donlon, 'Aboriginal skeletal collections and research in physical anthropology: an historical perspective', *Australian Archaeology*, No.39 (1994), pp.73 and 77.
95 M. Johnson, '"Cranial connections": Queensland's "Talgai skull" debate of 1918 and custodianship of the past', *Aboriginal History*, Vol.24 (2000), pp.117–118.
96 *Ibid.*, pp.119–120
97 S.A. Smith, 'The Fossil Human Skull Found at Talgai, Queensland',

Philosophical Transactions of the Royal Society of London: Series B, Vol.208 (1918), pp.382–383.
98   Flood, *Archaeology of the Dreamtime* (2004 ed.), p.56.
99   Anon., 'Prehistoric Man: Skull found in Victoria', *Queenslander* (Brisbane), 1 May 1926, p.11; N.G.W. Macintosh, 'The Cohuna Cranium: Physiography and Chemical Analysis', *Oceania*, Vol.23, No.4 (June 1953), pp.278–279.
100 J. Collette, 'Hermann Klaatsch's Views on the Significance of the Australian Aborigines', *Aboriginal History*, Vol.11 (1987), p.98.
101 Flood, *Archaeology of the Dreamtime* (1989 ed.), p.58.
102 Anon., 'The Mossgiel Man', *Australian Archaeology*, No.21 (December 1985), p.136.
103 Flood, *Archaeology of the Dreamtime* (1989 ed.), pp.62–63.
104 Bickel, 'Ancient man in Kow Swamp', p.97.
105 *Ibid.*
106 T. Stone and M. Cupper, 'Last Glacial Maximum ages for robust humans at Kow Swamp, southern Australia', *Journal of Human Evolution*, Vol.45, No.2 (August 2003), p.99.
107 Flood, *Archaeology of the Dreamtime* (2004 ed.), pp.73–74.
108 Mulvaney and Kamminga, *Prehistory of Australia*, pp.161–162.
109 J. Bowler *et. al.*, 'Pleistocene human remains from Australia: a living site and human cremation from Lake Mungo, western New South Wales', *World Archaeology*, Vol.2, No.1 (June 1970), p.56
110 Mulvaney and Kamminga, *Prehistory of Australia*, pp.162–163.
111 Flood, *Archaeology of the Dreamtime* (2004 ed.), p.70.
112 S. Webb, *The Willandra Lakes Hominids* (Canberra: Department of Prehistory, Research School of Pacific Studies, Australian National University, 1989), pp.67–70; S. Webb, 'Cranial Thickening in an Australian Hominid as a Possible Palaeoepidemiological Indicator', *American Journal of Physical Anthropology*, Vol.82, No.4 (August 1990), pp.408–409.
113 Flood, *Archaeology of the Dreamtime* (2004 ed.), pp.70–71.
114 Hiscock, *The Archaeology of Ancient Australia*, p.93.
115 Mulvaney and Kamminga, *Prehistory of Australia*, p.166.
116 Flood, *Archaeology of the Dreamtime* (1989 ed.), pp.63–64.
117 P. Brown, 'Artificial Cranial Deformation: a component in the variation in Pleistocene Australian Aboriginal crania', *Archaeology in Oceania*, Vol.16 (1981), p.165.
118 *Ibid.*, pp.156–157 and 166.

VI   DEMISE OF THE MEGAFAUNA

1   Anon, 'Wombat Ham: Pioneers Enjoyed It', *Gippsland Times* (Sale), 16 July 1934, p.4; E. Troughton, *Furred Animals of Australia* (Sydney: Angus & Robertson, 1967), p.142.
2   P. Stanbury and G. Phipps, *Australia's Animals Discovered* (Rushcutters Bay, NSW: Pergamon Press, 1980), p.11.
3   Clode, *Prehistoric giants*, pp.42–46.
4   J. Long *et. al.*, *Prehistoric Mammals of Australia and New Guinea: One Hundred Million Years of Evolution* (Sydney: University of New South Wales Press, 2002), pp.100 and 112.
5   Clode, *Prehistoric Giants*, pp.50 and 54.
6   *Ibid.*, p.56.
7   *Ibid.*, pp.36–37.
8   G.F. van Tets, '*Progure gallinacea*: The Australian Giant Megapode', in P.V. Rich

and G.F. van Tets (eds), *Kadimakara: Extinct Vertebrates of Australia* (Lilydale, Vic: Pioneer Design Studio, 1985), p.198; R.F. Baird, 'Centropus: The Giant Coucal', *Ibid.*, p.208.
9 Clode, *Prehistoric Giants*, pp.38–40.
10 E. Guiler, 'Tasmanian Devil', in R. Strahan (Ed.), *The Australian Museum Book of Australian Mammals* (Sydney: Angus & Robertson, 1983), p.28; G. Chaloupka, *Journey in Time: The World's Longest Continuous Art Tradition* (Chatswood, NSW: Reed, 1993), p.96.
11 J. Long, 'Marsupial Baby Killer or Aussie Big "Cat"?', *Australasian Science*, Vol.24, No.9 (October 2003), pp.31–32.
12 Flood, *Archaeology of the Dreamtime* (2004 ed.), p.179.
13 S. Wroe, 'A review of terrestrial mammalian and reptilian carnivore ecology in Australian fossil faunas, and factors influencing their diversity: the myth of reptilian domination and its broader ramifications', *Australian Journal of Zoology*, Vol.50, No.1 (2002), pp.6–7.
14 M.J. Smith, '*Wonambi naracoortensis* The Giant Australian Python', in Rich and van Tets, *Kadimakara*, p.159.
15 Clode, *Prehistoric giants*, p.33.
16 Flannery, *The Future Eaters*, p.184.
17 L. Dayton, 'Mass Extinctions Pinned On Ice Age Hunters', *Science*, Vol.292, No.5523 (8 June 2001), p.1819.
18 G. Haynes, 'The catastrophic extinction of North American mammoths and mastodons', *World Archaeology*, Vol.33, No.3 (February 2002), p.409.
19 Flannery, *The Future Eaters*, p.183.
20 G. Prideaux *et. al.*, 'An arid-adapted middle Pleistocene vertebrate fauna from south-central Australia', *Nature*, Vol.445, No.7126 (25 January 2007), pp.422–424; L. Dayton, 'Beasts hounded to extinction', *Weekend Australian* (Sydney), 27–28 January 2007, p.28; J. Long, 'Megafauna Theory Faces Extinction', *Australasian Science*, Vol.28, No.2 (March 2007), pp.18–19.
21 Haynes, 'The catastrophic extinction of North American mammoths and mastodons', p.391.
22 D. Grayson and D. Meltzer, 'A requiem for North American overkill', *Journal of Archaeological Science*, Vol.30, No.5 (May 2003), p.588.
23 Anon, 'Mammoth discovery', *Herald Sun* (Melbourne), 8 November 2019, p.28.
24 P. Martin, 'The Discovery of America', *Science*, Vol.179, No.4077 (9 March 1973), p.969.
25 R.E. Webb, 'Megamarsupial extinction: the carrying capacity argument', *Antiquity*, Vol.72, No.275 (March 1998), p.47.
26 Dayton, 'Mass Extinctions Pinned On Ice Age Hunters', p.1819.
27 Grayson and Meltzer, 'A requiem for North American overkill', p.586.
28 Martin, 'The Discovery of America', p.969; Grayson and Meltzer, 'A requiem for North American Overkill', pp.585–587.
29 J.C. Balouet and S.L. Olson, 'Fossil Birds from Late Quarternary Deposits in New Caledonia', *Smithsonian Contributions to Zoology*, No.469 (1989), pp.4 and 11; A. Anderson, 'Faunal collapse, landscape change and settlement history in Remote Oceania', *World Archaeology*, Vol.33, No.3 (January 2002), pp.377–379.
30 D. Grayson, 'The Archaeological Record of Human Impacts on Animal Populations', *Journal of World Prehistory*, Vol.15, No.1 (March 2001), pp.8–9.
31 S. Wroe, J. Field and D. Grayson, 'Megafaunal extinction: climate, humans and assumptions', *Trends in Ecology and Evolution*, Vol.21, No.2 (February 2006), pp.61–62.
32 A. Jelinek, 'Man's Role in the Extinction of Pleistocene Faunas', in P. Martin and H. Wright Jnr (eds), *Pleistocene Extinctions: The Search for a Cause* (New

Haven, Conn: Yale University Press, 1967), p.195; Gore, 'Neanderthals', p.22.
33 M. Stiller et, al., 'Withering Away – 25,000 Years of Genetic Decline Preceded Cave Bear Extinction', *Molecular Biology and Evolution*, Vol.27, No.5 (May 2010), p.975.
34 B. Bower, '"Dwarf" mammoths outlived last ice age', *Science News*, Vol.143, No.13 (27 March 1993), p.197.
35 A.J. Stuart et. al., 'Pleistocene to Holocene extinction dynamics in giant deer and woolly mammoth', *Nature*, Vol.431, No.7009 (7 October 2004), p.684; A.M. Lister, 'Mammoths in miniature', *Nature*, Vol.362, No.6418 (25 March 1993), p.288.
36 O. Ryder, 'Przewalski's Horse: Prospects for Reintroduction into the Wild', *Conservation Biology*, Vol.7, No.1 (March 1933), p.13; K. Kowalski, 'The Pleistocene Extinction of Mammals in Europe', in Martin and Wright, *Pleistocene Extinctions*, p.359.
37 Grayson and Meltzer, 'A requiem for North American overkill', pp.588–589.
38 A.M. Lister et. al., 'The phylogenetic position of the "giant deer" *Megaloceros giganteus*', *Nature*, Vol.438, No.7069 (8 December 2005), p.850.
39 Day, *The Doomsday Book of Animals*, pp.188–189.
40 A. Mysterud et. al., 'Population ecology and conservation of endangered megafauna: the case of the European bison in Bialowieza Primeval Forest, Poland', *Animal Conservation*, Vol.10, No.1 (February 2007), pp.77–79.
41 B. Brook and D. Bowman, 'The uncertain blitzkrieg of Pleistocene megafauna', *Journal of Biogeography*, Vol.31, No.4 (April 2004), p.518.
42 S. Weisburd, 'Creatures of the Dreamtime: A new exhibit digs into Australia's strange past lives', *Science News*, Vol.133, No.16 (16 April 1988), p.248.
43 S. Weisburd, 'Australia's animals of the past: A museum exhibit brings some of Australia's ancient and strange creatures to light', *Bioscience*, Vol.38, No.8 (September 1988), p.528.
44 M. French, 'What Fate Awaits? The Indigenous Peoples of the Darling Downs in 1851–52', *Queensland Review*, Vol.9, No.1 (May 2002), p.25.
45 R. Holden and N. Holden, *Bunyips: Australia's folklore of fear* (Canberra: National Library of Australia, 2001), p.175.
46 L. Dayton and L. Hall, 'Big bird rocks art', *Australian* (Sydney), 1 June 2010, p.3.
47 D. Welch, 'That Bird is not *Genyornis*', *Australian Archaeology*, Vol.82, No.2 (2016), pp.189–190. See also: D. Welch, 'Thy *Thylacoleo* is a thylacine', *Australian Archaeology*, Vol.80, No.1 (2015), pp.40–47.
48 Webb, 'Megamarsupial extinction', p.83.
49 *Ibid.*, p.51.
50 Clode, *Prehistoric giants*, pp.56 and 58–59.
51 Miller et. al., 'Pleistocene Extinction of *Genyornis newtoni*', pp.205–208.
52 G. Miller et. al., 'Ecosystem Collapse in Pleistocene Australia and a Human Role in Megafaunal Extinction', *Science*, Vol.309, No.5732 (8 July 2005), pp.288–290.
53 T. Flannery, 'Debating Extinction', *Science*, Vol.283, No.5399 (8 January 1999), pp.182–183.
54 White and O'Connell, *A Prehistory of Australia, New Guinea and Sahul*, p.93
55 R. Roberts et. al., 'New Ages for the Last Australian Megafauna: Continent-Wide Extinction About 46,000 Years Ago', *Science*, Vol.292, No.5523 (8 June 2001), pp.1888–1891.
56 C. Turney et. al., 'Late-surviving megafauna in Tasmania, Australia, implicate human involvement in their extinction', *Proceedings of the National Academy of Sciences of the United States of America*, Vol.105, No.34 (26 August 2008), pp.12152–12153.

Notes

57   Flannery, *The Future Eaters*, pp.203–205.
58   J. Field, 'Trampling Through the Pleistocene: Does Taphonomy Matter at Cuddie Springs?', *Australian Archaeology*, No.63 (December 2006), p.9.
59   B. Brook, R. Gillespie and P. Martin, 'Megafauna Mix-Up', *Australasian Science*, Vol.27, No.5 (June 2006), p.37.
60   R. Gillespie and B. David, 'The Importance, or Impotence, of Cuddie Springs', *Australasian Science*, Vol.22, No.9 (October 2001), p.43; R. Roberts *et. al.*, 'The Last Australian Megafauna', *Australasian Science*, Vol.22, No.9 (October 2001), p.40.
61   White and O'Connell, *A Prehistory of Australia, New Guinea and Sahul*, p.92.
62   Flannery, *The Future Eaters*, pp.183–184.
63   Johnson, 'Determinants of loss of mammal species during the Late Quarternary "megafauna" extinctions', p.2225.
64   C. Schrire, 'An Analysis of Human Behaviour and Animal Extinctions in South Africa and Australia in Late Pleistocene Times', *South African Archaeological Bulletin*, Vol.35, No.131 (June 1980), pp.6–7.
65   Haynes, 'The catastrophic extinction of North American mammoths and mastodons', p.400.

VII   PLEISTOCENE SAHUL: ADAPTATION AND INNOVATION

1   Flannery, *The Future Eaters*, p.234; Mulvaney and Kamminga, *Prehistory of Australia*, p.179.
2   Mulvaney and Kamminga, *Prehistory of Australia*, p.173.
3   Flannery, *The Future Eaters*, pp.182–183.
4   Hiscock, *The Archaeology of Ancient Australia*, pp.47–47 and 60.
5   P. Thorley, 'Pleistocene settlement in the Australian arid zone: occupation of an inland riverine landscape in the central Australian ranges', *Antiquity*, Vol.72, No.275 (March 1998), pp.34 and 44.
6   Hiscock, *The Archaeology of Ancient Australia*, pp.59–60.
7   *Ibid.*, pp.49–51.
8   *Ibid.*, p.52.
9   A. Gibbons, 'Aboriginal Genome Shows Two-Wave Settlement of Asia', *Science*, Vol.333, No.6050 (23 September 2011), pp.1689 and 1691.
10 Flannery, *The Future Eaters*, pp.182–183.
11 Mulvaney and Kamminga, *Prehistory of Australia*, p.175.
12 S. Bulmer, 'Waisted blades and axes: A functional interpretation of some early stone tools from Papua New Guinea', in R.V.S. Wright (ed.), *Stone tools as cultural markers: change, evolution and complexity* (Canberra: Australian Institute of Aboriginal Studies, 1977), pp.43–45.
13 Mulvaney and Kamminga, *Prehistory of Australia*, p.175.
14 R. Lampert, *The Great Kartan Mystery: Terra Australis 5* (Canberra: Department of Prehistory, Research School of Pacific Studies, Australian National University, 1981), pp.3 and 10.
15 H.M. Cooper, 'Large Stone Implements from South Australia', *Records of the South Australian Museum*, Vol.7 (1943), p.343.
16 Flood, *Archaeology of the Dreamtime* (2004 ed.), pp.141–142.
17 A. Brown, *Ill-Starred Captains: Flinders and Baudin* (Fremantle, WA: Fremantle Arts Centre Press, 2004), pp.189–190.
18 L. Brasil, 'The Emu of King Island', *Emu*, Vol.14, No.2 (October 1914), p.88; A. Morgan and J. Sutton, 'A Critical Description of Some Recently Discovered Bones of the Extinct Kangaroo Island Emu (*Dromaius diemenianus*)', *Emu*, Vol.28, No.1 (July 1928), p.2. While noting that the Kangaroo Island Emu

became extinct sometime between 1803 and 1836 and was regularly hunted by settlers, Morgan and Sutton subscribed to the idea that this species had been exterminated through bushfires rather than hunting.
19   W. Howchin, 'Further Notes on the Geology of Kangaroo Island', *Transactions of the Royal Society of South Australia*, Vol.27 (1903), p.90.
20   N. Tindale, 'Relationship of the Extinct Kangaroo Island Culture with Cultures of Australia, Tasmania and Malaya', *Records of the South Australian Museum*, Vol.6 (1937), pp.39–40.
21   N. Tindale and B. Maegraith, 'Traces of an Extinct Aboriginal Population on Kangaroo Island', *Records of the South Australian Museum*, Vol.4, No.3 (1931), p.286.
22   Tindale, 'Relationship of the Extinct Kangaroo Island Culture with Cultures of Australia, Tasmania and Malaya', p.39.
23   Flood, *Archaeology of the Dreamtime* (2004 ed.), p.139.
24   S. Holdaway and N. Stern, *A Record in Stone: The Study of Australia's Flaked Stone Artefacts* (Melbourne: Museum Victoria and Aboriginal Studies Press, 2008), pp.203–204.
25   Lampert, *The Great Kartan Mystery*, p.1.
26   Flood, *Archaeology of the Dreamtime* (2004 ed.), pp.141–142.
27   *Ibid.*
28   R. Lampert, 'Waisted Blades in Australia?', *Records of the Australian Museum*, Vol.35, No.4 (1983), p.148; Flood, *Archaeology of the Dreamtime* (2004 ed.), pp.143–144.
29   R. Lampert and P. Hughes, 'Early Human Occupation of the Flinders Ranges', *Records of the South Australian Museum*, Vol.22 (1988), p.165.
30   Lampert, *The Great Kartan Mystery*, p.190; Lampert, 'Waisted Blades in Australia?', p.149.
31   Flood, *Archaeology of the Dreamtime* (2004 ed.), p.144.
32   *Ibid.*, pp.145–146.
33   R. Lampert, 'Kangaroo Island and the antiquity of Australians', in Wright (ed.), *Stone tools as cultural markers*, p.217.
34   Tindale and Maegraith, 'Traces of an Extinct Aboriginal Population on Kangaroo Island', pp.285–286.
35   Lampert, *The Great Kartan Mystery*, pp.177–178.
36   Flannery, *The Future Eaters*, p.264.
37   Lampert, *The Great Kartan Mystery*, p.170.
38   *Ibid*, p.171.
39   *Ibid.*, pp.173–174.
40   G. Jenkin, *Conquest of the Ngarrindjeri* (Adelaide: Rigby, 1985), p.15; R. Berndt and C. Berndt with J. Stanton, *A World That Was: The Yaraldi of the Murray River and the Lakes, South Australia* (Melbourne: Miegunyah Press, 1993), p.86.
41   Flood, *Archaeology of the Dreamtime* (2004 ed.), p.140.
42   Mulvaney and Kamminga, *Prehistory of Australia*, pp.217–219.
43   M. Morwood and P. Trezise, 'Edge-Ground Axes in Pleistocene Greater Australia: New Evidence from S.E. Cape York Peninsula', *Queensland Archaeological Research*, Vol.7 (1990), pp.77 and 85.
44   Mulvaney and Kamminga, *Prehistory of Australia*, pp.213–214.
45   J. Specht *et. al.*, 'Prehistoric Obsidian Exchange in Melanesia: A Perspective from the Talasea Sources', *Australian Archaeology*, No.27 (December 1987), pp.3–4; Holdaway and Stern, *A Record in Stone*, p.23.
46   Mulvaney and Kamminga, *Prehistory of Australia*, p.214.
47   R. Jones, 'Ice-Age Hunters of the Tasmanian Wilderness', *Australian Geographic*, No.8 (October-December 1987), p.39; R. Jones, 'Tasmanian

Notes

Archaeology: Establishing the Sequences', *Annual Review of Anthropology*, Vol.24 (October 1995), pp.431 and 434.
48   Flood, *Archaeology of the Dreamtime* (2004 ed.), p.98.
49   E. King, 'The Origin of Tektites: A Brief Review', *American Scientist*, Vol.65, No.2 (March–April 1977), pp.512–514.
50   Mulvaney and Kamminga, *Prehistory of Australia*, p.216.
51   *Ibid.*, pp.221–222.
52   R. Bednarik, 'Cave Use by Australian Pleistocene Man', *Proceedings of the University of Bristol Spelaeological (Caving) Society*, Vol.17, No.3 (1986), p.227.
53   Flood, *Rock Art of the Dreamtime*, pp.25 and 30.
54   *Ibid.*, pp.29–30, 36 and 48.
55   *Ibid.*, p.35.
56   *Ibid*, pp. 30 and 38–39.
57   J. Flood, 'Copying the Dreamtime: Anthropic Marks in Early Aboriginal Australia', *Rock Art Research*, Vol.23, No.2 (November 2006), pp.240–241.
58   *Ibid.*, p.241.
59   Chaloupka, *Journey in Time*, p.122.
60   Mulvaney and Kamminga, *Prehistory of Australia*, p.212.
61   H. Allen, 'Reinterpreting the 1969–1972 Willandra Lakes archaeological surveys', *Archaeology in Oceania*, Vol.33, No.3 (October 1998), pp.211–213; Flood, *Archaeology of the Dreamtime* (2004 ed.), p.51.
62   K. Fitzsimmons *et. al.*, 'The Mungo Mega-Lake Event, Semi-Arid Australia: Non-Linear Descent into the Last Ice Age, Implications for Human Behaviour', *Public Library of Science One*, Vol.10, No.6 (17 June 2015), pp.1 and 11; Anon, 'Inland seafarers or good swimmers?', *Koori Mail* (Lismore), 1 July 2015, p.31.
63   Allen, 'Reinterpreting the 1969–1972 Willandra Lakes archaeological surveys', p.215.
64   Bowler *et. al.*, 'Pleistocene human remains from Australia', p.53; Flood, *Archaeology of the Dreamtime* (2004 ed.), pp.51–52.
65   Bowler *et. al.*, 'Pleistocene human remains from Australia', p.55.
66   *Ibid.*, p.49.
67   Hiscock, *The Archaeology of Ancient Australia*, p.104.
68   Flood, *Archaeology of the Dreamtime* (2004 ed.), pp.43–44.
69   *Ibid.*, p.44.
70   Johnston and Clark, 'Willandra Lakes Archaeological Investigations 1968-98', p.117.
71   Flood, *Archaeology of the Dreamtime* (2004 ed.), pp.268–269.
72   Bickel, 'Ancient man in Kow Swamp', p.254.
73   P. Hammond, 'Step back to the Ice Age', *Courier-Mail* (Brisbane), 7–8 April 2007, pp.26–27; A. Shoemaker, 'Ancient and modern footprints: music and the mysteries of Lake Mungo', in A. Chan and A. Noble (eds), *Sounds of Translation: Intersections of Music, Technology and Society* (Acton, ACT: ANU E Press, 2009), p.83.
74   M. Westaway, 'Footprints of the First Australians', *Australasian Science*, Vol.31, No.2 (March 2010), p.17.
75   S. Webb, M. Cupper and R. Robins, 'Pleistocene human footprints from the Willandra Lakes, southeastern Australia', *Journal of Human Evolution*, Vol.50, No.4 (April 2006), pp.411–412.
76   Hiscock, *The Archaeology of Ancient Australia*, pp.111–112.
77   *Ibid.*, p.113.
78   J. Balme and K. Morse, 'Shell beads and social behaviour in Pleistocene Australia', *Antiquity*, Vol.80, No.310 (December 2006), pp.799–801.

Australia's Ancient Aboriginal Past

79   Ibid., pp.801–802.
80   Ibid., pp.802–803.
81   Ibid, pp.805–807.
82   Ibid, pp.808–809.
83   C.E. Dortch, *Devil's Lair: a study in prehistory* (Perth: Western Australian Museum, 1984), pp.58 and 64.
84   Ibid., p.50.
85   C.E. Dortch, 'Devil's Lair, an Example of Prolonged Cave Use in South-Western Australia', *World Archaeology*, Vol.10, No.3 (February 1979), p.269.
86   Ibid., p.275; Flood, *Archaeology of the Dreamtime* (2004 ed.), pp.107–108.
87   Mulvaney and Kamminga, *Prehistory of Australia*, p.178.
88   Hiscock, *The Archaeology of Ancient Australia*, p.117.
89   Jones, 'Ice-Age Hunters of the Tasmanian Wilderness', p.44; Cosgrove, 'Late Pleistocene behavioural variation and time trends', p.100.
90   B. Brimfield, *Long Trek South: A Search for the History of the Palaeolithic Tasmanians* (Mowbray, Tas: Self-published, 2010), p.32.

VIII HOLOCENE AUSTRALIA AND REGIONAL CASE STUDIES

1   Flood, *Archaeology of the Dreamtime* (2004 ed.), p.257.
2   D.J. Mulvaney, 'The End of the Beginning: 6000 years ago to 1788', in D.J. Mulvaney and J.P. White (eds), *Australians to 1788* (Broadway, NSW: Fairfax, Syme & Weldon Associates, 1987), p.75.
3   S. Tutt (ed.), *Pioneer Days: Stories and Photographs of European Settlement Between the Pine and the Noosa Rivers, Queensland* (Caboolture, Qld: Caboolture Historical Society, 1974), p.7.
4   Mulvaney and Kamminga, *Prehistory of Australia*, pp.223 and 226; Hiscock, *The Archaeology of Ancient Australia*, pp.139–140.
5   P. Hiscock, 'Technological Responses to Risk in Holocene Australia', *Journal of World Prehistory*, Vol.8, No.3 (September 1994), pp.268–271.
6   Flood, *Archaeology of the Dreamtime* (2004 ed.), p.224.
7   Hiscock, 'Technical Responses to Risk in Holocene Australia', p.284.
8   Ibid., p.277.
9   Mulvaney and Kamminga, *Prehistory of Australia*, pp.267–269.
10   Lourandos, 'Swamp Managers of Southwestern Victoria', p..293; H. Builth *et. al.*, 'Environmental and cultural change on the Mt Eccles lava-flow landscapes of southwest Victoria, Australia', *Holocene*, Vol.18, No.3 (May 2008), p.414.
11   Builth *et. al.*, 'Environmental and cultural change on the Mt Eccles lava-flow landscapes of southwest Victoria, Australia', p.418.
12   R. McDowall and J. Beumer, 'Freshwater Eels', in R. McDowell (ed.), *Freshwater Fishes of South-Eastern Australia* (Terrey Hills, NSW: Reed, 1980), p.45; J. Merrick and G. Schmida, *Australian Freshwater Fishes: Biology and Management* (North Ryde, NSW: School of Biological Sciences, Macquarie University, 1984), p.57.
13   Lourandos, 'Swamp Managers of Southwestern Victoria', p.300.
14   P. Coutts, R. Frank and P. Hughes, 'Aboriginal Engineers of the Western District, Victoria', *Records of the Victorian Archaeological Survey*, No.7 (June 1978), p.24.
15   Lourandos, 'Change or stability?', pp.253–254; Flood, *Archaeology of the Dreamtime* (2004 ed.), p.242.
16   Flood, *Archaeology of the Dreamtime* (2004 ed.), p.242.
17   Lourandos, 'Swamp Managers of Southwestern Victoria', p.300; Flood, *Archaeology of the Dreamtime* (2004 ed.), p.245; I. McNiven and D. Bell,

'Fishers and Farmers: historicising the Gunditjmara freshwater fishery, western Victoria', *La Trobe Journal*, No.85 (May 2010), p.88.
18   G. Megalogenis, 'Rethinking the Noble Savage', *Weekend Australian* (Sydney), 3–4 August 2002, p.19.
19   Berndt, Berndt and Stanton, *A World That Was*, p.96.
20   *Ibid.*, p.11.
21   Lourandos, 'Swamp Managers of Southwestern Victoria', p.304.
22   McNiven and Bell, 'Fishers and Farmers', p.98.
23   Flood, *Archaeology of the Dreamtime* (2004 ed.), p.242.
24   Coutts, Frank and Hughes, 'Aboriginal Engineers of the Western District, Victoria', p.39; Lourandos, 'Swamp Managers of Southwestern Victoria', p.306.
25   Lourandos, 'Swamp Managers of Southwestern Victoria', p.298.
26   *Ibid.*, p.299.
27   P. Memmott, *Gunyah Goondie + Wurley: The Aboriginal Architecture of Australia* (St Lucia, Qld: University of Queensland Press, 2007), p.190.
28   E. Williams, 'Documentation and Archaeological Investigation of an Aboriginal "Village" Site in South Western Victoria', *Aboriginal History*, Vol.8 (1984), p.174.
29   *Ibid.*, pp.183–184; E. Williams, 'Earth mounds in south-west Victoria: What were they used for and how do we know they were cultural features?', in M. Sullivan, S. Brockwell and A. Webb (eds), *Archaeology in the North: Proceedings of the 1993 Australian Archaeological Association Conference* (Darwin: North Australian Research Unit, Australian National University, 1994), p.163.
30   Hiscock, *The Archaeology of Ancient Australia*, p.189.
31   D. Barwick, 'Mapping the Past: An Atlas of Victorian Clans 1835–1904 – Part 1', *Aboriginal History*, Vol.8 (1984), p.107.
32   I. McFarlane, *Beyond Awakening: The Aboriginal Tribes of North West Tasmania – A History* (Launceston, Tas: Fullers Bookshop, 2008), p.7.
33   Mulvaney and Kamminga, *Prehistory of Australia*, p.303.
34   S. Webb, 'Intensification, Population and Social Change in Southeastern Australia: The Skeletal Evidence', *Aboriginal History*, Vol.8 (1984), pp.157 and 160.
35   *Ibid.*, pp.169–170.
36   Coutts, Frank and Hughes, 'Aboriginal Engineers of the Western District, Victoria', p.24.
37   *Ibid.*, p.35; L. Black, 'Aboriginal Fisheries of Brewarrina', *South African Archaeological Bulletin*, Vol.2, No.5 (March 1947), pp.15–16; T.C. Roughley, *Fish and Fisheries of Australia* (Sydney: Angus and Robertson, 1966), pp.306–307.
38   Mulvaney, 'The End of the Beginning', p.89.
39   Flood, *Archaeology of the Dreamtime* (2004 ed.), p.250.
40   S. O'Connor, 'The Stone House Structures of High Cliffy Island, North West Kimberley, WA', *Australian Archaeology*, No.25 (December 1987), pp. 30 and 32–33.
41   *Ibid.*, p.38.
42   P. Thorley, 'Rock-art and the archaeological record of Indigenous settlement in Central Australia', *Australian Aboriginal Studies*, No.1 (2004), pp.82–83; M. Smith and J. Ross, 'What happened at 1500–1000 cal. BP in Central Australia? Timing, impact and archaeological signatures', *Holocene*, Vol.18, No.3 (2008), p.381.
43   I. McNiven, 'Tula Adzes and Bifacial Points on the East Coast of Australia', *Australian Archaeology*, No.36 (1993), p.23.
44   Flood, *Archaeology of the Dreamtime* (2004 ed.), pp.260–261.

45 Ibid.
46 R. Tonkinson, *The Mardu Aborigines: Living the Dream in Australia's Desert* (Fort Worth, TX: Holt, Rinehart and Winston, 1991), p.46.
47 Hiscock, *The Archaeology of Ancient Australia*, p.206.
48 R.J. Rowlands and J.M. Rowlands, 'An Aboriginal Dam in Northwestern New South Wales', *Mankind*, Vol.7, No.2 (December 1969), p.132.
49 *Ibid.*, pp.132–133 and 135.
50 J. Isaacs, *Bush Food: Aboriginal Food and Herbal Medicine* (Sydney: Ure Smith, 1991), p.86; T. Blake, '"This Noble Tree": J.C. Bidwill and the Naming of the Bunya Pine', *Queensland Review*, Vol.9, No.2 (November 2002), pp.41–42.
51 C. Petrie, *Tom Petrie's Reminiscences of Early Queensland* (Brisbane: Watson, Ferguson & Co., 1904), p.16.
52 *Ibid.*, pp.16–17; D. Horton, 'Bunya Nuts', in D. Horton (ed.), *The Encyclopaedia of Aboriginal Australia: Vol.1* (Canberra: Aboriginal Studies Press, 1994), p.166.
53 J. Flood, 'Moth Hunters of the Southeastern Highlands', in Mulvaney and White, *Australians to 1788*, pp.281–282.
54 *Ibid.*, pp.275–276.
55 *Ibid.*, pp.276 and 278.
56 *Ibid.*, pp.277–280.
57 J. Flood, *The Moth Hunters: Aboriginal Prehistory of the Australian Alps* (Canberra: Australian Institute of Aboriginal Studies, 1980), pp.54 and 56.
58 Flood, 'Moth Hunters of the Southeastern Highlands', pp.276 and 284.
59 Flood, *Archaeology of the Dreamtime* (2004 ed.), p.239.
60 *Ibid.*; Flood, 'Moth Hunters of the Southeastern Highlands', pp.284 and 287.
61 Flood, 'Moth Hunters of the Southeastern Highlands', pp.286–287.
62 Flood, *Archaeology of the Dreamtime* (2004 ed.), p.240.
63 B. Asmussen, '"There is likewise a nut ...": A Comparative Ethnohistory of Aboriginal Processing Methods and Consumption of Australian *Bowenia*, *Cycas*, *Lepidozamia* and *Macrozamia* species', *Technical Reports of the Australian Museum*, No.23 (2011), p.149.
64 Flood, *Archaeology of the Dreamtime* (2004 ed.), p.237.
65 Asmussen, '"There is likewise a nut ..."', pp.147–148.
66 Flood, *Archaeology of the Dreamtime* (2004 ed.), p.238.
67 Hiscock, *The Archaeology of Ancient Australia*, p.195.
68 Flood, *Archaeology of the Dreamtime* (2004 ed.), p.238.
69 *Ibid.*, p.230.
70 P. Savolainen *et. al.*, 'A detailed picture of the origin of the Australian dingo obtained from the study of mitochondrial DNA', *Proceedings of the National Academy of Sciences of the United States of America*, Vol.101, No.33 (17 August 2004), p.12390; L. Dayton, 'Long time here but dingoes were another China export', *Australian* (Sydney), 8 September 2011, p.3.
71 Mulvaney and Kamminga, *Prehistory of Australia*, pp.258–259.
72 *Ibid.*, p.259.
73 M. Carter, 'North of the Cape and south of the Fly: discovering the archaeology of social complexity in Torres Strait', in D. Bruno, B. Barker and I. McNiven (eds), *The Social Archaeology of Australian Indigenous Societies* (Canberra: Aboriginal Studies Press, 2006), pp.288–290.
74 I. McNiven, 'Inclusions, exclusions and transitions: Torres Strait Islander constructed landscapes over the past 4000 years, northeast Australia', *Holocene*, Vol.18, No.3 (May 2008), p.452.
75 B. David *et. al.*, 'Badu 15 and the Papuan-Austronesian settlement of Torres Strait', *Archaeology in Oceania*, Vol.39, No.2 (July 2004), pp.75–76.
76 Singe, *The Torres Strait*, pp.6–7.

Notes

77 Ibid., p.6.
78 Flannery, *The Future Eaters*, pp.283–284.
79 Singe, *The Torres Strait*, p.6.
80 Ibid., pp.4–5; D. Lawrence, 'Customary exchange in the Torres Strait', *Australian Aboriginal Studies*, No.2 (1998), pp.14 and 18.
81 Singe, *The Torres Strait*, p.5.
82 McNiven, 'Inclusions, exclusions and transitions', pp.456–457.
83 Singe, *The Torres Strait*, p.6.
84 Ibid., pp.18–19.
85 Mulvaney and Kamminga, *Prehistory of Australia*, pp.263–264; Johnson, '"A modified form of whaling"', p.28.
86 K. O'Dea, 'Traditional diet and food preferences of Australian Aboriginal hunter-gatherers', *Philosophical Transactions: Biological Sciences*, Vol.334, No.1270 (29 November 1991), p.235.
87 R. Gerritsen, 'Evidence for Indigenous Australian Agriculture', *Australasian Science*, Vol.31, No.6 (July-August 2010), p.37.
88 W.C. Dix and M.E. Lofgren, 'Kurumi: Possible Aboriginal Incipient Agriculture Associated with a Stone Arrangement', *Records of the Western Australian Museum*, Vol.3, Pt.1 (1974–1975), pp.73–77.
89 Flood, *Archaeology of the Dreamtime* (2004 ed.), p.262.
90 Mulvaney, 'The End of the Beginning', p.86.
91 Flannery, *The Future Eaters*, p.281.
92 Ibid., pp.281 and 284.
93 I. McBryde, 'Kulin greenstone quarries: the social contexts of production and distribution for the Mt William site', *World Archaeology*, Vol.16, No.2 (October 1984), pp.279 and 282.
94 Mulvaney, 'The End of the Beginning', p.92.
95 Flannery, *The Future Eaters*, p.288.
96 B. Gammage, '"... far more happier than we Europeans": Aborigines and farmers', *London Papers in Australian Studies*, No.12 (2005), p.6.
97 R. Jones, 'Firestick Farming', *Australian Natural History*, Vol.16, No.7 (15 September 1969), pp.226–227.
98 McFarlane, *Beyond Awakening*, p.21.
99 H. Reynolds, *The Other Side of the Frontier: Aboriginal resistance to the European invasion of Australia* (Ringwood, Vic: Penguin, 1995), pp.108–109.
100 B. Gammage, '"...Far more happier than we Europeans"', p.4.
101 B. Gammage, *The Biggest Estate on Earth: How Aborigines Made Australia* (Crows Nest, NSW: Allen & Unwin, 2011), p.303.
102 Ibid., pp.165–166.
103 B. Gammage, 'Australia Under Aboriginal Management', 15th Barry Andrews Memorial Lecture, Australian Defence Force Academy, Canberra, 31 October 2002, p.12.
104 Gammage, *The Biggest Estate on Earth*, pp.169–172 and 281–282.

IX TASMANIA: AN ISOLATED TRAJECTORY

1 R. Blench, 'The Languages of the Tasmanians and Their Relation to the Peopling of Australia: Sensible and Wild Theories', *Australian Archaeology*, No.67 (December 2008), p.14.
2 J. Wunderly, 'The Origin of the Tasmanian Race', *Man*, Vol.38 (December 1938), p.201.
3 M. Johnson and I. McFarlane, *Van Diemen's Land: An Aboriginal History* (Sydney: University of New South Wales Press, 2015), p.16.

4   F.A. Allen, 'The Original Range of the Papuan and Negrito Races', *Journal of the Anthropological Institute of Great Britain and Ireland*, Vol.8 (1879), p.49.
5   Ibid., pp.40–41.
6   Wunderly, 'The Origin of the Tasmanian Race', p.199.
7   J. Bonwick, 'On the Origin of the Tasmanians Geologically considered', *Journal of the Ethnological Society of London*, Vol.2, No.2 (1870), p.122.
8   J. Mathew, *Eaglehawk and Crow: A study of the Australian Aborigines including an inquiry into their origin and a survey of Australian languages* (London: David Nutt, 1899), p.5.
9   Johnson and McFarlane, *Van Diemen's Land*, p.17.
10 Taylor, 'The Tasmanian Languages', p.45.
11 J. Taylor, 'The Aboriginal Discovery and Colonisation of Tasmania', *Tasmanian Historical Research Association Papers and Proceedings*, Vol.50, No.4 (December 2003), p.220.
12 Ibid., p.217.
13 G. Calder, *Levee, Line and Martial Law: A History of the Dispossession of the Mairremmener People of Van Diemen's Land 1803–1832* (Launceston, Tas: Fullers Bookshop, 2010), p.15.
14 Ibid.
15 Ibid.
16 Z. Edwards, 'Bypass site set for human history claim', *Examiner* (Launceston), 11 March 2010, p.7; D. Brown, 'Bypass finds date to 40,000 years', *Mercury* (Hobart), 27 April 2010, p.3.
17 J. Allen, 'Peer Review of the Draft Final Archaeological Report and Test Excavations of the Jordan River Levee Site Southern Tasmania', J. Allen Archaeological Consultancies, 22 October 2010, p.22.
18 Lourandos, *Continent of Hunter-Gatherers*, pp.268–269; Calder, *Levee, Line and Martial Law*, p.13.
19 Jones, 'Ice-Age Hunters in the Tasmanian Wilderness', p.34.
20 McFarlane, *Beyond Awakening*, p.3.
21 Lourandos, *Continent of Hunter-Gatherers*, pp.247–248.
22 Johnson and McFarlane, *Van Diemen's Land*, p.24.
23 R. Fudali and R. Ford, 'Darwin Glass and Darwin Crater: A Progress Report', *Meteoritics*, Vol.14 (September 1979), pp.284–287 and 295; Jones, 'Ice-Age Hunters of the Tasmanian Wilderness', p.39.
24 J. Flood, *The Riches of Ancient Australia: A Journey into Prehistory* (St Lucia, Qld: University of Queensland Press, 1990), p.327.
25 Jones, 'Tasmanian Archaeology', p.430.
26 Lourandos, *Continent of Hunter-Gatherers*, pp.246–247; J. Garvey, 'Preliminary zooarchaeological interpretations from Kutikina Cave, south-west Tasmania', *Australian Aboriginal Studies*, No.1 (2006), pp.57–58.
27 Garvey, 'Preliminary zooarchaeological interpretations of Kutikina Cave, south-west Tasmania', p.60.
28 R. Cosgrove, 'Forty-Two Degrees South: The Archaeology of Late Pleistocene Tasmania', *Journal of World Prehistory*, Vol.13, No.4 (December 1999), p.393.
29 J. Garvey, 'Surviving an Ice Age: The Zooarchaeological Record from Southwestern Tasmania', *Palaios*, Vol.22, No.6 (November 2007), p.584.
30 Garvey, 'Preliminary zooarchaeological interpretations of Kutikina Cave, south-west Tasmania', pp.59–60.
31 A. Pike-Tay, R. Cosgrove and J. Garvey, 'Systematic seasonal land use by late Pleistocene Tasmanian Aborigines', *Journal of Archaeological Science*, Vol.35, No.9 (September 2008), pp.2541–2542.
32 S. Harris, D. Ranson and S. Brown, 'Maxwell River Archaeological Survey 1986', *Australian Archaeology*, No.27 (1988), pp.94–95.

Notes

33   J. Thompson, 'Covered cave deposits hide mysteries of past', *Sunday Tasmanian* (Hobart), 2 April 1995, p.63.
34   S. Dix, 'New Aboriginal hand stencil discoveries at the Freycinet National Park, Tasmania', *Australian Archaeology*, Vol.82, No.1 (2016), pp.76–77.
35   Cosgrove, 'Late Pleistocene behavioural variation and time trends: the case from Tasmania', pp.83–85.
36   *Ibid.*, pp.92–93.
37   Johnson and McFarlane, *Van Diemen's Land*, p.28.
38   Lourandos, *Continent of Hunter-Gatherers*, p.264.
39   Cosgrove, 'Forty-Two Degrees South', p.365.
40   R. Sim, 'Prehistoric Sites on King Island in the Bass Strait: Results of an Archaeological Survey', *Australian Archaeology*, No.31 (December 1990), p.36.
41   R. Sim, 'Prehistoric human occupation in the King and Furneaux Island regions, Bass Strait', in Sullivan, Brockwell and Webb (eds), *Archaeology in the North*, pp.362–363.
42   *Ibid.*, p.369; Flannery, *The Future Eaters*, pp.263–264.
43   Plomley, *The Tasmanian Aborigines*, p.55.
44   Taylor, 'The Aboriginal Discovery and Colonisation of Tasmania', pp.13–14.
45   Ryan, *The Aboriginal Tasmanians*, pp.13–14.
46   R. Jones, 'Hunting Forbears', in M. Roe (ed.), *The Flow of Culture: Tasmanian Studies* (Canberra: Australian Academy of the Humanities, 1987), pp.28–29.
47   R. Jones, 'Tasmanian Tribes', Appendix in N. Tindale, *Aboriginal Tribes of Australia: Their Terrain, Environmental Controls, Distribution, Limits, and Proper Names* (Canberra: Australian National University Press, 1974), p.325.
48   *Ibid.*, pp.320–321; D. Woodward, 'Diet in Tasmania over a Thousand Generations: A Preliminary History', *Tasmanian Historical Studies*, Vol.3, No.1 (1990–1991), p.144.
49   I. McFarlane, 'Aboriginal Society in North West Tasmania: Dispossession and Genocide' (unpublished PhD thesis, University of Tasmania, 2002), p.5.
50   Ryan, *The Aboriginal Tasmanians*, p.14.
51   I. McFarlane, 'Pevay: A Casualty of War', *Tasmanian Historical Research Association Papers and Proceedings*, Vol.48, No.4 (December 2001), p.282.
52   Plomley, *The Tasmanian Aborigines*, p.2.
53   McFarlane, *Beyond Awakening*, p.30.
54   H. Ling Roth, *The Aborigines of Tasmania* (Halifax, UK: F. King & Sons, 1899), pp.128–129.
55   Plomley, *The Tasmanian Aborigines*, p.29.
56   Roth, *The Aborigines of Tasmania*, p.131.
57   Plomley, *The Tasmanian Aborigines*, p.30; Flood, *Archaeology of the Dreamtime* (2004 ed.), p.202.
58   N.J.B. Plomley, *The Baudin Expedition and the Tasmanian Aborigines 1802* (Hobart: Blubber Head Press, 1983), p.168.
59   Plomley, *The Tasmanian Aborigines*, pp.32 and 35.
60   N.J.B. Plomley, *Jorgen Jorgenson and the Aborigines of Van Diemen's Land: being a reconstruction of his 'lost' book on their customs and habits, and on his role in the Roving Parties and the Black Line* (Hobart: Blubber Head Press, 1991), p.58.
61   McFarlane, *Beyond Awakening*, p.27.
62   *Ibid.*, p.27; Flood, *The Riches of Ancient Australia*, p.338.
63   I. McFarlane, 'Adolphus Schayer: Van Diemen's Land and the Berlin Papers', *Tasmanian Historical Research Association Papers and Proceedings*, Vol.57, No.2 (August 2010), p.112.
64   J. Clark, 'Devils and Horses: Religion and Creative Life in Tasmanian Aboriginal Society', in Roe (ed.), *The Flow of Culture*, p.59; Plomley, *The Tasmanian*

Aborigines, pp.61–62.
65 Plomley, *The Tasmanian Aborigines*, p.62; McFarlane, *Beyond Awakening*, pp.30–31.
66 N.J.B. Plomley (ed.), *Friendly Mission: The Tasmanian Journals and Papers of George Augustus Robinson 1829–1834* (Launceston, Tas: Queen Victoria Museum and Art Gallery and Quintus Publishing, 2008), p.284.
67 McFarlane, *Beyond Awakening*, p.31.
68 Clark, 'Devils and Horses', pp.53–54.
69 *Ibid.*, pp.56–57.
70 Ryan, *The Aboriginal Tasmanians*, p.11; McFarlane, *Beyond Awakening*, p.31.
71 C. Lord, 'A Note on the Burial Customs of the Tasmanian Aborigines', *Papers and Proceedings of the Royal Society of Tasmania for the Year 1923*, p.45.
72 F. Noetling, 'A Native Burial Ground on Charlton Estate, Near Ross', *Papers and Proceedings of the Royal Society of Tasmania for the Year 1908*, pp.37–39.
73 Jones, 'Tasmanian Archaeology', pp.426–427.
74 Lourandos, *Continent of Hunter-Gatherers*, p.271.
75 Plomley, *The Tasmanian Aborigines*, pp.45–46.
76 *Ibid.*, pp.46–47.
77 McFarlane, *Beyond Awakening*, p.9.
78 *Ibid.*, p.17.
79 McFarlane, 'Pevay', p.281.
80 Johnson and McFarlane, *Van Diemen's Land*, pp.40–41.
81 Plomley (ed.), *Friendly Mission*, p.788.
82 B. Hiatt, 'The Food Quest and the Economy of the Tasmanian Aborigines [Part 2]', *Oceania*, Vol.38, No.3 (March 1968), pp.206–208.
83 Plomley, *The Tasmanian Aborigines*, pp.51–52 and 54.
84 Hiattt, 'The Food Quest and the Economy of the Tasmanian Aborigines [Part 2]', p.210.
85 J. Taylor, 'The Palawa (Tasmanian Aboriginal) Languages' (unpublished MA thesis, University of Tasmania, 2004), pp.6–7.
86 Breen, 'Tasmanian Aborigines – Making Fire', p.43.
87 Plomley, *The Baudin Expedition and the Tasmanian Aborigines 1802*, p.168.
88 Plomley, *The Tasmanian Aborigines*, pp.40–41.
89 Plomley (ed.), *Friendly Mission*, p.599.
90 G. Volger, 'Making Fire by Percussion in Tasmania', *Oceania*, Vol.44, No.1 (September 1973), pp.60–61; McFarlane, 'Aboriginal Society in North West Tasmania', p.25.
91 Plomley, *The Tasmanian Aborigines*, p.40.
92 Hiatt, 'The Food Quest and the Economy of the Tasmanian Aborigines [Part 2]', pp.202–203.
93 Thompson, 'Covered cave deposits hide mysteries of past', p.63.
94 Hiatt, 'The Food Quest and the Economy of the Tasmanian Aborigines [Part 1]', *Oceania*, Vol.38, No.2 (December 1967), pp.110–111.
95 Plomley (ed.), *Friendly Mission*, p.665.
96 *Ibid.*, pp.559–560.
97 Hiatt, 'The Food Quest and the Economy of the Tasmanian Aborigines [Part 1]', pp.110–111.
98 *Ibid.*, p.115.
99 D. Collett, 'Endangered space and Aboriginal settlement on the coast of Tasmania: A preliminary model', in Sullivan, Brockwell and Webb (eds), *Archaeology in the North*, p.346.
100 Jones, 'Hunting Forbears', pp.38–39.
101 Mulvaney and Kamminga, *Prehistory of Australia*, p.354.
102 R. Jones, 'The Tasmanian paradox', in Wright (ed.), *Stone tools as cultural*

markers, p.203.
103 R. Taylor, 'The polemics of eating fish in Tasmania: the historical evidence revisited', *Aboriginal History*, Vol.31 (2007), p.10.
104 Hiscock, *The Archaeology of Ancient Australia*, p.133.
105 Flood, *Archaeology of the Dreamtime* (2004 ed.), p.206; Taylor, 'The polemics of eating fish in Tasmania', p.10.
106 Flannery, *The Future Eaters*, pp.268–269.
107 Taylor, 'The polemics of eating fish in Tasmania', pp.11 and 14.
108 McFarlane, 'Aboriginal Society in North West Tasmania', pp.12–13.
109 Johnson and McFarlane, *Van Diemen's Land*, p.45.
110 Plomley (ed.), *Friendly Mission*, p.757.
111 Johnson and McFarlane, *Van Diemen's Land*, p.47.
112 Taylor, 'The polemics of eating fish in Tasmania', pp.15–16.
113 *Ibid.*, pp.19 and 22.
114 McFarlane, *Beyond Awakening*, p.15.
115 Hiatt, 'The Food Quest and the Economy of Tasmanian Aborigines [Part 1]', p.119.
116 *Ibid.*, p.111; B. Plomley and M. Cameron, 'Plant Foods of the Tasmanian Aborigines', *Records of the Queen Victoria Museum, Launceston*, No.101 (1993), pp.2–11.
117 Woodward, 'Diet in Tasmania over a Thousand Generations', p.142.
118 J. Taylor, 'Aboriginal Language of Health and Well-being in Van Diemen's Land: Palawa (Tasmanian Aboriginal) Health and Nutrition', in P. Richards, B. Valentine and T. Dunning (eds), *Effecting a Cure: Aspects of Health and Medicine in Launceston* (Launceston, Tas: Myola House of Publishing, 2006), p.13.
119 Plomley, *The Tasmanian Aborigines*, p.57.
120 D.J. Mulvaney, *Encounters in Place: Outsiders and Aboriginal Australians 1606–1985* (St Lucia, Qld: University of Queensland Press, 1989), pp.34–36.
121 Plomley, *The Tasmanian Aborigines*, p.58.

INDEX

absolute dating 17
accelerator mass spectrometry 23
Acheulean technology 42, 45–8
Andaman Islands xiv, 99
Adelaide, SA 77, 126
Adventure Bay, TAS 187, 190
Afghanistan 98
Africa xiii, 14, 24, 27, 29–34, 36–7, 42–6, 49–51, 67, 81, 85, 93, 108, 114–15, 124, 139, 170
agriculture xvi, 13, 60, 88, 102, 143, 147, 156, 163–7
Ainu xiv, 100
Albert River, QLD 150
Allen, Francis 170
Allen, Harry 186
America xvi, 4, 10, 17, 22, 34, 51, 53, 91, 99, 112–13, 115, 118
Amiens 45
Amsterdam 44
Anderson, William 187
Anglian Glaciation 120
Anja Peninsula, WA 69
anthropophagi *see* cannibalism
ape x, xi, xiii, 28–32, 41, 44, 52, 59
Arafura Sea 87–8
archaeology vii, xiii, xiv, 1–4, 6–7, 9–11, 13–22, 25, 40, 42, 46–8, 52, 60, 64, 69–71, 74–6, 78, 84, 89–91, 93–6, 101–02, 105–07, 113, 123–5, 127–8, 132, 134, 136, 138–9, 141–4, 148–9, 151, 160, 162, 171–3, 175, 178, 185–6
archaeomagnetism 25
Ardipithecus 31–3
Argue, Debbie 81
Armidale, NSW 69
Arnhem Land, NT 100, 116–17, 134, 138–9, 144
art 10, 21, 24, 52, 65, 116–17, 133–4, 138–9, 144, 146, 175

Asia xi, xv, xvi, 2, 14, 29–30, 37, 43–6, 49, 51, 55, 57, 61, 66, 71, 81–2, 85, 88, 99–100, 109, 114–15, 127, 156, 169
Atherton Tablelands, QLD 99
auroch 60–1, 63, 115
Australian Alps 159
Australian Institute of Aboriginal Studies 18
Australian National University vii, 18, 20, 77, 81, 93–4
Australian Research Council 74
australopithecines xi, 14, 33–8, 40–2, 69, 78, 80–1

baboon 29, 33, 47
Babylon 3
backed blades 15–16, 127, 148–9, 156
Backstairs Passage, SA 125, 130
Badu Island, QLD 163
Ballawinne Cave, TAS 175
bamboo 45, 75, 87, 164–5
Banda Aceh 73
Bangladesh 98
Barrier Ranges, NSW 136
Barrow Island, WA 89, 93
Barwon River, NSW 155
Bassian Plain xvii, 171–2, 176, 181
Bass Strait 126, 170, 175, 177, 181, 188
Baudin, Nicolas 187
beads 139–41
Beckershoff, Wilhelm 57
Belgium 57, 60
Bel-Shalti-Nannar 3
Ben Lomond people 185
Berger, Lee 81
Berger, Thomas 62
Beringia 51
bipedalism xii, 29, 31–2, 34, 39
'big game tracker' hypothesis 91

Index

Big River people 185, 189
bioturbation 92
Birdsell, Joseph 87, 99–101
Bismarck Archipelago 131
bison 61, 91, 113, 115
Blackall Range, QLD 158
Black, Davidson 44
Bligh, William 187, 190
'blitzkrieg theory' 55, 113, 120–1
Blue Mountains, NSW 17
body decoration 95
Bogong moth 159–62, 166
Bogong Mountains, VIC 159
Bohlin, Birger 44
bone tools xvii, 16, 64, 131, 134, 141, 186–7
Bonn University 58
Bonwick, James 170
Booligal, NSW 104
boomerang xvii, 134, 138–9, 144, 147, 181
Borneo xii, 170
Botany Bay, NSW 15
Boucher de Perthes, Jacques 6
Boule, Marcellin 59
Bowdler, Sandra 90, 94, 123, 186
Bowler, Jim 93–4, 136
brain xi, xii, 34, 37, 39–41, 43–4, 52, 56–7, 60, 64, 69, 76–8, 80, 174
Braithwaite, Don 107
Brazil 51
Brewarrina, NSW 155
Brisbane, QLD 147, 158
British Association for the Advancement of Science 103
British Museum 11, 14
Brixham Cave 6
Broca's area 40–1
Bronze Age 3, 6, 11
Brown, Peter 69, 77–8, 81, 107
Buccaneer Archipelago, WA 155
Budgeongutte Swamp, VIC 152
Builth, Heather 151
Buka 88–9
Bulloo River, NSW 158
Bundaberg, QLD 158
Bunya Mountains, QLD 158
Bunya pine 158–61, 166
burials 4, 14, 63, 81, 105, 136, 144, 181
Burrill Lake, NSW 17

Calvert, Frank 11
Cambridge 8, 14, 19
Canada 113
Canberra, ACT 18, 77, 93
cannibalism 64, 151, 164
Cape Jervis, SA 130
Cape Martin, SA 92
Cape Otway, VIC 171
Cape Portland, TAS 180
Cape York, QLD xvii, 18, 107, 131, 143, 164–5
Carnac 3
Carnarvon, Lord 12
carnivores 38–9, 41, 45, 72, 110, 121, 185
Carpenter's Gap, WA 89
Carter, Howard 12–13, 17
Cave, A.J.E. 59
cave bear 114
ceremonies 133, 146, 154–6, 158, 167, 180, 185
Chad 30–1
Champollion-le-Jeune, Jean Francois 2
Chardin, Pierre Teilhard de 52–3
Cheetup Cave, WA 162
Childe, Vere Gordon 13
children 38, 63, 137, 147
chimpanzee x, xi, 29, 31–2, 38, 53, 75
China 28, 42, 44, 48, 51, 101, 115, 162
cicatrices 179
cider gum 189
circumcision 179
Clarence River, NSW 158
Clark, Julia 180
Cleland Range, NT 123
climate xii, xv, xvi, xvii, 20, 29–30, 32–3, 45, 48–9, 56, 85, 90, 93, 97, 101–02, 111–13, 115, 118, 120–1, 123, 125, 130, 146–9, 156, 162, 166, 177, 179, 184, 186
Clovis people 112
Cohuna skull 104–05, 107
Colless Creek Cave, QLD 123
Colt Hoare, Sir Richard 4
Columbia University 40
Coobool Creek, VIC 107
Cook, James 187, 190
Cooper, Harold 126–7
Cooper's Ferry, Idaho 51
Coorong, SA 151
Copenhagen 6

253

Cossack 58
Cossack skull 104–05, 108
Cox's Bight, TAS 180
crania 16, 37, 41, 44, 56, 102, 104, 106–07, 169
cranial capacity xii, 31, 34, 39–40, 49, 75
Crawford, E.H.K. 103
creation myths 180
cremation 27, 136, 144, 181
Crete 11, 72, 77
cretinism 80
Croatia 59, 63–4
Cro-Magnon 66, 139
Cuddie Springs, NSW 119–20, 132
cuneiform 2
Cuvier, Georges 5
cycads 161, 166
Czech Republic 65, 139

daisy yam 152, 154, 159
Dalby, QLD 158
dance 181
Darlots Creek, VIC 151
Darius I 2
Dart, Raymond 33
Darwin, Charles ix, 7–9, 12, 44, 58, 97
Darwin, Erasmus 7
David, Edgeworth 103
Davidson, D.S. 17
Dawson, Charles 52–3
dendrochronology 24
dendroglyphs 180
Denisovans xi, 46, 51, 68, 70, 84–5, 108
dentition x, 28, 30–1, 37, 40, 46, 75, 79, 101–02, 110
D'Entrecasteaux, Tobias 187
Devil's Lair, WA 18, 89–90, 94, 141
Devon Downs, SA 15–17, 19
diet 20, 25, 28, 32, 36, 38, 45–7, 60, 64, 74, 101, 114, 118, 121, 128, 132, 140–3, 153, 166, 174, 176–7, 185–6, 188–9
di-hybrid theory 101
Diluvian Theory 4
dingo 38, 41, 94, 101, 131, 147, 162–3
Diprotodon xv, 109, 117
disease 14, 47, 58–9, 120, 130, 178, 189–90
Dixon, Robert 100
DNA x, xi, 50, 56–7, 66–7, 70, 78, 85, 100, 162

Dordogne 59
Dorset 12
Doyle, Sir Arthur Conan 53
Dravidian people 98, 100–01, 162
Dreaming, The 83, 98, 116
dryopithecines 29–30
Dubois, Eugene 44–5
Duc d'Elbeuf 9
dugong 15, 163, 165
Dun, J.W. 15
Dusseldorf 57
dwarfism 37, 72, 78
dwellings 48, 153, 155, 179
Dynamic Phase 138

echidna 109–10, 135, 138, 185
Egypt 2, 12, 21, 23, 50, 98
electron spin resonance (ESR) 24–5, 43
emu xv, 109–10, 116, 118, 126, 134–5, 141–2, 174, 181, 185
England 3–4, 6–8, 12, 19, 52, 103
ENSO (El Nino Southern Oscillation System) 148–9, 166
environment xiv, xv, xvi, xvii, 20–1, 27, 30–1, 33, 35, 37, 43, 48, 53, 61, 74, 90–1, 95, 97, 99–101, 112–13, 118, 124, 145, 147, 149–50, 158–9, 161, 178
Erub Island, QLD 163
Etheridge, Robert 15
Ethiopia 31, 34
Eurasia 29, 49, 68
Europe xvi, 3–6, 14, 19, 29–30, 45–6, 49, 51, 53, 55–7, 61, 66, 85, 97, 100, 103, 109, 113–15, 126, 128–30, 133, 139–40, 154, 156–8, 162, 164–9, 171, 175, 178, 180–2, 184–5, 187–90
European bison 115
Evans, John 6
Evans, Sir Arthur 11
evolution ix, x, xii, xiii, xiv, 7–9, 12, 27–8, 30–3, 38–9, 41–2, 44, 46, 53–5, 58, 70–1, 78, 82, 84, 97, 101–02, 108
exchange networks 137, 139, 141, 144, 146, 164, 167
extinction xvi, 8, 36, 50, 71, 81, 91, 108, 111–20, 129, 143, 145, 168, 177

Falconer, Hugh 6
Falk, Dean 77–8
fast tracker hypothesis 90, 123
femur 31, 80

Index

Field, Judith 119
Figueira Brava 60–1
finger flutings 133, 144
Fiorelli, Guiseppe 10
fire xvi, xvii, 60, 64, 66, 75, 82, 90, 97, 118–19, 121, 152–3, 161, 165, 167–8, 180–2, 184–5, 188
fish xvii, 20, 60–1, 91, 95, 123, 134–6, 144, 149–52, 155, 160, 163, 176, 183, 186–9
Fitzroy Crossing, WA 89
Fitzroy River, VIC 151
Flannery, Timothy 'Tim' 119–20, 166, 187
Flinders Island, TAS 177, 188
Flinders, Matthew 12, 126, 130
Flinders Ranges, SA 125–6, 128–9
Florentine Valley, TAS 174, 176
Flores 46, 68–73, 75, 77–8, 81–2, 84, 86
Flores Giant Rat 72, 76
Florida State University 77
Flood, Josephine 101, 148, 166, 186
fluorine dating 22
Forth Valley, TAS 175
FOXP2 gene 57
France 3, 6, 45, 59, 63–5, 139
Fraser Cave, TAS *see* Kutikina Cave
French Riviera 48
Friendly Mission 188
Fromm's Landing, SA 19, 162
Fuhlrott, Johann 58

Gadja Madu University 76
Galapagos Islands 8
Gallus, Alexander 132
Gammage, Bill 167
Geissler, Elizabeth 97
gender 20, 42, 62, 107, 179
Genyornis newtoni xv, xvi, 110, 116–18
Germany 28–9, 42, 56–7, 65–6, 139
Giant Marabou Stork 72–3
Gibraltar 27, 57, 67
gigantopithecines 28
Giles, Ernest 157
Gill, Edmund 19
Glass House Mountains, QLD 147
Gordon-below-Franklin Dam, TAS 173
Gorham's Cave, Gibraltar 67
Great Barrier Reef, QLD 122
Great Dividing Range 94, 122, 152
Great Sandy Desert 89, 100

Great Victoria Desert 157
Greece 3, 11
Gregory, J.W. 98
Groote Eylandt, NT 15
Groves, Colin 81
Gubbi Gubbi people 147
Gulf of Carpentaria 123
Gunditjmara people 150

hairstyles 179
Hale, Herbert 15–16
Hamelin, Emmanuel 187
Hamersley Range, WA 157
Harris Lines 154
hearths 48, 60, 66, 75, 89, 134–6, 144, 151, 153–4
Hegira 22
Henneberg, Maciej 77–80
Henslow, John 8
herbivores 28, 90, 110, 113–14, 120–1
Herculaneum 9–10
Hesiod 2–3, 6
Hiatt, Betty 185
hieroglyphics 2, 21
High Cliffy Island, WA 155
Himalaya Mountains 29
Hiscock, Peter 123, 186
Hissarlick 11
HMS *Rattlesnake* 169
Hoare, Sir Richard Colt 4
Hobart, TAS 188
'Hobbit' xi, xiv, 37, 46, 68–70, 72–84
Holland 70
Holocene epoch xvi, 19, 85, 99, 101, 107–08, 128, 131–4, 138, 144–50, 153, 155–6, 159, 162, 165–8, 172, 175–6, 178, 182
Holloway, Ralph 40
Homer 10–11
Homo antecessor 49
Homo erectus xi, xii, 28, 34, 37, 42–9, 70–2, 75, 78, 80–1, 84, 88, 93, 99, 101, 104–08, 129
Homo ergaster 42–3
Homo floresiensis see 'Hobbit'
Homo habilis 36–42, 45–6, 75, 81, 84
Homo heidelbergensis 49
Homo luzonensis 81–4
Homo neanderthalensis see Neanderthals
Homo rhodesiensis 49
Homo rudolfensis 37

255

Homo sapiens vi, x, xi, xiii, 27, 37, 43,
    45–6, 49–52, 54–5, 61, 65–6, 82, 84,
    88, 99, 102, 104–05, 108, 114, 139
Hooker, Joseph 8
Hope, Jeanette 106
Horton, David 186
Howchin, Walter 126
human behaviour xii, 27, 52, 134, 136,
    138–40, 144
hunter-gathering 38, 42, 48, 121, 149
Hunter Island, TAS 177
Hunter Valley, NSW 21
Huon Peninsula, PNG 88, 125, 143
Hutton, James 5, 9
Huxley, Thomas 169
hyoid bone 57

Ice Age xvi, 85, 111, 120
India 13, 45, 98, 100–01, 162
Indian Ocean xiv, 95, 99
Indonesia xiv, 37, 46, 68–9, 71, 74, 76,
    78, 82, 87, 106, 171
Institute of Archaeology 107
Iran 2, 98
Iraq 60, 63
Ireland 4, 58, 115
Irish Elk 61, 115
Iron Age 3, 6
Islam 22
Israel 50, 57
Italy 3, 56

Jacob, Teuku 76–9
Jaimathang people 159
Jakarta 76
Japan xiv, 51, 100
Java 43–4, 70–1, 76, 84, 87, 101
Jefferson, Thomas 4–5
Jinmium, NT 96–7
Johannesburg 33
Jones, Rhys 93, 95–6, 171, 173, 178,
    186–7
Jordan River, TAS 172

Kadimakara 116
Kakadu National Park, NT 95
kangaroo xvi, xvii, 93, 110, 112, 117,
    120, 126, 128, 167–8, 174, 179, 181,
    183, 185
Kangaroo Island, SA 92, 122, 125–32,
    143, 147

Kartan culture 92, 126–31, 143
Katherine, NT 133
Keilor skull 104, 106, 176
Keith, Sir Arthur 52–3
Kennedy, E. 17
Kenniff Cave, QLD 19, 92
Kenya 13, 30, 47
Kiandra, NSW 159
Kiernan, Kevin 172–3
Kimberleys, WA 69, 74, 89, 100, 117,
    140–1, 161
King Charles III 10
King, William 58
King Island, TAS 126, 171, 176–7
Kingston, SA 130
Klaatsch, Hermann 104
Knossos 11
Komodo dragon 72–3, 75
Koonalda Cave, SA 132–3, 144
Kosipe, PNG 125, 129
Kow Swamp, VIC 18, 101–03, 105, 107,
    137
Kulpi Mara, NT 123
Kutikina Cave, TAS 172–3

La Chapelle-aux-Saints 59
Lachlan River, NSW 93–4, 135
Laetoli 34–5
Lake Alexandrina, SA 151
Lake Barrine, QLD 99
Lake Condah, VIC 149, 151–5
Lake Eyre, SA 118, 122–3
Lake Frome, SA 125
Lake Garnpung, NSW 106, 138
Lake George, NSW 97
Lake Gregory, WA 89
Lake Leaghur, NSW 134
Lake Mungo, NSW 18, 93–4, 101, 134–
    7, 141, 176
Lake Torrens, SA 126
Lamarck, Jean-Baptiste de 7, 9
Lampert, Ronald 127–30
Lancefield Swamp, VIC 117, 119–20
language xiii, 40–2, 71, 90, 98, 100, 126,
    170–1, 178
Lapstone Creek, NSW 17
Laron syndrome 78
Laron, Zvi 78
Lashmars Lagoon, SA 130
Last Glacial Maximum 51, 86, 95, 111,
    122–3, 125, 143, 171, 173, 175

Index

La Trobe University 173
Laurentide ice sheet 113
Lawn Hill Gorge, QLD 123, 143
Leakey, Louis 13–14, 36–7
Leakey, Mary 14, 34–5
Leakey, Richard xii, 36
Leeuwin-Naturaliste Ranges, WA 89
Leipzig University 56, 66
Le Moustier 63
Levant 50–1
Levi Range, NT 123
Liang Bua Cave, Flores 74–8, 80
Libby, Willard 22
Linnean Society 8
London 8, 13–14, 103, 107
Lourandos, Harry 20–1, 149
Lovejoy, C. Owen xi
Lubbock, John 6, 12
Lyell, Charles 5, 8–9

Maatsuyker Island, TAS 184
Mabuiag Island, QLD 107
Macintyre, Michael 106
Mackay, QLD 128
Mackintosh Cave, TAS 176
Madagascar 170
Madjedbebe, NT 19, 95–6
Madura Cave, WA 162
Malakunanja II, NT 95–6
Malaysia 99
Malo-Bomai cult 164
Malta 72
Malthus, Thomas 9
Macquarie Harbour, TAS 172
Mandu Mandu, WA 140–1
Mannum, SA 15
Maori 62
marsupial lion xvi, 110, 112
marsupial tapir 109
Martin, Paul 113, 120
mastodons 91
Mata Menge 70, 75
Mathew, John 97–8, 170
Matthews, J. 20
Max Planck Institute for Evolutionary Anthropology 66
Maxwell River, TAS 175
Maya 22
Mayer, August 58
McCarthy, Frederick 17–18, 20
McCormack, Robert 8

McFarlane, Ian 188
McLaren, Charles 11
MCIR gene 56
Mecca 22
medical disorders 67, 190
Mediterranean 23, 48, 72
megafauna xv, 90–1, 108–22, 128, 138, 145, 168
Megalania prisca xvi, 110
megaliths 3
Megantereon sp 42
Meiolania sp 111
Melanesians xi, xv, xvii, 85, 107, 154, 163
Melbourne x, 105, 132
Mer Island, QLD 163
Mesopotamia 2
Meston, Archibald 170
Mexico 112
microcephaly 77–8, 80
Micronesia 81
Miller, Geritt 53
Miller, Gifford 118–19, 121
Mimi Caves, WA 89
Mina Cave, TAS 175
Minjiwarra, WA 89
Minoan 11, 23, 77
Miocene epoch 28–9
Mississippi River 4
moa 114, 118
mollusc *see* shellfish
Mongolia 58, 115
monkey xi, 28, 73
monogamy 87, 178
monsoon 86–8, 122, 156
Montgomery Islands, WA 156
Morwood, Mike 69, 74, 76–81
Mossel Bay 49
Mossgiel skull 104–05
Moula-Guercy 63
mound builders xii, 4, 14, 154
Mount Beerwah, QLD 147
Mount Coonowrin, QLD 148
Mount Darwin, TAS 132, 173
Mount Eccles, VIC 150
Mount Gambier, SA 150
Mount Jukes, QLD 128–9, 143
Mount Perry, QLD 158
Mount Tibrogargan, QLD 148
Mount Vesuvius 9
Mount William, VIC 149, 152, 166

Mousterian 64, 67
multiregional theory 46
Mulvaney, John vii, 19, 92–4
Mungo I 105, 136, 138
Mungo II 106
Mungo III 106, 136, 138
Murray River 15, 101, 130, 150, 154–5, 171
Murray's Lagoon, SA 126–7
Mycenaean 11, 23

Nabonidus 3
Naish, William 103
Nanwoon Cave, TAS 176
Napier, John 36
Napier Ranges, WA 89
Naracoorte Caves, SA 112
National Centre for Archaeology, Indonesia 76, 78
National Museum of Australia 94
National Museum of Victoria 105
Native American Indians xiv, 4, 65, 113
natural selection 9, 33, 72
Nauwalabila, NT 95–6
Neanderthals xi, 27, 49, 55–67, 85
Neander Valley 57–8
Near East 17, 19, 27, 45, 55, 156
Neolithic 13
New Archaeology *see* Processual Archaeology
New Britain 131, 137
New Caledonia 113, 150, 169–70
New Guinea singing dog 94, 162
New Ireland 89
New South Wales 15, 17–18, 21, 69, 90, 93, 97, 103–04, 118–19, 132, 134, 144, 154–5, 158–9, 161–2, 175–6, 180
New York 40, 59
New Zealand 62, 114, 118
Ngarigo people 159
Ngarrindjeri people 126, 130, 151–2
Nice 48
Nicol, Mary *see* Mary Leakey
Ninjemys sp 111
Northern Illinois University 64
Northern Territory 15, 17, 19, 95–6, 120, 133, 137
Nullarbor Plain 112, 123, 132, 144, 162
Nunamira Cave, TAS 176

obsidian 131, 137, 143
ochre 27, 48, 63, 95, 123, 136–7, 141, 144, 164, 175, 179, 182–3
Oldowan technology 42, 70–1, 88
Old Testament 4
Olduvai Gorge 14, 36, 42
Oligocene epoch 28
Olorgesailie 47
optically stimulated luminescence 24, 89, 96, 137
ornamentation 65, 139–41, 144
Orrorin tugenensis 30–1
Out of Africa theory xiii, 46
Oxford 12

Paabo, Svante 66
Pacific Islands 112
Pacific Ocean 87–8, 91, 150, 154, 187
paintings 52, 65, 95, 116, 138–9, 144, 174–5, 180
Pakistan 28, 98
Palauan Archipelago 81
Palestine 12
palynology 97
Papua New Guinea xi, xiv, xv, xvii, 70, 85, 87–8, 94, 100, 122, 124–5, 129, 131–3, 143, 147, 163–5
Paranthropus 33–4, 36
Pardoe, Colin 107
Parmerpar Meethaner Cave, TAS 175–6
Patagonia 170
Pathology Group 79
Pedra Furada 51–2
Peking Man *see* Homo erectus
pelvis 31–2, 35, 57, 78
Pengelly, William 6
Perth 89
Perthes, Jacques Boucher de 6
Petrie, William Flinders 11–12
petroglyphs 16, 180
Philippines 37, 81, 84, 99
Phillip, Arthur 14–15
pigmentation 43, 56, 169
Piltdown Man 52–3, 103
Pintupi people 137–8
Pitt-Rivers, Augustus 11–13
Pittwater, NSW 17
Pleistocene epoch xvi, 19, 28, 85–9, 92–4, 99, 101–04, 107–08, 113–14, 118, 120–1, 123–8, 131–47, 149, 153, 156–7, 162, 172, 174–6

Index

Plomley, Brian 178, 181
Poland 62
Polynesia 87, 114, 154
Pompeii 9–10
Port Augusta, SA 91, 118
Portugal 60
potassium argon dating 24
pottery 12
Pre-Estuarine Period 138–9
Prestwich, Joseph 6
primates x, xii, 27–30, 32–3, 38–40, 42, 73
Principle of Uniformitarianism 5
Processual Archaeology 20–1
Proconsul 28
Procoptodon goliah 110
Przewalski's horse 115
Puritjara, NT 123
Pygmies 70–2, 78

Queensland 16, 19, 92, 99–100, 102–03, 116, 122–3, 128–9, 132, 143, 147, 150, 158–61, 169, 180
Queenstown, TAS 132
Quinkana fortirostrum xvi, 110

racemisation 25, 118
radiocarbon dating 17–19, 22–3, 92, 94, 96, 105, 116, 133, 140, 162, 175
ramapithecines 30
Rathje, William 25
Rawlinson, Sir Henry 2
Rebecca Creek, TAS 177
Redd, Alan 100
red-necked wallaby 142, 173–4, 176
Red Sea 51
relative dating 22
Rhine River 58
Rhone River 63
Richards, Gary 78
Richmond River, NSW 158
rickets 58
Riwi, WA 140–1
Roberts, Richard 119
Robinson, George Augustus 107, 178, 181, 183–5, 188
Rocky Cape, TAS 186
Romans 4, 12
Rosetta Stone 2
Ross, TAS 181
Royal Society of Great Britain 53

Saadanius hijazensis 28
Sahelanthropus tchadensis 30
Sahul vii, xiv, xv, xvi, 27, 68–70, 76, 84–91, 93–5, 97, 108–11, 116, 119, 122, 124–5, 131–2, 143, 171
Saudi Arabia 28
Scandinavia 114
Schaaffhausen, Hermann 58
Schliemann, Heinrich 10–11
Schofield, John 79
Schouten, Peter 79
Seton Cave, SA 127–9
Shanidar Cave 63
Shark Bay, WA 15, 130, 187
Sheard, H.L. 16
Shea's Creek, NSW 15
shellfish 49, 60, 74, 95, 123, 128, 134, 139–41, 163, 177, 183, 186, 189
shells 3, 65, 67, 135, 139–41, 155, 164, 183, 187–8
short-finned eel 150
Shropshire 7
Siberia xi, 100, 114–15
Sicily 72
Singh, G. 97
Sivapithecus 29
skins xvii, 48, 128, 131, 134, 160, 179, 181
skull 1470 41
Smith, Fred 64
Smith, Grafton Elliot 52–3, 103
Smith, James Joynton 103
Smith, Stewart 103
Soa Basin 74
social organisation 37–9, 42, 46
Solomon Islands 88
Solo River 44
South Africa 33–4, 36, 44, 49, 81
South America 8, 170
South Australia 15–16, 19, 91–2, 112, 118, 125, 134, 143, 150–1, 162, 172
South Australian Museum 126
Southern Forests Archaeological Project 173
Spain 10, 47, 49, 56
spear 61, 64, 133, 135, 138–9, 148–9, 151, 155, 159, 164–5, 182, 185–7
spear-thrower xvii, 134, 138, 144, 147, 164, 181
speech 40–2, 57
Spencer, Herbert 9

259

Spring Creek, VIC 119
Sri Lanka xiv, 98
stegodon 70–3, 75, 84–6, 88
Steno's Law 5
Stone Age xvii, 6, 14, 16
Stonehenge 3
Stoneking, Mark 100
stone tools xvii, 6, 15, 17, 24, 36, 42, 46, 51, 59, 64–5, 70–1, 73, 75, 79, 88, 90, 92–3, 119–20, 126–9, 131–3, 135–6, 141, 143, 173, 175, 177, 182
stratigraphy 11, 15–17
Straus, William 59
Strzelecki Desert 123
Stukeley, William 3
Sulawesi 71, 87
Sumatra 44, 73, 82
Sumbawa 71
Sunda 71, 85–6, 93
Swan Hill, VIC 107, 155
Sydney 14–15, 17–19, 103
Seychelles 170

Talgai Skull 16, 102–05
Tanimbar xiv, 87
Tanzania 14, 34, 36, 42
Tartanga, SA 15–17
Tasmania xiv, xv, xvii, 18, 20, 24, 90, 94–5, 98–100, 111, 119, 122, 126, 132, 142, 147–8, 150, 154, 168–90
Tasmanian devil 94, 110, 138, 163, 185, 188
Tasman Sea 169
Taung 33
Taylor, John 171–2, 176
Taylor, Rebe 188
teeth 28, 30, 35, 39, 43, 47, 56, 60, 65, 73, 75, 79, 102, 104, 110, 182
tektites 132, 143
Terra Amata 48
Teshik Tash 63
Thailand 28
The Brecknells, SA 126
therianthropes 139
thermoluminescence 24, 96
Thomsen, Christian 6
thorium uranium dating 119
Thorne, Alan 45, 77–9, 93–4, 101, 105–06
Thorpe, W.W. 17
thylacine 94, 110, 138, 163, 185

Thylacoleo carnifex see marsupial lion
Thylacoleo Caves, SA 112
Tibet 51
Tibooburra, NSW 158
Timor xiv, xv, 69–70, 74, 87–8
Timor Trough 88
Tindale, Norman 15–17, 19, 126–7, 129
Tobias, Phillip 36, 53
Tolkien, J.R.R. 69, 79
Toolondo, VIC 149, 152
tooth avulsion 179
Torquay 6
Torres Strait 88, 107, 163–5, 169
tri-hybrid theory 98–9, 170
Trinkaus, Erik 62
Trojan War 10–11
Troy 10–11
Tucson Garbage Project 25
Tula adzes 156
Turkey 11
Turner, William 169
Tutankhamen 12, 17
typology 12

Ugar Island, QLD 163
Ukraine 65
University of Adelaide 77
University of Amsterdam 44
University of Manchester 52
University of Melbourne 19, 98, 169
University of New England 69, 76
University of Sydney 18–19, 103, 175
Upper Mersey Valley, TAS 176
Ur 3, 17
uranium series dating 25, 119
Usher, James 4–5
Uzbekistan 63

Vanguard Cave, Gibraltar 67
Verhoeven, Theodor 70–1, 74
Veth, Peter 89, 124
Vedda xiv
Victoria 18, 20, 104–07, 116–17, 119, 148–50, 152–5, 159, 162, 166, 172, 176, 178
Vietnam 28
Virchow, Rudolf 58–9
Virginia 4
vitamin A 47
vitamin D 43, 56
Volger, Gisela 184

Index

Von Daniken, Erich 21

waisted axes 125, 128–9, 132, 143
Walgalu people 159
wallaby xvii, 110, 142, 173–4, 176, 179, 183, 185
Wallace, Alfred Russel ix, 7–8, 44
Wallace Line xv, 86
Walsh, John 53
Wardaman people 133
warfare 139, 144, 163–4
Warragarra rock shelter, TAS 176
water buffalo 120
water conservation 157
watercraft 51, 86–7, 130, 134, 146, 177, 183
Webb, Steve 106–07, 154
Weld Cave, TAS 175
Wernicke's area 40–1
Western Australia xv, 15, 69, 96, 117, 130, 140, 161, 165, 187
Westlake, Ernest 188
Wheeler, Robert Mortimer 13
Whitlegge, Thomas 15
wild millet 156, 165
Willandra Lakes, NSW 90, 93–4, 101–02, 105–06, 118, 134–5, 137, 144

Wilson's Promontory, VIC 171
Wiltshire 4
Winckelmann, Johann 10
wisent *see* European bison
Witwatersrand University 81
WLH50 106
wombat xvi, 95, 109–10, 118, 142, 174, 176, 185
women 38, 62, 87, 126, 128–30, 153, 157, 159–60, 179, 181, 183, 188–9
Wonambi naracoortensis xvi, 110–11
Wood-Jones, Frederic 169
Woolley, Leonard 17
woolly mammoth 5, 61, 65, 91, 112–14
woolly rhinoceros 5, 47–8, 61, 114
Wrangel Island 114
Wright, Richard 97
Wroe, Stephen 119
Wyrie Swamp, SA 134

Yeti 29
Yogyakarta 76
Young, James 188
Yowie x

Zhoukoudian 44, 48

www.ingramcontent.com/pod-product-compliance
Lightning Source LLC
Chambersburg PA
CBHW021349300426
44114CB00012B/1145